A Time of Coalitions

A Time of Coalitions
Divided We Stand

Paranjoy Guha Thakurta
Shankar Raghuraman

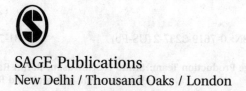

SAGE Publications
New Delhi / Thousand Oaks / London

First published in 2004 by

Sage Publications India Pvt Ltd
B-42, Panchsheel Enclave
New Delhi 110 017

Sage Publications Inc
2455 Teller Road
Thousand Oaks, California 91320

Sage Publications Ltd
1 Oliver's Yard, 55 City Road
London EC1Y 1SP

Published by Tejeshwar Singh for Sage Publications India Pvt Ltd, typeset in 10/12 Utopia at S.R. Enterprises, New Delhi and printed at Glorious Printers, New Delhi.

Library of Congress Cataloging-in-Publication Data

Thakurta, Paranjoy Guha.
A time of coalitions: divided we stand / Paranjoy Guha Thakurta, Shankar Raghuraman.
      p. cm.
   Includes index.
      1. Political parties—India. 2. Coalition governments—India. I. Raghuraman, Shankar. II. Title.
JQ298.A1T43   324.254—dc22   2004   2004003260

ISBN: 0-7619-3237-2 (US-Pb)   81-7829-372-2 (India-Pb)

Sage Production Team: Smita P Srinivasan, Rahul Rajagopalan, Anupama Krishnan, Ena M Joseph and Rajib Chatterjee

Table of Contents

List of Abbreviations

AASU	All Assam Students' Union
ABCD	Akhil Bharatiya Congress Dal
AGP	Asom Gana Parishad
AIADMK	All India Anna Dravida Munnetra Kazhagam
AIADMK(JL)	All India Anna Dravida Munnetra Kazhagam (Jayalalithaa)
AIADMK(JR)	All India Anna Dravida Munnetra Kazhagam (Janaki Ramachandran)
AICC	All India Congress Committee
AIMPLB	All India Muslim Personal Law Board
BALCO	Bharat Aluminium Company Limited
BAMCEF	Backward and Minority Communities Employees' Federation
BHEL	Bharat Heavy Electricals Limited
BJD	Biju Janata Dal
BJP	Bharatiya Janata Party
BJS	Bharatiya Jana Sangh
BKD	Bharatiya Kranti Dal
BKU	Bharatiya Kisan Union
BLD	Bharatiya Lok Dal
BMS	Bharatiya Mazdoor Sangh
BPCC	Bombay Pradesh Congress Committee
BPCL	Bharat Petroleum Corporation Limited
BSP	Bahujan Samaj Party
CAG	Comptroller and Auditor General of India
CBI	Central Bureau of Investigation
CBSE	Central Board of Secondary Education
CFD	Congress for Democracy
CII	Confederation of Indian Industry
CM	Chief Minister
CMP	Common Minimum Programme

CPI	Communist Party of India
CPI(M)	Communist Party of India (Marxist)
CPI(ML)-L	Communist Party of India (Marxist-Leninist)-Liberation
CSDS	Centre for the Study of Developing Societies
CWC	Congress Working Committee
DMK	Dravida Munnetra Kazhagam
EC	Election Commission
EPFO	Employees' Provident Fund Organisation
EVR	E.V. Ramaswamy Naicker
FIR	First Information Report
HPCL	Hindustan Petroleum Corporation Limited
HRD	Human Resources Development
HVC	Himachal Vikas Congress
HVP	Haryana Vikas Party
ICHR	Indian Council for Historical Research
ICSSR	Indian Council for Social Science Research
IMDTA	Illegal Migrants (Determination by Tribunal) Act
IMF	International Monetary Fund
INLD	Indian National Lok Dal
IPCL	Indian Petrochemicals Corporation Limited
IPF	Indian People's Front
IRA	Insurance Regulatory Authority
J&K	Jammu & Kashmir
JD	Janata Dal
JD(S)	Janata Dal (Samajwadi) and Janata Dal (Secular)
JD(U)	Janata Dal (United)
JKD	Jan Kranti Dal
JMM	Jharkhand Mukti Morcha
JP	Jayaprakash Narayan
KMPP	Kisan Mazdoor Praja Party
LDF	Left Democratic Front
LJSP	Lok Janshakti Party
LoC	Line of Control
LTTE	Liberation Tigers of Tamil Eelam
MBC	Most Backward Classes
MCC	Maoist Communist Centre
MCOCA	Maharashtra Control of Organised Crime Act
MDMK	Marumalarchi Dravida Munnetra Kazhagam
MGR	M.G. Ramachandran

MISA	Maintenance of Internal Security Act
MLA	Member of Legislative Assembly
MP	Member of Parliament
MPCC	Maharashtra Pradesh Congress Committee
NALCO	National Aluminium Company Limited
NC	National Conference
NCERT	National Council for Educational Research & Training
NCP	Nationalist Congress Party
NDA	National Democratic Alliance
NTR	Nandamuri Taraka Rama Rao
OBC	Other Backward Classes
PDP	People's Democratic Party
PDS	Public Distribution System
PEPSU	Patiala and East Punjab States' Union
PMK	Pattali Makkal Katchi
PMO	Prime Minister's Office
POCA	Prevention of Crime Act
POTA	Prevention of Terrorism Act
POTO	Prevention of Terrorism Ordinance
PSP	Praja Socialist Party
PSU	Public Sector Undertaking
PT	Puthiya Tamizhagam
PWG	People's War Group
PWP	Peasants & Workers Party
RJD	Rashtriya Janata Dal
RJP	Rashtriya Janata Party
RKP	Rashtriya Kranti Party
RLD	Rashtriya Lok Dal
RPI	Republican Party of India
RSP	Revolutionary Socialist Party
RSS	Rashtriya Swayamsevak Sangh
SAD	Shiromani Akali Dal
SC	Scheduled Caste
SGPC	Shiromani Gurudwara Prabandhak Committee
SIMI	Students' Islamic Movement of India
SJM	Swadeshi Jagaran Manch
SJP	Samajwadi Janata Party
SOG	Special Operations Group
SP	Samajwadi Party

ST	Scheduled Tribe
TADA	Terrorist and Disruptive Activities (Prevention & Regulation) Act
TANSI	Tamil Nadu Small Industries Corporation
TDP	Telugu Desam Party
TMC	Tamil Maanila Congress
TRC	Tamizhaga Rajiv Congress
TUJS	Tripura Upajati Juba Samiti
UDF	United Democratic Front
UF	United Front
ULFA	United Liberation Front of Asom
UP	Uttar Pradesh
UTI	Unit Trust of India
VAT	Value-Added Tax
VHP	Vishwa Hindu Parishad
VKA	Vanvasi Kalyan Ashram
VSNL	Videsh Sanchar Nigam Limited
WTO	World Trade Organisation

Preface
Diversity in Unity

Till the turn of the 21st century, conventional wisdom in India had it that coalition governments were an aberration, a brief and temporary phase that would soon give way to single-party governments led either by the Bharatiya Janata Party (BJP) or the Indian National Congress (INC). Over the term of the third Union government headed by Atal Bihari Vajpayee, which came to power in October 1999, most political participants and observers have grudgingly come to accept that this phase of coalition governments might be less shortlived than they had initially anticipated. Yet, they often seek to underplay the significance of this development by arguing that the polity remains essentially bipolar.

To claim that the BJP and the Congress represent two poles of the Indian polity would be too simplistic a view of the complex reality. Indeed, it can even be forcefully argued that Indian politics is becoming less, not more, bipolar. There are strong indications that the process of fragmentation of the polity is far from over.

While at the all-India level there may appear to be only two fronts or political formations of any significance, this picture of a uniformly bipolar polity disappears the moment we examine what's happening in the states. Yes, there are states in which the BJP and the Congress are the only major political players. But these states—Himachal Pradesh, Uttaranchal (carved out of Uttar Pradesh in 2000), Rajasthan, Gujarat, Madhya Pradesh, Chhattisgarh (earlier a part of Madhya Pradesh) and the national capital territory of Delhi—between them account for less than one-fifth of the total number of seats in the Lok Sabha, the lower House of Parliament. Then there are states where either the Congress or the BJP is one of the major political players, but the other is minor or insignificant.

Such states include Uttar Pradesh and Bihar, where the Congress is at best a marginal player, and Kerala, Andhra Pradesh and much of the north-east, where the BJP is no more than a fringe participant. Finally, there are states like Tamil Nadu and West Bengal where neither the BJP nor the Congress can claim to be one of the poles of the polity.

The elections to the state assemblies of Madhya Pradesh, Chhattisgarh, Rajasthan and Delhi in December 2003 provided evidence that the so-called bipolarity of Indian politics is being threatened even in states that have traditionally witnessed straight electoral battles between the BJP and the Congress. In the 2003 elections, the combined vote share of the BJP and the Congress was a little over 74 per cent in Madhya Pradesh, a significant drop of 3.2 per cent from the combined vote share in the 1998 assembly elections. Thus, one in every four voters in Madhya Pradesh is not voting for either the BJP or the Congress and this share is increasing, not decreasing. The picture in Rajasthan was even clearer. The BJP and Congress between them mopped up a little over 74 per cent of the votes cast in 2003, a 5.3 per cent decline from their combined tally in 1998. Similarly, in Chhattisgarh the BJP and Congress put together lost 5.4 per cent of the votes between the 1998 and 2003 assembly elections.

Even at the national level, the hypothesis of an increasingly bipolar polity is scarcely borne out by facts. The Congress and the BJP put together did increase their tally in the 543-member Lok Sabha by barely 22 seats between the May 1996 and February 1998 general elections. However, in the 1999 elections, the combined tally of the BJP and the Congress came down to below the level in 1996. In fact, the combined strength of 296 Lok Sabha MPs for the BJP and the Congress is the lowest since the BJP came into existence in 1980.

If at all one can talk in terms of two poles in Indian politics, it would have to be in terms of the pole of sectarian politics on the one hand, and inclusive politics on the other. The BJP, the caste-based parties and the regional parties are all parties that base themselves on a sectarian appeal, though this would certainly not be acknowledged officially. The Congress and the left, on the other hand, seek to make a genuinely pan-Indian appeal. In the contest between these two types of political mobilisation, the coalition era has seen the ascendancy of sectarian forces and the marginalisation of political forces that try to appeal across the social spectrum.

Those who believe that the Indian polity is becoming bipolar overlook the fact that coalition politics can create compulsions for the larger party to woo the smaller ones and not the other way round. Take an extreme example. In a Parliament with, say, 100 seats, assume there are three political parties. Party A has 49 seats; party B has a similar number while party C has only two seats. In such a situation, party C could be the most powerful party because its decision to align itself with either party A or party B would determine who comes to power.

The very description of two large parties as poles suggests that they are the ones that call the shots, which is not necessarily the case in India. This hypothetical example may seem absurd, but something akin to it has actually taken place in Indian politics more than once. In Uttar Pradesh, for instance, the Bahujan Samaj Party (BSP) has on three different occasions formed the government in the state with the support of the BJP after having opposed the party during the election campaign. On two of these occasions, the BSP has held the upper hand despite the fact that the BJP was by far the larger of the two parties in the Uttar Pradesh assembly. This was possible because the BJP's stake in keeping the rival Samajwadi Party (SP) out of power was greater than that of the BSP.

In Himachal Pradesh, events came as close to our hypothetical example as possible. In the state assembly elections in 1996, coinciding with the May 1996 general elections, the BJP won 29 of the 68 seats in the assembly seats, the Congress 33 seats, while the Himachal Vikas Congress (HVC, headed by former Union Communications Minister Sukh Ram who was expelled from the Congress after corruption charges were filed against him following the recovery of large sums of unaccounted money from his residences) won four seats. There was one independent candidate who won while elections were not held in one constituency. After the elections, the BJP had to align with Sukh Ram's HVC though the two parties had opposed each other. In the state government, the BJP had to concede the post of Deputy Chief Minister to Sukh Ram's son. The point is simple: the BJP needed the HVC more than the latter needed it in order to form the government in Himachal Pradesh.

A common fallacy that is related to the conviction that India's polity is essentially bipolar and contributes to it is the notion that the decline of the Congress and the rise of the BJP bear almost a one-to-one correspondence. Put differently, the rise of the BJP is seen as a process of the party occupying the space vacated by the Congress. Though this view is very widely held, the reality is far more complicated.

It is true that the period that witnessed the fastest growth of the BJP as an electoral force—from two seats in the 8th Lok Sabha elected in 1984 to 182 seats by the 12th Lok Sabha elected in 1998— has coincided with the phase of the most rapid decline of the Congress—from 415 seats in 1984 to 112 seats in the 13th Lok Sabha elected in 1999. That is perhaps why the two phenomena are seen as completely correlated with each other. However, what such a view misses is the fact that in areas where the Congress has been almost completely marginalised, it has been displaced not so much by the BJP as by smaller regional parties.

To take the most obvious case first, the marginalisation of the Congress in India's largest state, Uttar Pradesh (accounting for 80 out of the 543 seats in the Lok Sabha) has not led to the BJP becoming a party with unquestioned dominance in the state. On the contrary, the party was in 2002 reduced to third position in Uttar Pradesh, behind the SP and the BSP. Even at its peak in the mid-1990s, the BJP in UP never managed to get close to 40 per cent of the popular vote, though it was at that stage the single-biggest party in the state assembly.

The story in neighbouring Bihar has not been very different. Here again, the Congress has been reduced to a marginal presence over the last decade-and-a-half, but its decline has not led to the BJP becoming the dominant party. Laloo Prasad Yadav's Rashtriya Janata Dal (RJD) or its forerunner the Janata Dal (JD) were the main agents of the erosion of the Congress party's vote banks while the Samata Party—itself a breakaway group of the erstwhile JD—has a strength in Bihar that is equal to if not more than the BJP in terms of its political influence.

Could Uttar Pradesh and Bihar represent the exception to the rule that the BJP grows to fill the vacuum created by a shrinking Congress? Not quite. In states like Orissa, Assam and Karnataka, for instance, the BJP has grown rapidly, more often than not by consolidating the anti-Congress political forces. It is another matter that other anti-Congress groups—like the Janata Dal (United) in Karnataka, the Biju Janata Dal (BJD) in Orissa and the Asom Gana Parishad (AGP) in Assam—have at some stage decided that rather than compete with the BJP for the Opposition space, they could gain by aligning with the party.

Also, if we look back to the period before the decline of the Congress accelerated, that is, between the late 1960s and the mid-1980s, there were already signs of the party losing ground gradually but quite consistently to regional parties. The most obvious example would be Tamil Nadu, where the Congress today has little choice but to align with one or the other of the two main Dravidian parties in the state—the Dravida Munnetra Kazhagam (DMK) and the All India Anna Dravida Munnetra Kazhagam (AIADMK). But Tamil Nadu is not the only example. Andhra Pradesh and Maharashtra, traditional strongholds of the Congress, witnessed similar trends even if the process did not lead to the complete marginalisation of the Congress. In Andhra Pradesh, the Telugu Desam Party (TDP) rose from almost nowhere to become a powerful challenge to the Congress in the mid-1980s and has remained the main contender for power with the Congress. Similarly, in Maharashtra it was the rise of the Shiv Sena rather than the BJP which first raised questions about just how firm the Congress' grip on power in the state was.

Therefore, our main assertions so far are:

- The process of fragmentation of the Indian polity is not yet over.
- The polity is not becoming bipolar with smaller parties, including regional parties and caste-based parties, having no choice but to become appendages of either the BJP or the Congress either before or after elections.
- The decline of the Congress has not automatically resulted in the rise of the BJP—in other words, the political tussle between the two largest political parties in India has not been a zero sum game in which the losses of one inevitably result in the other gaining by filling a so-called political vacuum.

In this book, we argue that the new era of coalition politics does not necessarily signify a nightmarish scenario for India. As the polity of the world's largest democracy evolves and as institutions of governance mature, political instability would reflect the internal dynamics of a highly heterogeneous and deeply divided nation-state. Coalitions, in spite of their ideological contradictions, are perhaps better equipped to deal with the tensions of such a divided society than single-party governments that have a tendency to centralise and homogenise.

It might help here to examine the factors that have led to the fragmentation of India's polity and why these same factors work towards further fragmentation. Several political scientists have analysed the phenomenon of 'identity politics'. Sudipto Kaviraj has some interesting insights to offer on this question (*Contemporary Crisis of the Nation-State?* Edited by John Dunn, Oxford: Blackwell Publishers 1995). His contention is that the benefits of the Nehruvian model of economic development remained confined to a section consisting of the 'bourgeoisie, high managerial elites, state bureaucracy and agrarian magnates' and that this fostered resentment in the vast majority of the population. It is this resentment, he suggests, that has been tapped by various political groups leading to the fragmentation of the polity. Kaviraj also argues that the resentment against the elite extends to a rejection of all that the elite stood for, including the notion of the Indian identity overriding sub-national identities.

He writes:

Since this elite speaks the language of national integration and unity, the latter [movements of the non-elite] speak the negative language of localism, regional autonomy, small-scale nationalism, in dystopias of ethnicity—small xenophobic, homogeneous, political communities. This does violence to the political imagination of the Indian nation-state which emphasised diversity as a great asset and enjoined principles of tolerance as the special gift of Indian civilisation.... The world of political possibilities in India seems to be simplifying into the frightening choice before most of the modern world's political communities: to try to craft imperfect democratic rules by which increasingly mixed groups of people can carry on together an unheroic everyday existence, or the illusion of a permanent and homogeneous, unmixed single nation, a single collective self without any trace of a defiling otherness.

Kaviraj's point is well taken. The fragmentation of India's polity is undoubtedly an outcome of the feeling among very large sections of the population that they had been left out of the development process. What is interesting, however, is that this resentment hasn't always manifested itself through parties and groups that claim to be speaking for the excluded sections of society. The TDP, for instance, appeals to the Telugu identity across Andhra Pradesh. Clearly, it is not the case that all Telugus have been left out of the development process. Similarly, nobody can seriously argue that the Shiv Sena's appeal to a Maharashtrian identity arises from the feeling that all of Maharashtra has been denied the benefits of economic growth. Obviously, it has been possible for parties like the TDP and the Shiv Sena to use the resentment of specific sections of those speaking Telugu and Marathi and channelise it along lines of their choosing.

Yet, there is something that the TDP and the Shiv Sena have in common with caste-based parties like the SP in Uttar Pradesh or the RJD in Bihar. In each of these cases, the revolt of the underprivileged has been led by the most dominant of the intermediate castes—the Khammas in Andhra Pradesh, the Marathas in Maharashtra and the Yadavs in UP and Bihar. This is actually not very surprising. After all, even the ability to lead a revolt against the prevailing elite must presume some minimal access to the institutions of power and to resources of a sufficient magnitude. Such access and resources would be available only to the uppermost layers of the relatively underprivileged. These were indeed among the few sections outside the traditional elite that had not entirely been left out of the development process. As Kaviraj points out, 'the only rural group which secured benefits out of the development process were the large farmers whose compliance was bought by heavy subsidies, absence of income tax and slow cooptation into governmental power'.

The dalit movement might at first seem an exception to the rule, since dalits (or those at the very bottom of the caste hierarchy) have little or no control over land anywhere in the country. However, what is noteworthy is that even in this instance, the leadership has come from among the best-off sections of the dalits.

The fragmentation of India's polity, then, can be seen as the result of various sections deciding that an informal coalition like the Congress had failed to serve their interests. But what explains the tendency for coalitions to persist? It could well be the case that these sections perceive themselves as having gained from a process of explicit coalitions in which groups ostensibly speak for them. It is pointless, in this context, to debate whether Yadavs as a whole have actually gained because of the SP or the RJD, whether dalits are better off since the BSP was formed or whether Andhra Pradesh and Maharashtra have performed better after the formation of the TDP and the Shiv Sena. What matters is the popular perception among the relevant sections that their interests are being taken care of better than in the past.

Political scientist Arend Lijphart in his article, 'The Puzzle of Indian Democracy: A Consociational Interpretation' (*American Political Science Review*, June 1996), had contended that India largely conforms to what he described as consociationalism in a deeply divided society. He set out four parameters denoting consociationalism. These were: *(a)* a grand coalition government that includes representatives of all major linguistic and religious groups; *(b)* cultural autonomy for these groups; *(c)* proportionality in political representation and civil service appointments; and *(d)* a minority veto with regard to vital minority rights and autonomy. At the time Lijphart wrote this, it was true that the four characteristics were by and large present in the government of the day and had been present in all past Union governments in India as well.

Since 1998, however, with the National Democratic Alliance (NDA) government coming to power, the government in New Delhi could no longer be said to be meeting some of the parameters of consociationalism. Notably, the almost total exclusion of the Muslim community from the government was rather evident, despite the presence of a single Muslim Union Minister in the two NDA governments that came to power in 1998 and 1999. It is noteworthy that the 24 political parties comprising the NDA, the largest being the BJP, could not find more than one Muslim to hold a ministerial position in a country where roughly one out of seven individuals is a Muslim.

India is by no means unique among democratic nations in having coalition governments. In France, which has a system of proportional representation, and in Germany, which has a combination of proportional representation and constituency or seat-based direct elections, coalition governments have been more the rule than the exception after the conclusion of the Second World War in 1945. In both these countries, coalition governments have not usually brought about political instability.

For instance, there is in Germany a legal provision that an incumbent government cannot be voted out of power without simultaneously voting in an alternative government in between general elections. In recent years, for obvious reasons, many have suggested that India could adopt a similar system to avoid frequent elections that are expensive to conduct. Those opposed to this suggestion have argued that even if political instability results in frequent elections having to be conducted, this is a 'small price' to pay to ensure the existence of a vibrant and dynamic democratic polity. These arguments and counter-arguments have come to the fore in discussions on Indian politics for the simple reason that between May 1996 and October 1999, the country for the first time witnessed three general elections in quick succession.

If the experience of countries like Germany and France shows that coalitions and instability do not necessarily go together, Japan and Italy are proof of the fact that even unstable coalition governments do not automatically result in declining economic progress. Japan has had a series of coalition governments since 1976, when the Liberal Democratic Party lost its monopoly on power for the first time after the Second World War. That certainly did not prevent Japan from marching swiftly ahead of most of the world to become arguably the strongest economy in the world after the US, till the slowdown of the 1990s robbed it of some of the sheen. The Italian experience is even more remarkable. In the 58 years since the World War ended, Italy has had as many as 54 governments. Thus, a government in Italy lasts on average barely a year. Yet, Italy today is among the five most industrialised countries in the world. This, if nothing else, should make us wary about drawing any facile conclusions about the effects of political instability on the economy.

Even as this book was going to press in February 2004, important political developments were taking place in the run-up to the 14th general elections:

- Former Chief Minister of Uttar Pradesh Kalyan Singh had returned to the BJP after having been expelled from the party after the 1999 elections.
- The BJP had tied up with the AIADMK in Tamil Nadu though AIADMK leader J. Jayalalithaa had been instrumental in the fall of the second Vajpayee government in 1999.
- The Nationalist Congress Party (NCP) led by Sharad Pawar had broken up, with P.A. Sangma and V.C. Shukla forming their own political outfits.

- Congress President Sonia Gandhi's children Priyanka Vadra and Rahul Gandhi had started playing a more active political role and speculation on their entry into the electoral arena was rife.

- The BJP in Haryana jettisoned its partner, the Indian National Lok Dal (INLD), now seen as a liability.

Clearly, the process of fast-changing political alignments is far from over and pragmatism—or opportunism—continues to override ideological niceties.

India in a Time of Coalitions

The Introduction to the book briefly outlines why the Indian polity fragmented. It examines the political and social processes that led to the decline of the Congress and the rise of the BJP and regional parties, including caste-based parties. The new phase of coalition politics in the country is contextualised in this chapter and arguments are presented to support the contention that coalitions have had a positive influence on the working of the country's democratic polity. This introductory chapter explains why coalitions are not an aberration or a temporary phenomenon.

Bharatiya Janata Party: In Search of the 'Right' Strategy

Chapter 1 looks at the rise of the BJP from the time when it was virtually wiped out of Parliament in 1984. In the period since then, the party has not only provided India its first truly non-Congress Prime Minister, but also the first non-Congress Prime Minister to have remained in office for more than five years. The chapter documents the manner in which the BJP has periodically toned up or subdued its Hindutva rhetoric to come to power and retain it. The chapter attempts to answer the question: Which of the two faces of the BJP that have been seen in recent years—the hardline Hindutva face or the moderate, accommodative face—is likely to emerge as the party's real face over time?

The chapter also looks at the 'Congressisation' of the BJP, at how a party that once prided itself on its discipline is today as faction-ridden and corrupt as any other and has lost whatever claims it had to being 'a party with a difference'. Also examined is the rise and fall of the BJP in Uttar Pradesh, a state that is of crucial significance for the party in its search for power on its own at the centre. Of particular interest is the social combination that the BJP had seemingly forged successfully in the state and the reasons for this combination now apparently coming apart. Another aspect that the chapter deals with is the attempt by the Sangh Parivar (a term used to describe the Rashtriya Swayamsevak Sangh and the family of organisations associated with it, including the BJP) to appropriate part of the Opposition space in Indian politics. Will this attempt succeed in minimising the electoral damage done by the BJP's crumbling image? Or will the electorate see through this 'forked tongue' strategy?

During its tenure in office, the BJP has consciously tried to use foreign policy and defence policy as well as the issue of internal security as tools for enhancing its domestic support base. How successful has this strategy been? Has it persuaded unbiased voters that the party is more concerned about India's security than previous governments or has it only confirmed the suspicion that the BJP's communal agenda is by no means buried?

Indian National Congress: A Return to Family Values

Chapter 2 documents the dramatic decline of the Indian National Congress and its marginalisation in Uttar Pradesh and Bihar. It looks at how the large-scale desertion of the minorities (Muslims and Sikhs) and other sections like the scheduled castes and scheduled tribes in many parts of the country robbed the party of the 'umbrella' character it once had on account of its leadership of the independence movement. This chapter goes on to examine the Congress party's attempts to woo back these sections under the leadership of Sonia Gandhi and whether such attempts are succeeding or are likely to do so.

Can the Congress revive on its own, without depending on allies as the BJP is doing? Can a party that has barely one-fifth of the seats in the Lok Sabha continue to boast that it remains the only truly national party with around 28 per cent of the popular vote spread across the country? Can the Congress afford to ignore the fact that it lost important regional leaders like Sharad Pawar (Maharashtra), Mamata Banerjee (West Bengal), P.A. Sangma (Meghalaya) and the late G.K. Moopanar (Tamil Nadu)? The dearth of leaders with a mass base within the Congress was exacerbated by the sudden deaths in 2001 of two of the party's most popular young leaders—Rajesh Pilot and Madhavrao Scindia. Will these factors further centralise power within the Congress in the hands of the 'high command', which has become a euphemism for one person—party President Sonia Gandhi? What could this mean for the prospects of a revival of the Congress?

Caste in Stone: Politics of the Hindi Heartland

Chapter 3 deals with the fragmentation of the polity along caste lines in the states of Uttar Pradesh and Bihar. The social churning that most of southern India witnessed over a long period starting about half a century ago is now in evidence in the north in a more violent form. Some sections of the backward castes, which have for some time now exercised economic clout in Uttar Pradesh and Bihar, are clear that this influence has to be translated into political power as well. This attempt has succeeded in varying degrees in the two states. However, with the dalits also starting to assert themselves more vigorously and with fissures developing within the ranks of the other backward sections, the caste arithmetic in the country is not easy to decipher or interpret—even if class and caste tend to overlap in many parts of the country.

Small is Beautiful: Rooted in Region

Chapter 4 examines the rise of regional parties and looks into the question of how well established these parties are and how long their alliances are likely to last. Such political parties include the Telugu Desam Party in Andhra Pradesh, the Dravida Munnetra Kazhagam and the All India Anna Dravida Munnetra Kazhagam in Tamil Nadu, the Shiromani Akali Dal (SAD) in Punjab, the National Conference (NC) in Jammu & Kashmir, the Shiv Sena in Maharashtra, the Biju Janata Dal in Orissa and the Trinamool Congress in West Bengal. Regional parties have often been portrayed— particularly by supporters of the Congress and the BJP—as parties with narrow, partisan interests that are incapable of transcending the confines of their state or region. The interests of the country as a whole, it has been argued, cannot be safe in their hands. This chapter shows why this is a coloured view of regional parties. It illustrates situations in which the regional parties have shown that they are capable of looking at issues from a wider perspective.

Left Parties: Caged Birds?

Chapter 5 describes the changing tactics of the left in Parliamentary politics and the differences that have cropped up between them. While the Communist Party of India (CPI) became a part of the Union government for the first time in June 1996, the largest among the left parties, the CPI(M)—Communist Party of India (Marxist), remained wary of becoming part of an ideologically disparate United Front coalition. It had shunned the opportunity of even leading the Union government when the party's central committee voted against the party joining the United Front government thereby depriving the then West Bengal Chief Minister Jyoti Basu of a chance of becoming the Prime Minister. The chapter looks at how the left has been a key factor in shaping anti-BJP political formations and changing its once-adversarial relationship with the Congress. It also looks at what options the left has in the unfolding political scenario and what, if anything, it can do to further its dream of a 'Left and Democratic' front.

Friends in Need: Are Coalitions Inherently Unstable?

Chapter 6 deals with the question of whether coalitions can provide stable Union governments. It analyses coalitions in the past, in New Delhi and in various states, to see whether there are any credible guarantees for the longevity of coalitions. In New Delhi, the first non-Congress coalition government came to power in March 1977. Since then, there have been nine coalition governments at the centre. Why has only the last of these survived a full term? Why has it been relatively easier to forge stable coalitions in states but proved far more difficult to do so at the level of the Union government?

In explaining the instability of coalitions in New Delhi, various reasons have been cited. It has been argued that coalitions have been unstable because they were forged after elections rather than before them. Another popular argument is that coalitions can last only if there is one dominant party leading a pack of relatively insignificant partners. Do these theories stand the test of facts? Not quite, as this chapter reveals.

Friends in Deed: Can Coalitions Govern Effectively?

To what extent have political coalitions in India led to better governance? This is not an easy question to answer. Good governance has to be first defined and would include various considerations such as a lower incidence of corruption, greater transparency and accountability of bureaucrats and politicians, greater federalism, better distribution of the benefits of economic growth among the weaker sections and empowerment of those social sections which are less privileged in the country's caste-based society.

Chapter 7 focuses on some of these issues. Have coalition governments reduced the incidence of corruption in India? Some would argue that the fragmentation of the polity and the existence of coalition governments have brought about a slow and gradual process of cleansing in the economy and society. Others would contend that the incidence of scams and scandals would continue to rise as politicians, bureaucrats and those in business scramble to make a fast buck in a system in which the honest are penalised and a few have vast discretionary powers. The other issue is whether coalition governments have brought about a greater degree of federalism (or decentralisation) in India's polity. The answer to this question, we show, is an unequivocal: 'yes'.

Illusion of Consensus

Chapter 8 is on the economy. Is it true that coalition governments have slowed down or changed the course of economic policy making? We argue that they have not. At the same time economic decisions have certainly reflected the pulls and pressures of coalition politics. This chapter also shows how the notion that there is a consensus on the economic reforms programme within and across political parties is quite misleading. Very often the dissensions within parties—whether it be the BJP or the Congress—are as sharp as those between them. Finally, the chapter deals with whether the shifts in the polity and those in the economy are working in tandem or pulling in different directions.

Gazing at a Crystal Ball

The concluding chapter, Chapter 9, attempts to look ahead. The future of Indian politics has never been easy to predict at the best of times, more so now than ever before. The behaviour of nearly 700 million potential voters—over half of whom actually cast their votes—has become increasingly difficult to anticipate. If the view that ideologies are getting more and more blurred is accepted, the political matrix would get exceedingly complex and unpredictable. How well can a country with 20 officially-recognised languages, whose peoples practice over half-a-dozen major religions (though over 80 per cent of the Indian population is Hindu) and divide themselves along every conceivable line—be it language, religion, class, caste, region or race—not merely survive but also prosper as a nation-state? Read on.

Acknowledgements

This book has taken us all of six years to finish from the time we first started working on it. The delay has been thanks almost entirely to our own inability to set a deadline for ourselves and our desire to keep updating the book to take account of fresh developments. Anybody who has followed Indian politics over these last six years even cursorily would be aware of how rapidly the polity has been changing—and continues to change—and would, therefore, we hope be able to empathise with our predicament. The Vajpayee government's decision to advance the timing of the 14th general elections finally forced a deadline on us. We should, perhaps, be thankful to the government for deciding the issue for us.

We are especially thankful to our publishers, Sage Publications, who agreed to bring this book out at rather short notice. In particular, we wish to thank Omita Goyal, Sunanda Ghosh and Debjani M. Dutta, all of whom went out of their way to assist us.

We are grateful to Aditya Sinha, Arindam Sengupta, Hari Vasudevan, S. Jaipal Reddy, Kumaresh Chakravarti, Mahesh Rangarajan, Pradip Kumar Dutta, Prakash Patra, Sudipto Chatterjee, Swapan Dasgupta and Rahul Razdan for their comments on an earlier draft of the book. Their willingness to plough through a manuscript that was almost twice the size of the current book and their insightful comments have been of tremendous help to us in sharpening the focus of the book. Whatever shortcomings remain on this count are despite their suggestions and for which we are entirely responsible. Research support was provided by A. Srinivas, Urmi A. Goswami, and R. Sowmya Sri.

We wish to record our gratitude to our wives—Jaya and Aditi— who have had to put up with frequent disruptions in their normal routine to let us work. We hope that our children—Aranya, Trina, Triya and Purnajyoti—will also one day agree that the time we denied them was not wasted and that the result of that effort will remain relevant till they are old enough to understand what we have written.

The late Pranab Guha Thakurta, who unfortunately did not live to read the final version of his son's book, encouraged us to persevere, as did Krishna Guha Thakurta, K. Raghuraman and T.S. Kamalam. As parents, their anxiety to see the task completed and their constant queries on when the book would be published helped us to keep going. Thanks are due to Santwana Nigam and Rajendra Nath, who often had to adjust their schedules to take care of their grandchildren to enable us to work on the book.

We thank our friend Dilip Banerjee for the cover photograph he took of the two of us.

Our thanks are also due to many friends, colleagues and well-wishers but for whose encouragement we might have despaired of ever finishing the book.

Paranjoy Guha Thakurta & Shankar Raghuraman

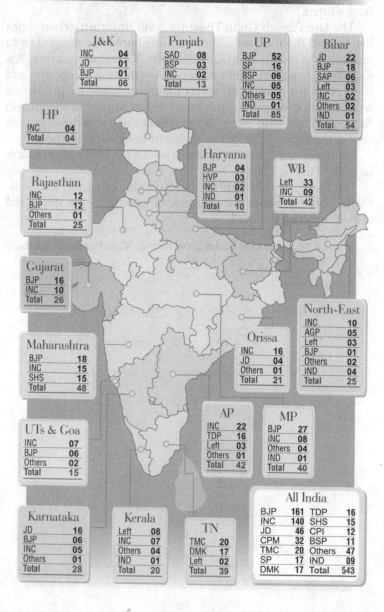

1996 ELECTIONS

J&K

INC	04
JD	01
BJP	01
Total	06

Punjab

SAD	08
BSP	03
INC	02
Total	13

UP

BJP	52
SP	16
BSP	06
INC	05
Others	05
IND	01
Total	85

Bihar

JD	22
BJP	18
SAP	06
Left	03
INC	02
Others	02
IND	01
Total	54

HP

INC	04
Total	04

Haryana

BJP	04
HVP	03
INC	02
IND	01
Total	10

WB

Left	33
INC	09
Total	42

Rajasthan

INC	12
BJP	12
Others	01
Total	25

Gujarat

BJP	16
INC	10
Total	26

North-East

INC	10
AGP	05
Left	03
BJP	01
Others	02
IND	04
Total	25

Maharashtra

BJP	18
INC	15
SHS	15
Total	48

Orissa

INC	16
JD	04
Others	01
Total	21

UTs & Goa

INC	07
BJP	06
Others	02
Total	15

AP

INC	22
TDP	16
Left	03
Others	01
Total	42

MP

BJP	27
INC	08
Others	04
IND	01
Total	40

Karnataka

JD	16
BJP	06
INC	05
Others	01
Total	28

Kerala

Left	08
INC	07
Others	04
IND	01
Total	20

TN

TMC	20
DMK	17
Left	02
Total	39

All India

BJP	161	TDP	16
INC	140	SHS	15
JD	46	CPI	12
CPM	32	BSP	11
TMC	20	Others	47
SP	17	IND	09
DMK	17	Total	543

1998 ELECTIONS

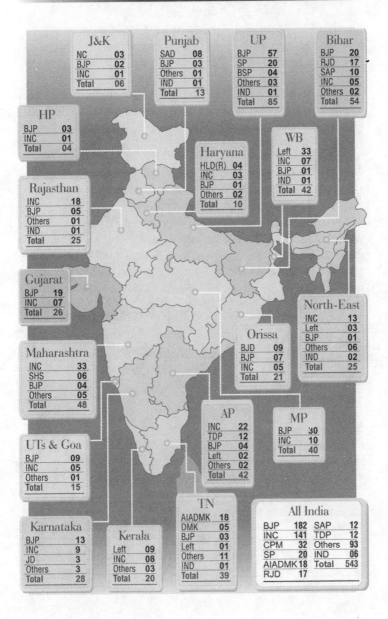

J&K

NC	03
BJP	02
INC	01
Total	06

Punjab

SAD	08
BJP	03
Others	01
IND	01
Total	13

UP

BJP	57
SP	20
BSP	04
Others	03
IND	01
Total	85

Bihar

BJP	20
RJD	17
SAP	10
INC	05
Others	02
Total	54

HP

BJP	03
INC	01
Total	04

Haryana

HLD(R)	04
INC	03
BJP	01
Others	02
Total	10

WB

Left	33
INC	07
BJP	01
IND	01
Total	42

Rajasthan

INC	18
BJP	05
Others	01
IND	01
Total	25

Gujarat

BJP	19
INC	07
Total	26

North-East

INC	13
Left	03
BJP	01
Others	06
IND	02
Total	25

Maharashtra

INC	33
SHS	06
BJP	04
Others	05
Total	48

Orissa

BJD	09
BJP	07
INC	05
Total	21

UTs & Goa

BJP	09
INC	05
Others	01
Total	15

AP

INC	22
TDP	12
BJP	04
Left	02
Others	02
Total	42

MP

BJP	30
INC	10
Total	40

Karnataka

BJP	13
INC	9
JD	3
Others	3
Total	28

Kerala

Left	09
INC	08
Others	03
Total	20

TN

AIADMK	18
DMK	05
BJP	03
Left	01
Others	11
IND	01
Total	39

All India

BJP	182	SAP	12
INC	141	TDP	12
CPM	32	Others	93
SP	20	IND	06
AIADMK	18	Total	543
RJD	17		

1999 ELECTIONS

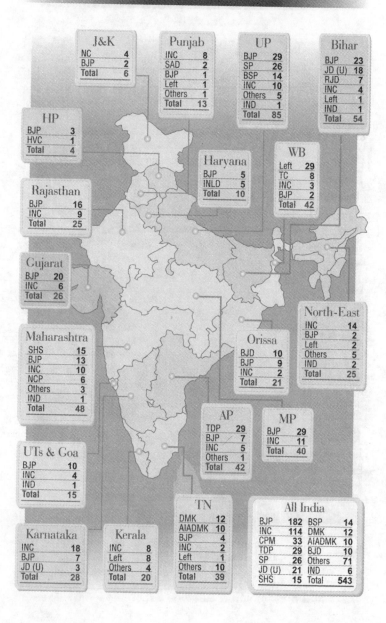

J&K

NC	4
BJP	2
Total	6

Punjab

INC	8
SAD	2
BJP	1
Left	1
Others	1
Total	13

UP

BJP	29
SP	26
BSP	14
INC	10
Others	5
IND	1
Total	85

Bihar

BJP	23
JD (U)	18
RJD	7
INC	4
Left	1
IND	1
Total	54

HP

BJP	3
HVC	1
Total	4

Haryana

BJP	5
INLD	5
Total	10

WB

Left	29
TC	8
INC	3
BJP	2
Total	42

Rajasthan

BJP	16
INC	9
Total	25

Gujarat

BJP	20
INC	6
Total	26

North-East

INC	14
BJP	2
Left	2
Others	5
IND	2
Total	25

Maharashtra

SHS	15
BJP	13
INC	10
NCP	6
Others	3
IND	1
Total	48

Orissa

BJD	10
BJP	9
INC	2
Total	21

UTs & Goa

BJP	10
INC	4
IND	1
Total	15

AP

TDP	29
BJP	7
INC	5
Others	1
Total	42

MP

BJP	29
INC	11
Total	40

Karnataka

INC	18
BJP	7
JD (U)	3
Total	28

Kerala

INC	8
Left	8
Others	4
Total	20

TN

DMK	12
AIADMK	10
BJP	4
INC	2
Left	1
Others	10
Total	39

All India

BJP	182	BSP	14
INC	114	DMK	12
CPM	33	AIADMK	10
TDP	29	BJD	10
SP	26	Others	71
JD (U)	21	IND	6
SHS	15	Total	543

Introduction
India in a Time of Coalitions

In March 2003, Atal Bihari Vajpayee became the first person who had never belonged to the Congress party to remain Prime Minister of India for five successive years. In fact, the Vajpayee government that came to power in October 1999 would almost certainly have lasted its full five-year term till October 2004, except for the fact that it voluntarily sought early elections, not because it could not continue in power.

Does this mean that India has entered a new era of stable coalition governments in New Delhi? At one stage it had appeared that the citizens of India would have to exercise their franchise every few years, that P.V. Narasimha Rao was destined to be the last Prime Minister to have completed his full term in office. The reasons for such a prognosis were obvious. Five successive general elections, starting with the one held in 1989, had failed to yield a single-party majority in the Lok Sabha. The last three of these elections were held within a span of less than three-and-a-half years, unprecedented in Indian history. The Narasimha Rao government was the only one among the seven governments in New Delhi that preceded Vajpayee's government of 1999 to have lasted the course. Even Rao's government was in a minority when it came to power in June 1991 and ultimately secured a majority only through defections.

The initial years of the Vajpayee government strengthened the apprehension that it too would prove to be an unstable coalition. With the support of over 300 of the 543 members in the 13th Lok Sabha, the third Vajpayee government, which came to power in October 1999, was apparently more secure than the previous one. However, halfway through the government's five-year term, the ruling National Democratic Alliance (NDA) led by the Bharatiya

Janata Party (BJP) was looking extremely shaky and threatening to collapse under the weight of its internal contradictions. The contradictions were not just between the BJP and its nearly two dozen allies in the NDA, but also within the Sangh Parivar. Whether one saw the second set of contradictions as a tussle between hardliners and moderates within the BJP and the Sangh Parivar or as a conflict of views between the BJP and the rest of the Parivar on the tactics to be adopted, the fissures appeared to have widened to a point where they threatened to destabilise the government. A string of electoral defeats for the BJP and its allies in the NDA in state assembly elections added to the doubts about the longevity of the government and the alliance.

One crucial event in the first half of 2002 dramatically altered the picture. Within days of the results of the February 2002 assembly elections being known, Gujarat was rocked by Hindu-Muslim riots. Over 1,000 died and several were injured in the worst communal violence witnessed anywhere in India since 1992–93, certainly the worst during the period the BJP has been in power in New Delhi. The orgy of violence began in the early hours of February 27, 2002 when *kar sevaks* (or volunteers for the building of a Ram temple at Ayodhya) travelling on the Sabarmati Express were torched to death by a Muslim mob near an obscure railway station called Godhra. The BJP used to claim that the minorities, especially Muslims, would be 'safest' under a government led by the party—that this claim had been effectively demolished was acknowledged in Parliament by none other than Union Home Minister L.K. Advani. This led to demands for the removal of Chief Minister Narendra Modi, not just from the Opposition, but also from several of the constituents of the NDA. Many of the BJP's allies threatened to withdraw support to the Vajpayee government if Modi was not replaced. But the BJP successfully called their bluff and refused to replace Modi.

In mid-March the same year the second crucial event took place. A number of the BJP's allies had taken exception to the government's position on the Ayodhya dispute (details of the dispute appear at the end of this chapter). The government's plea before the Supreme Court in March 2002 to allow a Hindu religious ceremony to take place at Ayodhya was perceived as violating the understanding among the NDA's constituents that this issue would not be raised. Some of the allies hinted that they would consider withdrawing from the NDA unless the government retracted its position. In this case too, as in the Modi episode, the BJP refused to budge from its position. In both cases, it became clear that if push came to shove the allies would not desert the BJP, even if the BJP periodically pursued its Hindutva agenda. The BJP's position in the NDA became even stronger after Modi led his party to a resounding victory in a communally polarised state by winning two-thirds of the seats in the Gujarat assembly elections held in December 2002.

By then, it became apparent that the threat of the BJP's allies withdrawing their support to the Vajpayee government had effectively dissipated. Remaining in power was clearly more important than maintaining ideological purity on the issue of secularism or politically correct postures. Whatever little doubts may have remained about the longevity of the NDA government were set at rest when two former foes—the All India Anna Dravida Munnetra Kazhagam (AIADMK) and the Bahujan Samaj Party (BSP)—became friends. Interestingly, it was in April 1999 that the AIADMK headed by Jayalalithaa withdrew support to the NDA government, which lost a vote of confidence in Parliament by a single vote in the 543-member Lok Sabha (more on that later). The government would have survived had two MPs of the BSP not abstained from voting.

Irony of ironies. By May 2002, the BJP had decided to support the BSP's Mayawati to run a coalition government in Uttar Pradesh (though the arrangement broke up after 15 months). The BJP was the junior partner in the government having obtained third position in the tally of seats in the 403-member state assembly after the Samajwadi Party (SP) and the BSP. That's not all. Evidence that yesterday's arch enemy could become tomorrow's bosom friend came in the form of Jayalalithaa—Chief Minister of Tamil Nadu—bending over backwards to repeatedly express her fondness for Vajpayee and his government at a time when the AIADMK's traditional rival in Tamil Nadu, the Dravida Munnetra Kazhagam (DMK), was very much a part of the NDA government. The DMK would time and again take a few snipes at the Vajpayee regime till it ultimately left the ruling coalition in December 2003. The AIADMK, on the other hand, would spare no opportunity to support the government while formally remaining outside the NDA. (Jayalalithaa was, in fact, the only non-BJP Chief Minister to have attended the ceremony in which Narendra Modi was sworn in as Chief Minister.)

The victory of the BJP in the December 2003 elections to the assemblies of three states in northern and central India—Rajasthan, Madhya Pradesh and Chhattisgarh—further strengthened the party and the NDA while weakening the Congress. The voters' verdict in the three states was evidently beyond the best expectations of the BJP and its partners in the NDA. Although the Congress was able to return to power in the national capital territory of Delhi, the party was terribly demoralised by its electoral losses. Congress leaders were particularly surprised and shocked that the party could not return to power in Rajasthan and also by the wide margin of defeat in Madhya Pradesh. The electoral outcome once again raised doubts about the ability of Congress President Sonia Gandhi to rejuvenate India's 'grand old party'.

A noteworthy aspect of the political situation in the four states of Delhi, Rajasthan, Madhya Pradesh and Chhattisgarh was that the electoral battle was primarily between the BJP and the Congress. Barring three other states, Himachal Pradesh, Gujarat and Uttaranchal, in each and every one of the other states in India, that is, 23 out of the 30 states in the country, the principal political opponents are not the BJP and the Congress. The other significant aspect of the December 2003 assembly elections was that while anti-incumbency sentiments were strong in Rajasthan, Madhya Pradesh and Chhattisgarh, this phenomenon was conspicuous by its absence in Delhi. What is anti-incumbency? It is when a larger proportion of the electorate votes against the incumbent (government, party or candidate) than in the previous elections.

The national capital used to be a stronghold of the Bharatiya Jana Sangh (BJS), the predecessor of the BJP. As recently as September–October 1999, the party had defeated the Congress in all the seven Lok Sabha seats it had contested in Delhi. Yet, the Congress led by Chief Minister Sheila Dixit was able to return to power with 48.1 per cent of the votes polled, 13 per cent higher than the proportion of votes polled by the BJP. Unlike the rest of the country, anti-incumbency sentiments were virtually absent in Delhi with 45 out of the 55 members of the legislative assembly who had been elected in 1998 being re-elected. The Congress retained 41 out of the 52 seats it had won, while the BJP held on to 10 out of the 15 seats it had earlier won.

The Congress was apparently more attuned to the fast-changing demographic pattern of the capital, which has been characterised by waves of migration from different parts of the country. Over and above the fact that a large section of the electorate was reasonably happy with the track record of the Dixit government in providing water, electricity and in improving roads, what helped the incumbent Chief Minister was the perception that she was more 'dynamic' than the BJP's Chief Ministerial candidate Madan Lal Khurana (who was later appointed to the post of Governor, Rajasthan).

That the 10-year old Congress government in Madhya Pradesh headed by Digvijay Singh was on a losing wicket was evident from the pre-election opinion polls that had been conducted. (The same opinion polls had been unable to predict the BJP's victories in Rajasthan and Chhattisgarh.) What did surprise political observers, especially Congress supporters, was the massive margin of defeat. Of the 228 assembly seats, the BJP won 171 seats representing a three-fourths majority while the Congress won only 39 seats. In terms of vote share, while the BJP's gain was only to the extent of 3.5 per cent, the Congress lost as much as 9.2 per cent of the votes cast resulting in a landslide defeat for the party given the working of the 'first-past-the-post electoral system'—a system which ensures victory to the candidate polling the maximum number of votes in an electoral constituency whether or not the candidate obtains a majority of the votes polled. The Congress polled 31.8 per cent of the vote and the BJP's share stood at 42.7 per cent.

The BJP was able to make massive inroads into what were considered traditional support bases of the Congress, particularly the tribal dominated areas of Mahakoshal and Malwa. The strategy of projecting Uma Bharati as its Chief Ministerial candidate clearly paid the BJP dividends. Bharati belongs to an intermediate caste, one of those officially called other backward classes (OBCs). Whereas the BJP received support from virtually all social strata and classes in Madhya Pradesh, only the Muslims remained solidly behind the Congress, which could hardly ensure victory for the party.

Despite the media hype in favour of former Chief Minister Digvijay Singh, it became amply clear that he had failed to deliver. Poor quality of governance, inadequate power supplies, a sharp decline in the condition of roads and insufficient availability of irrigation facilities contributed towards the defeat of the Congress government in Madhya Pradesh. The former Chief Minister's much-vaunted claims of having improved the education system and of decentralising power to grassroots-level bodies like the panchayats clearly did not convince the electorate of the state. Digvijay Singh's so-called 'soft Hindutva' line on issues like cow protection also failed to impress voters. That two relatively small parties—the BSP with two seats and the SP with seven—made their presence felt in the state certainly did not help the Congress, for they both ate into the vote share of the party.

The voters of Chhattisgarh were not particularly happy with the performance of Congress Chief Minister Ajit Jogi. Nevertheless, the electoral victory of the BJP in the state was not a sweeping one—the party won 49 out of the 90 seats in the assembly with 39 per cent of the popular vote. On the other hand, the Congress won 37 seats in the assembly with a 36 per cent vote share.

An important reason why the Congress lost in Chhattisgarh was not so much a surge in the BJP's popularity but the fact that two political parties played spoiler, the Nationalist Congress Party (NCP, which had broken away from the Congress on the issue of Sonia Gandhi being a candidate for the post of Prime Minister) and the BSP. Leading the NCP in the state was former Union Minister and Congress stalwart Vidya Charan Shukla, who was pitted against his own brother Shyama Charan Shukla. The NCP won only one seat but obtained 7 per cent of the votes while the BSP won two seats after polling 4.4 per cent of the votes after contesting in as many as 54 assembly constituencies.

The defeat of the Congress was also because the party performed rather poorly in the tribal-dominated Bastar region in the southern part of the state. The 10 seats the Congress lost in this region made all the difference between victory and defeat. Whereas the Congress has always claimed the support of the tribals all over the country, it lost 24 out of the 34 seats reserved for scheduled tribes in Chhattisgarh. (This phenomenon was not merely confined to Chhattisgarh—across the country, increasingly tribals are no longer voting for the Congress but for other parties, especially the BJP.) More importantly, there was widespread popular discontentment in Chhattisgarh about poor infrastructure facilities—availability of drinking water and electricity and the condition of roads—which found expression in the electoral verdict.

Whereas Jogi contended that he was a true leader of the tribals, his controversial image and the perception that he was authoritarian in his style of functioning certainly did not help his party. He was perceived to have turned a blind eye to his son, Amit Jogi, who had become politically influential. The less than complimentary perception of Ajit Jogi prevented the Congress from gaining political mileage out of the scandal involving the secret videotaping of Dilip Singh Judeo, former Union Minister of State for Environment and Forests and an important BJP leader in Chhattisgarh, allegedly accepting bribes for granting favours in the form of mining leases. Ajit Jogi was also foolish enough to sign a formal letter claiming that he had Sonia Gandhi's consent to support a breakaway faction of the BJP to form a government with a tribal as chief minister after the assembly election results were known, a move that led to his subsequent suspension from the Congress.

For the Congress, its biggest surprise was the defeat it suffered at the hands of the BJP during the elections to the Rajasthan assembly. This was because the former Chief Minister of the state Ashok Gehlot was considered clean and efficient. He is said to have endeared himself to the people by the sincerity with which he sought to handle the acute drought that the desert state had experienced in 2002. The question then would obviously arise as to why the BJP was able to win more seats in the Rajasthan assembly than it had ever been able to—120 seats in an assembly of 200 seats, more than double the Congress tally of 56 seats. Importantly, the BJP was able to bag 31 out of the 57 seats it had never won in Rajasthan.

The Congress had to eat humble pie in areas that were considered its traditional stronghold (in the eastern part of the state) and the party was rejected by large sections of its traditional supporters among the tribals—the BJP won 15 out of the 24 seats reserved for scheduled tribes in Rajasthan. The Congress used to get close to two-thirds of the tribal vote in the state but this time its share reportedly slumped to less than 40 per cent. A section of the Jats too ditched the Congress, but what was politically more significant was the fact that the BSP effectively helped the BJP by obtaining around 14 per cent of the dalit votes.

Whereas the BJP's Chief Ministerial candidate Vasundhara Raje was considered an outsider to politics in the state despite having won five Lok Sabha elections from Jhalawar in Rajasthan, she was able to reap the benefits of the BJP's strategy of micro-managing elections in each assembly constituency, a strategy that was said to have been masterminded by BJP General Secretary Pramod Mahajan. The BJP clearly paid a lot of attention to putting up good candidates. Gehlot, on the other hand, erred in allowing most sitting MLAs to offer themselves for re-election. Of the 129 sitting MLAs of the Congress who contested the elections, as few as 33 were re-elected. Interestingly, 12 out of the 30 sitting MLAs of the BJP also lost the assembly elections—a clear indicator of the strong anti-incumbency feelings that dominated the polls.

The results of the December 2003 assembly elections have clearly had an impact on the attitude of Congress leaders towards coalitions. Many sections in the party appear to be questioning the strategy of the Congress fighting elections on its own. While the Congress now seems more willing than before to strike alliances with other 'secular' parties, the big question of whether Sonia Gandhi would remain a contender for the post of Prime Minister remains unresolved. Significantly, on December 26, 2003, she said the Congress would not 'impose' its leadership on the secular alliance that would fight the NDA in the next Lok Sabha elections. She added that the Prime Minister would be 'chosen by the people' implying that the choice of who would be the candidate for the post would be decided only after the outcome of the elections was known. Sonia Gandhi's supporters claim she is the glue that is keeping the Congress together. Her opponents, on the other hand, argue that it is not merely her foreign origin but her political inexperience as well that is checking a revival of the Congress party under her leadership. The outcome of the 14th general elections could help clinch the argument either way.

* * *

In 1999, after the second Vajpayee-led government, which came to power in March 1998 and fell on April 17, 1999, the NDA (by then a pre-election alliance, unlike in 1998) secured a majority (299 seats) on its own. After the election results were announced, some others extended support to the government, taking the NDA's strength in the 543-member Lok Sabha to over 305. This meant that no single ally or constituent of the NDA had the numbers to reduce the government to a minority. Even withdrawal of support by the largest supporter or partner of the BJP-led alliance, the Telugu Desam Party (TDP), with 29 MPs, would have left the government with the support of around 275 members, a little more than the majority mark of 272.

Over the next two years, the NDA acquired new partners while some of its constituents—like the Trinamool Congress in West Bengal and the Pattali Makkal Katchi (PMK) in Tamil Nadu—deserted the alliance for a while, only to return to its fold after faring poorly in state elections. Despite the pulls and pressures of coalition politics, the constituents of the NDA by and large remained faithful to Vajpayee's government. If anything, the government faced stronger opposition to its policies from within the BJP and its ideological parent, the avowedly pro-Hindu RSS and its Parivar, than from the other partners in the alliance.

The NDA government's stability may have seemed inexplicable given the sheer number of coalition partners that had to be kept together, the number varying between 18 and 24 parties, and the fact that there was little ideological affinity among its constituents. The history of Indian politics also suggested that the longevity of alliances was uncertain, even when these were formed before elections. Most of the existing allies of the BJP were its political opponents almost till the day before they joined the NDA and had labelled the party Hindu chauvinist, if not downright 'communal' or 'fascist'. One of the former Ministers in Vajpayee's government formed in October 1999, Ram Vilas Paswan, had voted against the motion of confidence in April 1999 before he joined the government (though he left the NDA three years later). Despite ideological contradictions, however, the lust for power and opposition to the Congress—born of political compulsions in different states—have proved strong cementing forces binding the NDA.

The performance of constituents of the NDA in elections to state assemblies in May 2001 was uniformly poor, while the Congress, the leading Opposition party, put up a reasonably good show. As a result, the NDA and the Congress were ruling more or less the same number of states after these elections. One of the reasons cited for this poor performance of the BJP and its allies was a certain disillusionment among the electorate. It appeared that there was little to differentiate between the BJP and the Congress. The BJP had, at one stage, claimed that it was a 'party with a difference', that its supporters were less corrupt than politicians belonging to the Congress, that its cadres were more disciplined and less prone to factionalism, and that it believed in inner-party democracy unlike its political opponents. Within barely three years of being in power, many of these myths about the BJP had been shattered.

There were no discernible signs of a let-up in the incidence of corruption, internal bickering among contending groups within the party was rife and above all, the BJP's 'high command'—a revealing term once used only by the Congress to refer to the party president—was prone to replacing chief ministers in Uttar Pradesh, Gujarat and Uttaranchal at the proverbial drop of a hat without even going through the pretence of consultations among members of legislative assemblies. There was one important difference, however, between the two largest political parties in the country. Whereas the Congress took many decades in power to acquire its image of being a slothful, corrupt and decadent party, the BJP had achieved this dubious distinction in the span of just a few years.

The BJP's allies could read the writing on the wall even before elections to Uttar Pradesh, Punjab, Uttaranchal and Manipur took place in February 2002. While their unease grew, however, there was little they could immediately do about it, with the Congress preferring to bide its time rather than precipitate a political crisis. The BJP's allies were not the only ones to sense a decline in the NDA's popular support. Sections within the Sangh Parivar responded to the threat by seeking to appropriate some of the 'Opposition space' by criticising the government for its economic policies as well as its foreign policy.

If the BJP's allies were worried about the NDA's popular support prior to the state assembly elections of February 2002, the results of these elections confirmed their worst suspicions. The BJP and its allies lost in all four states that went to the polls and the Congress ended up forming a government in three of them. Prior to the polls, the BJP and its partners had held power in three of these states, while the fourth—Manipur—was under President's Rule.

In Uttar Pradesh, politically India's most significant state, the BJP put up its worst showing in over a decade, finishing third behind the SP and the BSP. The BJP-led alliance as a whole was only a handful of seats ahead of the BSP and well behind the SP. Considering that this was the state from which one out of every three BJP MPs in the Lok Sabha originated in the 1998 elections and that the party had cornered the single-largest chunk of Parliamentary seats from Uttar Pradesh even in the 1999 elections (29 out of 85 seats in the undivided state), the outcome of the February 2002 assembly elections was a really serious setback to the BJP and, by extension, to the NDA.

In Uttaranchal, the BJP was sitting pretty before the elections, with three-fourths of the legislators belonging to the party. But the 2002 assembly elections, the first in the state's history, saw the Congress gaining a majority and forming the government. In Punjab too, the Congress was a comfortable winner with the ruling Akali Dal–BJP alliance getting just over one-third of the seats in the 117-member assembly. What was significant was that the BJP fared much worse than the Akali Dal, winning just three of the 23 seats it contested.

Manipur, with a history of political instability, was arguably the state where the NDA's stakes were the lowest. None of the alliance partners had any history of electoral support in the state and it was only through a series of defections that first the Samata Party and then the BJP had managed to form governments in the state which lasted for very brief periods before continuing instability led to central rule being imposed on the state. If the elections to the Manipur assembly were significant in any sense in the national political scene, the significance lay in how the Congress would perform. The Congress finished as the single-largest party and though it won only 20 of the 60 seats in the assembly, it managed to cobble together a coalition that formed the government in Manipur.

What the two rounds of state assembly elections in May 2001 and February 2002 had done to the electoral map of India was quite dramatic. Prior to May 2001, the NDA was in power in as many as 16 out of the 30 assemblies in the country (including the ones at Delhi and Pondicherry which are not full-fledged states) while the Congress ruled in only nine assemblies. After February 2002, the situation had altered radically: the Congress was in power (or was sharing power) in 16 states while the NDA's tally had shrunk to only seven. Of these seven assemblies, the largest—and the only state assembly in which the BJP commanded a majority on its own—was Gujarat, which sends 26 MPs to the Lok Sabha. In four out of these seven state assemblies, the party was not a part of the government. (The December 2003 assembly elections saw the political map of India changing again, this time to the advantage of the BJP, with the party wresting from the Congress the three states of Madhya Pradesh, Rajasthan and Chhattisgarh.)

Soon after the results of the February 2002 assembly elections became known, Hindu-Muslim riots rocked Gujarat. Despite L.K. Advani's claim that Narendra Modi had acted with alacrity and contained the violence 'within 72 hours', the NDA government's opponents argued that the Modi administration had been deliberately negligent in containing the violence, if not actively colluding with those who sought 'revenge' against Muslims. Media reports of the riots indicated clearly that the state government had chosen to turn a blind eye to the 'retaliatory' acts of violence. It was not just the BJP's political opponents who attacked the Modi administration's role in the riots, some of the party's allies in the NDA were sharply critical of the Gujarat government in general and, more specifically, Modi's reported claim that the communal riots in different parts of the state were a 'reaction' to the 'action' against the *kar sevaks* at Godhra. (Modi was to subsequently deny that he had implicitly justified the violence by suggesting that Hindus had 'reacted' to the Godhra incident.)

The rift between the BJP and some of its alliance partners in the NDA—often described by the media as 'secular'—as well as the fissures between the so-called hawks and doves within the Sangh Parivar were further widened in early March over the Ayodhya issue.

Over and above the fact that the political temperature had risen on account of the Gujarat violence and the Ayodhya episode, two other incidents precipitated heated exchanges in Parliament. The first was a resolution by the RSS to the effect that the safety of the minorities in India depended on the goodwill of the majority. This statement was flayed by some of the NDA constituents on the ground that it was not just patronising towards the Muslims but also displayed the majoritarian or 'fascist' mindset of the Sangh Parivar. The second incident took place in Bhubaneshwar. A group owing allegiance to the Vishwa Hindu Parishad (VHP) and RSS ransacked a number of rooms in the Orissa assembly apparently on the ground that particular legislators had made statements that were termed 'offensive' by the VHP. This incident caused a fair amount of embarrassment to the Union government not merely because the state government in Orissa was controlled by the Biju

Janata Dal (BJD) in alliance with the BJP, but also on account of the fact that the mob had raised slogans in favour of Vajpayee. While the VHP later apologised for the incident, Orissa Chief Minister and BJD leader Naveen Patnaik claimed his political opponents had engineered the incident to discredit him and his government.

The series of apparently unconnected but dramatic developments in February–March 2002 made the NDA government appear more fragile and prone to internal strife than it had been at any stage since it came to power in November 1999. But, as already mentioned, this appearance was deceptive. In fact, the period February–March 2002 was, in retrospect, a kind of watershed in the NDA's evolution. It was from this period onwards that it became amply clear that the BJP's allies in the coalition had lost much of their ability to influence the agenda of the government, or at least of the BJP.

The declining clout of the BJP's allies and the increasing confidence of the BJP were starkly evident a year later. The Ayodhya issue came to the fore again in February 2003, with the government adopting a stance that was more favourable to the VHP's position than it had ever done in the past. Yet, there was no protest from the allies, unlike a year earlier. The results of the December 2003 assembly elections further strengthened the position of the BJP within the NDA. The BJP's victory in three out of four states that went to the polls was a significant departure from the trend since 1998. In the five years between November 1998 and December 2003, the BJP had won assembly elections only in the small state of Goa (that too, with a razor-thin majority) besides, of course, Gujarat. That the party was able to defeat the Congress in three states in the Hindi heartland was a major morale-booster in the run-up to the 14th general elections.

* * *

The 13th general elections, held in September–October 1999, marked a watershed in the contemporary political history of India. For the first time since 1984, a pre-electoral alliance was able to win a majority of seats in the Lok Sabha. Further, two clear trends that had persisted for a decade-and-a-half were either arrested or reversed. For the first time since 1984, the BJP was unable to add to its tally of seats. In fact, it lost around two percentage points of its share of the popular vote—roughly equal to 8 per cent of the total votes cast in favour of the party in the February 1998 elections. Though this decline in the vote share of the BJP was popularly attributed to the party having contested nearly 50 seats less in 1999 (339 against 388 in the 1998 elections), this was only partly true. Even a comparison of the vote share of the BJP in the 331 seats that it contested in both the 1998 and 1999 elections indicated a slight fall (of the order of 0.8–0.9 percentage points) in its support base.

The second trend that was arrested was the fall in the share of votes obtained by the Congress. The party's vote share had gone up by nearly 3 per cent between 1998 and 1999 though it lost nearly 30 seats in the Lok Sabha thanks to the 'first-past-the-post principle'. The support of the Congress was evidently spread relatively thinly across the country whereas the BJP's support base was concentrated in particular geographical regions, enabling the party to win more seats in the Lok Sabha even with a lower share of the popular vote. The net result of these two trends was that the expected polarisation between the BJP and the Congress did not take place (more on this later).

The 1999 general elections had also seen the most concerted attempt ever in Indian politics to project the electoral battle as some sort of a presidential referendum, with the BJP harping on a comparison between Atal Bihari Vajpayee and Sonia Gandhi. Another issue raised at this juncture was Sonia Gandhi's foreign origins. Some argue that this fact became a 'campaign issue' only after three senior Congress leaders broke away from the parent party after demanding that Sonia Gandhi make it clear that she would not be a Prime Ministerial aspirant. The leaders, who went on to form the Nationalist Congress Party (NCP), were Sharad Pawar, former Chief Minister of Maharashtra, Union Defence Minister in the Narasimha Rao Cabinet, and leader of the Opposition in the 12th Lok Sabha; P.A. Sangma, former Speaker of the Lok Sabha; and Tariq Anwar, a long-standing Lok Sabha MP from Katihar in Bihar. Their contention, in a letter circulated among members of the Congress Working Committee, was that no person of non-Indian origin should be entitled to hold the posts of President, Vice President or Prime Minister of the country. This dovetailed very well with the BJP's strategy for the impending 13th general elections, in which the party made it clear it would raise Sonia's Italian origin as a major issue. Another significant event that took place when Vajpayee's government was reduced to a 'caretaker' one was the infiltration of hundreds of people who crossed the Line of Control (LoC) in the Kargil area. The Indian defence forces responded by launching air and ground strikes.

As it turned out, the NCP did not make much of an electoral impact, except in Pawar's home state of Maharashtra, though Sangma too won from his constituency in the north-eastern state of Meghalaya. In Maharashtra, the NCP managed to win six of the state's 48 Lok Sabha seats, but severely damaged the Congress by splitting its traditional support base across the state. The NCP then went on to form an uneasy alliance with the Congress to form the state government in India's most industrialised province in western India.

The success in driving back infiltrators from Indian territory in the Kargil area in Jammu & Kashmir along the LoC between India and Pakistan in the middle of 1999 was also sought to be projected as a 'victory' of the Vajpayee government and was exploited for electoral mileage. The results and analyses based on post-poll surveys by the New Delhi-based research institution, the Centre for the Study of Developing Societies (CSDS), among others, suggested that Kargil did not have such a major impact on the electorate. The CSDS survey indicated that almost two-thirds (65 per cent) of the respondents questioned were aware of the skirmishes along the LoC but a mere 15 per cent acknowledged that the Kargil episode had influenced their voting. The same survey incidentally indicated that less than half (46 per cent) of the respondents were aware of the nuclear tests conducted by the Vajpayee government in May 1998.

The 13th general elections were the first after the 3rd general elections in 1962 in which polling was spread in five phases over a period of one month. A number of political analysts and psephologists claimed that the impact of Kargil had waned over this period, and that the throwing out of infiltrators to the Pakistan side of the LoC had a greater impact on the electorate in the first three phases of polling in September 1999. Much of this analysis was based on studying the gains and losses in terms of Lok Sabha seats over the five phases of polling. If, however, one studies the data on vote shares, the hypothesis that there was a 'Kargil effect' in the early phase of polling, which waned as the elections progressed, cannot be sustained.

The data revealed that the vote share of the BJP and its allies did not show an improvement over the 1998 figures (if one takes into account the new alliances) even in the early phases of polling. This means that the Vajpayee government's claims of having won a 'victory' at Kargil did not add votes to NDA's kitty. The 'Kargil effect' must, therefore, be seen as a myth. After all, if there was a Kargil effect in favour of the BJP and its allies in the early stages of the elections, it should have resulted in more voters voting for them than the number which did in the 1998 elections. This simply did not happen. A more plausible hypothesis is that the incidents in Kargil did help the BJP and its allies to stem, and reverse, what till early 1999 seemed like an upsurge in the fortunes of the Congress. Even so, the impact of Kargil seems at best to have prevented loss of seats for the NDA relative to the 1998 position, not added seats. The BJP certainly did not lose support on account of Kargil—but the extent to which the party gained remains debatable.

That the alliance won more seats in 1999 than in the 1998 elections was thanks entirely to the electoral arithmetic in different states. In particular, the split in the traditional Congress base in Maharashtra and the addition of the votes of new allies of the BJP like the TDP in Andhra Pradesh and the Janata Dal (United) (JD[U]) in Bihar drastically changed electoral equations in these states. These three states between them accounted for 144 seats in the Lok Sabha and the NDA had gained almost 50 seats in these states compared to the 1998 elections. Of these, 37 seats were gained in Maharashtra and Andhra Pradesh alone. The fact that both these states had completed polling by the third phase explains the huge gains made by the NDA in the initial phases of polling, rather than any so-called Kargil effect. It must be emphasised that the BJP–Shiv Sena (the BJP's oldest ally in the NDA) alliance lost a substantial chunk of its vote share in Maharashtra, but gained seats thanks to the split in the Congress on the eve of elections. Similarly, in Andhra Pradesh, the BJP and the TDP put together could not improve on their vote share between 1998 and 1999, while the Congress did—but not enough to counteract the consolidation of votes on the other side.

There is another, more obvious, explanation to counter the hypothesis of the Kargil effect. Evidence of this came in the form of the divergent results in different states that went to the polls in the initial part of the elections, in the first three weeks of September 1999. If Kargil did indeed boost the prospects of the NDA, why did the alliance sweep Haryana, Himachal Pradesh and Delhi (winning all 21 seats in these states) while, at the same time, being very nearly wiped out in neighbouring Punjab (winning just 3 of the 13 seats in the state) which borders Pakistan? Why did the BJP and its allies win 36 of the 42 Lok Sabha seats in Andhra Pradesh, but only 10 of the 28 seats in Karnataka, where they had won 16 seats in the previous elections in 1998? The explanation is rather mundane and, as stated earlier, has more to do with electoral arithmetic—the division of opposition votes or an addition of a new ally to the BJP's camp. In addition, there were strong anti-incumbency sentiments in states like Punjab and Karnataka, where the local governments were perceived to be less than responsive to popular aspirations.

The 1999 elections also disproved the hypothesis of 'voter apathy' due to frequent elections. The 60 per cent voter turnout in 1999 was a little lower than the 62 per cent recorded in the 1998 elections, but higher than the 58 per cent recorded in 1996. Even if many of the 670-odd million voters in India are poor and illiterate and should have good reason for being disillusioned with democratic institutions of governance, the fact is that they exercise their franchise in much higher proportion than do the educated and economically better-off urban middle class. The South Delhi constituency (regarded as having one of the most educated and prosperous electorates), for instance, recorded only a 42 per cent voter turnout. (This was the constituency from which former Finance Minister Manmohan Singh, considered the architect of economic reforms in the Narasimha Rao government, lost by 30,000 votes to the BJP's Vijay Kumar Malhotra.)

A related phenomenon, which might explain the continuing enthusiasm for voting, is the strong anti-incumbency trend witnessed in the last three general elections. On each occasion, between 40 per cent and 50 per cent of incumbent MPs were rejected, either by their own parties or by the voters. Thus, each of the last three Lok Sabhas has seen around 250 new faces in a House comprising 543 members. Considering that the last three elections have been held within a span of just three-and-a-half years, this is a telling indicator of the way the electorate punishes politicians perceived to be 'non-performing'. Anti-incumbency sentiments operate at both the central and state levels. As a result, it is not uncommon for a party's MPs to pay the price for the failure of its state government to deliver on its promises. The number of constituencies retained by political parties in the last three elections has barely exceeded half the 543 seats in the Lok Sabha: the exact figures are 264 in 1996, 263 in 1998, and 283 in 1999. Though it may seem unfair that an individual MP should be punished by the electorate for no fault of his, the flip-side is that good work by the party's government too pays off for the incumbent MP. This underlines the fact that while individuals do matter, the policies and performance of parties are more important in a Parliamentary democracy.

In the 1999 elections, there were strong anti-incumbency sentiments among voters in a number of states. These sentiments worked against the BJP-led NDA in Uttar Pradesh, Punjab, Maharashtra and Karnataka. The same sentiments worked against the Congress in Orissa and Rajasthan and the Asom Gana Parishad (AGP) in Assam. However, many state governments defied this trend. Among such states were the left-ruled states of West Bengal, Kerala and Tripura, the Congress-ruled Madhya Pradesh, the TDP-ruled Andhra Pradesh and the DMK-ruled Tamil Nadu. However, in the May 2001 assembly elections, anti-incumbency sentiments were strong in Tamil Nadu, Kerala and Assam, while West Bengal's voters continued to swim against the tide—helped by the CPI(M) led Left Front replacing the octogenarian Jyoti Basu with Buddhadeb Bhattacharjee (who is 25 years younger) as Chief Minister, despite the fact that Basu holds the distinction of having been India's longest-serving Chief Minister in a state (between 1977 and 2001).

The importance of anti-incumbency sentiments is best illustrated by the BJP's performance in undivided Uttar Pradesh which then had almost one-sixth of the total seats in the Lok Sabha (85 out of 543). In the 1998 elections, the BJP on its own had won 57 of the state's 85 seats and with its allies had won 60 seats. In 1999, however, the party could barely win 29 seats on its own and a total of 32 seats with its allies. While most political pundits and opinion polls or exit polls had predicted some reverses for the BJP in UP, the magnitude and scale of the party's losses, in a four-cornered contest in most parts of the state, came as a surprise even to them.

The surprising nature of the UP results in the 1999 Lok Sabha elections was attributed by many, including psephologists, to 'tactical voting' by those opposed to the BJP (a thinly-veiled reference to the Muslims in particular). However, the data does not bear out such a hypothesis. If indeed tactical voting was resorted to in larger measure, the voting patterns should have shown less of a division in the non-BJP votes in constituencies than it did in the past. On the contrary, what the data revealed was a significant increase in the division of votes in most constituencies. To be precise, the index of opposition unity (IOU), a statistical tool used by psephologists to measure the division of opposition votes, had increased vis-à-vis 1998 in 57 of the state's 85 Lok Sabha constituencies. The increased division of votes was thanks largely to the fact that the Congress, which had been reduced to no seats and just 6 per cent of the vote in 1998, increased its vote share by 8 percentage points to 14 per cent and won 10 seats while two more seats were won by its ally, the Rashtriya Lok Dal lead by Ajit Singh. (The RLD subsequently ditched the Congress for the BJP in 2001 and Ajit Singh, son of former Prime Minister Charan Singh, became Union Agriculture Minister in the Vajpayee government. Ajit Singh again parted ways with the BJP in 2002.)

The real reason for the BJP's debacle in Uttar Pradesh was an extremely strong anti-incumbency wave against the party. The BJP, which had won 36.5 per cent of the votes in the state in the 1998 elections, got only 27.6 per cent in 1999, a drop of about 9 per cent. This was by far the largest swing of votes away from an incumbent state government anywhere in the country in the 1999 elections. However, as we shall elaborate later, this swing away from the BJP was not uniform across all sections of UP society. There were clear indications of a marked disenchantment among the upper castes, who had in the 1990s been ardent supporters of the BJP. The result of this disenchantment was that Kalyan Singh, the man the BJP had projected through the 1990s as its most popular mass leader in the state and the automatic choice for Chief Minister, had to step down a month after the results of the October–November 1999 Lok Sabha elections were known and yield place to Ram Prakash Gupta, a man who was Deputy Chief Minister two decades earlier in 1977, but had since then been consigned to political oblivion. Despite the so-called dynamism displayed by Gupta's successor Rajnath Singh and his concerted efforts to woo the 'most backward classes', the BJP was unable to recover lost ground in the February 2002 assembly elections—as already mentioned, the party ended up third in the elections, after the SP and the BSP. Out of the 403 seats in the UP assembly, in the February 2002 elections the BJP obtained 88 seats, the BSP 98 and the SP 143.

While on the subject of anti-incumbency, it is worth pointing out that the viewpoint widely spread by the media and political analysts about the Rashtriya Janata Dal (RJD) in Bihar doing very poorly in the Lok Sabha elections in 1999 because of resentment against its state government's non-performance was simply not true. Election data reveals that the RJD and its major ally in the state, the Congress, both increased their share of the popular vote. Yet, the alliance (which also included the CPI[M]) could win just 12 (RJD: 7, Congress: 4 and CPI[M]: 1) out of the state's 54 Lok Sabha seats. This was, as in Andhra Pradesh, electoral arithmetic at work rather than anti-incumbency sentiments. While the Janata Dal had contested against the BJP–Samata Party alliance and the Congress–RJD alliance in 1998, it had joined the NDA in the 1999 elections. Since the Janata Dal had secured 9 per cent of the popular vote in the 1998 elections, this addition was always likely to be electorally significant, if the party's supporters were willing to accept such an alliance. As it turned out, the majority was comfortable with this arrangement. Thus, the addition of 6 per cent to the NDA's kitty of votes was enough to add 10 seats to its tally in Bihar.

Yet, it is true that by any yardstick of performance, the RJD government in Bihar cannot be said to have 'performed' if one looks at the economic indicators of one of India's poorest states. All of this suggests that the anti-incumbency factor too cannot be seen merely as a consequence of 'lack of performance' by state governments, as perceived by middle-class analysts or sections of the media. It is a rather more complex mix of developmental issues and of community identity and *izzat* (honour or pride).

* * *

After the 11th general elections in May 1996, Vajpayee's government had lasted barely 13 days. This was followed by the formation of a United Front comprising over a dozen political parties that ran the government with tenuous support from the Congress for a year-and-a-half under two Prime Ministers, H.D. Deve Gowda and I.K. Gujral. The slender majority of the next Vajpayee government that came to power after the February–March 1998 elections was despite the truly spectacular rise of the BJP's strength in

Parliament over the previous decade and a half. In the last decisive general elections held in India, in 1984, the BJP had won only two of the 543 seats in the Lok Sabha. The Congress, which had at that time run the Union government for all but six years since 1947, when India became politically independent, held as many as 415 seats in the Lok Sabha after the 1984 elections. The party, for the first and only time, had more than three-fourths majority in Parliament following the elections that were conducted after the assassination of former Prime Minister Indira Gandhi in October that year. The elections saw her son Rajiv Gandhi succeeding her with a thumping majority in Parliament, the likes of which was never enjoyed by Indira Gandhi herself or her father Jawaharlal Nehru, the first Prime Minister of independent India.

Since 1984, the BJP has gained the most from the decline of the Congress. But that is only the beginning of the story. The rest of it is about the mushrooming of myriad political formations, which, in turn, has resulted in five coalition governments since May 1996. For the first time, the chair of the Prime Minister of India was occupied by no less than four individuals in the span of less than a year, between May 1996 and April 1997.

Has India entered a new phase of coalition politics? Yes, it has. Is the country ultimately moving towards a two-party system or is it moving towards a multi-party system in which two dominant parties provide poles for the rest to cluster around? As already stated, we do not think so. In our view, the process of fragmentation of the polity is not yet over. This, in turn, could throw up unexpected possibilities and political realignments, including the formation of new political parties.

To what extent has the BJP succeeded in shedding its image of being a right-wing Hindu nationalist party dominated by the upper-caste sections of north India? To some extent, it undoubtedly has, and in fact went out of its way to shed it. Will the Congress, the 119-year-old party of the country, be able to revive and re-occupy the centrist political space as an umbrella organisation representing the interests of all sections of the world's most heterogeneous society, under the leadership of Sonia Gandhi? We are not so sure. Has the so-called 'third force', an amorphous combination of the left and largely regional parties, become irrelevant after just 18 months in power or will this section continue to play a pivotal role in shaping the country's politics? The answer is that smaller parties would be playing an even more important role in shaping the country's polity, whether or not they come together as a united front.

Virtually everybody, barring a few sections within the Congress, has now come to accept the new reality of Indian politics, namely that the era of single-party rule is over, at least in the foreseeable future. In fact, it can convincingly be argued that it is the Congress' failure to recognise this reality that has, to a great extent, been responsible for the party steadily losing seats in Parliament. After the 13th general elections, the Congress found itself with just 112 seats in the Lok Sabha, by far the lowest ever, despite increasing its vote share significantly. The results of the 1999 elections also suggest that the polity is far from becoming bipolar. The two largest parties—the BJP and the Congress—between themselves accounted for just over half the seats and votes polled. In other words, close to half the votes and seats went to roughly three dozen other political parties of varying sizes, many of which were not aligned with either the BJP or the Congress. Clearly, despite assertions to the contrary by both the BJP and the Congress, the political space for a 'third front' does continue to exist, however amorphous such a grouping might be.

That the BJP managed to woo close to two dozen allies from across the length and breadth of the country meant that, at least for some time, the BJP was forced to keep in abeyance some of its contentious and emotive slogans like the building of a Ram temple at Ayodhya, the abrogation of Article 370 of the Constitution (which confers special status to the state of Jammu & Kashmir in terms of autonomy from the central government) or the demand for a uniform civil code.

Any government in a polity as badly fractured as India's has been after the last three general elections—held in May 1996, February 1998 and September–October 1999—would almost inevitably not be very stable. On its own, the BJP, the single-largest party in the 13th Lok Sabha, had barely a third of the total number of seats. In 1998, even with its pre-poll allies, it did not command a majority. The party was, therefore, forced to depend on those willing to categorise it merely as a 'lesser enemy' in order to ensure the survival of its government.

One of the biggest surprises of the post-election scenario in March 1998 was the support given to the Vajpayee government by the TDP headed by Andhra Pradesh Chief Minister Chandrababu Naidu who, till that stage, was the convenor of the United Front. Naidu played a tantalising game of hide and seek with his erstwhile allies, insisting that the TDP would remain 'equidistant' from the Congress and the BJP. The first indication of what equidistance meant to the TDP was the surprise election of its nominee as the Speaker of the Lok Sabha with the support of the BJP and its allies. The drama reached its culmination with Naidu announcing just hours before the actual vote of confidence in the house that his party would be voting in favour of the Vajpayee government.

Also surprising was the decision of the National Conference (NC), a party that was then ruling the northern-most state of Jammu & Kashmir—India's only Muslim-majority state—to abstain in the vote of confidence sought by Vajpayee in March 1998. The decision of the NC, led by Chief Minister Farooq Abdullah, surprised many since the BJP has long been perceived as inimical to Muslim interests and also because the party in its election manifesto had argued in favour of abrogation of Article 370. Abdullah justified his decision on the ground that the state could ill afford to have an antagonistic relationship with whoever was in power in New Delhi. While the TDP subsequently had to part ways with the United Front (UF), the NC curiously never formally withdrew from the Front. It is another matter that the Front itself later ceased to exist without any formal process of dissolution ever taking place. After being a part of the NDA for more than four years, the NC left the alliance in 2003 after it had failed to form the government in Jammu & Kashmir.

What were the consequences of the fractured mandate and the unexpected shifts in allegiances after the 12th general elections held in February–March 1998? One was that the Vajpayee government had 18 parties supporting it at that time, including half a dozen parties with just one MP each. Yet, the government's survival of its first vote of confidence was thanks almost entirely to the TDP's last-minute decision to support the BJP-led government. The fact that the TDP insisted its support to the Vajpayee government was issue-based and not unconditional underlined the fragility of the government.

Vajpayee himself had felt that the mushrooming of regional parties—the 13th Lok Sabha had 38 political parties recognised by the Election Commission of India, the 12th Lok Sabha had representatives of 42 political parties while there were 26 parties in the

11th Lok Sabha—together with the arguably disproportionate clout these parties enjoy in a situation in which Parliament is 'hung', represents a phase that Indian politics could not have avoided but is also one which would not last for long. This was what the Prime Minister had asserted in his reply to the discussion on the motion of confidence moved by him in the Lok Sabha in March 1998. Vajpayee saw the fragmentation as an aberration in a polity that was gradually moving towards a more stable polarisation (a formulation that the BJP has since been careful not to emphasise).

This analysis was to a large extent a reflection of the outcome of the February 1998 polls in which the 13-party United Front, which ran the two previous governments for 18 months with grudging and uneasy support from the Congress, suffered a debacle. The UF's strength in the Lok Sabha had been reduced from close to 180 seats to less than 100 after the elections. Subsequent desertion from its ranks left it with less than 85 Lok Sabha MPs in March 1998. This convinced the votaries of the two-party theory that they were correct in writing off the 'third force' as a spent force in national politics. As they saw it, the smaller parties would either fade away or be forced to align themselves with one or the other of the two strong poles of Indian politics, the BJP and the Congress. Many shared this view. They suggested that there are distinct signs of the polity becoming bipolar, the BJP providing one pole and the Congress the other.

However, the outcome of the 13th general elections held in September–October 1999 indicated that this trend towards bipolarity was still not taking place and the 'third force' was far from becoming irrelevant. Significantly, the BJP too had subtly changed its assertions on the issue. Unlike the Congress, it had come to terms with the fact that prospects of it growing further on its own steam were dim in the immediate future. Hence, even leaders like L.K. Advani (who went on to become Deputy Prime Minister), perceived as ideological hardliners, conceded that the BJP's continuation in power would depend on its ability to tie up alliances with several regional partners.

Though the United Front itself may be virtually defunct, regional parties as a category have not lost out. On the contrary, these formations have come to hold the levers of power in the Union government. There are, therefore, many who argue that a third space will continue to exist in Indian politics, even if the parties that occupy this space keep changing.

The phenomenon of political parties extending 'outside' support to coalition governments is considered to be a reason why such governments have been unstable—in fact, five out of the seven governments formed in New Delhi between 1989 and 1998 have been brought down on account of withdrawal of support by various parties (especially the Congress and the BJP) that supported governments without participating in them. The exceptions were the Narasimha Rao government, which completed its full term of five years (June 1991 to May 1996) despite starting out as a minority government, and the Vajpayee government of 1998–99. Narasimha Rao had to face charges in court for having allegedly bribed MPs to win a vote of confidence in July 1993. India's premier investigating agency, the Central Bureau of Investigation (CBI), framed the charges. A lower court convicted Rao and one of his Ministers, Buta Singh, but the Delhi High Court acquitted them on appeal.

The other factor that arguably influences the stability of a coalition government is whether the alliance came into being before or after the elections. On the face of it, pre-poll alliances are likely to be more stable than post-poll ones. Yet, the BJP-led coalition found itself unable to muster a majority in the 12th Lok Sabha without the assistance of post-poll allies. As the BJP-led government realised within days of securing power, even pre-poll allies could prove to be troublesome partners—a case in point being the way in which the AIADMK and J. Jayalalithaa brazenly arm-twisted the Vajpayee government to accept their demands on more than one occasion. Eventually, she and her party went on to successfully destabilise the government, thus triggering off the process leading to the 13th general elections. The experience of the recent past lends weight to the contention that the only reasonable guarantee of the stability and longevity of a coalition government is ideological compatibility among partners. The Left Front government in West Bengal and the BJP–Shiv Sena alliance in Maharashtra are two such examples.

The United Front government under Deve Gowda was the first Union government in India that was formed following a post-poll alliance cobbled together in May 1996 and after a Common Minimum Programme (CMP) had been thrashed out. The earlier coalitions at the centre—the Janata Party government in 1977 headed by Morarji Desai and the Janata Dal government in

1989 headed by V.P. Singh—were formed on the basis of pre-poll alliances.

After the May 1996 elections, for the first time the Congress was not the single-largest party in the Lok Sabha. Of course, the Janata Party in 1977 had more seats in the House than the Congress, but the party came into being after various constituents of a pre-poll alliance merged after the elections. In the results of the 1977 elections, therefore, the Congress did emerge as the single-largest party. In 1996, in fact, the Congress became weaker than it ever was in Parliament, with barely 140 MPs in the Lok Sabha against nearly 200 MPs owing allegiance to the BJP and its allies. The BJP emerged as the single-largest party in the lower House despite getting just over one-fifth of the popular vote, while the Congress got just under 30 per cent of the votes. But Vajpayee's first government lasted only between 16 and 28 May 1996.

This was followed by the formation of the 13-party United Front coalition which was supported from 'outside' by both the Congress and the CPI(M), the second- and third-largest parties in the Lok Sabha. Unlike the Congress, the CPI(M) joined the Front (but not the government). While erstwhile political opponents came together to keep the BJP out of power, also for the first time, representatives of regional parties as well as nearly a dozen chief ministers of various Indian states started playing a more active role in the functioning of the central government.

The change from a situation in which a single party (the Congress) dominated the government to one of multi-party configurations has been accompanied by other significant changes in the working of India's polity. One such change has been the growing role of Constitutional institutions from the President to state Governors and the Election Commission. Yet, the instability of central governments has periodically resulted in an active debate on the need for fundamental alterations to the Westminster Parliamentary form of government itself. Arguments have been made in favour of and against different forms of government—an American-style presidential system or a French type of combination of the presidential and parliamentary systems.

The 1999 Lok Sabha election was sought to be projected as a 'presidential' election, one that pitted Vajpayee against Sonia Gandhi. But, it would be simplistic to perceive the elections in this manner. Personalities, separated from the political parties they represent or the issues and ideologies they stand for, have always influenced the Indian electorate to a lesser or greater degree. However, it can be contended that given India's tremendous diversities, the socially and regionally heterogeneous peoples of the country have to evolve their own system that could perhaps uniquely combine the systems existing in other countries.

The questions remain:

- Is India moving towards a two-party system or into an extended phase of coalition politics?
- If indeed coalition governments are here to stay, just how relevant are the experiences of coalitions in various states since 1957?
- Are there lessons to be drawn from these state-level experiences over four decades that are relevant at the all-India level?
- Is there reason to believe that coalitions at the centre are intrinsically more unstable than similar formations in states?
- Will the endeavour to ensure stability of governments lead to a further blurring of ideological distinctions within and among political parties?

The answer to these questions will have an important bearing not only on the future of individual parties or the composition of future governments, but also on the very nature of Indian politics.

In terms of the economy, there has been a subtle, but distinct, change in the debate on the merits of liberalisation, which was significantly accelerated by the minority government of P.V. Narasimha Rao, which came to power in May 1991 after Rajiv Gandhi's assassination. At present, sections of the Congress and the BJP want the Indian economy to integrate with the rest of the world at a faster pace. There is undoubtedly a consensus on the need for and virtues of de-bureaucratisation cutting across all political formations. However, the left and sections of the BJP, the Congress and other political parties have their own different notions about the nature of economic reforms required. One manifestation of this is the slogan of *swadeshi* raised by a section of the ideological fraternity of the BJP. The word literally means 'from one's own land' or 'indigenous', and is a term that was used by the 'father of the nation' Mohandas Karamchand Gandhi, or Mahatma Gandhi, as a call for the boycott of British goods during the anti-colonial struggle. Today, the *swadeshi* slogan has come to signify different things to different people: self-reliance, economic nationalism or even protection to domestic industry from international competition.

While it has been argued that its tenure in office has compelled the BJP to move away from its image of being a right-wing party and to adopt a less sectarian form of politics, there is the counter-argument that the Vajpayee government could confer a certain legitimacy to communal (anti-Muslim) politics that was not so far available to it. Either way, Indian politics could be changing fundamentally.

It is also worth examining how realignments of social forces are likely to influence the course of the country's politics. The growing confidence of the dalits, together with the consolidation of their influence in some of the country's largest states behind parties representing their interests, is one such phenomenon. The emergence of 'other backward classes' as a political force to reckon with is another.

- Does bickering among coalition partners lead to greater transparency and more accountability, which, in turn, reduces the incidence of corruption in public life?
- Or, will it result in greater cynicism among politicians, since today's accusers could become tomorrow's allies?
- Will the participants in governments with short tenures tend to adopt an approach of 'making hay while the sun shines'?
- Or will the fear of their actions being scrutinised by successor regimes act as a check on the propensity of politicians in power to earn a fast buck?

Even though a number of politicians facing charges of corruption have been re-elected (for, among other things, being seen to be fulfilling the aspirations of the electorate), corruption remains an important political and economic issue in India. Sections of the media and the judiciary have become more active in highlighting as well as following up instances of corruption involving persons holding positions of power. The manner in which Narasimha Rao's minority government won a vote of confidence in Parliament in July 1993 and became a majority government by 'allegedly' bribing MPs to defect was itself the subject of a protracted legal battle, as mentioned earlier.

The recent history of India has thrown up a number of crucial questions, the answers to which are not very clear.

- What impact would the process of economic liberalisation have on the functioning of the polity and on the development of a country which has entered the 21st century with the world's largest population of the poor and the illiterate?

- Will the political changes that have taken place lead to a greater integration of minorities and tribals within the national mainstream?

- Will future governments be better able to reflect the aspirations of different regional and ethnic groups?

- Will the redrawing of the internal political map of India be more than a cartographic exercise and heighten fissiparous tendencies?

- And, will the aggravation of contradictions in the world's second-most populated country and arguably the most heterogeneous nation-state bring about its disintegration, as some have claimed from time to time?

These questions are obviously too complex to be answered by specialists in any one discipline. In fact, it would be futile to pretend that any definitive answers can be provided at all. All that can be attempted is to present as many aspects of the totality as possible and provide pointers to some of the linkages. In this respect, the generalist approach of the journalist may perhaps make up in width and reach for what it might lose in terms of academic rigour.

A Short Note on the Ayodhya Dispute

Ayodhya, a small town in eastern Uttar Pradesh, has been at the centre of a major controversy since the mid–1980s. A section of Hindus claims that a mosque (the Babri masjid) built in this town by a general of Babar, the first Mughal emperor, in the 16th century had been constructed by demolishing a temple to mark the birthplace of the mythical lord Rama. For over half a century, ownership of the land on which the mosque existed has been disputed. Before the mid–1980s, few outside Ayodhya were aware of (or bothered about) this dispute. The VHP started a campaign to build a temple where the disputed structure stood at Ayodhya in 1986. This campaign received a major fillip in 1989 when the BJP threw its weight behind the VHP's campaign and Advani undertook a *rath yatra* (a procession led by a 'chariot') across the country to popularise the demand for building a Ram temple to replace the

Babri masjid. The dispute erupted on December 6, 1992, when a mob of Hindus chanting slogans, demolished the structure. Prime Minister Rao was the perfect picture of a helpless spectator as the official media provided a running commentary that afternoon of how the domes of the mosque were being reduced to rubble one by one. (Months later, Home Minister in Rao's government S.B. Chavan was to remark that all that the Prime Minister did that afternoon was watch television, a remark he later withdrew.) Vajpayee was not present at the site, but other BJP leaders like Advani, Murli Manohar Joshi, Uma Bharati, and Sadhvi Rithambara among others were. Communal riots ensued in different parts of India, particularly Mumbai and parts of Gujarat.

After December 1992, the Union government acquired the land around the site where the disputed structure had stood. The Supreme Court of India ordered the government to ensure that the status quo was maintained in the area and no fresh construction was allowed. Even as leaders of the VHP had periodically hyped up a demand to construct a temple at the site where the demolished mosque had stood, they had backed off from precipitating a direct confrontation with the authorities. Towards the end of 2001, Vajpayee declared that he was confident the dispute could be resolved through negotiations between Hindu and Muslim organisations and that he was hopeful the settlement would be reached by March 2002. In January 2002, the VHP issued an 'ultimatum' that it would start constructing the temple on March 15 irrespective of whether the various disputes had been resolved by the government or the courts of law. Shortly thereafter, the Prime Minister announced that his attempts to resolve the issue through negotiations had failed and that it was now up to the courts to give their verdict.

The VHP steadily stepped up its aggressive posture as the campaign for the Uttar Pradesh elections drew to a close, leading most observers to conclude that the timing was more than a coincidence. After the UP election results and the communal violence in Gujarat, the VHP's posture became even more strident and it started asserting that it would install the foundation stone (*shila*) for the Ram temple in Ayodhya on March 15, come what may. Many of the BJP's allies within the NDA, including the numerically most significant TDP, expressed their strong disapproval of the VHP's stance and publicly called upon the government to ensure that law and order was maintained in Ayodhya.

Meanwhile, a Muslim petitioner from Delhi pleaded with the Supreme Court to prevent the *shila pujan* (ceremony to consecrate the stone) at Ayodhya on March 15. With March 13 being set as the date for the court to deliver its verdict on this petition, the BJP's allies stepped up pressure on the government to ensure that the court's verdict was strictly implemented. At an all-party meeting Vajpayee assured those present that the government was committed to upholding the law and that it would strictly follow the directions of the apex court.

On March 13, the Supreme Court ordered that no religious activity of any sort should be allowed on the land acquired by the government in Ayodhya till further orders. While the order was widely welcomed by the Opposition in Parliament and by almost all the BJP's allies in the NDA, the pleadings of the Attorney General (Soli Sorabjee) while appearing in court on behalf of the Union government led to fresh controversy within the NDA and outside it. When asked for the government's response to the petition, Sorabjee told the court that the government was of the view that a symbolic ceremony could be allowed under strict conditions to ensure that no untoward incidents took place. Several of the BJP's allies took exception to this position taken by Sorabjee and protested that they had not been consulted before formulating the government's position. These allies further argued that this position smacked of a 'soft' or 'conciliatory' attitude towards the VHP. The opposition too attacked the government, charging it with actively colluding with the VHP.

The government immediately started a damage limitation exercise. Several of its ministers appeared on television channels to 'clarify' that the stand taken by Sorabjee in court was not the government's, but his own. The following day, Vajpayee reiterated this point of view in Parliament and Sorabjee too was at pains to suggest that he had merely offered a legal opinion and not put forward the government's views on what ought to be done or not done on March 15. The Opposition dismissed the entire exercise as an absurd claim. The Trinamool Congress and the TDP publicly appeared to accept the explanation, although many of them said they still disapproved of Sorabjee's intervention in court.

Meanwhile, security in Ayodhya had been stepped up to unprecedented levels. Trains and bus services to the town had been suspended after the Gujarat riots and outsiders seeking to enter Ayodhya had to obtain special passes. Sensing that it would not be able to mobilise enough people in Ayodhya on March 15 to precipitate a confrontation with the administration, the VHP toned down its rhetoric and said it was prepared to settle for a symbolic *puja* outside the acquired land. On March 15, the government finally acceded to the VHP's demand for a symbolic *puja* and for the presence of an official from the Prime Minister's office to accept the symbolic *shila* after the *puja* from Ramchandra Das Paramhansa, President of the Ramjanmabhoomi Nyas, a VHP front organisation set up for the specific purpose of constructing the Ram temple in Ayodhya.

While this strategy ensured that March 15 passed off peacefully, barring stray incidents of communal violence in Gujarat and some other parts of northern India, it led to fresh accusations from the Opposition of the government having become party to the VHP's programme. Though the BJP's allies did not publicly support this position, there was definite unease among many of them at the manner in which the VHP seemed to be setting the agenda. The unease grew as the VHP announced that it would be initiating a campaign (*asthi yatra*) in which urns carrying the ashes of the victims of the Godhra carnage would be carried to various parts of the country to be immersed in different rivers. Once again, the BJP's allies joined the Opposition in protesting that this was calculated to whip up communal passions and should not be allowed. Soon thereafter, the VHP claimed that it had no intentions of organising any such procession.

The Ayodhya issue came to the fore again in February 2003, when the government moved a petition in the Supreme Court urging it to vacate its March 2002 order banning religious activity on the acquired land. Interestingly, this time round there was no pretence that this was not the official position of the government or that it was the Attorney General's 'personal opinion'. Nor was there any protest from the allies, unlike a year earlier. It is another matter that the Supreme Court dismissed the government's petition on March 31, 2003.

Chapter 1
Bharatiya Janata Party
In Search of the 'Right' Strategy

The Bharatiya Janata Party has for long rightly been perceived as the political wing of the RSS. Recent electoral history, however, seems to have convinced the BJP that the militantly pro-Hindu image cuts both ways and may, therefore, have to be used more selectively than in the past. The pro-Hindu stance certainly served its purpose in the early 1990s and catapulted the BJP to within a stone's throw of power in New Delhi. Yet, this same image limited its further growth in the second half of the 1990s and on occasions was a distinct liability. It was a liability primarily in terms of alienating almost all the minority communities and also large sections of the majority Hindu community. It was also an image that made other parties wary of joining hands with the BJP. This latter fact was brought home to the BJP the hard way, when it failed to win over any new allies to its side in May 1996, despite having formed the Union government. Thereafter, the party's leadership has taken pains to project a more moderate and secular face, though the veneer has slipped from time to time.

It is not as if the entire rank and file of the BJP, or even all of the party's national leadership, has accepted the change in stance and strategy. There are sections within the BJP that still believe that the party would be best served by a single-minded focus on garnering votes from the majority community. This section has become more assertive after the BJP won a two-thirds majority in the December 2002 assembly elections in Gujarat after the communal riots which in fact resulted in a severely polarised electorate. Nevertheless, the party's practice in the last few years—and even after the Gujarat elections—shows that the dominant opinion within the leadership is in favour of a more flexible strategy.

As mentioned already, the BJP has also realised it cannot hope to form the Union government without the support of regional parties. Hence, from a party that insisted, till as late as 1998, that coalitions were temporary, the BJP did an about-turn and declared that coalitions are here to stay in India, at least in the near-term.

Yet, the BJP's opponents maintain that the party has only acquired a façade of moderation and its core agenda of Hindutva remains undiluted. This is what has been referred to as the BJP's and the Sangh Parivar's 'hidden agenda'. The notion that the 'hidden agenda' is merely a convenient stick for envious opponents to beat the BJP with is quite a common perception. However, it is not quite as much of a hoary old cliché as BJP spokespersons would have us believe. The most overt and blatant manifestation of the real agenda of the BJP is in the manner in which the party's functionaries have tried to impart a majoritarian bias—often described by the media as saffronisation, since the colour saffron is considered devout by Hindus—to the education system and syllabi and content of history textbooks in particular and also by making key changes in the academic establishment (more on this later in the chapter).

The party's reluctance to discard the Hindutva plank was also made evident in a series of incidents in February–March 2002. The clearest evidence of this was of course the Gujarat riots. Never after 1947 had communal riots in a state been so widespread and so sustained. Further, with the exception of the anti-Sikh riots that followed Indira Gandhi's assassination by Sikh members of her personal security team on October 31, 1984, there have perhaps been no other communal riots in which virtually all the victims belonged to one community—in this case the Muslims. It is this that led many observers to characterise the communal disturbances in Gujarat as a 'pogrom'. There was another unique feature about the Gujarat riots. These were the first major riots in India in the era of private television channels and hence the first riots to be telecast live, as it were. The Gujarat riots were unique in yet another respect. For perhaps the first time in India, large numbers of relatively well-to-do people actively participated in the looting of property owned by Muslims that accompanied the riots.

While the media and almost all political parties including most constituents of the NDA were unanimous in criticising the Modi administration for acting too late—whether it be in calling in the army to control the rioters or in arranging relief for those affected—spokespersons of the BJP (including the Prime Minister) blamed the media for allegedly inflaming communal passions and for playing a partisan role while reporting the incidents that had taken place.

The Modi administration's partisan role was highlighted again by the fact that while all of the 62 Muslims arrested for their alleged involvement in the Godhra incident were charged under the Prevention of Terrorism Act (POTA)—a law that puts the onus of proving innocence upon the accused—none of the 800-odd people arrested for the rioting that followed were charged under this law. Modi ultimately had to backtrack after the Opposition and some of the BJP's allies raised a furore in Parliament. He, of course, claimed that the POTA charges were being dropped because the state's Advocate General had advised him that all those arrested should be charged under the same legal provisions.

When Prime Minister Vajpayee visited Gujarat for the first time after the communal violence, he expressed regret for what had happened and advised Modi to follow *raj-dharma* (or the duty of the ruler) and not discriminate among his 'subjects'. On the same occasion, on the eve of a visit outside the country, Vajpayee lamented that the Gujarat violence had made India lose face before the rest of the world. Within weeks, however, Vajpayee had not-so-subtly changed his position. At a party conclave in Goa, he claimed that while the riots should not have taken place, the reasons why they occurred should not be ignored. He claimed that if Muslims and opposition leaders had condemned the Godhra incident strongly enough, the violence that followed might have been contained. He blamed the BJP's political opponents and the media for demonising the entire population of Gujarat—and this became an election slogan for Narendra Modi.

That the BJP was keen on garnering advantage from the communally charged atmosphere in the state became obvious when the party sought to hold elections in the state ahead of schedule. The Chief Election Commissioner J.M. Lyngdoh refused to oblige the party and, despite the fact that he was a Constitutional authority, was publicly and privately attacked by those in government.

Lyngdoh had been scathing in his criticism of the state administration for not having created an atmosphere in which large sections of the minority community living in rehabilitation camps
would have been able to exercise their franchise without fear of
intimidation. The elections were eventually conducted in December 2002. Modi led a vicious campaign not only against his main
political opponent from the Congress—Shankersinh Vaghela who
used to be a member of the BJP and the RSS—but kept referring
to the Chief Election Commissioner by his full name, James
Michael Lyngdoh, to establish Lyngdoh's Christian identity and
impute a motive that he was somehow favouring Sonia Gandhi
because of her Christian background. On more than one public
occasion, Modi rhetorically speculated if the two met in church.
It was, of course, a separate matter that Lyngdoh openly proclaimed that he is an atheist.

The clout of the hardliners within the BJP received a major
boost when Modi's strategy worked—the BJP swept to power in
Gujarat with a two-thirds majority in the 182-member state assembly. Modi's supporters within the party, including Arun Jaitley
who was General Secretary of the party at that time, were predictably exultant. The hardliners kept talking about how the 'Gujarat
experiment' should be replicated in other parts of the country. If
one excluded the outcome of the Goa assembly polls that the BJP
won with a slim majority, Gujarat was the first state assembly election won by the BJP since the third Vajpayee government came to
power in New Delhi in October 1999. But the so-called 'Modi
magic' had worn off by the time the next round of assembly elections took place a few months later, in February 2003. In the small
mountainous state of Himachal Pradesh, the BJP failed to return
to power. In December 2003, the BJP did win assembly elections
in three crucial states—Rajasthan, Madhya Pradesh and
Chhattisgarh—but the Hindutva agenda was conspicuous by its
absence, at least from the official campaign.

The BJP's claims that it had set aside the controversial Ayodhya
issue and adopted the NDA's agenda as the only one to be followed by the party while it shared power with its coalition partners also came under a cloud in February–March 2002. The party's
opponents saw a 'conspiracy' when the VHP stepped up the tempo
in its campaign to build the temple at the disputed site in Ayodhya
in the run-up to the assembly elections in Uttar Pradesh. The allies,

however, were not yet concerned, since the BJP publicly maintained that it had nothing to do with the VHP's campaign and that the Ayodhya dispute could ideally be settled through a negotiated settlement between Hindus and Muslims or by a court order. But Attorney General Soli Sorabjee ended up upsetting many of the BJP's allies in the NDA with his suggestion that a token foundation stone laying ceremony be allowed on land acquired by the government near the disputed site on March 15. Despite subsequent attempts at damage control, the BJP's 'secular' allies remained upset at the turn of events. The BJP, they felt, was not honouring its promise that it would abide by the Common Minimum Agenda of the NDA alone and set aside all contentious issues. The unease of the BJP's allies rose as the VHP and the RSS grew increasingly belligerent while the government sought to walk a tightrope, simultaneously attempting to placate the Sangh Parivar and the constituents of the NDA.

A year later, the Ayodhya issue was back in focus. In February 2003, the government moved a petition in the Supreme Court urging it to vacate its March 2002 order banning religious activity on the acquired land. There was, however, an interesting contrast from the situation just a year before. Gone was the pretence that Sorabjee's was a 'personal opinion' or his reading of the legal situation; the government was making no bones about the fact that it wanted to give part of the acquired land to the Ram Janmabhoomi Nyas, a VHP-supported trust to build a Ram temple.

The outcome of the February 2002 assembly elections in Uttar Pradesh had dealt a body blow to the BJP's ambitions to consolidate its position as the only alternative to the Congress in national politics. The party's attempts to project itself as a centrist party believing in the future of coalitions also took a beating as the outcome of the UP polls turned out to be much worse than the BJP had been expecting. Out of the 400 assembly constituencies that went to the polls, the BJP ended up a poor third with 88 seats after the SP with 143 seats and the BSP with 98 seats.

During the election campaign, the BJP was quite hopeful that it would be able to impress the electorate of India's most populous state that the party's Chief Minister Rajnath Singh (who had replaced the octogenarian Ram Prakash Gupta more than a year earlier) would be the most effective and efficient person to lead the economically backward state in which caste sentiments run deep. Rajnath Singh tried hard to rid his party of the image of being controlled by upper-caste individuals (mainly Thakur and Brahmin) by offering reservation of government jobs to the 'most backward classes' (MBCs). Though the Supreme Court shot down his plans, Rajnath Singh had clearly sought to divide the intermediate and lower castes and appeal to sections that were seen to be staunch supporters of the SP and the BSP. By playing the 'MBC card', he had also attempted to win back to the BJP's fold certain lower-caste groups (like the Lodhs) owing allegiance to former BJP Chief Minister Kalyan Singh who had been expelled from the party in 1999.

The results of the elections left no room for doubt that the strategy had failed to deliver the goods. Once again the BJP's focus in UP shifted to damage control. More specifically, an attempt was was made to ensure, by whatever means possible, that Mulayam Singh Yadav's SP would not be able to form the next government in the state, despite being by far the single-largest party in the assembly. In the days immediately following the election results BJP leaders kept insisting that the party was quite prepared to sit in the Opposition benches according to the 'mandate of the people'. However, at the same time, party leaders were conducting hectic negotiations with Mayawati, the BSP leader. Soon enough, the two parties had reached an understanding on power sharing in the state. Mayawati would head a coalition government with the BJP and sundry smaller groups and individuals as junior partners.

The BJP central leadership did not have an easy time trying to persuade its UP unit to accept such an arrangement. Several important leaders of the BJP in UP, including Rajnath Singh, were hostile to a tie-up with the BSP, with which the BJP had in the past had an extremely acrimonious parting of ways. These leaders did not bother to make a secret of their opposition to any alliance with the BSP. They argued that playing second fiddle to the BSP, a party whose support base was predominantly among the dalits, would further alienate many of the BJP's supporters belonging to the upper castes. These leaders of the BJP in UP—who were themselves from the upper castes—had to ultimately relent, when the central leadership reportedly bluntly told them that they had no choice but to support the coalition led by the BSP. Rajnath Singh, in what was seen as a face-saving move, was inducted into the Vajpayee cabinet.

The BJP–BSP tie-up nevertheless remained shaky till Deputy Prime Minister L.K. Advani in a public appearance on April 14, 2002 made it amply clear that the alliance was there to stay. April 14 is an important day in the BSP's calendar, since it marks the birth anniversary of Bhimrao Ambedkar, the only dalit leader with an iconic status cutting across rival dalit groups and parties in different parts of the country, who is also considered to be the architect of the Indian Constitution. At the annual rally to mark the occasion, Advani not only made it a point to be present, but also extolled Mayawati's virtues in no uncertain terms, making it clear that opposition to the BJP–BSP coalition would not be tolerated.

This remained the position of key central leaders like Vajpayee and Advani even a year later, when a large delegation of BJP MLAs from Uttar Pradesh came to meet the Prime Minister in New Delhi to complain about the 'step-motherly' treatment being accorded to them and their party by the Mayawati government. The two leaders are said to have ticked them off, pointing out that having failed to win the elections, they were in no position to be finicky. Without an alliance with the BSP, they were reportedly told, the BJP would be in dire straits in UP in the 2004 Lok Sabha elections.

The central leadership's anxiety to keep the coalition together was understandable. Not only was UP itself an electorally crucial state for the BJP, the possible support of the BSP in the neighbouring state of Madhya Pradesh could even mean the difference between winning or losing in that state. With the Madhya Pradesh assembly elections scheduled to take place in late–2003, the party did not want to rock the boat in UP. Unfortunately for the BJP, while the UP state unit could understand the compulsions of the central leadership, this did not prevent many of the MLAs from making their displeasure evident. They continued to maintain that the alliance would only work to the BSP's advantage, while the BJP's support base in the state would continue to shrink. Ultimately, as detailed in another chapter, the contradictions between the BJP and the BSP led to the alliance falling apart in August 2003.

Unlike the BJP's central leadership, Mayawati never bent over backwards to keep the coalition going. She was not averse to taking steps she knew would antagonise at least some sections within the BJP. A prime example of this was her decision to arrest independent MLA Raghuraj Pratap Singh—alias Raja Bhaiyya—and his father.

Raja Bhaiyya is an archetypal feudal lord and is notorious for 'ruling' his fiefdom with brute violence. Dozens of criminal cases had been pending against him for decades, but no progress was made as the administration had never before received the political support necessary to proceed against him and his family. Raja Bhaiyya was among the independent MLAs who supported Mayawati's government when it was formed in February 2002. Towards the end of that year, however, he was part of a group of independent MLAs and BJP dissidents who unsuccessfully sought to bring down the Mayawati government. Suddenly, the Mayawati government swung into action against Raja Bhaiyya. Cases that had been gathering dust for years were resuscitated and his estates in Kunda were raided. The police allegedly found caches of arms, buried treasures, a skeleton of a man in a pond and so on. The once untouchable feudal lord was put behind bars and charged under POTA for, among other things, conspiring to kill Mayawati.

The crackdown on Raja Bhaiyya was an astute political move that achieved several objectives. First, it sent out a clear message to all existing and potential dissidents that they should be prepared to face the wrath of the state if they did not fall in line. At the same time, it helped Mayawati establish her credentials as a dalit leader who was not scared of taking on even the most powerful among the upper castes. Finally, it left the BJP's leaders with the unenviable choice of either alienating their upper-caste supporters by backing her move or being seen as aligning themselves with a person with an unsavoury reputation.

After the BJP parted ways with the BSP in August 2003 and Mayawati resigned from the post of Chief Minister, speculation was rife that the party had tacitly supported Mulayam Singh Yadav in his bid to become Chief Minister. Mulayam's detractors alleged that the quid pro quo for the BJP's tacit support was that the state government would soft pedal the criminal cases pertaining to the demolition of the Babri masjid against BJP leaders like Advani, Joshi and Uma Bharti. What explained the BJP's changed attitude towards Mulayam, traditionally the party's prime rival in UP? The main factor seemed to be that the BJP wanted to buy time. When the alliance with the BSP broke up in August 2003, the BJP was clearly in disarray in UP and could ill afford an election at that stage. Also, it needed to get its act together before the 14th general elections.

The strategy appeared to be working well at the time of writing. In December 2003, Vajpayee had a much-publicised meeting with Kalyan Singh, sparking off speculation about the latter's 'home coming'. Kalyan Singh later rejoined the BJP. After Kalyan Singh (who was UP Chief Minister when the Babri masjid was demolished in December 1992) was expelled from the BJP in 1999, he bitterly criticised Vajpayee, saying that the BJP's central leadership was deliberately trying to evade their responsibility for demolition of the mosque. He formed his own Rashtriya Kranti Party (RKP) which then tied up with Mulayam Singh Yadav's SP and helped split votes that resulted in the defeat of a number of candidates of the BJP during the February 2002 assembly elections. Subsequent events, however, proved the old adage that in politics, there are no permanent friends or enemies.

The months since February 2002, thus, encapsulated the various contradictions that the BJP has been trying to resolve in its new *avatar* as a party in government rather than as one in opposition. Electorally, it was engaged in an attempt to reconfigure the caste coalitions it had traditionally banked on. Politically, it was struggling to find a way by which it could reconcile the conflicting interests of the Hindutva hardliners and the 'secular' allies of the BJP in the NDA. While Vajpayee, Advani, and the then Foreign Minister Jaswant Singh projected the 'moderate' or 'liberal' mask of the party in power, others like Human Resources Development Minister Murli Manohar Joshi were left free to vigorously pursue the party's Hindu nationalist agenda.

Saffronising Education

The very fact that Joshi and another hardliner, Uma Bharati, were chosen to head the HRD Ministry when Vajpayee became Prime Minister in 1998 was seen by observers as evidence of the party's hidden agenda. This was only one of two ministries in which both the senior as well as junior ministers were from the BJP, the other being the Ministry for Information and Broadcasting (which too could greatly help the party's propaganda efforts). Joshi's first stint in the job was surrounded by controversy, but he retained the portfolio in the third Vajpayee government as well. This only added to the misgivings of the BJP's political opponents about the party's hidden agenda.

In his first tenure as HRD Minister, Joshi had already made sweeping changes in key positions in the academic establishment, pertaining to both school and higher education. The Indian Council for Historical Research (ICHR) witnessed a complete revamp, at the end of which historians known to be inclined towards the BJP were at the helm. That this was not merely a 'jobs for the boys' move is evident from the pronouncements of historians close to the BJP, like K.S. Lal, who had earlier headed the Archaeological Survey of India. The right-wing historian was quoted (in an article by Akshay Mukul in *The Hindustan Times*) as arguing that there was nothing wrong with Joshi attempting to rewrite history, since the Congress and left intellectuals had (according to him) done the same thing. Said Lal: 'Historians like Nurul Hasan saw to it that books written during his stint as education minister hid the true face of Islam, which is essentially a barbaric religion. Instead, emphasis was laid on the study of economic history. Institutions like NCERT [National Council for Educational Research and Training] and ICHR were used to propagate this ideology.' Lal went on to assert that the 'corrections' would now be thorough. 'Textbooks should highlight the achievements of Hindus during the Vedic period; the role of religion during the medieval period; how Muslim rulers from [Allauddin] Khilji onwards deliberately kept Hindu farmers at subsistence level, forcing them to migrate as indentured labour to Mauritius and the West Indies.'

It is the communal bias that is evident in these statements, which have little basis in fact, that is the real cutting edge of the attempt to saffronise education. It is not as if Lal's positions are an aberration from the norm among those appointed or elevated to high positions in academia under Joshi's tutelage. Krishna Gopal Rastogi, Joshi's appointee to the NCERT, had in 1998 privately circulated a copy of his autobiography titled *Aap Beeti* (literally, 'My Experiences'). Rastogi has in his book graphically narrated how he shot dead a Muslim woman in Uttar Pradesh during Partition. Rastogi has justified his actions by writing that the woman's beauty had distracted his friends in the RSS from rioting and turned them into 'lusting human beings who were on the verge of raping her'.

The author stated: 'I have always felt sorry for the action' (which stunned his friends into returning to their 'task'). The RSS head

K.S. Sudarshan had, in his Foreword to Rastogi's book, lauded the author's wife for allowing his 'physical needs' to be fulfilled during his trips abroad. On his foreign travels, Rastogi writes that the three things most easily available in the West were food, liquor and women. He has, at the same time, claimed that he was reminded of divine fairies when he saw scantily clad women on a beach in Yugoslavia. Rastogi has also revealed his unhappiness about not having been earlier appointed as an adviser to the education minister because he 'did not like a more intelligent person to work under him'. After the contents of Rastogi's controversial autobiography became public, he claimed that sections of his account were 'fictionalised'.

Rastogi was not the only Joshi protege at the NCERT. A few months after he assumed office, in July 1998, Joshi appointed J.S. Rajput as Director. Rajput's mandate was clear: to 'indigenise' education. Guidelines issued by him made it clear that 'the remnants of the alien legacy of the pre-independence period have to be shed completely'. Nor are the ICHR and the NCERT the only institutions that have faced the sweep of Joshi's broom. The physics professor has also radically revamped the Indian Council for Social Science Research (ICSSR) and the governing body of the Indian Institute of Advanced Study, Shimla. Both these institutions are now packed with votaries of Hindutva.

The extent of Joshi's zeal for ensuring that the academic establishment was packed with those with the right worldview is best illustrated by what happened at the ICSSR in 2001. The late Manohar Lal Sondhi, a former MP belonging to the Bharatiya Jana Sangh, who had been appointed Head of ICSSR by Joshi, was sacked soon after he organised a seminar of 'intellectuals' from India and Pakistan. The seminar was organised days before the Agra summit meeting in July 2001 between Vajpayee and Musharraf. While Sondhi was allegedly removed for financial irregularities and replaced by a bureaucrat, it was no secret that the seminar was the real reason for his dismissal. The episode revealed how intolerant the ruling establishment was towards even a 'liberal' member of the Sangh Parivar. Another Joshi nominee who had to face the HRD Minister's wrath for being too independent was ICHR head M.G.S. Narayanan who, like Sondhi, was ostensibly removed for financial irregularities.

The BJP's determined efforts to 'saffronise' the education system became more evident when the Central Board of Secondary

Education (CBSE) issued a circular deleting certain references made in NCERT textbooks on history meant for school students. These references were, among other things, to Hindus eating beef during the Vedic ages and also on the question of whether there existed a Hindu civilisation at Ayodhya—the so-called birthplace of the mythical Lord Rama—around 2000 BC, the period to which Rama is sought to be dated according to Puranic tradition. These efforts saw the political Opposition coming together against the BJP and the NDA; Congress leader Arjun Singh even accused the government of 'Talibanising' education which led to members of the ruling coalition walking out of the Rajya Sabha.

BJP-ruled states too have contributed to the effort at saffronising education. The Kalyan Singh government in UP, for instance, had rewritten history textbooks (as reported by *Frontline* in November 1998) to portray the RSS founder, Dr. K.B. Hedgewar, as one of the leading lights of the freedom movement. Also, the entire period of rule by Muslims is presented as a 'period of resistance' by Hindus. The Sultanate period is characterised as one in which society was divided into two main classes—'ruling or Muslim class and ruled or non-Muslims of whom Hindus were the majority'.

Even in Rajasthan, a state that was ruled between 1993 and 1998 by the BJP's Bhairon Singh Shekhawat, a Chief Minister seen as very much in the same moderate liberal mould as Vajpayee and who went on to become India's Vice President, the party attempted to use textbooks for its propaganda. *Frontline* detailed how school textbooks in the state not only justified the Pokhran nuclear blasts, but also played up writings of RSS ideologues like Professor Rajendra Singh, the then RSS chief, Tarun Vijay, the editor of the RSS mouthpiece *Panchajanya*, and RSS head K.S. Sudarshan. These attempts are apart from the activities of RSS-run Vidya Bharati institutions. These include 14,000 schools at the nursery, primary and secondary levels with 18 lakh students, 60 colleges and 25 other institutions of higher education. An NCERT report in 1996 had warned that many of the Vidya Bharati textbooks were 'designed to promote bigotry and religious fanaticism'.

Thus, there can be little doubt that the BJP and the RSS do have an agenda distinct from that of the NDA's, even if the agenda is not exactly hidden. At the same time though, the party has succeeded in ensuring that this agenda does not acquire too high a profile, except on rare occasions like the states' education ministers' conference in 1998, where Joshi's eagerness to thrust a report drawn up by a known RSS votary and to use the controversial *Saraswati vandana* song as a substitute for the national anthem in opening the conference drew flak from allies and foes alike.

Historians like Bipan Chandra and Romila Thapar, two so-called left-wing historians, passages from whose textbooks were deleted by the NCERT/CBSE dictat, have argued that changing the manner in which history is taught to young people is crucial for the RSS and the BJP. For them, it is crucial that India's ancient past be glorified so that the country's subsequent decline can be largely attributed to the onset of Mughal rule. For the propagandists of the Sangh Parivar, the achievements of Muslim rulers like Akbar need to be underplayed just as they seek to lay less emphasis on the degeneration of Hindu society because of the ills of the caste (varna) system which were responsible for the rapid spread of Jainism, Buddhism and later, Islam in the subcontinent. If this slant is not imparted to the interpretation of ancient and medieval Indian history, Chandra contends that the entire edifice of the communal ideology of the RSS and the BJP would collapse.

Controlling the Organs of the State

The BJP's attempts to propagate its Hindutva agenda have not been confined to the educational establishment. The party's supporters and sympathisers have over the years come to occupy key positions in various organs of the state, while those seen as inimical to its ideology and interests have been marginalised in the bureaucracy, the defence services, the judiciary and in non-government organisations. A large number of retired judges, bureaucrats and senior officers of the armed forces have joined the BJP in recent years.

As a part of this process, some individuals have also acquired power and influence disproportionate to their official position. The most obvious example is the Principal Secretary who doubles up as National Security Advisor, Brajesh Mishra, a former career diplomat. Mishra was catapulted to the pinnacle of administrative power during the second and third Vajpayee governments. So powerful did he become that at one point in 2000, the media, the Opposition and even sections within the Sangh Parivar were of the view that he was the power behind the throne. While some went as far as to suggest that he was the 'real prime minister', most analysts agreed that Mishra's ability to influence government policy and decisions was considerably greater than most members of the Vajpayee cabinet. At one stage, the RSS as well as the Shiv Sena gunned for Mishra and another bureaucrat, Nand Kishore (N.K.) Singh. Vajpayee however, stood behind Mishra like a rock. He made it clear in no uncertain terms that any attack on his Principal Secretary amounted to a personal attack on him. Though an official panel suggested that Mishra be divested of one of his two responsibilities, nothing of the sort took place. Mishra, whose father was former Congress Chief Minister of Madhya Pradesh in 1963, continued to wield considerable clout—he merely adopted a lower public profile.

The importance of Mishra in the Vajpayee regime is indicative of a bigger strategy followed by the BJP in the ruling coalition—allies and partners were given considerable 'autonomy' to pursue their political interests provided they did not object to the BJP using the levers of power to try and fulfil its long-term goals. It was, therefore, no coincidence that barring the Ministry of Defence, all crucial ministerial portfolios (including Home, External Affairs, Finance, and Human Resources Development) were 'reserved' for the BJP. The party had no problems in handing over the stewardships of many of the economic ministries perceived as lucrative to its partners, ministries such as Telecommunications, Civil Aviation, Industry and Commerce, Railways, and Power.

In early January 2000, the Gujarat government ruled by the BJP, which had a majority in the assembly on its own, announced a controversial decision to lift the ban on government employees joining the RSS. The conduct rules for government employees not only barred them from joining or aiding any political party or movement, but also specifically listed 14 organisations including the RSS as those which they could not join. The Gujarat government's order, by lifting the ban on the RSS alone, certainly created the impression that the state government was bent on appeasing Hindu organisations. This impression was strengthened by the track record of the BJP government in Gujarat and the timing of the order on the eve of a major RSS gathering. Gujarat, through 1998 and 1999, had witnessed a spate of violent incidents against the Christian community, particularly in the tribal-dominated Dangs district. Towards the end of 1998, Vajpayee himself came under considerable criticism for suggesting that a national debate on religious conversions take place after a visit to some of the communally disturbed areas of Gujarat. Since the VHP, which was seen as instrumental in the attacks, had also taken the position that conversions of tribals by Christian missionaries had led to communal tension, Vajpayee's call for a national debate on conversions was seen as dovetailing into a communal Hindu agenda.

While the BJP in Gujarat had to climb down from its position following instructions from the party 'high command' and after its allies kicked up a fuss, the BJP, prior to the Gujarat riots of 2002, had always claimed that it was the best guarantor of protection of the rights of minorities and that communal disturbances had not taken place in states ruled by the party. More than one judicial commission of inquiry has indicted supporters of the Sangh Parivar for instigating communal riots, but often such riots have occurred in states in which the BJP has not been in power. Significantly, the brutal murder of Australian missionary Graham Staines and his two sons in January 1999 took place in a remote forest area in Orissa, a Congress-ruled state at that time. This impression that minorities are most safe under BJP rule has, however, taken a beating after the series of attacks on Christians in Gujarat followed by the 2002 communal violence against Muslims.

Earlier, the BJP–Shiv Sena government in Maharashtra had tried its very best to delay the publication of the report of the Justice Sri Krishna Commission, which inquired into the December 1992 communal riots in Mumbai and the bomb blasts in March 1993. The waves of riots which rocked India's commercial capital in the wake of the demolition of the Babri masjid left some 3,000 dead and many more injured, most of them belonging to the Muslim minority. The Manohar Joshi government in Maharashtra refused to initiate any action against those who had been indicted in the Sri Krishna Commission report for inciting the riots, including some of his own ministers as well as the Shiv Sena supremo Bal Thackeray.

Reworking Caste Equations

At the same time, the so-called moderate sections of the BJP continue their efforts to rid the party of its exclusivist image by actively wooing tribals and lower-caste Hindus, with varying degrees of

success. In December 1999, Vajpayee announced that the government was committed to amending the laws relating to job reservations for those from the scheduled castes (SCs) and scheduled
tribes (STs). Under the existing provisions, while 22 per cent of all
government jobs at the entry level are reserved for these catego-
ries, promotions are 'merit-based'. Various SC/ST organisations
have for long been demanding that the 22 per cent reservation be
extended to promotions as well. Merit as a criterion, they argued,
was used by upper-caste superiors to deny the SC/ST employees
promotion. The courts, however, have ruled in the past that promotions without merit as a criterion were violative of the law.
Vajpayee's assurance now is that the laws will be suitably amended to ensure that merit is no longer a necessary criterion for
promotion.

This move is out of character with the BJP's traditionally implicit apathy towards low-caste Hindus. In fact, it was the perception that the BJP was essentially a party anaemic to the lower rungs
of Hindu caste society that helped the party make the most of the
upper-caste backlash against the implementation of the Mandal
Commission's report in the Hindi belt. Though not in tune with
the BJP's track record, Vajpayee's attempt to woo the SC/ST sections was a response to the imperatives of the times. In Uttar
Pradesh, in particular, the expulsion of Kalyan Singh from the BJP
led to an erosion in the party's support base among the intermediate castes. This was sought to be countered by Rajnath Singh as
Chief Minister of UP, by a concerted pre-election effort to woo the
so-called 'most backward castes' by reserving government jobs
for them within the quota reserved for the 'other backward classes'
(OBCs). The BJP justified its strategy by arguing that the relatively
advanced sections of the OBCs had cornered most of the jobs that
had been reserved for this section. While there was certainly considerable merit in this argument, the party's detractors were also
not wrong in claiming that this marked the BJP's attempts to create a rift within the ranks of the OBCs, a substantial proportion of
whom were aligned to either the SP or the BSP in the state.

What is interesting here is that the BJP in UP had attempted to
cobble together a caste alliance very similar to what the Congress
had done in the 1970s and 1980s. The Congress after 1967 had
lost the support of substantial sections of the intermediate castes,
who saw in Charan Singh a leader of their own ilk, but retained its

hold over power thanks to the support of the upper-most and lower-most castes of the Hindu hierarchy. Yet, the BJP is a long way from replicating the situation. For one, the party, unlike the Congress of yore, has virtually no support among the sizeable Muslim population (in both the 12th and the 13th Lok Sabhas, the BJP had just one Muslim MP). Moreover, given the consolidation of the BSP, it seems unlikely that the BJP will be able to win over large sections of the dalits to its fold.

Among the tribals of northern India, on the other hand, the BJP has made impressive inroads in the last few years. Seats reserved for candidates from the scheduled tribes—whether in Parliament or in the state legislatures—have traditionally been the bastion of the Congress since independence. This was true more or less across the length and breadth of India, except in some pockets where local groups specifically espousing the cause of tribals challenged the dominance of the Congress. Thus, groups like the Jharkhand Mukti Morcha (JMM) in Jharkhand (earlier the southern districts of Bihar) or the Mizo National Front in Mizoram were the only serious challenge the Congress faced in tribal-dominated areas.

Today, that situation has undergone a drastic change in wide areas of northern India stretching from Gujarat to Orissa and Jharkhand. In this band cutting across the heart of India, it is the BJP that now dominates tribal seats, with the Congress struggling to catch up. Here are some telling statistics: In the elections to the state assembly in Bihar (which then included Jharkhand) held in 2000, the BJP won 14 of the 28 seats reserved for STs, the Congress and the JMM could do no better than six each. In neighbouring Orissa, where elections were held at the same time, the BJP contested 23 of the 34 ST seats, leaving its partner the Biju Janata Dal (BJD) to contest the remaining 11. The BJP won 13 seats and the BJD won eight, the same number as the Congress.

Two-and-a-half years later, the same trend was visible in the December 2002 Gujarat assembly elections. The BJP won 13 of the state's 26 ST seats, the Congress 11. Fast-forward another year to December 2003 and move to Rajasthan, Madhya Pradesh and Chhattisgarh—the trend is if anything even clearer. In Madhya Pradesh, the BJP won 37 of the 41 ST seats, the Congress just two. In Chhattisgarh, the 34 ST seats were split 25–9 in favour of the BJP and in Rajasthan the Congress won five of the state's 24 ST seats against the BJP's 15. In these six states put together, therefore, the BJP holds 117 of the 187 assembly seats reserved for tribal candidates. The second biggest party, the Congress, holds a mere 41 by comparison.

What explains this dramatic turnaround among tribals? Much of the credit for this impressive performance by the BJP must go to the Vanvasi Kalyan Ashram (VKA), an RSS front working among tribals. For the record, the VKA does various things for the benefit of the tribals, including setting up schools and health centres. The cutting edge of its activities, however, remains its campaign to prevent tribals from being converted to Christianity. The VKA has been quite successful in polarising tribals along communal lines, pitting the 'Hindu' tribals (many of whom are actually followers of animist religions) against the Christians. Partly, it has been helped by the fact that successive Congress governments were quite content to pay lip service to developing tribal areas, while doing precious little. The fact that tribals who have converted to Christianity also typically have better access to education and hence to jobs has also helped the VKA in its attempts to drive a wedge between tribals belonging to different religions.

There are many who believe, somewhat simplistically, that the BJP has succeeded in government by becoming increasingly like the Congress, a centrist political party that had attempted to reconcile the interests of different sections of society. In the early 1990s, BJP insiders who were sympathetic to the more rabid sections within the Sangh Parivar would jocularly remark that Vajpayee was the best-known Congressman in the BJP. One BJP leader, K.N. Govindacharya, was even quoted as claiming before a foreign diplomat that Vajpayee was the *mukhota* (mask) of the party—although this statement was denied, the message stuck. Little could these BJP 'hardliners' have realised—as they did in June 1996 after the first 13-day Vajpayee government fell—that they would have to eat their words, that the BJP would have to shed its exclusivist stance and compromise with its erstwhile political opponents to remain in power. The BJP has subsequently had to justify these political compromises as a choice between 'lesser evils'.

To understand the manner in which the BJP has evolved from a mere adjunct of its ideological parent, the RSS, to a political party that has sought to occupy the centrist space in the country's polity vacated by the Congress, it is necessary to go back in time. In the course of this chapter, we juxtapose the current face of the BJP with references to the past to examine how the party has become what it is today.

Living Down the Past

The Bharatiya Janata Party is the successor to what was the Bharatiya Jana Sangh (BJS) between 1951 and 1977, but most of the political party's supporters and cadre owe allegiance to the Rashtriya Swayamsevak Sangh, ostensibly a social association of Hindu nationalists, the largest organisation of its kind in India and the world. Whereas the Indian National Congress was formally established in 1885, the growth of the RSS and some other Hindu nationalist organisations like the Hindu Mahasabha can be traced to the second decade of the 20th century.

The RSS was founded by Keshavrao Baliram Hedgewar in 1925 and consolidated by M. S. Golwalkar (better known as Guruji, meaning teacher or guide) from 1940 onwards. But it was only in the wake of the January 30, 1948 assassination of Mahatma Gandhi and the widespread condemnation of the assassin, Nathuram Godse, and his links with the RSS that the Sangh felt the need for a political front. The circumstances which led to the founding of the BJS in 1951 were explained by the former BJP Vice President, the late K.R. Malkani, in an article on the party's history posted on the BJP's official website:

> The RSS, along with millions of people, did not approve of Gandhiji's Muslim appeasement policy…but it had the greatest respect for the Mahatma. Indeed, Gandhiji had visited the RSS winter camp in Wardha in December 1934 and addressed the Delhi RSS workers in a *bhangi* [low caste] colony in September 1947. He had deeply appreciated the 'noble sentiments' and 'astonishing discipline' of the RSS…. But after his killing, 17,000 RSS workers—including Shri Guruji—were accused of conspiracy of the murder of Mahatma Gandhi…. But during all this time, not one MLA or MP raised the issue in any legislature. For the RSS, it was the moment of truth…unless the RSS grew political teeth and wings, it would always be at the mercy of unscrupulous politicians.
>
> This was the context in which Shri Guruji blessed the birth of the Bharatiya Jana Sangh under the leadership of Dr. Shyama Prasad Mookerjee.

This account of the origins of the BJP clearly establishes that the party is the political 'teeth and wings' of the RSS and is contrary to the position adopted by certain BJP spokespersons in recent years that while many party leaders are members of the RSS, the BJP as a party only has fraternal links with the Sangh and is independent of, and autonomous from, the RSS.

For the better part of the first half-century of independence, the Congress ruled India while the BJP remained a party in Opposition. The BJP and its predecessor participated in a number of coalition governments both at the Union as well as in a number of states in northern India from the 4th general elections in 1967. However, it was not until as late as May 1996, nearly three decades later, that a representative of this political stream for the first time came to occupy the highest post in the country when Vajpayee headed the Union government for a period of barely two weeks. While this was the shortest tenure of any Indian Prime Minister, Vajpayee—the first Prime Minister who did not have his origins in the Congress—returned to the seat of power in New Delhi for a second time after the February 1998 elections by forming a shaky and fragile coalition of over a dozen political parties. This government lasted 13 months (for the superstitious, Vajpayee's first term as Prime Minister had lasted 13 days!) before it lost a dramatic vote of confidence in the Lok Sabha by a single vote. Vajpayee returned as Prime Minister for the third time in October 1999 after the 13th general elections—the third in barely three-and-a-half years—this time heading a larger and more stable coalition of some two dozen partners.

The BJP's political opponents have always dubbed the party's followers as communal, exclusivist, majoritarian, fanatical and fundamentalist. The more militant supporters of the BJP and its fraternal organisations believe that Hindus in India are in danger of losing their identity in the land of their birth because successive Congress governments have pandered excessively to the interests of minorities (read Muslims). An extreme viewpoint—articulated by persons like Acharya Giriraj Kishore of the VHP—is that India, which is home to the world's second-largest population of Muslims (after Indonesia), is unique in the sense that the minority community has been able to control if not dominate the Hindus who comprise a majority (around 80 per cent of the Indian population). This could happen, it is claimed, because past Congress

governments were willing to excessively placate Muslims and con-
done extremist and fundamentalist elements among them.

Some of those from the BJP's ideological fraternity also contend
that because Hindus are divided into hundreds of castes, while
the Muslims are less divided, the Muslims effectively become the
single biggest group in India rather than a minority community.
The more moderate sections of the BJP, on the other hand, acknowledge that Indian society is diverse, plural and multi-cultural
and Hindus as the dominant community should accommodate
the interests of the minorities. Nevertheless, those belonging to
even this liberal section within the BJP are not always comfortable condemning majority communalism in terms as strong as
they use for the communalism that is displayed by fringe sections
of the Muslims in India.

Many BJP supporters frequently invoke the violent memories
of Partition and the formation of Pakistan. The Congress has
always attacked the BJP (and earlier the BJS) because Nathuram
Godse was a supporter of the RSS and the Hindu Mahasabha. RSS
spokespersons have, on the other hand, claimed that Godse had
publicly rejected the views of the RSS and joined the Hindu
Mahasabha before he started planning his assassination of
Gandhi. The Congress has always claimed a right to rule the country on the ground that its organisation was at the forefront of the
struggle for independence that culminated in 1947. At the same
time, the Congress has criticised the BJP because its supporters
did not play an active enough role in throwing British colonial
rulers out of the country. Congress leader Arjun Singh once challenged the BJP and the RSS to place before the nation the names
of those among its supporters who had opposed British rule.
Vajpayee's official curriculum vitae (in the Lok Sabha 'Who's Who')
does, of course, state that he was jailed in 1942 during the time of
the Quit India movement against colonial rule, but more on that
later (see profile of Vajpayee at the end of the chapter). The BJP's
sympathisers, on the other hand, don the mantle of being the 'true'
nationalists, the 'genuine' patriots who did not collaborate with
the British.

In a critique of the RSS, *Khaki Shorts and Saffron Flags*, Tapan
Basu, Pradip Dutta, Sumit Sarkar, Tanika Sarkar and Sambuddha
Sen, all of whom are left academics based in Delhi, argued that
the events of December 6, 1992 reaffirm the conviction that the

RSS and the VHP dictate the politics of the Hindu right and define the limits within which the BJP can manouevre. The editor's preface to the book states:

> The Hindu right has for long operated with two faces.... On the one hand, it has sought to present a gentle face symbolised in L.K. Advani's beatific smile; on the other it has widely projected an angry, aggressive and savagely sectarian face expressed in the speeches of Sadhvi Rithambara and Uma Bharati. These two faces are iconically represented...in the twin images of Ram...the image of *Ram lalla,* the child god and the image of Ram as the masculine warrior god. The Hindu right also talks in two languages: the language of democracy and that of authoritarianism, the language of law and that of force. The BJP claims to function within a constitutional, democratic, legal framework; but the activities of the RSS, the VHP and the Bajrang Dal mock this framework.

Over the years, the RSS has sought to gain greater acceptability by appropriating icons of Indian history. The list includes spiritual leaders like Swami Vivekananda, Ramakrishna Paramahansa and Sister Nivedita, and leaders of the freedom movement like Netaji Subhash Chandra Bose, Bhagat Singh, Annie Besant, Vallabhbhai Patel and even Gandhi. In fact, most members of the Sangh Parivar have more than a hint of admiration for independent India's first Union Home Minister Sardar Vallabhbhai Patel in Jawaharlal Nehru's government who presided over the construction of a temple at Somnath that had been destroyed by Muslim conquerors. It is no coincidence that Home Minister-turned-Deputy Prime Minister, L.K. Advani, has often been affectionately compared to Sardar Patel. So has Narendra Modi, who was dubbed the 'Chhota (small) Sardar'. The supporters of the Sangh Parivar predictably ignore the fact that Patel was, on many occasions, a trenchant critic of the RSS. In projecting Patel as a great hero of the national movement, it also likes to drive home the point that the Congress has not adequately appreciated the contribution of leaders like him in the national movement while lauding the role of the Nehru–Gandhi family.

The need to associate itself with leaders identified with the freedom movement stems from the fact that the RSS has for long, and rightly, been perceived as an organisation that stayed aloof from the mainstream of the anti-colonial struggle. The fact that Gandhi's assassin had for long been a member and activist of the RSS (though at the time of the assassination he was a member of the Hindu Mahasabha) only added to this need. RSS publications (and now the website) prominently display statements by many of these leaders allegedly praising the activities of the RSS. They, of course, do not bother to point out that these same leaders had on several occasions scathingly criticised the RSS as a communal organisation or that Bhagat Singh was a communist.

The RSS' selective quoting of Gandhi perhaps best illustrates the point. Their propaganda material keeps emphasising the fact that Gandhi had been impressed by the discipline of the RSS cadre when he visited an organisational camp at Wardha in Maharashtra (not far from Gandhi's own Sevagram) at the invitation of the RSS founder, Dr. Hedgewar, in 1934. Dr. Hedgewar himself had been a former member of the Congress party and had been jailed briefly during the Civil Disobedience Movement of 1930–31. What the RSS and the BJP conveniently overlook is what Gandhi said about the RSS 12 years after his visit to the RSS camp at Wardha in the wake of the communal riots of 1946. When one of Gandhi's supporters praised the RSS cadre for the work done by them in helping Punjabi refugees at the transit camp in Wagah (now a border post between India and Pakistan), Gandhi had answered: 'But don't forget even so had Hitler's Nazis and the fascists under Mussolini.' He went on to describe the RSS as a communal body with a totalitarian outlook and asserted: 'the way [to independence] does not lie through *akhadas*…if they are meant as a preparation for self-defence in Hindu–Muslim conflicts, they are foredoomed to failure. Muslims can play the same game, and such preparations, covert or overt, do cause suspicion and irritation. They can provide no remedy.'

That Gandhi should have drawn an analogy between the RSS and the Nazis was hardly surprising. M. S. Golwalkar was an unabashed admirer of Hitler's methods as this excerpt from his *We or Our Nationhood Defined* (1938) reveals: 'German national pride has now become the topic of the day. To keep the purity of the nation and its culture, Germany shocked the world by her purging the country of the semitic races—the Jews. National pride at its highest has been manifested here. Germany has also shown how well-nigh impossible it is for races and cultures, having differences going to the root, to be assimilated into one united whole, a good lesson for us in Hindustan to learn and profit by.'

Golwalkar was not reticent when it came to elaborating on exactly what the lessons for India were: 'The non-Hindu people in Hindustan must either adopt the Hindu culture and language, must learn to respect and revere Hindu religion, must entertain no idea but the glorification of the Hindu nation, i.e. they must not only give up their attitude of intolerance and ingratitude towards this land and its age-old traditions, but must also cultivate the positive attitude of love and devotion instead; in one word, they must cease to be foreigners or may stay in the country wholly subordinated to the Hindu nation, claiming nothing, deserving no privileges, far less any preferential treatment, not even citizen's rights.'

Khaki Shorts points out that Golwalkar developed his exclusivist logic to target one more enemy: the communists who were branded as being of foreign origin. Even after Nehru's government banned the RSS in February 1948 following Gandhi's assassination, in his letters to Nehru and Patel, Golwalkar argued for lifting the ban on the RSS as it could help the government of independent India fight against the 'menace' of communism. There were many within the Congress at that time, not excluding Acharya Kripalani and Patel himself, who were sympathetic to his pleas and the RSS won back its legality in July 1949.

Legitimising the Hindutva Agenda

The BJP and the BJS, even when they were part of coalition governments in New Delhi or in various states, had sought to retain their distinctive identity despite being part of bigger coalitions. The Janata Party government, which came to power in March 1977 after 19 months of Emergency rule by defeating the Congress headed by Indira Gandhi, broke apart in 1979 on the issue of 'dual membership' of its constituents, namely, the BJS group led by External Affairs Minister Vajpayee and Information and Broadcasting Minister L.K. Advani, who both refused to disown their association with the RSS. It is ironic to recall how 'socialist' George Fernandes—who later became Vajpayee's ardent supporter, close confidante and Defence Minister—was at the forefront of the campaign to remove the BJS section from within the Janata Party government on this issue. More than a decade later, in September–October 1990, the V.P. Singh government collapsed soon after the BJP withdrew its support in the wake of Advani's arrest in Bihar during his *rath yatra* to build the Ram temple at Ayodhya.

It was the BJP and its allied organisations like the RSS, the VHP and the Bajrang Dal which took the initiative to mobilise the group which demolished the Babri masjid. The destruction of what the BJP's supporters euphemistically called a 'disputed structure' was sought to be projected as a dramatic assertion of the victory of the Hindus over the Muslims who had conquered and ruled India for centuries and as a righting of a historical wrong. Many of those who participated in the demolition were young lumpens who wanted to return to their nondescript villages with a handful of rubble (symbolically referred to as Babar's bones). The demolition of the mosque, preceded by Advani's *rath yatra*, resulted in a violent fallout thousands of miles away in places like Mumbai and Surat in Gujarat where waves of anti-Muslim riots occurred leaving hundreds dead and thousands more traumatised. In March 1993, a series of bomb blasts in public places occurred which were apparently in retaliation for the demolition of the mosque.

In 1997, Ainslee T. Embree, professor and India-watcher at Brown University in the US, argued that describing the groups responsible for the demolition of the mosque as fundamentalist or fanatic can be misleading as these terms suggest a primarily religious motivation.

> Hindu nationalists is a more accurate description, for, their leaders insisted, they were inspired not by religious fervour but by a desire to assert the pre-eminence of Hindu culture in the life of the Nation. The unifying ideology of Hindu culture, to which they gave the name 'Hindutva', was an explicit rejection of secular nationalism, which, they argued, was a deceptive mask for enemies of the Hindu nation, including the westernised, denationalised intellectuals that had made common cause with Muslims, communists, and other alien ideologies, to seize control of the state.

The rise in the BJP's political support base was closely linked to the Ram temple/Ayodhya controversy although the party has consciously sought to play down the issue in recent times. The BJP's supporters argue that the party has not given up its intention of building a temple at the site where the mosque stood but is not pressing the issue since the party on its own does not command a majority in Parliament.

The BJP's allies contend that secularism has been made into a 'bogey' to disguise opportunistic opposition to the BJP. Despite the presence of many persons in the Vajpayee government whose secular credentials have never been in doubt, it is also a fact that very few Muslims have come forward to join the BJP in recent years. In the second Vajpayee government, for instance, there were only two Muslim ministers, one of them being Mukhtar Abbas Naqvi who also happened to be the only Muslim MP belonging to the BJP in the 12th Lok Sabha. Naqvi lost his seat in the 13th Lok Sabha elections and was made party General Secretary and spokesperson. In that Lok Sabha, the only Muslim MP belonging to the BJP was Shahnawaz Hussain who also happened to be the youngest minister in Vajpayee's council of ministers. Also significant is the fact that Hussain represents Kishenganj in Bihar, the only Lok Sabha constituency with a Muslim majority outside Kerala and Jammu & Kashmir. Despite the efforts made by sections of the BJP to project the party as secular, Muslims in India have remained by and large wary of aligning themselves with the BJP. This is hardly surprising given the fact that virtually every single judicial commission of inquiry into incidents of communal violence in independent India had indicted either members of the BJP or persons and parties which have been allied to the party.

At the time of the demolition of the Babri masjid, most senior leaders of the BJP, especially Vajpayee and Advani, publicly expressed their sorrow and unhappiness at what happened at Ayodhya. The party, however, stopped short of condemning those responsible for the demolition. In fact, it virtually provided a justification for the act by its stance that the incident was unfortunate but a result of the Narasimha Rao government not heeding the people's religious sentiments. The BJP also harps on the fact that it was during the tenure of the Congress government headed by Rajiv Gandhi that the locks on the gates to the Babri complex were opened following a court order.

The Sangh Parivar has long practiced the art of speaking with a forked tongue. As early as 1956 when the States Reorganisation Act was enforced, Guru Golwalkar favoured a more unitary India whereas Deen Dayal Upadhyay, the then head of the BJS, favoured the formation of as many as 40 states (against 28 at present). In a more contemporary context, the VHP and the Bajrang Dal have typically taken harder and more strident positions, while the BJP seeks to project itself as a liberal, cosmopolitan organisation.

Despite an antipathy towards minorities in most cases, the BJP has been able to strike a close rapport with sections of the Sikh community, especially the supporters of the Shiromani Akali Dal (SAD), because the Sangh Parivar views Sikhs as 'essentially' Hindu. The alliance between the BJP and the Akalis, which had its origins in the late 1960s, was cemented after the anti-Sikh riots that took place in and around New Delhi after the assassination of Indira Gandhi by a Sikh member of her bodyguard on October 31, 1984.

In order to win new allies and influence political leaders, the BJP has, particularly since the February 1998 general elections, sought to play down three controversial aspects of its election manifesto, as already mentioned: namely, the building of a Ram temple at Ayodhya, the formulation of a uniform civil code for citizens of all religious denominations, and the abrogation of Article 370 of the Constitution of India. Each of these issues was central to the BJP's manifesto for the 1998 Lok Sabha elections.

Though the BJP played down these issues after coming to power, other organisations of the Sangh Parivar have not had any qualms about continuing to emphasise these and other sensitive issues. As a matter of fact, the VHP and the Bajrang Dal keep talking about the need to demolish mosques at Kashi and Mathura (two other cities in Uttar Pradesh) that had been built centuries ago, allegedly over Hindu religious sites. The RSS too has periodically supported this move. Their repeated assertions caused quite a bit of embarrassment to the Vajpayee government. Advani met representatives of the hardliners in the Sangh Parivar, like Ashok Singhal of the VHP, to try and convince them to moderate their statements.

There are many in the RSS and allied organisations who desperately feel the need to correct the wrongs of history and who passionately argue that the main reason why Hindus have been oppressed over the centuries is on account of the community being too passive and too accommodating. At the same time, the moderate voices within the Sangh Parivar acknowledge the plurality of Hinduism and its non-partisan character. The one-time militant proponents of Hindutva (or Hindu-ness) currently spare no effort in highlighting the accommodative and 'melting pot' nature of Hinduism; they agree that Hinduism is perhaps less an organised religion and more a philosophy of life.

Swaminathan Gurumurthy, a leading ideologue of the Swadeshi Jagaran Manch (SJM), a frontal organisation of the RSS which concerns itself with economic issues, stated in 1993:

> We must realize that we have a problem on hand in India, the problem of a stagnant and conservative Islamic society. The secular leaders and parties tell us that the problem on our hands is not Islamic fundamentalism, but the Hindutva ideology. This view is good only for gathering votes. The fact is that we have a fundamentalist Muslim problem, and our problem cannot be divorced from the international Islamic politics and the world's reaction to it…the apparently unorganized and diverse Hindu society is perhaps the only society in the world that faced, and then survived, the Islamic theocratic invasion.

He goes on to add: 'The assimilative Hindu cultural and civilisational ethos is the only basis for any durable personal and social interaction between the Muslims and the rest of our countrymen…. A national effort is called for to break Islamic exclusivism and enshrine the assimilative Hindutva. This alone constitutes true nationalism and true national integration.'

The BJP's 1998 election manifesto also sought to project Hindutva as a civilisational concept and not a narrow religious one. It also said, 'Every effort to characterize Hindutva as a sectarian or exclusive idea has failed as the people of India have repeatedly rejected such a view and the Supreme Court, too, finally endorsed the true meaning and content of Hindutva as being consistent with the true meaning and definition of secularism. In fact, Hindutva accepts as sacred all forms of belief and worship. The evolution of Hindutva in politics is the antidote to the creation of vote banks and appeasement of sectional interests. Hindutva means justice for all.'

The reference to the Supreme Court is to the December 1995 judgement of a Constitutional bench of the apex court headed by the then Chief Justice of India, J. S. Verma (who went on to become Chairman of the National Human Rights Commission). The judgement came in response to a petition filed in the court challenging the validity of the election of Maharashtra Chief Minister Manohar Joshi of the Shiv Sena on the grounds that he had appealed to religious sentiments by stating that industrially prosperous Maharashtra would become India's first Hindu state. This, the petition argued, was a corrupt electoral practice. The judgement stated: '...no precise meaning can be ascribed to the terms "Hindu", "Hindutva" and "Hinduism"; and no meaning in the abstract can confine it to the narrow limits of religion alone, excluding the content of Indian culture and heritage. It is difficult to appreciate how...the term "Hindutva" or "Hinduism" per se, in the abstract, can be assumed to mean and be equated with narrow fundamentalist Hindu religious bigotry....'.

Not surprisingly, the BJP's ideologues were jubilant about this judgement, while its opponents felt it had given the party an opportunity to claim that its secular credentials had been upheld by the apex court of the land.

Speaking with a Forked Tongue

Within the BJP, and especially within the larger Sangh Parivar, members have voiced various shades of political opinion from the extreme right to the relatively moderate. While speaking in many voices can confuse political opponents when a party is out of power, the same trait can prove to be a liability when the party is governing. This was what the BJP realised within months of the Vajpayee government coming to the helm of power in New Delhi. The BJP's critics in the Congress and the left had always claimed that the party and its allies spoke in a forked tongue and that its public pronouncements concealed a hidden agenda.

Here's one example of the kind of vitriol that was spewed by VHP functionaries. At a public rally in New Delhi's Ramlila Maidan in late January 2002, Acharya Dharmendra attacked Vajpayee in downright abusive terms. He suggested that the Prime Minister, who had had his knees operated, should get his eyes operated as well if he was unable to see the mass upsurge in favour of building the Ram temple at Ayodhya. He also pointed out that the money spent on the knee operation had come from the exchequer and asked whether the people had paid so that Vajpayee could kneel before George Bush and Tony Blair.

Dharmendra then went on to accuse Vajpayee of being a betrayer to the Ram temple movement and said the Prime Minister ought to remember the fate of villains like Hiranyakashyap, Ravana, Taimur, Aurangazeb and even Tony Blair's aunt, Queen Victoria, who could not retain power forever. The VHP leader, somewhat unusually, used an Urdu couplet to hint that Vajpayee should quit if he couldn't ensure the construction of the Ram temple. The couplet went: '*Had-e-gham-e-hasti se guzar kyon nahin jaate, Jeena nahin aata hai to mar kyon nahin jaate, Manzil ko paana hai to toofan bhi milenge, dar agar hai to kashti se utar kyon nahin jaate.*' (Why don't you reach beyond the limits of the perils of being? Why don't you die if you don't know how to live? If the goal is to be reached, storms will have to be braved. If you are afraid, why don't you get off the boat?) Advani too was not spared, with Dharmendra pointing out that those who described the demolition as a shameful incident would not have reached where they had but for that incident.

BJP president M. Venkaiah Naidu created a stir in June 2003 when he described Vajpayee as a *vikaspurush* (development man) and Advani as a *lohpurush* (iron man) and said that his party would contest the 2004 general elections under the leadership of both these stalwarts. The media interpreted the statement to mean that Vajpayee could hand over the mantle of leadership of the BJP as well as the NDA (and future governments as well) to his deputy Advani. Advani promptly said Vajpayee was his leader but Vajpayee's own statement at a party gathering soon after returning from a visit abroad made it apparent to all concerned that he was the real boss. He said that he was neither 'tired' nor 'retired' and added: 'Let the party fight the elections under Advani's leadership'. Naidu went into a tizzy clarifying that he had not questioned Vajpayee's position nor was he in any way trying to drive a wedge between the two tallest leaders of the BJP. While the dust raised by his remarks took some time to settle, this episode revealed once again that much of the so-called differences between Vajpayee (the 'liberal') and Advani (the 'hardliner') lay in the minds of mediapersons and that if it came to the crunch, Advani too was clear that Vajpayee was the most suitable person to lead the coalition and the government even if Advani controlled some of the key portfolios and was responsible for taking many crucial decisions.

To some extent, Advani's position was a bit vulnerable because his name figured in the court cases relating to the demolition of the Babri masjid. Though the cases had remained largely forgotten for over a decade, the issue came to the fore in July 2003, when the CBI filed fresh chargesheets against some of the key accused including Advani and one other Minister in the Vajpayee cabinet, Murli Manohar Joshi. (The fresh filing of chargesheets had become necessary after the Allahabad High Court had rejected the earlier chargesheets on technical grounds.) It was revealed that the CBI had dropped the charge of conspiring to demolish the masjid that was part of the earlier chargesheet. The Opposition accused the government of having unduly influenced the CBI, while the government predictably denied the charge. The Opposition also pointed out that it was untenable for those who were the prime accused in a case to also be the political masters of the prosecuting agency in the case. As on previous occasions, the issue ultimately died down, but it did, even if only briefly, put the spotlight back on an aspect of Advani's past that the BJP's allies and many of its new-found supporters have not been very comfortable about.

Ayodhya remained in the news throughout June and early July 2003 for other reasons as well. The Sankaracharya of Kanchipuram was in this period making an effort to bring about a negotiated settlement to the dispute between Hindu and Muslim groups. While the government had nothing to do with this effort formally, it was an open secret that the Kanchi Sankaracharya, Jayendra Saraswati, had the blessings of the Prime Minister. This raised hopes—unduly as it later transpired—that the conflict that had raised communal tensions for over a decade-and-a-half could finally be resolved peacefully. Reports in the media in early June suggested that the Sankaracharya had mooted a proposal under which both Muslims and Hindus would agree to abide by the court's verdict on the disputed site and the Muslims would give a 'no-objection certificate' to the Hindus for the latter to build a Ram temple on the land near the disputed site that had been acquired by the government. In return for this, the Sankaracharya promised to get an assurance from Hindu groups like the VHP that similar disputes about places of worship in Kashi and Mathura would be permanently shelved. The All India Muslim Personal Law Board (AIMPLB), with whom the Sankaracharya was corresponding, called a meeting on July 6 to consider the proposal and submit its response.

As soon as media reports on the Sankaracharya's proposal appeared, leaders of the VHP threw a fit. Not only did they reject the proposal outright, they launched a tirade against the Sankaracharya questioning his locus standi and even going so far as to suggest that as the leader of a Shaivite sect he had no business interceding in a dispute that pertained to Ram, an *avatar* of Vishnu. Unlike in the past, the RSS was also quick to back up the VHP's stance, rubbishing the idea that the Hindus should give up their claims on Kashi and Mathura and suggesting that the Sankaracharya was out of his depth. The VHP went a step further and started attacking the Prime Minister as well, warning him that if he reneged on the BJP's campaign promise on the Ram temple, he would pay for it.

Soon thereafter, RSS chief K.S. Sudershan had a meeting with the Kanchi seer. Emerging from the meeting, he declared that there were no differences between the RSS and the Sankaracharya on the Ayodhya issue. The reason for this was to become clear on July 6, when the AIMPLB met and rejected the Sankaracharya's proposal. It then revealed that the Sankaracharya had modified his proposal at a late stage. Not only was there no longer any assurance that Hindus and Muslims would agree to abide by the court's verdict on the disputed site, the Sankaracharya had made it clear that the Muslims should also 'mentally prepare' themselves to hand over the mosques at Kashi and Mathura 'at some point in the future'.

The same VHP that had viciously attacked the Sankaracharya just a couple of weeks earlier, now went to town about how the AIMPLB had 'insulted' a revered Hindu religious leader like the Sankaracharya by rejecting his offer outright. Interestingly, throughout this episode, Vajpayee chose to remain silent. He neither confirmed nor denied the speculation that he had initiated the Sankaracharya's peace efforts, nor did he clarify whether the sudden change in position was known to him and/or had his approval. Vajpayee was again at his ambiguous best barely a month later, at the cremation of Mahant Ramchandra Paramhans, one of the key leaders of the Ram temple movement, in Ayodhya in early August. He declared that the Paramhans' 'last wishes' on the construction of the temple in Ayodhya would be fulfilled. When the Opposition raised a hue and cry in Parliament, he 'clarified' that he had said nothing new and that there had been nothing in his speech to suggest that the temple would be built by force or necessarily at the disputed site. The government's position on the issue, he insisted, had not changed one bit.

On the economic front, the BJP had often been derogatorily dismissed as a party of upper-caste traders who had little or no influence in large parts of the country in the south, east and northeast. The economic policies articulated by the party have been in favour of free enterprise capitalism. When the Finance Minister in the P.V. Narasimha Rao government, Manmohan Singh, unveiled his policies of economic liberalisation in July 1991, the BJP accused the Congress of hijacking its economic agenda. This was the same political party that, despite its avowed pro-business stance, had earlier agreed to follow the tenets of 'Gandhian socialism' in its economic policies. Active advocacy of the virtues of capitalism was not considered desirable in the Indian context, not even for the BJP, which (together with the Swatantra Party in the 1960s) had vociferously espoused the cause of free enterprise. While there is a lot that is common between the economic policies of the Congress and the BJP, within the Sangh Parivar itself there are deep divisions on a number of issues. Thus, while one section of the BJP is in favour of the government rolling out the red carpet for foreign investors, another section argues for a cautious and selective approach towards multinational corporations. 'Computer chips not potato chips' was a slogan that became popular in the run-up to the May 1996 general elections.

One section of the Sangh Parivar, the Swadeshi Jagaran Manch, has time and again opposed decisions of the Vajpayee government that have been perceived to be against the interests of local entrepreneurs. In fact, the extreme right and the left have often made common cause in articulating the need to protect domestic industries from international competition (by increasing tariff barriers in the form of higher customs duties as well as other restrictions on inflows of foreign capital). The SJM as well as the Bharatiya Mazdoor Sangh (BMS), the trade union wing of the RSS, have opposed some of the economic policies of the Vajpayee government, which caused considerable embarrassment to the ruling party.

RSS leaders like Dattopant Thengadi (also a founder of the BMS) openly criticised the government at public meetings where the then Finance Minister Yashwant Sinha's competence was questioned. Later, this section of the Sangh Parivar was persuaded to tone down its criticism. The then BJP President, late

Kushabhau Thakre, had to personally intervene with RSS leaders to ensure that the government's sympathisers spoke in one voice. As stated earlier, what was a diversionary tactic for the Sangh Parivar when in Opposition became a distinct liability for the Vajpayee government.

Party with a Difference?

The BJP and the RSS have always emphasised the importance of 'discipline'—the *shakhas* or gatherings of RSS volunteers clad in khaki shorts and holding sticks usually begin by a chanting of prayers and physical exercises. For many years, the leaders of the BJP claimed that theirs was the most disciplined, cadre-based party in the country (ironically, as disciplined as members of the communist parties which have always been their biggest political rivals). But this perception was more media hype than reality.

The BJP's claims of being a disciplined party, a party different from others especially the Congress, were shattered by a series of incidents which took place in Gujarat in 1995 and 1996. Infighting and factional conflicts between rival groups culminated in unprecedented physical violence inside the assembly at Gandhinagar on September 19, 1996. In the state assembly elections in February 1995, the BJP had secured 121 seats or two-thirds of the total and Keshubhai Patel was sworn in as Chief Minister in March. Dissensions were evident from day one and within six months, the fight was out in the open. On September 27, a group of 46 MLAs headed by Shankersinh Vaghela signed a memorandum to the state's Governor, Naresh Chandra, staking claim to form a new government after contending that Keshubhai Patel had lost his majority in the assembly. In a dramatic gesture, Vaghela took his group of legislators to Khajuraho, apparently to protect them from the ruling faction of the BJP in Gujarat. In November, the party's national leaders led by Advani intervened to defuse the crisis. Keshubhai Patel resigned and was replaced by Suresh Mehta as CM.

The truce between the warring factions lasted barely six months. On May 20, 1996, factional infighting within the BJP resulted in supporters of the official group assaulting the octogenarian Cabinet Minister Atma Ram Patel, seen as sympathetic to the Vaghela group, and stripping him naked in the presence of thousands of people at a public meeting addressed by Vajpayee. Three months later, in August, Vaghela led a group of 46 MLAs in submitting a memorandum to the Governor that the BJP had been reduced to a minority in the assembly. Legislators complained that they were being kept under 'house arrest' by members of the ruling faction. Soon, Vaghela split the party to form the Rashtriya Janata Party (RJP).

With both factions prepared to do anything to ensure they formed the government in Gujarat, matters reached a point where the Governor had no option but to submit a report to the Union government in September stating that he had come to the 'painful conclusion' that there had been a Constitutional breakdown in the state and he was left with no alternative but to suggest invocation of Article 356 to impose President's rule in the state. He recommended that the assembly be kept in suspended animation. The Union government headed by H.D. Deve Gowda did not act on this report, but after Chandra sent in a similar report again within days, the Union Cabinet decided to impose President's rule in Gujarat.

Vaghela went on to become Chief Minister of Gujarat, but not for long. By March 1998, Keshubhai Patel was again Chief Minister of Gujarat after fresh assembly polls were held in the state with Vaghela's RJP suffering a major electoral reverse. Nevertheless, the infighting within the BJP in Gujarat and its eagerness to form coalitions and find new allies highlighted how the party had become prone to all the ills plaguing the Congress.

Factional fighting was to erupt again in the Gujarat BJP on the eve of the December 2002 state assembly elections. Narendra Modi, who was seeking re-election after the communal violence in the state, decided to make it clear who was the boss in the state. As part of his attitude of brooking no opposition, he refused to let Haren Pandya, another prominent BJP leader in Gujarat, be nominated as the party's candidate for the Ellis Bridge constituency in Ahmedabad, the state's largest city. Pandya, who had served as Home Minister in the Keshubhai Patel government, had represented this constituency for several terms and won each time with impressive margins. Yet, Modi put his foot down and made it clear that Pandya would not be nominated again. Even attempts by senior central leaders of the BJP, like Advani, to persuade Modi to relent proved futile. Modi had made it a 'prestige issue' and his views prevailed.

Three months after the 2002 assembly election, in March 2003, Pandya was shot dead by 'unidentified gunmen' outside a public park in Ahmedabad where he went for his morning walk. He lay bleeding to death in his car for two hours before he was discovered. It is a measure of the hostility between Modi and Pandya and the public perception of this hostility that the opposition Congress was not alone in insinuating that Pandya's killing was a 'political murder'. As a matter of fact, the same phrase was used during a memorial meeting by Keshubhai Patel and by Pandya's father, in the presence of Advani and Modi. Interestingly, on the same occasion Advani acknowledged that 'injustice' had been done to Pandya by not allowing him to contest the election.

The virus of indiscipline that the BJP first contracted in Gujarat later spread to the state that was of paramount importance in its bid to win and retain power at the centre—Uttar Pradesh. Despite serious efforts by the BJP's central leadership to contain the damage of an ugly factional fracas, it ultimately led to the party's most high-profile mass leader in the state at the time, Kalyan Singh, being expelled. While Kalyan Singh's threats of causing a vertical split in the UP unit of the BJP ultimately proved exaggerated, his expulsion did alienate sections of the OBCs from the party.

Soon after the 1998 Lok Sabha elections, it became clear that the BJP in UP was a badly divided house with a section of the party's MLAs publicly demanding the ouster of Chief Minister Kalyan Singh, the man who was seen as the architect of the party's dramatic rise in electoral fortunes in the 1990s. There was little doubt that Kalyan Singh was by far the most popular leader of the party in UP. Yet, within his own party he faced a growing challenge to his leadership from a group predominantly of MLAs and organisational leaders from the upper castes. It was also widely believed that while Kalyan Singh enjoyed the confidence of Advani, Vajpayee's own sympathies lay more with the dissident group.

The dissidents, who included prominent party leaders like Lalji Tandon, Kailashpati Mishra and Rajnath Singh, were ostensibly opposed to Kalyan Singh's leadership because of his autocratic style and the favours he was alleged to have done for some of his close associates like the corporator Kusum Rai. They argued that the Chief Minister's undemocratic ways were fast eroding public support for the party and could deliver a body blow to its electoral prospects if he was not ousted. The media, political analysts and the lay public, however, remained convinced that their real grouse against the Chief Minister was the fact that he was from one of the intermediate castes—a Lodh—and his tenure had loosened the upper castes' grip on institutions of power in the state.

Ironically, when Kalyan Singh was first chosen by the BJP in June 1991 to head the state government, it was this same caste background that played a major role. The entire northern region of the country was at the time severely divided along caste lines in the aftermath of the decision by the Janata Dal (JD) government at the centre to implement the report of the Mandal Commission. The report had essentially recommended reservations in government jobs for the intermediate castes and though most major political parties had consistently promised in their election manifestoes to implement the report, there was an unstated understanding that the promises would not be honoured—till V.P. Singh's own political compulsions provoked him to announce as Prime Minister that the government would in fact implement the report. The violent agitations against this decision, led largely by upper-caste students, laid the foundation for a caste-based division that was more overt than ever before. It was with a view towards exploiting these caste divisions that the BJP groomed Kalyan Singh as its foremost leader in UP through the 1990s.

By the time of the 1999 general elections, it was quite evident that there was considerable resentment against Kalyan Singh within the BJP's state unit. However, the BJP leadership was unable either to discipline the dissidents or replace Kalyan Singh on the eve of the crucial Parliamentary elections of 1999, though virtually everybody in the state, from political pundits to the layman, was clear that the Chief Minister would be removed from his post, whatever be the results of the elections. During the elections, Kalyan Singh refused to condemn the activities of his former associate Sakshi Maharaj (who, like him, had been named as an accused in the Babri masjid demolition case) who openly campaigned against the BJP and for the Samajwadi Party, a party Sakshi Maharaj later joined. Soon after the Lok Sabha elections, this reckoning was proved right. The fact that the BJP fared rather poorly in UP only helped the dissidents to raise their campaign for the removal of Kalyan Singh as Chief Minister. It was the severe anti-incumbency factor against the Chief Minister, they said, which had led to the BJP winning just 29 Lok Sabha seats in the state, almost half the number it won in 1998.

The party's central leadership too was now willing to play along with the dissidents and, in November 1999, it decided to ask Kalyan Singh to step down. The man named to replace him, however, came as a surprise. Ram Prakash Gupta, it is true, had once been Deputy Chief Minister of the state, but that was more than two decades earlier, in 1977. Since then, he had maintained a relatively low profile in politics. What might have swung the decision in his favour were two facts: first, he was neither from the upper castes, nor quite from the backward castes. As a Bania (a trading community), he could possibly manage to strike a balance in the fight for power between the two contending caste factions in the BJP's UP unit. Equally, Gupta was seen neither as a prominent dissident, nor as a Kalyan Singh loyalist. Clearly, the BJP's central leadership was still hoping that a truce could be negotiated in a factional fight that was threatening to do severe damage to the party in the state. As part of this attempt at a truce, Kalyan Singh was offered a berth in the Union Cabinet, as was a prominent dissident leader, Rajnath Singh. While Rajnath Singh accepted the offer, Kalyan Singh refused it, giving the first indications of what was to come.

Immediately after he stepped down as Chief Minister, Kalyan Singh launched a frontal attack on Vajpayee, blaming him for orchestrating the revolt against him. He also chose to single out Vajpayee for 'betraying' the party's ideology and its commitment to its voters to build a Ram temple in Ayodhya. It was this jettisoning of the BJP's core agenda, he insisted, that had led to its electoral defeat in the state. Kalyan Singh also attempted to drive a wedge between Vajpayee and Home Minister Advani, by maintaining that Vajpayee had 'hijacked' the party, while Advani was feeling suffocated in a party which had parted from its ideological moorings. All he succeeded in doing in the process was to force Advani, and other leaders who had earlier been seen as sympathetic to his travails, to condemn him and deny any rift within the central leadership. Kalyan Singh's deliberately provocative statements against Vajpayee had the predictable result of forcing the party's central leadership to expel him from the BJP.

Speculation that Kalyan Singh's expulsion would lead to a significant split in the party's leadership and ranks in UP was belied. While a few individual leaders spoke in defence of him, there was no significant desertion from the BJP's ranks. However, the departure of Kalyan Singh did cost the BJP dear in the February 2002 assembly elections. Kalyan Singh's RKP managed to win in only four constituencies (Kalyan Singh himself winning from two of them), but damaged the BJP's prospects in dozens of seats. The result was that the BJP finished third behind the SP and the BSP.

It is not as if the BJP was unaware of the implications of expelling Kalyan Singh. Yet, faced with the choice of alienating Kalyan Singh's support base or much of its leadership in the state, the party chose what it felt was the lesser evil. In a significant development in December 2003, four years after he was forced to resign as Chief Minister of UP, Kalyan Singh met Vajpayee at the residence of Lalji Tandon, signaling a thaw in their strained relationship—yet again, what became apparent was that there are no permanent friends or enemies in politics after Kalyan Singh rejoined the BJP. His confidantes, including Kusum Rai who was by then a minister in Mulayam Singh Yadav's government, reluctantly quit their positions to return to the BJP.

The Himachal Pradesh assembly elections of February 2003 saw factional feuds within the BJP coming out in the open. The party's campaign was led by Prem Kumar Dhumal, the incumbent Chief Minister, who was seeking re-election. The BJP was convincingly beaten by the Congress, which managed to win a majority in the assembly despite also being faction-ridden. Shanta Kumar, former Union Minister for Civil Supplies and Consumer Affairs in the Vajpayee Cabinet, and the senior-most BJP leader in Himachal Pradesh, who had been elected Chief Minister of Himachal Pradesh on two previous occasions in 1977 and 1990, was quick to blame Dhumal's 'non-performance' for the debacle. Dhumal, in turn, accused Shanta Kumar of sabotaging the BJP's prospects by propping up 'rebel' candidates in several constituencies. The party officially blamed 'infighting and factionalism' for the electoral defeat and Shanta Kumar was dropped from the Union Cabinet.

Another episode which badly battered the image of the BJP as the 'party with a difference' and the attempts of the NDA to present itself as a 'clean' coalition was the Tehelka incident in March 2001. Two journalists belonging to the website Tehelka masqueraded as arms dealers and secretly videotaped a number of defence officials and politicians. The most sensational of these recordings was a sequence showing the then BJP President Bangaru Laxman accepting a wad of currency notes from the two journalists.

Laxman, who belongs to a scheduled caste and was Vajpayee's nominee as party president presumably to rid the BJP of the image that it was a party dominated by Hindu upper-caste members, had to resign in ignominy. There was an attempt to rehabilitate Laxman more than six months later when he was made the head of a Parliamentary committee on housing. Though he bitterly complained that he had merely done what all Indian politicians do, namely, accept funds on behalf of his party, and that he was made a scapegoat because of his caste background, the damage to the BJP had already been done.

The bigger fallout of the Tehelka episode was the resignation of Defence Minister George Fernandes, a socialist, a non-practising Christian, and an individual who had revealed his amazingly dexterous skills in acting as Vajpayee's handy-man and troubleshooter when it came to placating troublesome allies like Jayalalithaa and Mamata Banerjee. Fernandes put in his papers since the secretly-filmed Tehelka tapes indicated that the journalists had entered the Defence Minister's official residence and had spoken to his party president and companion Jaya Jaitly about donating funds to their party (the Samata Party). Even as the one-judge commission of inquiry was questioning witnesses to determine the correctness or otherwise of the charges thrown up by the Tehelka tapes, Fernandes was re-instated as Defence Minister in October 2001, seven months after he resigned. The Opposition attacked the government and took the novel step of refusing to ask Fernandes questions as Defence Minister in Parliament, arguing that he could not legitimately hold the post till he was cleared of wrongdoing by the commission.

Going beyond the Cow Belt

Unlike the Congress, the BJP, ever since it was formed in 1980, and the BJS before it, has never hesitated in becoming part of a coalition. After the 4th general elections in 1967, many states in northern India including Punjab, Uttar Pradesh and Bihar saw the formation of non-Congress state governments which were cobbled together by opportunistic alliances among those opposed to India's grand old party. The BJS even agreed to sink its differences with the communist parties to keep the Congress out of power in these states, even if the coalition governments that were formed were shortlived and prone to implosion, since there were no ideological bonds to bring together the politically diverse groups. Despite such alliances, the BJS was not a serious force to reckon with in Indian politics till 1977.

In the 1st general elections held in independent India between October 1951 and February 1952, the BJS won three out of the 94 Parliamentary seats it had contested (two from West Bengal and one from Madhya Pradesh) out of 489 seats in the first Lok Sabha. In the 2nd general elections held in 1957, the BJS contested more seats (130) but was able to gain only one extra seat in the aggregate while losing all four seats it had won earlier. Of the BJS's four seats in the second Lok Sabha, two came from Uttar Pradesh and two from Bombay. It was after the 3rd general elections in 1962 that the presence of the BJS on the national political scene became more evident: the party won 14 out of the 196 seats it contested, increasing its tally in Madhya Pradesh (to three) and Uttar Pradesh (to seven) while opening its account in Punjab (with three seats) and Rajasthan (one seat). The party's share in total votes polled went up steadily in the first three general elections from just over 3 per cent in 1952 to just under 6 per cent in 1957 and 6.4 per cent in 1962.

The 4th general election in 1967 was the first that saw the Congress' hold on Indian politics diminishing. The BJS won 35 seats in a Lok Sabha with 520 seats. The party obtained 9.4 per cent of the votes polled. It expanded its position in Uttar Pradesh with 12 seats, six in Delhi, 10 in Madhya Pradesh and three in Rajasthan. The three seats held earlier in Punjab were subdivided into Haryana and Chandigarh. The BJS opened its account not only in Bihar by winning a seat but also in south India, by returning an MP from Andhra Pradesh for the first time. The period that followed saw the beginning of coalition politics in the states of north India with BJS members participating in various non-Congress governments in states like Bihar, Uttar Pradesh, Punjab, Haryana, Orissa and Madhya Pradesh. For the first time, the BJS gained experience of working with diverse political groupings including ideological opponents like the communists.

The rise of Indira Gandhi eclipsed the growth of the BJS for a while thereafter. Indira Gandhi headed the Union government for the first time on January 24, 1966, after her father and India's first Prime Minister, Jawaharlal Nehru. She split the party three years later in 1969 to establish the Congress(I), as also her supremacy. She successfully projected herself as an upholder of socialistic values while painting her opponents within the Congress as those in favour of a conservative status quo. Her *garibi hatao* (banish poverty) slogan caught the imagination of the people as did her stance on issues like bank nationalisation, abolition of privy purses to feudal lords, and land reforms.

The 1971–72 war with Pakistan and the formation of Bangladesh saw Indira Gandhi riding the crest of a popularity wave. The first nuclear test was conducted in Pokhran, Rajasthan, in 1974—this event was welcomed by the BJS in Opposition, a fact that the party sought to repeatedly emphasise to garner domestic support after the second set of nuclear tests were conducted in the second week of May 1998. At this time the Congress was striding ahead with as many as 342 MPs in a Lok Sabha of 518 members in the 1971 elections. The BJS got 22 seats while its share of the votes polled came down to 7.4 per cent.

By the mid-1970s, Indira Gandhi's authoritarian tendencies and imperious attitude had become apparent. She was accused of promoting her younger son Sanjay Gandhi as an 'extra-constitutional' authority. This phase culminated in the imposition of an internal Emergency that lasted 19 months—this was the only time in independent India's history when citizens' fundamental rights were brutally curbed, and censorship enforced on the press. The result? Indira and Sanjay Gandhi and her party suffered a humiliating defeat, and India saw the re-emergence of the Sangh Parivar from the shadows. While many within the BJS actively opposed Indira Gandhi's authoritarian actions and supported the 'total revolution' movement led by Jayaprakash Narayan (JP), there were others in the Parivar who 'tactically' accepted her 20-point programme to escape the rigours of jail. There was limited opposition within the Parivar to merging with the Janata Party. Indira Gandhi was routed by Raj Narain in Rae Bareilly and her younger son, Sanjay Gandhi, lost the elections in Amethi, both in Uttar Pradesh. The Congress had been routed in the elections, surviving mainly in the south, with 154 MPs elected to the 542-member 6th Lok Sabha. The Janata Party government, which came to power on March 24, 1977 with Morarji Desai as Prime Minister, had Vajpayee as External Affairs Minister and Advani as Minister for Information and Broadcasting. This was the first time that representatives of the Sangh Parivar participated in a coalition government in New Delhi.

What followed is well known. Morarji Desai started faltering in late July 1979, ostensibly on the issue of the 'dual membership' of Vajpayee, Advani and others who refused to disown their allegiance to the RSS, thus culminating in the fall of the Janata Party government. The Congress went on to support a minority government led by Charan Singh which lasted barely six months. There were many internal contradictions that had dogged the shortlived Janata Party government. But to some, like socialist firebrand George Fernandes, who almost overnight switched loyalties from Morarji Desai to Charan Singh, the issue of dual membership was most significant. Fernandes had, by then, been accused in the Baroda Dynamite Case. (There is an interesting sidelight here: among the lawyers who supported him then was a young man, Swaraj Kaushal, and his wife Sushma Swaraj, who was, five years later, to move from the Janata Party—as the youngest MLA and minister in two governments in Haryana headed by Devi Lal—to become an important figure in the BJP.) Chaudhury Charan Singh's government lasted from July 28, 1979 to January 14, 1980. He was the only Indian Prime Minister who never faced Parliament during his entire tenure.

Having been unceremoniously rejected by the electorate three years earlier, Indira Gandhi strode back to power in the 7th general elections helped by the mileage the Congress extracted from the rising prices of onions: the Congress(I) won 353 out of 529 seats in the Lok Sabha with nearly 43 per cent of the votes polled. After Indira Gandhi's assassination on October 31, 1984 which led to the most brutal attacks on the Sikh community by goons—some of them associated with Congress politicians—the Congress, headed by Rajiv Gandhi and riding a 'sympathy wave', won a massive mandate—415 out of 517 seats in the Lok Sabha—unprecedented in the annals of Indian history. This was also the period which saw the BJP going through its politically weakest phase: the party had won two out of the 229 seats it had contested in the 1984 elections and its share of the popular vote stood at 7.4 per cent—the BJS had obtained an identical proportion of votes polled in the 1971 elections. The 1980s were truly a lost decade for the BJP. It was only towards the end of Rajiv Gandhi's term as Prime Minister, between 1987 and 1989, that the BJP's political support base started picking up and since then, its rise has been truly spectacular.

In the 1989 elections, racked by charges of corruption and inefficiency, the Congress headed by Rajiv Gandhi collapsed. The BJP bounced back with 11.5 per cent of the votes polled which translated into a big jump in the number of seats in the Lok Sabha: the party had 86 members in a house of 543 seats making it the third largest after the Congress with 197 seats and the Janata Dal with 142 seats. The BJP chose to support V.P. Singh's minority coalition government without participating in it. More than the internal contradictions within the JD that led to Chandra Shekhar being sworn in as Prime Minister on November 10, 1990 with 'outside' support from the Congress headed by Rajiv Gandhi, there was another more important reason for the collapse of the V.P. Singh government. This was the clash between his Mandal Commission agenda—aimed at reserving government jobs for backward castes—and the agenda of the BJP to build a Ram temple at Ayodhya after demolishing the Babri masjid, symbolised by Advani's *rath yatra* across the length of north India, whipping up support to build the temple, before his arrest at Samastipur, Bihar, a state led at that time by Laloo Prasad Yadav.

The first round of voting in the 10th general elections took place on May 20, 1991. The next evening, Rajiv Gandhi was assassinated by a 'human bomb' at Sriperumbudur, Tamil Nadu. The elections were completed on June 15 and a minority government of the Congress party headed by former Minister for Human Resources Development in Rajiv Gandhi's government, P.V. Narasimha Rao, assumed power in New Delhi on June 21, 1991. The BJP's tally of 120 seats in a Lok Sabha with 543 seats made it the biggest Opposition party. The rush to build the Ram temple picked up in 1992. In late November, Narasimha Rao cut short his trip to Dakar in Senegal, where heads of state of the Group of 15 (G-15) developing countries were gathered, to attend a meeting of religious leaders to sort out the Ayodhya issue which was threatening to get out of hand. Among the so-called religious leaders was one of Narasimha Rao's cronies, controversial 'godman' Chandra Swami, also known as Nemi Chand Gandhi, aka Nemi Chand Jain.

Ayodhya and After

On December 6, 1992, the Babri masjid's structure was demolished by gangs of hooligans. As described earlier, it was one of *the* worst moments in independent India's history. India's image as a tolerant, secular nation took a battering in the eyes of the world. Vajpayee and Advani, both in Parliament and outside, expressed regret for what happened. But the BJP was a divided house. The official bio-data of Uma Bharti, who took an active role in urging the mob to demolish the structure, describes her as a 'religious missionary'. Clad in saffron and sometimes derogatorily referred to as the 'sexy *sanyasin*' by her political opponents, Bharti and Vajpayee openly clashed in public years later in 1998 when the BJP government was seeking to change its position on privatising the insurance industry.

Right through the better part of 1994 and 1995, the BJP tried assiduously to convey the impression that it was indeed the party of the future, that Vajpayee was the Prime Minister-in-waiting. The fractured mandate thrown up by the May 1996 general elections disappointed the BJP, which was hoping it would be able to comfortably form the Union government, led for the first time by a truly non-Congress Prime Minister. Even when it was apparent that a majority would elude the BJP-led alliance, party ideologues convinced Vajpayee and Advani that they stood a faint chance of convincing others to support the alliance. As temperatures rose in the capital city of New Delhi in more than just the metaphorical sense, Vajpayee remained Prime Minister for just two weeks starting May 16, 1996. During this fleeting period in Indian history, a significant event took place—Union Finance Minister Jaswant Singh formally approved the counter-guarantee to the loans taken to set up the country's first power project fully financed by a foreign corporate group, Enron of the US.[1]

The first Vajpayee government may have lasted barely 13 days, but even that short period was enough for dissidence to raise its ugly head. The BJP's only Muslim MP at that time (from the Rajya Sabha) Sikandar Bakht had been given the ministerial portfolio of Urban Development. But he was most unhappy, refused to attend

---

[1] The Enron project had more than its share of controversies. The BJP and the Shiv Sena had made common cause with environmental groups to oppose tooth-and-nail the giant project located near the coast at Dabhol before the 1995 assembly elections in Maharashtra, India's most industrialised state. The Congress government in the state headed by Sharad Pawar had first approved the project. After the BJP–Shiv Sena combine came to power in the state, it did an about-turn and renegotiated a larger project at Dabhol with the same Houston-based energy group.

office or stop sulking till he was made External Affairs Minister. By then, the BJP's power brokers, armed with cellular phones, had come back with the news that no new MPs, individually or in groups, would be willing to switch their allegiance. The Telugu Desam Party led by the Andhra Pradesh Chief Minister Chandrababu Naidu was firmly with the 'third force' as convenor of the United Front and busy confabulating on the formation of the next government. It was apparent that Vajpayee was bound to lose a vote of confidence in the Lok Sabha.

In the meantime, the United Front, comprising 13 political parties, had been formed and had chosen an unlikely 'dark horse' candidate, former Chief Minister of Karnataka H.D. Deve Gowda, as the man to head its government. After the BJP government fell, Deve Gowda was invited to form the government and did so with the support of the Congress. The BJP thus became the main opposition party in the Lok Sabha for the 18-month period in which the UF remained in office.

During this period in Opposition, the BJP often appeared divided about its future strategy. Should it stress the accommodative 'Vajpayee line' on welcoming new alliance partners to form coalitions or should it continue with contentious issues like the building of the Ram temple, the uniform civil code, and so on, which could alienate existing and potential allies? The hardline view prevailed and these issues (together with the old BJS issue of a ban on cow slaughter) were mentioned in the BJP manifesto issued before the February 1998 elections.

The elections saw India's voters giving an even more fractured verdict. While in most states the battle-lines were clear and the polity was bipolar, by the time the numbers were totted up and aggregated, it was apparent to all that the 12th Lok Sabha, like the earlier house, would not be able to provide a government with some degree of stability for any length of time. Based on the results of 534 seats (in a lower house of Parliament with 543 seats), the BJP and 12 of its alliance partners would be able to muster the support of just under 250 MPs. The Congress and its allies won just over 170 seats, the United Front was considerably weakened with less than 100 seats (93 to be precise), while independents and 'others' took up the remaining seats.

The BJP's pre-election alliance partners were the Samata Party in Bihar led by Nitish Kumar and George Fernandes; the Biju Janata

Dal headed by Naveen Patnaik, the son of the late Chief Minister and 'strongman' of Orissa, Biju Patnaik, and a relative greenhorn in politics; the Shiromani Akali Dal of Punjab; the Trinamool Congress of West Bengal led by Mamata Banerjee; the Shiv Sena; five parties in Tamil Nadu: the AIADMK led by Jayalalithaa, the PMK (Pattali Makkal Katchi) led by Dalit Ezhilmalai, the MDMK (Marumalarchi DMK or the DMK for resurgence) led by Vaiko, the Tamizhaga Rajiv Congress (TRC) led by K. Ramamurthi, the Janata Party of Dr. Subramaniam Swamy; and the Lok Shakti led by the late Rama Krishna Hegde, former Chief Minister of Karnataka.

In addition, the BJP alliance included one MP from the Haryana Vikas Party led by Haryana Chief Minister Bansi Lal. His arch opponent in the state, Om Prakash Chautala of the Haryana Lok Dal with four MPs, while opposing Bansi Lal in Haryana, chose to support the Vajpayee government with the HVP. Such indeed are the curious twists and turns in Indian politics. Also interesting is the fact that one member of Parliament belonging to the Janata Party, the colourful Dr. Subramaniam Swamy, was at this juncture an ardent supporter of Vajpayee and the coalition government he would head.

While Vajpayee formed his council of ministers that was sworn in on March 19, 1998, even with the 12 alliance partners, the BJP was still falling short of the magic majority mark in the Lok Sabha. The National Conference, as already mentioned, had abstained in the vote of confidence sought by the Vajpayee government. The final act in the drama was played out a week later, on the fateful morning of March 28, 1998.

Till that morning, on the issue of who would hold the post of Speaker of the lower house of Parliament, the BJP and its partners had conveyed the impression that they would settle for the candidature of P.A. Sangma, Congress leader, former Speaker who had received quite a few compliments for his stewardship of the 11th Lok Sabha, and the first and only tribal to hold the post. In fact, even that morning, the then Parliamentary Affairs Minister Madan Lal Khurana had spoken to him about the BJP's support for his candidature while, at around the same time, the TDP had decided to jump the UF ship and go along with the BJP-led alliance. Chandrababu Naidu, who was no less than the Convenor of the United Front, justified his position on the plea that there was no way the TDP could support a government led by the Congress. The 'reward' received by the TDP for the support of its 12 MPs to the Vajpayee government was that one of them, G.M.C. Balayogi, became the new Speaker of the 12th Lok Sabha. While the other constituents of the UF predictably screamed blue murder and accused Naidu of being a betrayer, the deed had been done.

Defeated by a Single Vote

The second Vajpayee government, which lasted 13 months between March 28, 1998 and April 17, 1999, was a fragile coalition from the start. The AIADMK-led group (including the PMK, the MDMK, the Tamizhaga Rajiv Congress led by K. Ramamurthy, and the Janata Party) that commanded the support of 27 MPs at that time, kept the BJP on tenterhooks because Jayalalithaa delayed her letter to the President of India committing the group's support to a government led by Vajpayee. From the word go, when the ruling alliance confabulated on its National Agenda for Governance, the AIADMK and Jayalalithaa proved to be rather troublesome and unreliable partners. The portly former film actress from Poes Garden, Chennai, put her foot down (and got her way) when it came to ministerial appointments. Her loyalists occupied crucial positions which, it was believed, was aimed at ensuring that the 42 corruption cases instituted against her and her associates by the DMK regime would proceed as slowly as possible.

Among the AIADMK MPs who occupied key posts were M. Thambi Durai, who became Union Minister for Law, Justice and Company Affairs and R. Muttaiah, who became Minister of State for Revenue in the Ministry of Finance (but had to quit after his name appeared as an accused in one of the court cases against Jayalalithaa and her associates and was replaced by R.K. Kumar). K. Ramamurthy of the TRC became Minister for Petroleum and Natural Gas. Predictably, Thambi Durai was later accused of trying to influence the transfer of prosecutors in Tamil Nadu who were handling cases against Jayalalithaa and her associates. Similar accusations were levelled when there were large-scale transfers of officers belonging to the Income Tax Department. The government—and even the BJP's spokespersons—claimed that these transfers and new appointments were 'routine' and the prerogative of the government, but very few were fooled. The Vajpayee government also took the initiative to sort out the apparently irreconcilable differences primarily between two states in southern India, Tamil Nadu and Karnataka, over sharing the water of the river Cauvery.

The first major decision of the Vajpayee government that stunned the world was his decision to conduct a series of nuclear tests at Pokhran in the second week of May 1998. These explosions were conducted almost exactly 24 years after the first tests were conducted at the same arid desert zone in Rajasthan's Jaisalmer district. Even as international attention was focused on the subcontinent, Pakistan conducted its 'tit-for-tat' tests.

Just over a fortnight after the nuclear tests, on June 1, 1998, Finance Minister Yashwant Sinha presented the first Union budget of the Vajpayee government, which turned out to be quite a disaster. What was unprecedented was the fact that within days of the announcement of the budget proposals, the government backtracked on a number of key proposals (detailed in the chapter on the economy). The entire sequence of events following the presentation of the budget conveyed a distinct impression (even to the BJP's sympathisers) that the government was being pulled apart on account of internal dissensions.

As the fragility of the coalition government became more apparent, the AIADMK continued to put pressure on Vajpayee and his colleagues to dismiss the DMK government in Tamil Nadu headed by Karunanidhi on the ground that the state government was not being able to check the activities of anti-national terrorists and Tamil rebels in Sri Lanka. Other partners in the BJP-led alliance like the Trinamool Congress obtained a 'Bengal package' of concessions from the Union government, which included an extension to the underground railway in Kolkata.

At around this juncture, the Vajpayee government came under a lot of criticism for failing to prevent attacks on the Christian community in the tribal-dominated district of Dangs in Gujarat on Christmas Day (which coincidentally also happens to be Vajpayee's birthday). The Prime Minister returned from a visit to the state and was quoted by the media as saying that a national debate on religious conversions was needed. A group of nuns had earlier been gang-raped in Madhya Pradesh while an Australian missionary Graham Staines and his two young sons were brutally burnt to death in their vehicle in a village in northern Orissa. Both

Orissa and Madhya Pradesh were ruled by Congress governments and the BJP sought to dismiss as 'politically motivated' the criticism that attacks on Christians had mounted after the party came to power in New Delhi.

By the end of December, another major controversy engulfed the Vajpayee government even as the Prime Minister made his much-publicised plans to undertake a bus ride across the border to Lahore to meet his Pakistani counterpart Mian Nawaz Sharif. This was the sacking of the former Chief of Naval Staff, Admiral Vishnu Bhagwat on December 30, 1998. The same day, the Cabinet Committee on Appointments also transferred the former Defence Secretary Ajit Kumar and made him Industry Secretary. Defence Minister George Fernandes came into the eye of an unprecedented storm after it was disclosed that he had been approached by all three Chiefs of Staff of the Army, Navy and Air Force to persuade him to stop the government (the Defence Ministry) from intervening in what are considered to be 'mandated' and 'routine' operations to check the inflow of illegal arms through sea routes in the Bay of Bengal. The entire operation was code-named Operation Leech and the insinuation that was later made was that Fernandes for some reason did not want to prevent the inflow of arms to those opposed to the military regime in Myanmar. It was pointed out that refugee students of Myanmar had been guests in the official residence of Fernandes.

The Defence Minister, who had earlier sought to convey an impression that he was in favour of upholding the interests of ordinary service personnel by making frequent trips to visit troops in the Siachen glacier, eating with them and hauling up bureaucrats who were slow in sanctioning expenses of army jawans in inhospitable terrain, painted the entire Vishnu Bhagwat episode quite differently. Fernandes accused Bhagwat of insubordination, of trying to undermine civilian authority over the defence forces, and for refusing to make Vice Admiral Harinder Singh the Deputy Chief of Naval Staff. Singh had accused Bhagwat of discriminating against him in a public complaint and also described Bhagwat's wife, Niloufer Bhagwat, as a communist sympathiser and pointed out that she was half-Muslim. A distinct impression was created that the government was trying to kill two birds with one stone: the Shiromani Akali Dal was keen on Harinder Singh's appointment because he was a Sikh, while the BJP's ally in Maharashtra, the Shiv Sena, was already quite upset with Admiral Bhagwat's lawyer-wife who had vociferously protested against functionaries of the Shiv Sena who had been accused of abetting the anti-Muslim riots in Mumbai before the Justice Sri Krishna Commission of inquiry.

As allegations and counter-allegations flew thick and fast, selected media persons sympathetic to the Vajpayee government were fed selective bits of information purporting to indicate how Bhagwat was a troublesome and treacherous character. Bhagwat, in turn, accused the Defence Minister of having become a victim of the lies spread by corrupt officials and former senior defence personnel turned arms agents. Fernandes and Defence Ministry officials, on the other hand, claimed that Bhagwat was a 'habitual' litigant on the ground that he had gone to court earlier against the decision of the then Chief of Naval Staff who had not promoted him to the rank of Vice Chief. What did not help Bhagwat's cause was that he had eventually been promoted under former Admiral L. Ramdas who had, by then, become an important pillar of the anti-nuclear movement in the country and a bitter critic of the government. Around this time, former Prime Minister Deve Gowda levelled another accusation at the Defence Ministry headed by Fernandes. On the basis of leaked confidential correspondence, he claimed that new Russian tanks were being sought to be hastily inducted into the Indian Army without proper evaluation and trials. Vajpayee stood by Fernandes in his fight against the sacked Admiral and his wife. He even spent New Year's Eve at the residence of Harinder Singh who was then the Fortress Commandant of the Navy stationed at Port Blair in the Andaman & Nicobar Islands in the Bay of Bengal.

The Bhagwat episode did not die down as quickly as Vajpayee and Fernandes may have hoped even after Vajpayee made his 'historic' trip to meet Mian Nawaz Sharif. It was not just the Congress that attacked the government in general and Fernandes in particular for having sacked Admiral Bhagwat. The BJP's largest ally, the AIADMK, too later demanded that Fernandes be removed from the post of Defence Minister. There was more than a touch of irony in this demand because Fernandes had, on more than one occasion, been despatched by Vajpayee to Chennai to meet and placate Jayalalithaa.

In April 1999, Jayalalithaa's confidante Subramaniam Swamy (who had, incidentally, many years earlier been instrumental in instituting a number of corruption cases against her) organised a tea party at a Delhi hotel which was attended by, among many others, the Congress President Sonia Gandhi. The BJP was hoping against hope that the AIADMK would not pull out from the alliance. The party had weaned away the AIADMK's former supporters to its side. But the writing on the wall was clear: there was no way that Jayalalithaa could be persuaded not to withdraw the support of 18 AIADMK MPs from the Vajpayee government. The inevitable took place on April 14, 1999 after the AIADMK withdrew its support to the government and the President of India asked Vajpayee to seek a fresh vote of confidence in the Lok Sabha.

The following day, Vajpayee moved the vote of confidence in his 13-month government and stated that while all his political opponents had ganged up opportunistically to defeat his government, they would not be able to form an alternative government. He was proved correct. The Lok Sabha debated the motion that evening and the whole of the following day with the Lok Sabha session stretching till past 6.00 AM. On April 16, the Indian National Lok Dal (INLD) led by Om Prakash Chautala with four MPs in the Lok Sabha decided to abstain from voting after earlier claiming that the party would vote against the Vajpayee government and in favour of a pro-farmer leader like Deve Gowda. Also unexpected was the position adopted by the five MPs of the BSP led by former Uttar Pradesh Chief Minister Mayawati. On the floor of the house, Mayawati claimed that the BSP would abstain from voting but when the votes were cast the next morning, it became evident that the BSP had voted against the Vajpayee government.

In the cliff-hanging vote of confidence, the government obtained 269 votes while one extra vote (or a total of 270 votes) was cast against the motion of confidence. Just before the voting took place, objections were raised against Giridhar Gamang of the Congress casting his vote since he had by then become Chief Minister of Orissa although, technically, he remained a member of the lower house of Parliament since he had not been elected to the state legislative assembly. The Speaker, Balayogi, asked Gamang to use his 'good sense' to decide whether or not he should vote. Gamang did. Another MP who said his conscience dictated that he flout his party's directive to vote in favour of the Vajpayee government was Saifuddin Soz of the National Conference. Soz had never been comfortable with his former leader, Chief Minister Farooq Abdullah's decision to ditch the UF and support the Vajpayee government.

After the Vajpayee government was reduced to a 'caretaker' status on April 17 and he had put in his papers, unsuccessful attempts were made to form an alternative. Congress President Sonia Gandhi first claimed before the President of India that 272 MPs would support an alternative government led by the Congress (and presumably under her leadership). Thereafter, the Samajwadi Party led by Mulayam Singh Yadav stated that it could not under any circumstances support a minority government comprising the Congress. The Congress, in turn, claimed that it would not be part of a coalition government. The CPI(M), which had been actively trying to woo its partners among the left parties, found that there was dissension in the ranks of the left as well. Two small left parties, the All India Forward Bloc and the Revolutionary Socialist Party, stated that their MPs would not support a government of which the Congress was a part. Even after the four MPs of the Janata Dal (including two former Prime Ministers, Deve Gowda and Gujral) agreed to support a Congress government, Sonia Gandhi realised much to her chagrin that instead of 272 MPs, just about 233 MPs would go along with a Congress government.

At this time, BJP supporters carried out a systematic 'whisper campaign' against President K.R. Narayanan, hinting that he was biased in favour of the Congress because he had served as a bureaucrat in successive Congress governments and had been a Congress MP too. It was claimed that the President should not have asked Vajpayee to prove his majority but instead let the government be defeated on the floor of the house in the normal course. It was also argued that Narayanan gave Sonia Gandhi 'too much time' to try and cobble together an alternative government. Eventually, the 12th Lok Sabha was dissolved. The President asked all parties to come together to pass the Union budget (which had been presented as usual in end February) without any amendment and without any discussion to avert a possible financial crisis.

- Within a fortnight of the fall of the Vajpayee government, as already mentioned, dramatic developments occurred. In early May, hundreds of armed infiltrators crossed the LoC in the Kargil area.

- Three senior Congress leaders broke away from the parent party and formed the NCP, after demanding that Sonia Gandhi make it clear that she would not be a Prime Ministerial aspirant.

Kargil and Sonia's foreign origins thus became the two key issues in the BJP's election campaign. As Kargil gripped the country and became India's first televised war, the Vajpayee government and its supporters sought to play up jingoistic sentiments. Many believe the Kargil war was a key factor that ensured that the BJP and its allies returned to power after the 13th general elections in October 1999. Yet, as already observed, the impact of Kargil was not uniform: there was no apparent impact in states like Punjab, Karnataka or Uttar Pradesh. The 'mandate' of the 13th general elections may have been widely welcomed by the BJP but clearly there was no euphoria. For the first time since 1984, the BJP had not been able to increase the number of Lok Sabha seats it held nor its share of the popular vote. In fact, the BJP's share of the total vote came down by roughly 2 per cent between the 12th and the 13th general elections.

The results of the 13th general elections meant two things for the party: On the one hand, they gave Vajpayee's third government a firmer hold on power than his previous attempts. On the other, they greatly increased, at least initially, the dependence of the BJP on its allies for remaining in power. This latter fact was crucial in ensuring that the so-called Vajpayee line of moderation prevailed. Not only were functionaries of the BJP in the Union government at pains to deny they had any agenda other than the National Agenda for Governance adopted by the National Democratic Alliance, even state-level BJP leaders making contrary noises were quickly chastised. The former Chief Minister of UP, Ram Prakash Gupta, for instance, sought to clarify that the BJP had not forgotten its promise to its supporters on building a Ram temple at Ayodhya. Following predictable protests from the allies, Vajpayee declared in the Lok Sabha that Gupta had assured him that he never said the temple was part of the UP government's agenda.

More significant was a BJP National Council meeting held in Chennai in December 1999. The meeting adopted a resolution putting all contentious issues on hold. The initial draft of the resolution had, in fact, contained a paragraph suggesting that the party had no agenda apart from the NDA agenda. This was clearly too much for the hardliners in the 1,400-member National Council to stomach and had to be dropped. Thus, the struggle between the hardliners and the moderates within the BJP continued and if the moderate position prevailed more often than not, it was largely because of political compulsions.

These compulsions have tested Vajpayee's ability to walk the tightrope, a skill he has mastered over the years. For example, soon after a trip to the United States where, while addressing a group of non-resident Indians, Vajpayee described himself as a true *swayamsevak* (a member of the RSS, literally, one who volunteers to serve society before self), he put out a long, written treatise entitled 'Musings from Kumarakom'—a holiday resort in Kerala. In that treatise, Vajpayee described the Ram Mandir issue as one involving 'national prestige' even as he asserted that no person was above the law, in an apparent attempt to counter the assertion of the VHP, the Bajrang Dal and others that a temple would be constructed at the disputed site at Ayodhya irrespective of the outcome of lawsuits which were pending in various courts.

Vajpayee and the BJP have thus continued to equivocate on the Hindutva issue. The question about whether Hindutva will remain the main vote-catching plank for the party or will it evolve into a more moderate, secular organisation has been kept alive. If Gujarat convinced most observers that the BJP would continue to rely on its communal card to deliver votes, the victories in Rajasthan, Madhya Pradesh and Chhattisgarh led political analysts to suggest that the party had discovered the virtues of making governance a primary election issue. The BJP, it was suggested, had realised that the communal card was yielding diminishing returns and hence was unlikely to use it aggressively in future.

Such a prognosis might be more than a little premature. True, the assembly elections of December 2003 have shown that the BJP can win elections even without using the communal card. However, what has not been demonstrated yet is whether the BJP can retain power without resorting to an election campaign that polarises the electorate along communal lines. The only state in which the BJP has won two successive terms in the recent past has been Gujarat, where its return to power seemed threatened till the post-Godhra riots took place in the first half of 2002.

Monopoly 'Nationalists'

The Sangh Parivar has always projected itself as the only truly nationalist group. It has traditionally portrayed the left as a political force whose patriotism is questionable, as one that has owed greater allegiance to 'masters' in Moscow (when the Soviet Union was still a communist regime) and Beijing than to India. The minorities have been painted as people whose patriotism cannot be taken for granted since they too owe allegiance to authorities or holy places outside Indian soil, whether it be the Vatican or Mecca and Medina. Guru Golwalkar did not mince words in saying as much. In one of his books, *Bunch of Thoughts,* he described the Muslims, the Christians and the communists as post-independent India's three 'internal enemies'. In more recent times, the Sangh Parivar, and in particular the BJP, have not been quite as candid about this formulation, but the mindset has not changed very much, nor has any leader of the RSS or the BJP ever disowned these views. Nor has the BJP ever taken exception to one of its staunchest allies, the Shiv Sena, periodically voicing such sentiments about the minorities.

The questioning of the Congress' nationalist credentials has been somewhat more subtle. In the immediate post-independence phase, it was obviously not easy to sell the line that the Congress was not a nationalist party. Hence, the Sangh Parivar concentrated its criticism of the Congress on pointing out that it had acquiesced in partitioning the country, that its leaders were 'appeasing' Muslims and in general were too corrupt and self-serving to bother about the interests of the country at large. With Sonia Gandhi becoming President of the Congress, the BJP stepped up its propaganda against her origins, a position that went down well with sections of the middle class.

Since it came to power in 1998, the BJP has assiduously sought to propagate its more-patriotic-than-thou image. The first attempt to 'monopolise' the nationalist agenda was seen when the government decided to conduct a nuclear blast in Pokhran in May 1998 and announced to the world that India was now capable of weaponising its nuclear programme. The blasts were justified by citing 'threat perceptions' not just from Pakistan, but also from China. Those who spoke against the nuclear weapons programme were dubbed anti-national, if not agents of Pakistan's infamous spy agency, the Inter-Services Intelligence (ISI).

Nine months later, in February 1999, Vajpayee made the famous bus ride to Lahore for the summit with Nawaz Sharif. The trip was played up as one that could provide a new direction to India–Pakistan relations and reduce tensions between the two neighbours. Those who had said the Pokhran blasts would vitiate the atmosphere between the two countries were being proved wrong, the government claimed. On the contrary, India's nuclear blasts had forced Pakistan to take a more conciliatory position, the BJP argued. Within a month of the fall of the Vajpayee government in April that year, the Kargil war took place. As the facts revealed themselves, it became clear that Pakistan's intrusion in Kargil was on even as Vajpayee and Sharif were discussing plans to meet each other.

No longer could the BJP and the government claim that Pakistan had been brought to heel by the Pokhran blasts. The tack, therefore, changed. Kargil became a rallying point for jingoistic posturing. Once again, those who questioned the wisdom of the Pokhran blasts or suggested that the government had been too complacent about the Lahore trip or claimed that Kargil took place on account of intelligence failure were sought to be clubbed into the 'anti-national' category by the BJP and its supporters. The BJP claimed its critics had 'politicised' what was a matter of national concern and that these misguided sections should be training their guns on Pakistan instead of attacking the government.

When the Taliban regime in Afghanistan destroyed the world's largest statues of Buddha carved out of mountainsides at Bamiyan, leaders of the BJP spared no efforts in condemning the move. These leaders were extremely uncomfortable when media commentators sought to compare the destruction of the Bamiyan Buddhas with the destruction of the Babri mosque at Ayodhya.

In May 2001, Vajpayee and General Pervez Musharraf (who replaced Nawaz Sharif as Pakistan's head of state in October 2000) met at Agra. The summit meeting, which had been preceded by considerable media hype, turned out to have raised more expectations than it fulfilled. Vajpayee sought to unsuccessfully change Pakistan's position that Kashmir was at the 'core' of the dispute between India and Pakistan—his close friend and then External Affairs Minister Jaswant Singh had said Kashmir was at the core of Indian nationhood. At Agra, Musharraf did not bend one bit and managed to hog much of the media limelight after his meeting with senior Indian journalists (which was supposed to be off-the-record) was broadcast over television channels.

The terrorist attacks on the World Trade Centre in New York and the Pentagon on the outskirts of Washington on September 11, 2001, provided yet another occasion for the Vajpayee government to propagate its view that some Muslims were not to be trusted. Even before September 11, the Vajpayee government had displayed its affinity towards American interests when it enthusiastically welcomed the new George W. Bush administration's announcement of a missile development programme to militarise space. Weeks before the American air attacks on Afghanistan started, Foreign Minister Singh had told a journalist that the Indian government would be happy to provide military support to the US by offering its airports as bases.

Despite obvious pointers that the US was not interested in extending its 'war on terror' to Kashmir, at least in the immediate context, the government kept trying to portray American intervention in Afghanistan as a golden opportunity. The suggestion was that the US would become more appreciative of India's concerns about terrorism in Kashmir and exert pressure on Pakistan to stop its 'proxy war'. In reality, of course, the US restricted itself to paying lip service to the Indian government's concerns and refused to pressurise Pakistan to stop its support for 'freedom fighters' in Kashmir. In fact, the attacks on Afghanistan gave the Pakistani President an opportunity to demand, and get, various financial sops in the form of write-off of loans from multilateral aid agencies.

A month after the September 11 attacks, the government banned the Students' Islamic Movement of India (SIMI), charging the organisation with having links with Osama bin Laden and his Al-Qaeda network and with having participated in acts of terrorism in India. Riots broke out in Lucknow, a city with a sizeable Muslim population, when the authorities followed up the ban by arresting several SIMI leaders. Fortunately, however, the riots neither spread to other parts of the country nor lasted very long. The timing of the ban on SIMI, just four months before the elections to the Uttar Pradesh assembly were to be held, was seen not just by Muslims but also by most political analysts as motivated.

Most commentators not identified with the BJP or the Sangh Parivar also pointed out that the ban betrayed a communal bias.

While not defending SIMI, they asked why organisations like the Bajrang Dal, which made no secret of their aggressive intent against Muslims, had not been included in the ban. Advani disingenuously sought to explain this by saying that while there was specific evidence of SIMI's connections with terrorist acts and organisations, nobody had presented any evidence of the Bajrang Dal being involved in such 'anti-national' activities. The Opposition pointed out that there had been any number of reports in the media on the Bajrang Dal distributing arms and organising camps to train its cadres in the use of these weapons.

In the last quarter of 2001, the ruling party mounted a concerted campaign to push through a law ostensibly aimed at curbing terrorism. In October, the Union Cabinet suddenly got the President to promulagate an ordinance called the Prevention of Terrorism Ordinance (POTO). This was done without consulting even the BJP's allies in the NDA, leave alone the Opposition. The ordinance raised a big hue and cry. The political Opposition, civil rights groups, several jurists and most journalists protested against the promulgation of the ordinance. Even some allies of the BJP, like the DMK, publicly announced their opposition to POTO.

The opposition to POTO was on several counts. The most common cause for resistance was the experience with the Terrorist and Disruptive Activities Act (TADA) that had been in force between 1987 and 1995. Critics pointed out that POTO was simply TADA reincarnated. In fact, they said, the new law included some provisions that were even more draconian than those in TADA. For instance, under POTO, the accused need not be given the identities of 'witnesses' deposing against him. TADA had been allowed to lapse in 1995 since Parliament agreed that it had not served the intended purpose. Worse, it had been severely misused by the police against the minorities, particularly the Muslims, or to settle personal scores. The fact that at a time when terrorism was rampant in Punjab, Kashmir and much of the north-east, the largest number of those detained under TADA came from Gujarat, a state with no history of terrorism, was seen as clinching evidence of its misuse. That barely 1 per cent of the 76,000-odd people charged under TADA had been convicted was also cited as evidence of its ineffectiveness and of the fact that its preventive detention provisions had been misused on a large scale.

Apart from these general reservations on TADA and hence POTO, the media had a specific cause for worry. A provision in

POTO made it mandatory for journalists with any information about terrorists to pass it on to the authorities. Failure to do so would make the journalist liable to prosecution under POTO. Thus, for instance, if a journalist were to secure an interview with, say, the commander of the Hizb-ul-Mujahideen, it would be mandatory for him or her to tell the authorities where, when and through whom the interview was arranged. This provision, journalists pointed out, would severely curtail their ability to gather information without fear of being labelled as abettors of terrorism.

The government initially took the attack to the critics, accusing them of effectively helping the terrorists by trying to block the passage of the Act to replace POTO. Like President George Bush, Advani presented everybody with a choice of being 'with-us-or-with-them'. Those who did not support POTO were playing into the hands of terrorists, he argued. His Cabinet colleagues like Arun Jaitley, Union Law Minister, argued that POTO had in-built safeguards that did not exist in TADA. Jurists like Fali Nariman, former Attorney General and now a member of the Rajya Sabha, were not impressed by these 'safeguards'. The law, he maintained, was too draconian and in any case not needed since existing laws were enough to deal with most of what POTO was trying to tackle.

The government also attacked the Opposition, accusing it of being hypocritical. States like Madhya Pradesh and Maharashtra, both ruled by the Congress either by itself or in an alliance, and West Bengal, which was ruled by the CPI(M), it pointed out, had enacted similar laws to deal with organised crime. While the CPI(M) responded by announcing that it would withdraw the Prevention of Crime Act (POCA) that it was proposing to pass, the Congress governments argued that the Maharashtra Control of Organised Crime Act (MCOCA) and the corresponding Act in Madhya Pradesh were not similar to POTO and that the BJP was being disingenuous in making the comparison.

After a standoff in Parliament lasting weeks and after growing protests against POTO, the government changed its tack somewhat. While still insisting that POTO was essential to combat terrorism and that there could be no compromise on it, the Prime Minister admitted that the government should have consulted all political parties before promulgating the ordinance. He also said that the government was willing to consider suggestions on how the law could be fine-tuned, but would not relent in its resolve to get the legislation through Parliament. An all-party meeting was convened in early December 2001, but failed to make any difference to the entrenched positions. Shortly thereafter, the government made more conciliatory gestures, saying that the law would not be misused against journalists.

POTO eventually became POTA, after the government convened a joint session of the two houses of Parliament. This became necessary since the government was not sure that it would be able to muster a majority in support of the Bill in the Rajya Sabha. Under the Indian Constitution, legislation must be adopted by both houses before it becomes law. In the event of the Rajya Sabha rejecting a Bill that has been adopted by the Lok Sabha, it can still become law provided a joint sitting of both houses votes in favour of the Bill. This provision in the Constitution had been used only on two previous occasions in the history of independent India. The fact that the government chose to use it to pass POTA was clearly intended to prove that it was committed to fighting terrorism.

Ironically, one of the first occasions on which the law was used was to jail Vaiko (formerly known as V. Gopalaswamy) who was arrested by the Tamil Nadu government headed by Jayalalithaa for allegedly supporting the Liberation Tigers of Tamil Eelam (LTTE) of Sri Lanka—the organisation had been banned in India after its leader Velupillai Pirabhakaran was accused of conspiring to assassinate Rajiv Gandhi. Vaiko's arrest was ironical for more than one reason. First, his party, the Marumalarchi Dravida Munnetra Kazhagam (MDMK) was a partner in the NDA government headed by Vajpayee. Second, he was arrested at a time when the AIADMK under Jayalalithaa was making a concerted effort to come close to the Vajpayee government. Finally, Vaiko himself had vociferously argued in Parliament in favour of enacting POTA and, in fact, had rubbished suggestions from the Opposition that the enactment was 'draconian' and that its provisions were liable to be misused against political opponents.

Also significant was the fact that whereas POTA was used against all the persons accused in the Godhra incident on February 27, 2002, the law was not used even once against any person involved in the subsequent violence that took place in Gujarat that was specifically targeted at Muslims. POTA, as already mentioned, was also used by the Mayawati government in Uttar

Pradesh against MLA Raja Bhaiyya and his father for allegedly conspiring to kill the Chief Minister.

POTA once again figured prominently in the BJP's attempts to portray itself as the only 'nationalist' party and the Opposition—the Congress in particular—as suspect on this count, in the context of Jammu & Kashmir. This state as we know has been gripped by terrorist violence since 1989 that has claimed over 60,000 lives. The terrorists—who have received moral and material support from Pakistan, not to mention training in the use of arms—have undoubtedly been helped by a sense of alienation from the Indian mainstream within large sections of the population in the Kashmir Valley, which is predominantly Muslim. Elections over the years have been perceived as rigged, with the government in New Delhi conniving with the one in Srinagar to keep out genuine representatives of the people who might have demanded greater autonomy or perhaps even secession. As is typical in such situations, the Indian security forces' attempts to counter the militants involved some excesses, which added further fuel to the fire and accusations of large-scale violation of human rights by groups like Amnesty International.

It was in this context that the state assembly elections of October 2002 were held. Unlike in the past, these elections were perceived as being relatively free of official coercion or manipulation. The fact that the BJP and the National Conference, the parties in power in New Delhi and Srinagar respectively, were trounced, helped buttress this feeling. No single party managed to get a majority, but the Congress in the Hindu-majority Jammu region of the state and the People's Democratic Party (PDP) in the Muslim majority Kashmir Valley emerged as the winners. Though the Congress overall had more MLAs than the PDP, it was ultimately the PDP that headed the coalition government formed by the two parties along with some smaller parties and independents. One of the key campaign promises of the PDP had been that it would disband the Special Operations Group (SOG) of the J&K police. This group, formed specifically for counter-insurgency operations, was seen as particularly ruthless and unconcerned about human rights.

Not surprisingly, among the first announcements made by PDP leader Mufti Mohammed Sayeed when he became Chief Minister of the state was a declaration that the SOG personnel would be absorbed into the main police force and that POTA would not be used by his government. This policy, which he described as a 'healing touch', was immediately attacked by the BJP as 'going soft on terrorists'. These developments took place barely two months before the Gujarat elections. As a result, the BJP made the 'fight against terrorism' one of the major issues of the Gujarat election campaign and Modi constantly accused the Congress of playing into the hands of terrorists. In fact, he even kept referring to the Congress as sympathisers of 'Mian Musharraf' (the Pakistani President) in his election speeches.

Pragmatism, BJP Style

An interesting feature of the alliances that the BJP has forged since 1998 has been what the party likes to describe as 'pragmatism', which others might see as opportunism or ruthlessness. As already mentioned, the BJP forged a coalition with the BSP in Uttar Pradesh for a third time, despite having gone through two previous acrimonious alliances with the same party. This is not because the BJP leadership was under any illusion that the latest tie-up with the BSP would be long-lived or less problematic. It was simply because the BJP believed it needed the BSP to survive the short term in Uttar Pradesh and to pose a serious threat to the Congress in Madhya Pradesh.

Uttar Pradesh is not the only state where the BJP has shown such clinical 'pragmatism' in deciding its alliances. Andhra Pradesh, Haryana and Tamil Nadu are three states where the party has jettisoned pre-election allies without even a pretence of any differences merely because other parties in these states had become more 'useful'. The first of these instances was in Andhra Pradesh in 1998. In the Lok Sabha elections that year, the BJP had partnered the Lakshmi Parvathi faction of the Telugu Desam Party, contesting against the faction headed by Lakshmi Parvathi's stepson, Chandrababu Naidu. Unfortunately for the BJP, Naidu's faction got 12 out of the 42 Lok Sabha seats in the state, while Lakshmi Parvathi's faction could not win a single seat. Without even a formal announcement of the alliance with the Lakshmi Parvathi faction being broken, immediately after the election results were known, the BJP started negotiations with Naidu to form the government in New Delhi.

In 1999, the BJP acted equally ruthlessly in Haryana. The previous year, the BJP had fought the assembly elections in the state in alliance with Bansi Lal's Haryana Vikas Party (HVP) and come to power. When the second Vajpayee government fell in April 1999 and it became clear that another general election was round the corner, the BJP decided that Om Prakash Chautala's INLD was the horse to back in Haryana. It withdrew support to the Bansi Lal government, resulting in its fall, and helped Chautala form a government in July 1999. Its assessment about the INLD being a more useful ally proved right, with the BJP–INLD alliance winning all 10 Lok Sabha seats in the state in the September–October general elections.

What happened in Tamil Nadu was perhaps the most bizarre example of the BJP's 'pragmatism'. On the one hand, the DMK was a constituent of the NDA and its leaders were members in the Vajpayee Council of Ministers till December 2003. Yet, it was evident that the AIADMK, which was formally an Opposition party, was closer to the BJP than the DMK. Similarly, Vaiko had been in jail for over a year, charged under POTA, but there was hardly any protest from the BJP or any acknowledgement that the case against the MDMK leader was politically motivated. The reason was simple enough: in the last assembly elections held in Tamil Nadu in May 2001, the AIADMK won close to three-fourths of the seats, the DMK and the MDMK had to eat humble pie. In December 2003, the DMK and the MDMK both finally left the NDA.

In the mountainous state of Himachal Pradesh, an interesting development occurred after the assembly elections in the state coinciding with the May 1996 general elections. Out of 68 seats, the BJP won 29 seats, the Congress 33 seats, the HVC (headed by former Union Communications Minister Sukh Ram who was expelled from the Congress after corruption charges were filed against him, won four seats, there was one independent candidate who won, while elections were not held in one constituency.

The BJP—which had attacked Sukh Ram in 1995 and, together with other Opposition parties, paralysed the Lok Sabha which was debating the Narasimha Rao government's telecommunications policies for two weeks—realised the only way it could form a government in Himachal Pradesh was by aligning with Sukh Ram. By aligning with the HVC to come to power in the state, the BJP proved that it could act as opportunistically as any of its political opponents.

There is an interesting aside to this episode. Fortuitously for the BJP, the HVC split down the middle with two of its MLAs joining the BJP. Interestingly, Sukh Ram later described this split as his 'master stroke'. It might seem strange that a party leader should welcome a split in his own party and treat it as a master stroke. But Sukh Ram was not being facetious. Given the provisions of the anti-defection laws as they were at the time, the four-member HVC would have been open to the threat of defections from its ranks to the Congress, which would then have been in a position to form the government. Under the prevailing law, if one-third or more of a legislature party's members left the parent party it would qualify as a 'split' rather than a defection and the members would not be disqualified from the legislature. By 'making' two of his MLAs join the BJP, Sukh Ram had effectively ensured that they could not defect, since they were now part of a much bigger group in the legislature.

There is little doubt, therefore, that the BJP's much-touted 'coalition *dharma*' is not far from being a euphemism for crass opportunism, principles and loyalty be damned.

A Man for All Seasons:
A Profile of Vajpayee

Atal Bihari Vajpayee, the first person to become Prime Minister of India without ever having been a member of the Congress party, has been in the political limelight for most of the past four decades. Though he was a founder member of the Bharatiya Jana Sangh when it was formed in 1951, and a protégé of the first President of the BJS, Dr. Shyama Prasad Mookerjee, he was first noticed on the national stage when he got elected to the Lok Sabha in 1957 from Balrampur, having failed in his earlier attempt to enter Parliament from Lucknow in a by-election in the mid-1950s. In 1957, he was just one of four successful BJS candidates all over the country, though Vajpayee too lost from two other constituencies, forfeiting his security deposit in one of them. In all, Vajpayee has been elected to the Lok Sabha on nine occasions and lost elections twice. His losses came in 1962 from Balrampur in Uttar

Pradesh and from Gwalior in Madhya Pradesh in 1984, when he was defeated by Madhavrao Scindia, in an election that saw just two BJP members being elected MPs. Vajpayee is the only person to have been elected to the Lok Sabha from four different states— Uttar Pradesh, Madhya Pradesh, Gujarat and Delhi.

India's first Prime Minister, Jawaharlal Nehru, impressed with Vajpayee's Parliamentary interventions had, as early as the 1960s, picked him out as one with a bright future in Indian politics and a man who could even one day become Prime Minister—an insight that has proved truly prophetic. Along the way to becoming India's 10th Prime Minister (and later the 13th and 14th as well), Vajpayee has had an impressive political career in his party, in public office, and above all in being able to steer (but not entirely, as we shall see) clear of controversy.

He has been awarded the country's second-highest civilian award, the Padma Vibhushan, and was the first recipient of the Best Parliamentarian Award in 1994. In the citation for the latter award, he was described as a 'multifaceted personality' and as 'an eminent national leader, an erudite politician, selfless social worker, forceful orator, poet, litterateur and journalist'. The extent to which this opinion is shared by people cutting across the political spectrum is best illustrated by two facts. For one, it was noticeable that when the Lok Sabha was debating the motion of confidence in his government in May 1999, speaker after speaker from the Opposition ranks castigated the government for its failures on all fronts, but made it a point to shower praise on Vajpayee the individual. For another, many of the partners in the coalition led by Vajpayee, like Mamata Banerjee of the Trinamool Congress, pointedly observed that their support is to the leadership of Vajpayee, not to the BJP.

This non-partisan appreciation of his qualities, which few Indian political leaders have been able to command, has also been the reason for Vajpayee's participation in, and on one occasion leadership of, Indian delegations to international fora. He was part of the Indian delegations to the United Nations General Assembly in 1988, 1990, 1991, 1992, 1993, 1994 and 1996. He also led the Indian delegation to the UN Human Rights Commission meeting in Geneva in 1993 (when he was in the Opposition) and was widely acknowledged as having done a commendable job of forcefully presenting the Indian position on human rights.

As the External Affairs Minister in the Janata Party government of 1977, Vajpayee was credited with having taken a significant step towards normalisation of Sino–Indian relations by initiating a visit to the Chinese capital. During this period, he also created a minor flutter by insisting on addressing the UN General Assembly in Hindi, the first time anybody had done so.

Vajpayee has long been perceived as having views that are not always fully in tune with his party's, even if he has been content with merely expressing a divergent view rather than aggressively countering the party's stance. Invariably, such differences have seen Vajpayee espousing a moderate line against the more hardline Hindu nationalist positions of his party colleagues. The most striking example of this divergence between Vajpayee's position and his party's came immediately after the Babri masjid demolition. Vajpayee described the incident as India's 'darkest hour', while the rest of the party was busy celebrating privately and publicly refusing to condemn the incident. It is another matter that with the passage of time the two positions have converged into what is now the official party position—the demolition was 'unfortunate' but the inevitable outcome of playing with the people's religious sentiments.

The differences Vajpayee has often expressed from the party's official position has contributed in great measure to large sections of people who do not agree with the BJP's ideology, and the media, describing him as 'the right man in the wrong party', an image that has helped immensely in winning him support from outside the BJP's spheres of influence. The same image, however, has also periodically resulted in those within his party and the larger Sangh Parivar viewing him with suspicion, or at least seeming to do so publicly. The BJP's General Secretary, K.N. Govindacharya, for instance, started quite a controversy when he allegedly contemptuously dismissed Vajpayee as little more than the party's public 'mask' only to later claim he had never made such a statement. There are many who argue that such apparent distinctions between Vajpayee's positions and those of other BJP leaders are no more than an elaborately played out charade scripted by the Sangh Parivar to appeal both to militant Hindus and more moderate elements. A conspiracy theory of this sort would normally have found no takers, but for the Sangh Parivar's well-established penchant for speaking in different voices.

However, despite all his perceived or real differences with the BJP's official stance, Vajpayee has been its most acceptable public face and no non-entity in the party organisation either. He led the BJS from 1968 to 1973 and into its merger with the Janata Party in 1977 and subsequently became the BJP's first President when the party was formed in 1980 with the BJS sections of the Janata Party breaking away. He has also been the undisputed choice of the party and its electoral partners for the post of Prime Minister since the 1996 elections.

Vajpayee himself has not only denied that he has any differences with the ideology and the philosophy of the RSS, he has categorically stated in an article published in *Panchajanya*: 'The single reason for my long association with the RSS is that I like the sangh, I like its ideology and above all, I like that RSS attitude towards people, towards one another which is found only in the RSS.' Having elaborated on his first links with the RSS, which was then dominated in Gwalior by Maharashtrians, Vajpayee described how his own brother had changed after he joined the RSS and was persuaded to give up his 'elitist' habit of cooking his own food and not eating the same fare offered to others in a camp.

Vajpayee's attitude towards Muslims as revealed in this article does not seem very different from the dominant view in the RSS. '[The] Congress has not correctly understood the Muslim problem. They continue to carry on their policy of appeasement. But to what effect? The Muslims of this country can be treated in three ways. One is *tiraskar* which means if they will not themselves change, leave them alone, reject them as out-compatriots. [The] second is *puraskar* which is appeasement, that is, bribe them to behave, which is being done by the Congress and others of their ilk. The third way is *parishkar*, meaning to change them, that is, restore them to the mainstream by providing them *samskaras* [a Sanskrit word whose meaning is a complex amalgam of culture, tradition and etiquette]. We want to change them by offering them the right *samskaras*…'. While Vajpayee is clearly not implying that violence or force be used against Muslims, it is revealing that he too sees the Muslim 'problem' as one of a community that has to be provided the 'right *samskaras*'. On the Ayodhya issue, Vajpayee has in the same article stated: 'We [meaning, the Hindus] did pull down the structure in Ayodhya. In fact, it was a reaction to the Muslim vote bank. We wanted to solve this problem through negotiation and legislation. But there was no "*puraskar* for *burai*" [no reward for an evil act]. We change "*burai*" also with "*parishkar*" [cleanliness]. Now I think the Hindu society has been regenerated which was the prime task of the RSS. Earlier, Hindus used to bend before an invasion but not now. This change in Hindu society is worthy of welcome. So much change must have come with the new-found self-assertion. This is a question of self-preservation. If the Hindu society does not expand itself, it will face the crisis of survival...'.

Vajpayee is obviously a highly complex personality—one who can write poetry expressing empathy with the victims of the nuclear holocaust at Hiroshima and Nagasaki, and yet spearhead the government's decision to go ahead with the nuclear tests in May 1998. It is said that as early as the 1950s, Vajpayee publicly said that one could live with half a piece of bread (*adha-roti*) but India must have its own atomic bomb to earn the respect the country deserves in the comity of nations.

It would, however, be incorrect to state that Vajpayee has never had a taste of controversy since he was initiated into public life while still a student by the senior RSS leader Balasaheb Deoras in the late 1930s. In fact, the controversy that has dogged him most over the last two decades pertains to his role in the Quit India Movement launched by Mahatma Gandhi against the British rulers in 1942. Life sketches sponsored by the Sangh Parivar and the BJP have invariably included a reference to Vajpayee being jailed during the Movement, without providing any further details. Vajpayee himself describes the incident rather blandly in his own article 'The Sangh is my Soul'. The third paragraph of the article ends: 'I also participated in the Quit India movement in 1942 and was jailed. I was then studying for my Intermediate examination. I was arrested from my native village Bateshwar in Agra district. I was then 16.' (This would imply that Vajpayee was born in 1926, but more of that later.) The unstated, but clearly intended, implication of all the references to Vajpayee's term in jail is that he indeed played a heroic role during the Quit India Movement, a major milestone in the history of India's freedom movement. Interestingly, a hagiography of Vajpayee written by two of his longstanding associates (including one who is a Union minister) makes no mention whatsoever of the Bateshwar episode or the Prime Minister's role in the Movement.

In *India under Atal Behari Vajpayee: The BJP Era*, C.P. Thakur and Devendra P. Sharma (UBS Publishers, 1999) have devoted a full chapter to detailing Vajpayee's career in politics. The chapter entitled 'Gwalior to New Delhi: A Short Distance But a Long Journey' goes into considerable detail about Vajpayee's childhood, his family background, his early education and his rise in the Sangh Parivar and the BJP. The authors are notably silent on Vajpayee's involvement, if any, in the freedom movement.

Since 1974, charges have been levelled from time to time by his political opponents that Vajpayee's testimony before a magistrate in his native village of Bateshwar, near Agra in Uttar Pradesh, on September 1, 1942 was, in fact, responsible for at least one 'freedom fighter', Liladhar Bajpai, being sentenced to five years' rigorous imprisonment. It is ironical to recall today that one of those who made this charge against him in 1989, the late P. Rangarajan Kumaramangalam, was later a prominent member of the BJP and Cabinet Minister in the second and third Vajpayee governments. Earlier, Kumaramangalam, as a Congress MP at the time, was a signatory to a letter by 52 MPs accusing Vajpayee of playing a 'nefarious role' in the Quit India Movement and suggesting that 'he implicated a number of freedom fighters to save his own skin'. In fact, the letter even insisted that Vajpayee has signed a confessional statement that was 'the only basis for sentencing a whole group of freedom fighters for long terms of imprisonment'.

Every occasion on which this charge has been raised since 1974 (when *Blitz* published an article on the topic), Vajpayee, his party, and the Sangh Parivar have responded by dismissing the allegations as totally baseless and even threatening to sue those who made the accusations. The controversy, however, refused to die down. Ultimately, in early 1988, the facts of the case were brought to light by a detailed investigation by a team of journalists for *Frontline* magazine and were confirmed by Vajpayee himself.

As is often the case, the truth lies somewhere in-between the two extreme positions taken by the supporters of the accused and the accusers. While it is true that Vajpayee's testimony was not used as evidence in court, it is also equally true that Vajpayee did sign a confessional statement absolving himself of any role in an incident that had taken place in September 1942 in which a government building at Bateshwar village had been damaged by a group opposed to British rule in India. In that statement, Vajpayee also named Liladhar Bajpai alias Kakua as one of those who led the mob that had damaged the building.

Clearly, therefore, while Vajpayee was not directly responsible for Liladhar Bajpai being sentenced to five years' rigorous imprisonment, he was also by his own admission not an active participant in the Quit India Movement. That Vajpayee was arrested on the occasion was merely due to the fact that he, with his brother, was present among a crowd. In defence of his having named Liladhar Bajpai, Vajpayee has clarified that his confessional statement was recorded in Urdu, a language he cannot read, and it was not read out to him later. However, Vajpayee did confirm (in an interview with *Frontline* editor N. Ram) that he had indeed signed the statement. Liladhar Bajpai himself contended that though the confessional statement signed by Vajpayee was not used as evidence in court, it was a major factor in his being sentenced since the Vajpayee brothers were, unlike the rest of the village, educated and hence considered more dependable in their testimony by the police and the court. He also suggests that the case of the prosecution very closely mirrored the testimony of the Vajpayee brothers.

Another occasion on which Vajpayee created a bit of a flutter in political circles was when he described Indira Gandhi soon after the 1971 war with Pakistan as Durga, a reference to one of the most popular mother goddesses in the Hindu pantheon. Just a few years later, during the Emergency declared by Indira Gandhi in 1975, he was jailed as were most prominent Opposition leaders.

There is also a relatively trivial controversy surrounding Vajpayee's age. Official records say he was born on December 25, 1926. Vajpayee's own article, quoted earlier, bears this out. So too does the hagiography of Vajpayee written by Thakur and Sharma. However, his confessional statement of September 1, 1942 records his age as 20, by which logic he should have been born in 1922. In recent years, his supporters have taken to celebrating his birthday, Christmas Day, with great fanfare. Special supplements were brought out in leading national dailies on his '75th birthday' both in 1997 and in 1998. Interestingly, there were posters on Delhi's walls again in December 1999 announcing celebrations of the Prime Minister's 75th birthday, till newspapers reported that Vajpayee had decided not to celebrate his birthday as a gesture of solidarity with those being held hostage in a hijacked Indian Airlines aircraft at that time.

In the middle of 2000, Vajpayee's knees were operated on. Many felt that by then he had lost the metaphorical spring in his step.

He seemed to be smiling less and his famous wit and oratory skills were less in evidence. His critics claimed he had started resembling former Prime Minister Narasimha Rao who would often make a virtue out of inaction. To many, Vajpayee remained more than a bit of an enigma. The same man who described himself as a *swayamsevak* to a gathering of non-resident Indians at Staten Island, New York, would in his 'Musings from Kumarakom' talk of the Ram Mandir problem as an issue of 'cultural nationalism' even as he asserted that the verdict of the courts would be respected in the Ayodhya case.

Vajpayee revelled in trying to be everything to everybody. He would seek to placate the hawks in the RSS by stating that the writing of history should not be one-sided. At the same time, he would project a moderate 'Nehruvian' image of himself as the archetypal liberal politician who would strive to attain a balance between conflicting viewpoints. While the media would often highlight the differences between the two 'camps' in the BJP, one led by Vajpayee and the other by Advani, Vajpayee himself would periodically attempt to paper over such alleged differences by suddenly dropping in, unannounced, to Advani's home for lunch. Advani too would from time to time assert that Vajpayee was his senior and leader and that there was no man he admired more. Nevertheless, the differences in their styles were apparent to all observers of the Indian political scene: Vajpayee's approach was indeed laid-back and conciliatory. He loved his good food and his jokes. Advani, on the other hand, was the man who was in charge of things, a 'modern-day Sardar Patel' who would not fight shy of controversy in stating his positions. His lifestyle, unlike that of Vajpayee, was spartan, almost puritanical. The two were a study in contrasts.

It is clear that Vajpayee has never quite adhered to the ascetic and austere image that many other leaders from the Sangh Parivar have sought to project. For instance, he makes no bones about the fact that he is a bachelor and not a *brahmachari* (celibate). He told a group of children in a jocular vein that he hadn't married because no woman was willing to marry him. His love for poetry, music and cinema has only added to his image as a charming and multi-dimensional personality.

Chapter 2

Indian National Congress

A Return to Family Values

India's oldest and largest political party, the Indian National Congress (INC), is far from being the dominant party that it was for the better part of the first half century of independent India's existence. True, the Congress was not merely the single-largest Opposition party in Parliament, but was also, in early 2003, in power—alone or in coalition with others—in 15 of the country's 30 assemblies. In fact, at one stage immediately after February 2002, it ruled or shared power in 16 assemblies. By way of contrast, in early 2003, the BJP—the single-largest constituent of the ruling NDA coalition—ruled in only three states (Gujarat, Jharkhand and Goa) and even the NDA as a whole controlled only seven state governments. Even after the December 2003 state assembly elections in Madhya Pradesh, Chhattisgarh, Rajasthan and Delhi, in which the Congress lost power in all the states except Delhi, the party still ruled in 12 states, while the BJP was in power in only six states and the NDA in ten.

These statistics might seem to suggest that the Congress is not doing all that badly. What they do not reveal is the fact that the party is extremely weak in at least four states that between them account for over 200 of the 543 seats in the Lok Sabha. These states include Uttar Pradesh (80 Lok Sabha seats), besides West Bengal (42 seats), Bihar (40 seats) and Tamil Nadu (39 seats).

Die-hard supporters of the Congress insist that it is the 'natural party of governance' in India. This phrase was used by Sonia

Gandhi at the Guwahati conclave of Congress chief ministers in April 2002. Yet, even in a best-case scenario for the party, it is difficult to see the Congress winning more than 35 seats in the 14th general elections from the four states mentioned. What that means is that the Congress would have to win at least 240 seats from the remaining 341 in 24 states and seven Union territories to win a majority in the Lok Sabha, certainly a tall order if not impossible. It would seem, therefore, that the best the Congress can hope for is to lead a coalition government in New Delhi.

Yet, until as late as December 2003 the party appeared strangely reluctant to concede that the country had entered an era of coalition politics in which single-party governments were ruled out in the foreseeable future. This presents an interesting contrast with the BJP. Like the Congress, the BJP till 1998 saw coalitions as an aberration of sorts and insisted that they were a temporary phenomenon. The polity, the BJP then maintained, was inevitably becoming bipolar, with the Congress and the BJP representing two poles. Subsequently, following the 1998 and 1999 general elections, which threw up hung Parliaments, the BJP modified its earlier position and accepted that coalitions were here to stay at least for some time. The Congress, on the other hand, continued to staunchly assert that it was capable of governing India on its own. Statements to this effect were made by party leaders every now and then despite the fact that the Congress had alliances in several states and continues to do so—in Maharashtra, Kerala, Jammu & Kashmir, and Manipur.

Ironically, the Congress was less rigid about governing India on its own at a point when its dominance in the country's polity was unchallenged. The very first elected Union government formed in independent India included not only people from outside the Congress or any other political party—like the eminent scientist C.H. Bhabha, Dr. John Mathai and C.D. Deshmukh—but even members of Opposition parties like B.R. Ambedkar of the Republican Party of India and Shyama Prasad Mookerjee of the Bharatiya Jana Sangh. Of course, it was the fact that the Congress had an overwhelming majority in the Lok Sabha and was under no threat from any other party that allowed Jawaharlal Nehru to show such magnanimity towards his political opponents. Conversely, it is the fact that the Congress is today fighting for its political survival that makes it very difficult for the party to cede any ground to other parties, except when it is compelled to do so.

One such example of the party being compelled to face reality was witnessed not very long ago. In June 2003, the Congress party convened a conclave (*vichar manthan shivir* or, literally, a meeting to churn ideas) at Shimla, the capital of Himachal Pradesh where the party had just been returned to power. During the conclave, the party diluted its position somewhat on forming coalitions to oppose the BJP-led NDA. Unlike the similar session held five years earlier in September 1998 at Pachmarhi, Madhya Pradesh, this time round the Congress did not expressly state that coalition governments were an aberration in Indian politics and that the party should fight on its own under most circumstances and seek allies only when absolutely necessary and in states where the party was especially weak. At Shimla, however, the Congress seemed to be coming to terms with the fact that its weakness in states like Uttar Pradesh, Bihar, West Bengal and Tamil Nadu would not be a passing phase and that given the reality on the ground, the party would have to be more open to the idea of a broad anti-BJP coalition.

The Congress President—like all Congress presidents in the past—has been surrounded by sycophants and they ensured that the message coming through from Shimla was that the Congress would not be averse to tying up with 'secular' parties provided the partners accepted Sonia Gandhi's candidature as Prime Minister. This predictably aroused the ire of parties like the Samajwadi Party and, of course, the Nationalist Congress Party whose very existence was founded on the premise that a person of foreign origin should not aspire to hold the highest political position in the country. These parties pointed out that it was premature on the part of the Congress to decide who would lead a coalition even before such a coalition came into existence. While Mulayam Singh Yadav had been 'soft' on the issue of Sonia's foreign origin and so also was a section within the NCP, Sharad Pawar and others were of the view that the Congress should not adopt a 'big brotherly' attitude even before an anti-NDA front was formed. The left had, in any case, contended that Sonia's foreign origin was a non-issue, particularly after the Supreme Court had categorically rejected a petition challenging her Indian citizenship.

After the shock of the results of the December 2003 state assembly elections, the Congress party seemed to have realised that it would need allies if it were to put up a serious challenge to the

NDA in the 14th Lok Sabha elections. In late December, after Sonia Gandhi addressed a public rally at Mumbai's Shivaji Park, she told journalists that the Congress would not impose its leadership on the secular alliance that it was trying to forge. This was interpreted as a signal from the Congress to parties like the NCP and the SP to join a broad anti-NDA alliance without the apprehension that they would necessarily have to accept Sonia as the leader of the alliance and hence a prime ministerial candidate. The decision on who should become Prime Minister, Sonia said, would be left to the people. The day after her statement to the media, however, Congress spokesperson S. Jaipal Reddy and other party leaders bent over backwards to clarify Sonia's remarks, insisting that she remained the leader of the Congress and, therefore, the party's candidate for the post of Prime Minister. Not surprisingly, neither the NCP nor the SP were particularly enthused by the 'clarification'. The Congress' position on coalitions remained as nebulous as ever.

Whatever be the formal position of the Congress party on coalitions or on the issue of building a 'secular' alliance of parties opposed to the BJP and the NDA, the reality on the ground is far more complex. Barely a week after the confabulation of top leaders of the Congress party at Shimla in July 2003, the party's MP from Malda, West Bengal, A.B.A. Ghani Khan Chowdhury decided to tie up with the BJP to control the board of the Malda *zila parishad* (or district council). The *parishad* had been controlled by the ruling Left Front in the state for 15 years. In 2003, out of the 33 members in the council, the Congress had wrested 15, the Left Front had 16 while the BJP and the Trinamool had one member each. Ghani Khan Chowdhury successfully wooed the BJP councillor to support the Congress-led alliance, at a time when the two largest political parties in the country were bitterly opposed to one another in every other part of the country.

Incidentally, Ghani Khan Chowdhury has been elected on the Congress ticket no less than seven times in a row since 1980, that too, from a constituency in a state that has been a bastion of the communist parties and where the Left Front has been in power continuously since 1977. When he was asked why he had allied with the BJP to control the Malda *zila parishad*, he stated categorically: '[To] hell with party policies. To me people come first.'

By capturing the board the Congress will bring relief to the people oppressed under the CPI(M). That's my first priority,' he told the *Indian Express* on July 14, 2003.

Performing on the Periphery

In recent years, the electoral performance of the Congress has hardly been consistent. The outcome of the 1998 and 1999 general elections was the worst in the history of the party. Yet, the party put up a creditable show in assembly elections, not just those held after 1999, but even in those held between the two general elections. This is because the electoral performance of the Congress has in most cases merely mirrored the rise and fall of the NDA's popularity. In other words, the Congress has done little on its own to win over new sections of the electorate, but has been content to cash in on anti-incumbency sentiments.

When the Vajpayee government fell in April 1999 and mid-term elections to the Lok Sabha soon became inevitable, the Congress saw itself as a serious contender for power. Six months later, when the election results were in, it had to face the bitter reality. The party had the lowest number of seats ever in the Lok Sabha. The anticipated 'magic' of the Nehru–Gandhi family name clearly had not done the trick despite the leadership of Sonia Gandhi. Yet, the results of the 13th general elections were far from being an unmitigated disaster for the Congress. For the first time since the 1984 elections, the party had increased its share of the popular vote by nearly 3 per cent between the 1998 and the 1999 general elections.

What explains the dramatic decline of the Congress in the span of a decade-and-a-half since 1984 and its inability to adapt to the changing political scenario? One important factor was its unwillingness to recognise that India has entered an era of coalition politics, in which no single party can expect to govern the country on its own. Related to this is the failure to accept that the Congress can no longer claim to be 'a coalition within a party'. While the party acknowledges that some sections of the population have deserted its ranks in recent years, it does not seem to realise that this is part of a pattern and not just stray unrelated phenomena.

Congress supporters argue that it has lost the support of these sections due to specific circumstances: for instance, the Muslims deserted the party because they held it responsible for the demolition of the Babri masjid in December 1992 and the Sikhs because of the anti-Sikh riots of November 1984 following the assassination of Indira Gandhi. These are at best elements of a larger trend: the Congress has been losing its coalitional character because it has failed to live up to the aspirations of those very sections of the country that constituted its 'traditional' support base. Instead of crumbs, these sections have tasted power and become empowered through their association with regional as well as caste-based political parties. For the Congress, what is worse is that the party seems to be unsure about the strategies it should pursue to win back its traditional supporters among the religious minorities as well as intermediate and backward castes. Within the party, there are many who still believe that coalition governments have been and remain aberrations; that single-party rule is superior. This view, the Congress' opponents believe, is born out of arrogance and is also responsible for the decline of the party.

Why has the Congress found it so difficult to read the writing on the wall? Why do influential sections in the party still believe it has an almost divine right to rule and that any other political formation is doomed to be shortlived and ineffective? A crucial reason is the 'ivory tower' nature of the Congress leadership. Many of the party's leaders have led and continue to lead cloistered lives in the capital's spacious bungalows, their political survival dependent on loyalty to the party president instead of their popularity among the electorate. It is hardly a secret that many of those who are at the helm of the party's affairs are individuals who would find it tough to win an election from any part of the country. During the post-independence period, especially the period when Jawaharlal Nehru served as Prime Minister, the Congress truly represented a federation of state units and its state leaders commanded considerable clout in influencing the central leadership. Many analysts see the roots of the decline of the Congress in the party's highly centralised structure that was imposed by Indira Gandhi and was continued by all subsequent party presidents, particularly Rajiv Gandhi and now Sonia Gandhi.

Under what circumstances can the Congress hope to regain its lost glory? Anti-incumbency sentiments against the Vajpayee government may work in its favour. But this alone may not be sufficient. One view within the Congress is that the party should no longer hesitate to strike alliances with regional political parties even if it means the Congress accepting that it is a junior partner in these states. But there are many within the party opposed to this line of thinking; this section clearly believes it is worth waiting for the time when voters would return to the Congress because of the non-performance of incumbent governments. If the latter view prevails, the lost glory of the Congress may never be regained, that paradise would be lost forever. Marking time does not always work. In the fluid world of Indian politics, stagnation almost inevitably leads to decline. Even if it would be rather premature to write the political obituary of the Congress, the party's revival is in serious doubt.

A Single-Party Coalition

The Congress is India's grand old political party: it was set up in December 1885 and was at the forefront of the struggle against the British. It represented a coalition of various sections of the country that had fought for independence from colonial rule. The Congress has ruled India by forming the Union government for all but roughly 11-and-a-half years between August 1947 and January 2004. During this period of four-and-a-half decades of Congress rule, a member of the Nehru–Gandhi family has headed the government for all but six years (when Lal Bahadur Shastri and P.V. Narasimha Rao served as Prime Ministers).

Till 1984, when the influence of the Congress reached a peak in terms of seats in the Lok Sabha, the party had its share of ups and downs, particularly when it suffered major setbacks in the 4th general elections in 1967 and the 6th general elections 10 years later. During this period, however, the Congress managed, by and large, to maintain its 'umbrella' character and no major social groups could be said to have become hostile or completely alienated from the party. In fact, the Congress could rightfully claim that it was the only political party that not only represented all sections of the population but also had a base in virtually every single village across the length and breadth of the country. The Congress could also rightly contend that it was unique among political parties in India, in that it afforded an opportunity for all sections to put forward their claims and points of view even if these conflicted often with one another. The party believed in a consensus-building approach and, in that sense, acted like a coalition. Academics like Rajni Kothari have analysed this phenomenon at great length and pointed out that this was in fact the strength of the party and a legacy of its leading role in the anti-colonial struggle.

The fact is that the Congress is the only major Indian political party that still believes it can single-handedly rule a diverse country. The party believes it has been able to internalise this diversity and thus, at best, needs a few minor 'regional' partners to come along with it. It is worth noting that even when Congress governments in the past have required the support of other parties (the ones led by Indira Gandhi in the late 1960s and by Narasimha Rao in the early 1990s), the party has preferred not to form coalition governments.

Congress spokespersons have forwarded another reason for the party not forging too many alliances with regional partners. The logic is disarmingly simple: in many states, the Congress is either ruling or is the principal opposition party where a regional party is in power. The argument is that if one looks at the list of allies of the BJP, almost all of these alliance partners are from states where the BJP itself is relatively weak and has never been in power. Examples: Andhra Pradesh where the TDP rules, Punjab where the Akalis were in power, Tamil Nadu where the DMK or the AIADMK is the ruling party, Orissa where the Biju Janata Dal is the main opponent of the Congress, Karnataka, West Bengal, Bihar and so on. In other words, it is the relative weakness of the BJP in these states that does not threaten the regional parties and hence, makes the formation of alliances easier. The argument of the Congress thus runs something like this: if the Congress is perceived as a threat to its regional ally, where is the question of forming a coalition? While there is considerable weight in this argument, it still begs a critical question. Why has the Congress not been successful in forging an alliance in one state where it is weak (specifically, Uttar Pradesh) and been a reluctant ally in another (Bihar)?

In Uttar Pradesh, the Congress is vying with the Samajwadi Party and the Bahujan Samaj Party for specific political constituencies: with the SP for the support of the Muslims and with the BSP for the votes of lower castes (dalits). Clearly, the Congress is left without any option in Uttar Pradesh, because neither the SP nor the BSP wants to help revive the Congress because it would almost inevitably imply erosion in their respective areas of support.

Unlike in Uttar Pradesh, in Bihar it was the Congress that was reluctant to tie-up with the RJD and not the other way round. This would seem inexplicable given the fact that the Congress and the RJD in Bihar—before Jharkhand was carved out of the state on November 15, 2000—had fairly distinct areas of influence, geographically as well as among social sections (castes). In the southern, mineral-rich part of the undivided state, which has a significant population of tribals, the Congress was the dominant partner in the Congress–RJD alliance, while the reverse was true for the central and northern regions of Bihar. As far as caste equations were concerned, the RJD had the support of an overwhelming majority of Muslims and Yadavs, but had very little support from the upper castes while the Congress did. This was remarkably similar to the pattern of the rival BJP–Janata Dal (United) alliance's support base. The BJP commanded the support of the upper castes in Bihar while the JD(U), which at that time included the Samata Party, appealed to sections of the intermediate and the lower castes. Again, the JD(U) was the stronger of the two allies in northern and central Bihar, while the BJP was by far the bigger political force in southern Bihar, later Jharkhand.

If the BJP and the JD(U) could effectively forge an alliance in Bihar, what prevented the Congress from doing the same with the RJD? The situation in Bihar was a clear illustration of the refusal of the Congress to accept the reality on the ground: that coalition politics had become the order of the day and in coalitions, the smaller partner often has to accept its position as a junior ally and be more accommodating (or less cussed).

A Democratic Party?

The Congress boasts that it is the 'largest democratic party in the world'. The epithet 'democratic' may once have described the grand old party of the Indian freedom movement quite accurately, but many would now question the validity of such an adjective to describe the Congress. The reality is that, barring a period of a little less than seven years between May 1991 and January 1998, the Congress has been seen more as a party that has willingly submitted itself to dynastic rule by the Nehru–Gandhi clan ever since Indira Gandhi acquired unquestioned control over the party by splitting it in 1969. The assumption of the reins of the party by

Sonia Gandhi from 1998 and the events that have followed have only further buttressed this view of the Congress.

If the party has surrendered its moral right to be called democratic, it still retains the status of being the largest party in the world, with the exception of the Chinese Communist Party. The Congress also, till the last Lok Sabha elections held in 1999, had obtained a larger share of the popular vote in India than any other party. However, the steady decline in the electoral fortunes of the party since its peak performance in the 1984 general elections has put even that status in jeopardy. In those elections, the party won just over 48 per cent of the popular vote, the highest it had ever achieved. Never before, not even in the first general elections held in 1952, had the party managed as high a share of the votes polled. From that peak, the decline has been steady, indeed even precipitous at times. In each of the four general elections that followed, in 1989, 1991, 1996 and 1998, there was erosion to the point where the Congress could win only 25.8 per cent (just over one in four) of the valid votes polled in the February 1998 Lok Sabha elections.

In the 1989 elections, which Rajiv Gandhi faced after a roller-coaster ride on the popularity charts during his tenure as Prime Minister, the Congress' share of the popular vote had already been drastically reduced to 39.5 per cent, a decline of almost 9 per cent from the 1984 peak. Only once before, in 1977, had the party got less than 40 per cent of the popular vote. The loss in the number of Lok Sabha seats was even more damaging. The party won just 197 seats, less than half the number it had won in 1984 (415). In the 1991 elections, the situation should have been ideal for the Congress. As in 1980, the elections were being fought at a time when a puppet government supported by the Congress had been brought down after it had replaced another non-Congress government. The non-Congress government, like the previous one in 1977–79, had collapsed because of internal squabbles. This should have given the Congress the ideal platform to recapture power.

As it happened, the Congress did come back to power after the 1991 elections, but not with a majority of its own. The party won just 232 seats and had to depend on allies (and later defections) to form the government and then survive for five years. Even this figure of 232, most analysts agree, was thanks largely to the sympathy wave generated by the assassination of Rajiv Gandhi halfway through the elections. Most pollsters who have analysed the results of the two phases of polling, one held before the assassination and the other after it, believe that the Congress tally would not have been significantly higher than the 197 seats it got in 1989, but for this tragic event. In any case, there were alarm bells for the Congress, which had seen its share of the vote dip even further, despite increasing its tally of seats. The 39.5 per cent of votes that it secured in 1989 had slipped further to 36.5 per cent in 1991. This trend continued in 1996, with the vote share coming down further to 28.8 per cent, and the number of seats coming down to 140. As we have noted earlier, there was to be a further decline in 1998 (to 25.8 per cent of the vote), before the trend got reversed in 1999.

What should be worrying for the Congress is that at the current level of its vote share, the BJP is close on its heels. The Congress had already, in the 1996 elections, ceded its position as the single largest party in terms of the number of Lok Sabha constituencies won, to the BJP. However, it was still comfortably ahead in terms of the share of the popular vote, with almost 29 per cent to the BJP's 20 per cent. The results of the 1998 elections suggested that the Congress was, for the first time, in serious danger of losing its pride of place even in terms of the share of the popular vote, the gap being narrowed down to just 0.2 per cent. Though the rise in the Congress' vote share in 1999 by nearly 3 per cent and a fall in the BJP's vote share has widened this gap to almost 4 per cent, this left little room for cheer in the party, particularly since the Congress had less seats in the 13th Lok Sabha than it has had in any previous one.

This slump from a position of seeming invincibility in 1984 to a party in danger of being relegated firmly to second place in the Indian polity took less than a decade-and-a-half. In retrospect, it must be said that much of the blame for this state of affairs rests squarely on the shoulders of the Congress leadership. At a time when major changes were taking place in Indian society and politics, particularly in the northern Indian states, or the Hindi heartland as it is often referred to (see next chapter), the Congress was unable either to intervene actively to influence the course of these changes or even to react adequately to them to ensure its survival. The result was that in India's two most populous states, undivided Uttar Pradesh and Bihar, which at that time between them accounted for 139 of the 543 Lok Sabha MPs, that is more than one in every four, the Congress was reduced to a virtual non-entity by 1998.

In the 1998 elections, the Congress drew a blank in Uttar Pradesh and its share of the vote in that state was down to single digit figures. In the 1999 elections, the Congress staged a recovery in the state, increasing its share of the votes from 6 per cent to 14 per cent and winning 11 Lok Sabha seats where it had none in 1998. It seems ironical to recall that during the first three decades after independence (1947–77), all the Indian Prime Ministers (barring Gulzari Lal Nanda), who were from the Congress, were elected from Uttar Pradesh. Of the Prime Ministers who followed Morarji Desai, Charan Singh was elected from Baghpat in the state. Whereas Indira Gandhi was re-elected from Medak (Andhra Pradesh) in 1980, Rajiv Gandhi, V.P. Singh and Chandra Shekhar were all elected from constituencies in Uttar Pradesh.

The importance of Uttar Pradesh in Indian politics is not merely on account of the fact that nearly one out of every five Indians lives in the state and it accounts for 80 out of the 543 seats in the Lok Sabha. Only twice in independent India has a party formed or led a government in New Delhi without having won the single-largest chunk of the 85 seats that the state had till Uttaranchal was carved out of it in October 2000. These were during the Congress regime of Narasimha Rao (1991–96) and the following United Front government under two Prime Ministers (Deve Gowda and Gujral) that lasted 18 months. On both occasions the ruling party or front did not have a majority in the Lok Sabha.

In Bihar, arguably one of the most economically backward states in the country, the Congress has been reduced to a marginal political force. The figures of the number of Lok Sabha seats won by the Congress in the state (which sent 54 MPs to the Lok Sabha before its division in 2000) tell their own story: 48 in 1984, four in 1989, one in 1991, two in 1996, four in 1998 and five in 1999. The failure of the Congress to revive in Bihar in the 12th and 13th general elections was despite the party striking an alliance with the ruling party in the state, the RJD headed by Laloo Prasad Yadav. The Congress continues an uneasy love–hate relationship with the RJD and the party's leaders in Bihar have often protested against the foisting of an alliance by the high command.

The decline of the Congress party since 1984, particularly in the Hindi-speaking heartland of Uttar Pradesh and Bihar, cannot be understood merely in terms of numbers. The fall of the party has been precipitated by specific communities and social groups deserting its fold almost en masse. Indira Gandhi's assassination led to the biggest-ever electoral victory of the party under Rajiv Gandhi. Ironically, however, this was also the first election that witnessed almost the entire Sikh community turning hostile to the Congress. By the time the 1991 elections were completed, after Rajiv Gandhi's assassination in May the same year, large sections of the backward castes of northern India (especially Uttar Pradesh and Bihar) had also become alienated from the Congress. In any case, this section that is loosely referred to as the OBCs had never been particularly loyal to the Congress. After the December 6, 1992 demolition of the Babri masjid at Ayodhya when P.V. Narasimha Rao was Prime Minister, the Muslims—large sections of that community had by then already started doubting the ability and willingness of the Congress to protect and promote their interests—started withdrawing their support to the Congress. In states like UP, the Muslims switched their allegiance to parties like the SP led by Mulayam Singh Yadav.

There are other groups, like the scheduled castes and tribes in many parts of the country, which have moved away from the Congress not because of any strong dislike for the party, but because of two broad factors. On the one hand, there is a growing disillusionment with the Congress and a belief that the party has 'used' them as vote banks without sincerely addressing their concerns and aspirations. This feeling is perhaps best epitomised in the slogan that the BSP used to telling effect in wooing the scheduled castes in UP—'*vote hamara, raj tumhara, nahin chalega*' ('our vote and your rule, this cannot go on'). On the other hand, alternate platforms have emerged which arguably provide the dalits superior options. This is a sort of vicious circle. For instance, the very fact that Muslims and Yadavs in Bihar had left the Congress and got together under the Janata Dal in 1989 meant that the Congress was no longer seen as a viable political force by the dalits, who saw the Janata Dal as a better prospect. This, in turn, meant that the upper castes in Bihar—as in Uttar Pradesh—who had by and large stayed with the Congress till that stage, had to look for a more viable alternative to counter the consolidation of the lower castes. They turned to the BJP in these states. Thus, the Congress became the victim of a chain reaction of group desertions in these two states.

After the May 1996 elections, the fact that the Congress had perceptibly lost support in the north also meant that social groups in other parts of the country had to re-examine their options. This was an important reason for the party ceding ground to the BJP in various parts of the country. For example, it was arguably the feeble state of the Congress at the national level that emboldened the maverick Mamata Banerjee to break away from the parent Congress in West Bengal, float the Trinamool Congress and fight the 1998 elections in alliance with the BJP. Similarly, in Tamil Nadu and Orissa, where the BJP had never had a significant political base, there were regional parties willing to ally with it, because of the perception that it was the BJP and not the Congress that was more likely to form the government in New Delhi. The BJP also found allies in the north-east, another area which had been outside its sphere of influence. The decision of the National Conference of Jammu & Kashmir to not oppose the formation of a BJP government was also dictated by similar pragmatism (some would call it opportunism) rather than any fondness for the BJP's policies.

Yet, it is precisely this feature of its decline—the chain reaction—that makes the Congress believe it can engineer a dramatic revival. The party believes that the process can be reversed just as easily. The argument is that since many of those groups which deserted the party over the last 15 years have done so not out of animosity, but due to pragmatic considerations, they would not hesitate to return to the Congress fold if the party shows signs of recovering lost ground. For example, the Congress believes that if it can win back the Muslims in UP, it would be better placed to woo the upper castes and the dalits too. However, the results of the February 2002 assembly elections in the state indicate that most Muslims are either with the SP or the BSP and have not returned to the fold of the Congress, except in specific constituencies where individual Congress leaders are better placed to defeat the BJP than either the SP or the BSP.

The fact that the Congress believes the SP and the BSP in UP have vote bases that could easily be brought back to the party's fold has often dictated its tactics. For instance, in early 2003, when the Mayawati government was threatened by dissidence from among the BJP and some independent MLAs, the SP was keen to hasten the government's demise by staking a credible claim to forming the government. For this, the SP, which had 143 MLAs in the 403–member assembly, clearly needed the support of the 25 MLAs belonging to the Congress and others belonging to smaller political parties, besides any dissidents who could be persuaded to switch sides. The SP tried to convince the Congress that if the party were to publicly announce its support to an SP–led government, other groups and dissident MLAs would be quick to jump on to what would appear to be the winning bandwagon. The Congress, however, kept saying that it would extend support to the SP only if the latter could convince the party that it would be able to garner a majority. With the standoff remaining unresolved, the ruling coalition had been given enough breathing space not only to keep its flock together, but ultimately, to even break the Congress party in the UP assembly. Of the 25 MLAs belonging to the Congress, eight left the party's fold to form a separate group, which joined the ruling coalition.

The official explanation given by the Congress for dithering on that occasion was that the party did not wish to destabilise elected governments and would rather wait for such governments to collapse under the weight of their internal contradictions. Many political observers saw this as camouflage. The real reason, they insisted, was that the Congress wanted to get back at the SP for not having supported Sonia Gandhi's candidature for Prime Ministership in April 1999, when the second Vajpayee government lost a vote of confidence. There could well be some merit to this argument. However, hard-nosed political calculations also seemed to have been a factor in the Congress' reluctance to back the SP in its bid for power in UP. As already mentioned, there is a considerable overlap in the potential support bases of the two parties. Hence, it is not particularly surprising that the Congress has no desire to strengthen the SP's position in the state any further.

After the Glorious Days

The decline of the Congress as the 'natural party of governance' in India took place over a long period of time, as already seen. From the heady days of *garibi hatao* and the formation of Bangladesh, to the Emergency which brought an end to the glorious days.

The assassination of Indira Gandhi was followed first by the Congress' most spectacular electoral victory ever in the December

1984 general elections and then a period of steady decline right till the 1996 elections. After these elections, what was particularly worrying for the Congress was its dismal performance in three of the country's most populous states from the crucial Hindi heartland—Uttar Pradesh, Bihar and Madhya Pradesh—and in two other states which had long been regarded as secure bastions of the party in parliamentary polls—Maharashtra and Tamil Nadu. Between them, these five states accounted for 266 of the 543 Lok Sabha seats, that is, almost half of the Lok Sabha. The combined score of the Congress in these five states in the 1996 elections was only 30 seats. But if the decline in the party's Hindi heartland had been apparent for some time, what came as a rude shock was its performance in Maharashtra and Tamil Nadu. These two states had always elected an overwhelming majority of MPs from the Congress and its allies, not breaking that pattern even in the most disastrous elections for the Congress till that stage, the 1977 elections. In 1996, the Congress drew a complete blank in Tamil Nadu and won just 15 of the 48 seats in Maharashtra.

Predictably, the man seen as responsible for this debacle was the one who was then party President and Prime Minister, P.V. Narasimha Rao. Party supporters who had till that stage eulogised Rao as the man who, by ushering in a bold package of economic reforms, had placed the Indian economy on a new high growth path, suddenly started finding inadequacies in their leader that they had carefully overlooked till that time. After being unexpectedly catapulted to the Prime Minister's post as a 'compromise' choice between powerful rivals in the aftermath of Rajiv Gandhi's assassination in 1991, Rao had kept the party in power for five years despite starting out with a minority government, which remained in a minority for a considerable part of the tenure of the government. This had earned him the loyalty of his colleagues in the Congress and grudging admiration for his policy of 'masterly inactivity' in times of crisis.

With his hold over power gone, Rao was now put under the microscope for all his faults. What was thus far seen as masterly inactivity was now held up as the inability to respond to situations. Party activists argued that the Rao government's failure to prevent the demolition of the Babri masjid and the apparently callous attitude of Rao himself during the event had finally driven the Muslims away from the party's fold and contributed in no small measure to its debacle. It was also pointed out that Rao's insistence on forging an electoral alliance with the AIADMK in Tamil Nadu had proved disastrous on two counts. For one, it had forced most party supporters in Tamil Nadu, who had vehemently opposed the tie-up, to quit the party and form the Tamil Maanila Congress (TMC).

To add insult to injury, while the Congress–AIADMK alliance failed to win a single seat from Tamil Nadu, the polls had vindicated the TMC's decision to align with the DMK and the CPI instead. This three-party alliance won all of the 39 Lok Sabha seats in the state. It was also pointed out that the Rao government's image of being one of the most corrupt in India's history badly dented the party's electoral prospects. A final addition to this litany of complaints against Rao was that he lacked the charisma that had been the hallmark of Congress leaders of the past, notably of those from the Nehru–Gandhi family. Rao, the party seemed to be suggesting now, was not a vote winner and while he may have proved adept at retaining power, he could not be expected to win an election for the Congress. Those familiar with the internal politics of the Congress would suggest that despite the poor showing at the hustings, Rao might have been spared these barbs if he had somehow been able to get the party a share in power. As it turned out, that was not to be.

Out of Power

The 1996 elections had delivered a hung verdict in which the BJP and its allies had by far the largest block of seats, but were still more than 70 seats shy of the halfway mark of 272. The Congress and its allies had just about 150 seats, while the National Front and other regional parties shared close to 190 seats. Since well over 100 of these 190 seats were shared between the Janata Dal, the left, the TDP of Andhra Pradesh and the AGP of Assam, and none of these parties was prepared to support the Congress, this led to a peculiar situation for Rao. As leader of the second-biggest party in the Lok Sabha, he had to agree to extend support to the United Front.

The alternative would have been either to let the BJP form the government or to precipitate another round of elections immediately, both of which were considered worse options for the Congress. For the Congress, the BJP represented the long-term threat, the party that was growing at an alarming pace and seemed on the verge of replacing it as the premier party in India. The United Front, on the other hand, was seen as a motley group, which would most probably collapse under the weight of its own internal contradictions and was, therefore, unlikely to pose a challenge to Congress supremacy in the foreseeable future, a perception that subsequent events partially bore out.

Despite the fact that supporting the UF seemed to be the only course open to the Congress under the circumstances, Rao took enough time to decide upon it for the BJP to be invited to form the government by President Shankar Dayal Sharma before he had written to Sharma informing him of the Congress' decision to support the UF's claim to form the government. However, the BJP's stint in power proved really shortlived, with the party and its allies holding office for less than a fortnight before being forced to resign as it became clear that they would lose the mandatory vote of confidence.

Thus, the Congress ultimately ended up supporting the UF government headed by H.D. Deve Gowda, former Chief Minister of Karnataka, who emerged as the unlikely consensus choice for the post of Prime Minister from among the 13 parties in the UF, that is, after former Prime Minister V.P. Singh and Jyoti Basu, Chief Minister of West Bengal and leader of the CPI(M), both turned down offers to head the government.

The Congress extended support to the Deve Gowda government without participating in it. Within the party there were two points of view. One school of thought held that it would be best for the party not to be directly associated with a government that was likely to be seen as a squabbling ineffective bunch, while another felt that the Congress must extract the price for its support in the form of a share in power. As it turned out, the decision was in a sense taken out of the party's hands, since most constituents of the UF had made it amply clear that not only were they unwilling to support a Congress government, they were equally against sharing power with the Congress, even if it were a minor partner. Congress support was thus strictly from 'outside', no different from the kind of support it had extended in the past to the Charan Singh government in 1979–80 or the Chandra Shekhar government in 1990–1991.

The UF was expected to have its share of internal wrangles and it did. However, the differences within the Front never quite reached flashpoint. For the Congress, therefore, which had banked on the coalition collapsing on its own to get a second chance at grabbing power, the wait was proving to be a test of its patience. It was a matter of time before the party would have to take the initiative to change the power equations in New Delhi. Developments within the Congress helped precipitate such an initiative. This came after the chargesheeting of Rao in the JMM bribery case (detailed later in the book) and of his son in the infamous 'urea scam'. The two chargesheets provided just the ideal excuse that dissidents within the party had been waiting for. Sitaram Kesri, who had for long been treasurer of the Congress, deposed Rao as the President of the party and immediately started issuing statements that revealed that the Congress was not prepared to play second fiddle to the UF any longer.

Among the many statements that Kesri issued over a few months in late 1997 and early 1998 was one in which he 'warned' the government that his party's support could not be taken for granted. Kesri's new aggressive posture was widely interpreted in political circles and among analysts as an attempt to get the Congress a share in power. The UF, however, was unwilling to respond to these threats in the manner in which the Congress President expected it to. Finally, after it became clear that the Congress would once again have to take the next step, Kesri sent a formal letter to the President announcing that his party had withdrawn its support to the government. Since that effectively meant that the Deve Gowda government was reduced to a minority in the Lok Sabha, the President directed it to seek a vote of confidence.

Even at this stage, it seemed that Kesri thought the UF would be willing to share power with the Congress rather than face a complete loss of power and the prospect of fresh elections. The second best scenario being viewed by the Congress was one in which the UF would break apart and large sections of it would then be either willing to join a Congress-led government or support one from the outside. So transparent were Kesri's motives that even the *Times* of London editorially dubbed him an 'old man in a hurry', a sobriquet that Deve Gowda repeatedly referred to in his last speech in Parliament as Prime Minister. As events unfolded, neither of these wishes of Kesri was fulfilled. Despite severe pressure from first-time MPs, who were horrified at the prospect of their tenure in the Lok Sabha proving even more shortlived than they had anticipated, the UF refused to succumb to the Congress' tactics. Deve Gowda retained the support of the entire UF in the vote of confidence.

But, the situation changed after he was voted out, as was inevitable. Though the UF still refused to consider sharing power with the Congress, the choice was now between forming a government under a new leader acceptable to the Congress, or facing elections. The UF settled for a change at the top and thus gave Kesri a face-saver. Kesri immediately declared that the Congress would have no problems in supporting a UF government led by anybody other than Deve Gowda. In fact Kesri insisted rather unconvincingly that he had at no stage objected to the UF per se. His objection, he maintained, was restricted to Deve Gowda himself, ostensibly because the former Prime Minister had not given the Congress the respect it deserved as the single-largest party supporting the government and had also failed to provide adequate leadership to the fight against communalism.

Kesri's explanation may have fooled nobody, but what mattered was that another Congress-supported UF government was in office. Inder Kumar Gujral thus became Prime Minister, but Kesri's toying with the UF was not done yet. Within a year of Gujral becoming Prime Minister, the interim report of a Commission of inquiry into the assassination of Rajiv Gandhi provided the Congress President another opportunity to turn the screws on the UF. The Congress by this time was clearly restless out of power and willing to try any trick in the book to get it. The Commission, headed by a retired judge, Milap Chand Jain, indicted the DMK government that was in office in Tamil Nadu in 1991, for having failed to protect Rajiv Gandhi despite intelligence reports indicating a threat to his life. The interim report was characterised by sweeping indictments that earned the wrath of not just the DMK and the UF but also of the media. Yet, the Congress found it extremely useful, because it provided the fig leaf that the party was searching for to camouflage its blackmail of the UF. Kesri jumped at the opportunity and demanded that the UF should dissociate itself from the DMK, failing which the Congress would withdraw support to the government. The ostensible argument was that the Congress could not possibly support a government in which one of the partners was being held responsible for contributing, even if only through negligence, to the assassination of a former Congress president and Prime Minister.

Once again, the Congress' calculations seemed to be that whatever position the UF took it would work to the benefit of the Congress. If it refused to expel the DMK from the Front, the Congress could pull down the government and then hope to be given a chance to form the next one. If such a chance were given, the Congress was sure that it would be able to muster up enough support from within the UF itself to form the government and win the vote of confidence in the Lok Sabha. If, on the other hand, the UF succumbed to Congress blackmail, the party would gain further ascendancy in the coalitional arrangement.

As it turned out, the Congress had once again miscalculated and underestimated the cohesion within the Front. While there were a few murmurs to the effect that the DMK should withdraw from the government of its own accord and thereby make things easier for the other UF partners, these were quickly squashed. The TDP and the left were prominent among those who insisted that the Front should not succumb to pressure tactics. The government rejected the Jain Commission's interim report and the UF declared that the DMK would stay, as part of the Front and of the government. As soon as the Congress withdrew support, as it was forced to, on November 28, 1997, the Union Cabinet met and decided to resign without seeking a fresh vote of confidence. More importantly, the Cabinet also decided to recommend fresh elections, a recommendation K.R. Narayanan, who was now President, immediately accepted. The Congress move had misfired once again and the party was to face an election for which it was clearly less well prepared than its main rival, the BJP.

Most Congressmen were aware that Sitaram Kesri would, if anything, be even less effective than Narasimha Rao at attracting voters. While Rao had a long experience of electoral politics, having been Chief Minister of his home state of Andhra Pradesh, Minister in several Union governments and finally Prime Minister, Kesri had for most of his career remained an organisational man. His rare forays into electoral politics had been embarrassing. Clearly, he could not be the face the party presented to the electorate, particularly when the BJP and its allies were basing much of their electoral strategy on the undoubted popularity of their

Prime Ministerial candidate, Atal Bihari Vajpayee. Yet, Kesri himself could not afford to let any of the other leaders within the
Congress emerge as the man to lead the party's election campaign.
Given the history of the Congress since Indira Gandhi, it was clear
that the man who would electorally lead the party would ultimately also call the shots organisationally, especially if the party
performed well.

Back to the Family

Given Kesri's dilemma and the unwillingness of rival leaders to
let each other gain an edge in the organisational stakes, it was
hardly surprising that the Congress turned once again to a member of the Nehru–Gandhi family to bail it out of a crisis of its own
making. The fact that Sonia Gandhi was born an Italian may have
seemed to rule her out of contention for party leadership to many
outside the party. Yet, within the Congress, it appeared the most
obvious course. Why was this so? New York-based Shashi Tharoor,
who works with the United Nations, asks this question and then
goes on to offer an interesting explanation in his book (*India: From
Midnight to the Millenium*, Penguin 1997): 'What, then *is* this
mystique made of, that it can make an Indian ruler out of an Italian whose only patrimony is matrimony', is the question Tharoor
asks. He says the real strength of the Nehru–Gandhi dynasty lies
in its members being perceived as truly national figures. 'Displaced
Kashmiris to begin with, the Nehrus' family tree sports Parsi, Sikh
and now Italian branches, and its roots are universally seen as
uncontaminated by the communal and sectarian prejudices of
the Hindi-speaking "cow belt". Nehru himself was an avowed ag-
nostic, as was his daughter until she discovered the electoral advantages of public piety. All four generations of Nehrus in public
life remained secular in outlook and conduct. Their appeal tran-
scended caste, region and religion, something impossible to say
of any other leading Indian politician.'
   Sonia Gandhi, who had first been offered the leadership of the
party immediately after the assassination of her husband, Rajiv
Gandhi, in 1991, had steadfastly stuck to her stance that while she
remained a well-wisher of the Congress and was willing to intervene to settle internal disputes, she had no desire to participate
in active politics. For reasons best known to her, she shifted her

position and in early 1998, with just over a month to go for the general elections, she agreed to take over as President of the Congress, ostensibly because the party was facing an electoral and organisational crisis from which she could help it emerge. Sonia Gandhi still insisted that she would not contest the elections, but became the main campaigner for the party.

Her entry into the thick of the election campaign undoubtedly galvanised the party organisation that till that stage had seemed distinctly uninspired. It also meant that the focus of the campaign became increasingly personality-oriented, with both the major parties—the Congress and the BJP—projecting individuals rather than issues. The BJP, which conveyed the impression of being rattled by Sonia Gandhi's entry into the fray, chose to pick on her Italian origins and portray it as the bankruptcy of the Congress that it could not throw up an 'Indian' leader and had to depend on someone of foreign origin to rescue it. The Congress countered by pointing out that Sonia Gandhi had married into a family that had not only provided India three Prime Ministers, but had sacrificed two of them—Indira Gandhi and Rajiv Gandhi—to 'protect national integrity'.

The results of the elections, when they emerged, became the subject of much debate on exactly how much of an impact Sonia Gandhi had had on the Congress' performance. Her detractors pointed out that the party had won just as many seats in the 1998 elections as it had in the 1996 elections (140) and, therefore, the claimed impact was more hype than reality. Her supporters, on the other hand, argued that but for her intervention the Congress would definitely have lost further ground in the 1998 elections since it was seen as the party which had forced a mid-term election on the people, and it was only because of Sonia Gandhi that the Congress had managed to hang on to its tally in the Lok Sabha.

Sonia Gandhi herself had some interesting things to say on the issue. In her first speech as Congress President to the session of the All India Congress Committee (AICC) on April 6, 1998, she said: 'I have come to this office at a critical point in the history of [the] party. Our numbers in Parliament have dwindled. Our support base among the electorate has been seriously eroded. Some segments of the voters—including our tribals, dalits and minorities—have drifted from us. We are in danger of losing our central place in the polity of our country as the natural party of governance.' In the same speech, she also quoted extensively from the hard-hitting introspective speech made at the centenary session of the Congress in 1985 by Rajiv Gandhi. In that speech, she reminded the AICC, Rajiv Gandhi had said: 'What has become of our great organisation? Instead of a party that fired the imagination of the masses throughout the length and breadth of India, we have shrunk, losing touch with the masses.' Sonia Gandhi reiterated her husband's assertion that the only way in which the Congress could once again fire the imagination of the people was by 'a politics of service to the poor'.

She also reminded the AICC that Rajiv Gandhi had, in the same speech, made some incisive remarks on the de-ideologisation of the party: 'The ideology of the Congress has acquired the status of an heirloom, to be polished and brought out on special occasions. It must be a living force to animate the Congress workers in their day-to-day activity. Our ideology of nationalism, secularism, democracy and socialism is the only relevant ideology for our great country.' And, said Sonia Gandhi, 'the instrument for carrying the Congress policies to the people had, of course, to be the humble Congress worker. But the genuine Congress worker remains unheeded and unrecognised. He is not only the last to be heard but also the least heard. I see it as my primary task as Congress President to restore to the Congress the vision of the Congress centenary—power to the people through the panchayats; and power to the Congress worker through democracy within the party.' This last remark of Sonia Gandhi seems particularly ironic in the context of all that followed, as we shall elaborate later.[1]

In the same speech, Sonia Gandhi also cautioned her party against seeing her entry as some kind of a magic wand that would overnight revive the Congress. She said: 'I am no saviour, as some of you might want to believe. We must be realistic in our expectations. The revival of our party is going to be a long drawn process, involving sincere hard work, from each and every one of us.... It

---

[1] It is worth noting that as late as 1998, a good seven years after the economic reforms programme had been initiated by a Congress government, the party's leader was still referring to socialism as the only relevant ideology for India. Clearly, the Congress was unable to decide whether it should go the whole hog in adopting an economic ideology that was market-friendly or stick to the socialist rhetoric that had served the party well over the years. The equivocation on this crucial issue continues to this day.

was our party which lowered the voting age to 18 from 21; yet, as the average Indian voter gets younger and more educated, it is our party which has suffered reverses. To this large and influential segment of the electorate, some of their disenchantment with us arises from our party being seen as soft on corruption and criminalisation. The impression has gained ground among them that we want to cling to power or achieve it at any cost.'

This was a surprisingly candid observation at that time, but Sonia Gandhi's practice as Congress President and as the Chairperson of the Congress Parliamentary Party (to which post she was elected soon after the elections despite not being a member of either house of Parliament) has hardly shown any departure from the party's desire to 'cling to power or achieve it at any cost'.

Immediately after the 1998 election results were announced, the Congress believed it had an outside chance of forming the government, since the leading left party, the CPI(M), had declared that it would be prepared to support a Congress government to keep the BJP out of power. However, such hopes were soon dashed as it became clear that most other constituents of the UF would not be prepared to support the Congress. In fact, the Front ultimately disintegrated rather rapidly on the question of support to the Congress. The TDP's Chandrababu Naidu, Chief Minister of Andhra Pradesh, objected to the CPI(M)'s position saying that it was the Front as a whole (of which he was the convenor) to take a decision. The CPI(M), by taking such a unilateral stand, he felt, had forced other Front constituents to also chalk out their individual strategies. While Naidu at this stage was still talking in terms of maintaining 'equidistance' from the BJP and the Congress, it soon became apparent that he considered the Congress the bigger enemy. As the CPI(M) and others called him a traitor and worse, Naidu switched his allegiance to the BJP. He argued that there was no way he could support the Congress that, among other things, had pulled down two successive UF governments.

Vajpayee agreed to G.M.C. Balayogi, MP, TDP, becoming the Speaker of the Lok Sabha after days of high drama, as a quid pro quo for the TDP's support. It was not just the TDP, but by that time a number of smaller parties including the INLD and the Sikkim Democratic Front had announced that they would support a government headed by Vajpayee while the National Conference decided to abstain from the voting. What was amply clear by then was that the Congress could under no circumstances form the government. Sonia Gandhi went to President K.R. Narayanan and said the Congress would henceforth play a constructive role as an Opposition party.

For much of the first year of the Vajpayee government, the Congress repeatedly emphasised that it would do nothing to destabilise or pull down the Vajpayee government, but would fulfil its 'constitutional responsibility' as the single-largest Opposition party if and when the government fell. Throughout this period, other parties opposed to the BJP, like the CPI(M) and the Samajwadi Party, kept urging the Congress to take the initiative to 'rescue the country from the misrule of the BJP', but Sonia Gandhi remained adamant. The Congress, she said, would not make the first move. This seeming reluctance to pull down the government was seen as the right strategy for the party till the November 1998 assembly elections to Delhi, Rajasthan, Madhya Pradesh and Mizoram.

The Pachmarhi Session

At the Congress' 'brainstorming session' in September 1998 in Pachmarhi, Sonia's comments were revealing of the Congress strategy at the time. In her opening remarks, she said:

> In less than two hundred days, the BJP-led coalition has proved its inability to govern India. There is no evidence of firm and decisive direction in any branch of its activities. The economy is stagnant, inflation is on the rise. Investor and business confidence is at an all time low. Foreign policy is in a shambles. The coalition in Delhi is at war with itself. Internal contradictions are being exposed day by day. The BJP and its allies are speaking with different voices on vital national and international issues.... Our stand of not rushing into bringing this government down has been appreciated all round. I once again wish to make it clear that as and when the need arises our party will fulfil its constitutional obligations without hesitation and provide stability and purpose. We have never opposed for the sake of opposition. We have highlighted the failures and follies of the government. We will continue to do so.

In her speech at the conclusion of the Pachmarhi session, Sonia Gandhi reflected the mood of the Congress, which seemed to believe it was on a major upswing. She said:

Friends, there has been much talk about the Congress' attitude towards a coalition government. The fact that we are going through a coalitional phase at national level politics reflects in many ways the decline of the Congress. This is a passing phase and we will come back again with full force and on our own steam. But in the interim coalitions may well be needed.... In the last few months, I get the feeling that the country, fed up with over two years of non-governance, is waiting to give us another chance. I get the feeling that more and more people who moved away from us are once again coming around to the point of view that only the Congress has the experience, the expertise, the energy and the enthusiasm to provide an effective government that will revive the stagnant economy, arrest the price rise, get new investments flowing once again and improve our standing in the world. We should, however, not be complacent. But we must recognise that the tide seems to be turning.

At the same time, the Pachmarhi session also recognised that there were several major weaknesses in the Congress organisation that needed urgent attention. Sonia Gandhi had pointed to these as well in her opening remarks:

The question we must ask ourselves is whether we have, in any way, diluted our commitment to the fight against communal forces. It would perhaps be tempting to say we have not. However, there is a general perception that we have at times compromised with our basic commitment to the secular ideal that forms the bedrock of our society. During our deliberations we must all apply our minds to this vitally important question.

Second, we must acknowledge that we have not successfully accommodated the aspirations of a whole new generation of dalits, adivasis and backward people particularly in the northern parts of the country. Could this be one of the reasons for our decline in states like Uttar Pradesh and Bihar? Regrettably, we have not paid enough attention to the growth of such sentiments and feelings and consequently have had to pay a heavy price. It is not enough to make promises. The Congress Party must ensure to this section of our people full and equal representation. Great damage has been done to national-level politics itself on account of our decline in north India particularly. Electoral reverses are inevitable and are, in themselves, not cause for worry. What is disturbing is the loss of our social base, of the social coalition that supports us and looks up to us.

An interesting feature of the discussions at Pachmarhi was that the Congress chose to identify organisations like the Samajwadi

Party, the Rashtriya Janata Dal, and the Bahujan Samaj Party as 'casteist' and as parties that would have to be fought if the Congress' fortunes were to revive in northern India. This was to have a major impact later when the Congress tried to form a government after the collapse of the Vajpayee government in April 1999.

So Near, Yet So Far

Events proved that the Congress gameplan for the November 1998 elections to four state assemblies was well conceived. In fact, the party's showing in these elections exceeded even its own expectations. The Congress won three-fourths of the seats in Rajasthan, two-thirds in Delhi and got a comfortable majority in Madhya Pradesh, where most pollsters had predicted a BJP victory. The result was seen largely as a reflection of popular disenchantment with the Vajpayee government's abysmal mismanagement of onion supplies. A 15 per cent drop in the output of this essential vegetable had sent its prices soaring in September–October to as much as 10 times the normal price. This was, in a sense, a repetition of history. Earlier, in 1980, Indira Gandhi had also used the rise in onion prices during the Janata Party's tenure to devastating effect in the election campaign to return to power.

The Congress itself saw the November assembly election results as a sign that the time was ripe for it to start sending out signals that it might not be averse to forming an alternate government in New Delhi. The signals were quite enthusiastically picked up by the AIADMK, which had been an uncomfortable ally of the BJP throughout the tenure of the Vajpayee government. J. Jayalalithaa, through her emissary Subramaniam Swamy, arranged a meeting with Sonia Gandhi at a 'tea party' given by Dr. Swamy in March 1999. The maverick Dr. Swamy himself referred to it as the most talked-about tea party after the Boston Tea Party. The reasons were obvious. Nobody was fooled by the apparent casualness of the meeting and it was clear that a serious challenge was being mounted against the Vajpayee government. Jayalalithaa meanwhile kept up the pressure on Vajpayee through a series of demands that she knew would not be conceded. Among them was the demand for the reinstatement of sacked naval chief Admiral Vishnu Bhagwat and the 'transfer' of Defence Minister George Fernandes to some other position. The Congress too was pressing for a parliamentary discussion on the Bhagwat episode, as was most of the Opposition.

The chain of events that began with the 'tea party' culminated in Jayalalithaa withdrawing the support of her 18 MPs to the Vajpayee government on April 14, 1999. The President, K.R. Narayanan, on the same day asked Vajpayee to seek a vote of confidence on the floor of the Lok Sabha. While Narayanan himself did not indicate the time within which this would have to be done, the BJP decided that the vote of confidence would be moved the very next day in Parliament. Party insiders say this was done because the BJP felt it would give the Opposition no time to arrive at a consensus on the contours of the alternate government. Confusion on this score, the BJP felt, would force many of the smaller parties to play safe by voting for a government that already existed rather than risk dissolution of the Lok Sabha if the Vajpayee government fell and no alternate government could be formed.

The BJP's calculations proved incorrect, but only just. After a two-day discussion on the vote of confidence, in which one session lasted through the night, it was still not clear which way the numbers would stack up. In fact, even after the votes had been cast, at noon on April 17, the MPs themselves were still not sure whether the government had survived or lost. It was only after the results of the electronic count were modified through physical checks that it became clear that the Vajpayee government had lost the vote of confidence by a single vote.

With the Vajpayee government reduced to a 'caretaker' status, attempts began to form an alternative government. The CPI(M) and the CPI had already made it clear that in their opinion the only party that could form such a government was the Congress and that all other secular parties should lend the Congress support in doing so. Two other left parties, the All India Forward Bloc and the Revolutionary Socialist Party, maintained that their MPs would not support a government led by the Congress or one of which the Congress was a part. Mulayam Singh Yadav of the Samajwadi Party made similar statements. He also made an attempt to drum up support for a government led by Jyoti Basu, but these were nipped in the bud by the CPI(M) itself refusing to consider such a proposal. Despite these hurdles, Congress and left leaders felt the differences would ultimately be ironed out.

This misplaced confidence provoked Sonia Gandhi to meet the President and claim that she had the support of 272 MPs. The

Congress had also made it clear that it would not be part of a coalition government. Soon, Sonia Gandhi realised that instead of the claimed 272 MPs, just about 233 MPs would go along with a Congress government. There was once again an attempt to bring about a consensus on a government led by Basu. The CPI(M), seeing that the choice was between accepting this and facing an election or perhaps even giving the BJP a second chance to form a government, indicated that it might be willing to accept such an arrangement if the Congress were prepared to do so. However, the Congress made it clear that it was in no mood to succumb to Mulayam Singh Yadav's 'blackmail'. That brought to an end the Opposition's attempts to cobble together a government. Though sections of the BJP did tentatively suggest that it should once again be called upon to form a government, the Cabinet ultimately decided to go along with the President's view that the only solution to the impasse was to dissolve the Lok Sabha and call for fresh elections.

Sonia Gandhi later justified the Congress' position in the following words at a meeting with chiefs of the party's state units on May 6:

As we had promised all along, as soon as the government fell, we prepared to take upon ourselves our Constitutional responsibilities. The parties of the secular Opposition wanted us to take up the leadership of an alternative government. Differences among different parties of the Opposition quickly made it clear that a stable, viable coalition government could not be put together. Only a minority Congress government, supported from the outside by the other secular parties, could give the country the assurance of a stable government. This was well understood by almost all members of the secular Opposition.

If such an alternative minority Congress government did not come about, much to the disappointment of the left and the Third Front, as also the country at large, the blame lies squarely at the door of a small, regional party, which placed its narrow interests above the larger interest of the secular future of the country. We were not prepared to succumb to political blackmail. Bending at the knee is a BJP habit. It is entirely appropriate that the Samajwadi Party has found its destiny in the arms of the communal forces of this country. The clandestine contacts between leaders of the SP and the BJP have ruthlessly revealed the nexus between them, a nexus which has led us to the present situation. These nefarious links, now exposed, must be rejected through the ballot box by defeating both the BJP and its secret partner.

The Foreign Hand?

Within a fortnight of the fall of the Vajpayee government, several dramatic developments occurred within the Congress. As already mentioned, Sharad Pawar, P.A. Sangma, and Tariq Anwar, broke away after demanding that Sonia Gandhi make it clear she would not be a Prime Ministerial aspirant. Their contention, in a letter circulated among members of the Congress Working Committee (CWC), was that no person of non-Indian origin should be entitled to hold the posts of President, Vice President or Prime Minister of the country. It became clear that the BJP would raise Sonia Gandhi's Italian origin as a major issue.

Sonia Gandhi took the issue as a personal affront to her and dramatically submitted her resignation from the post of party President after walking out of the meeting of the Congress Working Committee where it was being discussed. In her letter of resignation, she said: 'Though born in a foreign land, I chose India as my country. I am Indian, and I will remain so till my last breath. India is my motherland, dearer to me than my own life.... I came into the service of the party not for a position of power but because the Party faced a challenge to its very existence, and I could not stand idly by. I do not intend to do so now.... I will continue to serve the Party as a loyal and active member to the best of my ability.'

What followed was high drama. It began with all the Congress Chief Ministers submitting their resignations to Sonia Gandhi saying they had no desire to continue in her absence. Leaders of various state units also sent in their resignations. Even the CWC, barring the three 'offending' members, submitted letters of resignation en masse to Sonia Gandhi. Congress workers in various parts of the country threatened to immolate themselves unless Sonia Gandhi withdrew her resignation. The three leaders who had raised the issue were dubbed traitors and their effigies burnt.

After this farcical show of loyalty had lasted for over a week, the CWC met once again and expelled Pawar, Sangma and Anwar from the party. Sonia Gandhi still maintained that she would not withdraw her resignation. However, that this was merely a posture became clear when a special session of the AICC was organised a few days later at the Talkatora Stadium. Sonia Gandhi returned triumphantly to preside over this session. In her emotional speech on the occasion, she said: 'The very people who had come to me with folded hands to plead that I emerge from my seclusion to save the Congress began questioning my patriotism. They sought to sow seeds of suspicion about me in the minds of my fellow countrymen and women. And they did this in concert with those very forces whom I had entered the political arena to combat.'

Apart from the issue of her foreign origin, the stick that has been repeatedly used by her opponents to beat her is the Bofors scandal. The scandal erupted during Rajiv Gandhi's tenure as Prime Minister. The Swedish armaments manufacturer Bofors was allegedly awarded a major contract to supply Howitzers (field guns) to the Indian army after it paid bribes to various influential individuals who were reportedly close to Rajiv Gandhi. Thirteen years after the contract was awarded and a decade after the Central Bureau of Investigation (CBI), filed a first information report (FIR), charges were framed against a number of accused persons, including former bureaucrats and businessmen, among whom was the Italian Ottavio Quattrocci, reportedly a close friend of the Gandhi family. The CBI chargesheet also named Rajiv Gandhi as an accused, though he obviously could not be legally proceeded against, simply because he was no longer alive.

The manner in which the Congress headed by Sonia Gandhi reacted to the development is significant. The party not only blocked Parliamentary proceedings demanding the removal of Rajiv Gandhi's name from the chargesheet, but it mobilised a large rally of its supporters in the Capital in late November 1999 to back up its demand. The fact that the Congress chose to focus on this issue to attack the Vajpayee government spoke volumes for the absence of issues with a wider political appeal in the Congress gameplan.

Another source of embarrassment for Sonia Gandhi was the charge made by Subramaniam Swamy that precious Indian antiques had been smuggled out of the country and were being sold at a shop in Italy owned by Sonia's sister. Swamy also referred to allegations in a book by a Russian author that Sonia Gandhi and her son Rahul Gandhi had received payments from the KGB before the Soviet Union broke up. The Vajpayee government referred these allegations to the CBI, which instituted cases which are pending in court. While these allegations have not become a major political issue, they could well be used by the BJP if and when necessary.

Congress in No Hurry

During the tenure of the third Vajpayee government, the Congress at no stage made an attempt to destabilise it, nor did it appear restless out of power. This was a marked change from previous occasions when the Congress was not in power in New Delhi. What explained this willingness on the part of the Congress to rest content as an Opposition party? The BJP and its allies had lost almost every state assembly election held after the general elections of September–October 1999, while the Congress had won many of these elections. The NDA's only successes came in the assembly elections in Haryana and Orissa, which were held in February 2000, within four months of the general elections. Since then, the NDA has had no success in any state election. In the May 2001 elections to the state assemblies of Kerala, West Bengal, Tamil Nadu, Assam and Pondicherry, the Congress won on its own in Assam and was part of the winning alliance in Kerala, Tamil Nadu and Pondicherry. The NDA fared miserably in each of these states. In February 2002, it was no different. The NDA lost in each of the four states that went to the polls—Uttar Pradesh, Punjab, Uttaranchal and Manipur—despite having been in power in three of these states prior to the elections. The Congress won a majority of the seats in Punjab and Uttaranchal and managed to form a coalition government in Manipur.

It was this sequence of assembly elections that seemed to have convinced the Congress leadership that the longer the NDA remained in power, the more of an 'anti-incumbency' burden it would accumulate. It was also the party's belief that if the NDA government was given enough time to thoroughly discredit itself, the electorate would have no option but to turn to the 'natural party of governance' in the next general elections. That, the Congress believed, represented the party's best chance of coming back to power on its own, or at least forming a coalition government in which it would not merely be the largest constituent, but also be able to call the shots.

Anti-incumbency votes against the NDA were not all that the Congress was banking on. The party was also anticipating a re-alignment of political alliances by the time of the next general elections. For starters, it was expecting the Nationalist Congress Party to be part of a Congress-led alliance for the next elections. The Congress had also anticipated that some of the BJP's partners in the NDA, like the DMK in Tamil Nadu, could dissociate themselves from the BJP by the time the 14th general elections took place and join hands with the Congress. The merger of the Tamil Maanila Congress (TMC)—which had broken away from the Congress in 1996—with the parent party in May 2002, could significantly improve the electoral prospects of the Congress in Tamil Nadu, a state whose polity is dominated by the two Dravidian parties, the DMK and the AIADMK, and where the Congress had become an almost non-existent political force.

The Congress' expectations about political realignments before the 14th Lok Sabha elections were not entirely unrealistic. In 1999, the Congress and the NCP had contested against each other, thereby benefiting the BJP–Shiv Sena alliance in Maharashtra. Subsequently, the Congress and the NCP came together to form a coalition government in the state. However, this alliance has never looked secure. The Vajpayee government, in 2001, tried to woo Sharad Pawar by giving him a Cabinet-ranking position as head of an official all-party disaster management committee. In December 2003, Advani met Shiv Sena chief Bal Thackeray apparently to ascertain his reaction to a situation in which the NCP became a part of the NDA. Thackeray said he was not averse to the idea provided the NCP dissociated itself from former Deputy Chief Minister of Maharashtra Chhagan Bhujbal (who was earlier in the Sena). Despite repeated attempts by the BJP to woo the NCP, the Congress–NCP coalition in Maharashtra had not broken down at the time of writing. Meanwhile, the DMK and the MDMK, both of which had seemed quite uncomfortable within the NDA, finally broke away from the ruling coalition in December 2003 and tied up with the Congress in the run-up to the 14th general elections.

Apart from the electoral arithmetic, the Congress also devised a new strategy to refurbish the party's image among the electorate.

For long, the Congress leadership was perceived as the party President assisted by a group of geriatrics, most of whom would find it difficult to win even a local election. These individuals have been perceived as being more cut out for palace intrigues than for mass politics, though some of them may have had genuine popular support in their heyday. There is no dearth of examples of this breed of Congress 'leader'—Ambika Soni, Arjun Singh, Ghulam Nabi Azad, R.K. Dhawan and M.L. Fotedar, to name just a few. Sonia Gandhi consciously went about projecting a different image of the Congress. Chief Ministers like Digvijay Singh of Madhya Pradesh, Ajit Jogi of Chhattisgarh, S.M. Krishna of Karnataka, Ashok Gehlot of Rajasthan, A.K. Antony of Kerala, Tarun Gogoi of Assam and Sheila Dixit of Delhi were projected as efficient and dynamic administrators capable of galvanising development in their respective states.

The projection of Congress chief ministers had acquired a new fillip after the untimely deaths of two prominent young party leaders, Rajesh Pilot and Madhavrao Scindia. This was a dramatic shift from the culture inculcated in the Congress by Indira Gandhi and continued by her son Rajiv as well as his successors, P.V. Narasimha Rao and Sitaram Kesri. Since the late 1960s, when Indira Gandhi assumed leadership of the Congress, Chief Ministers from the party were treated with complete disdain by the party high command. Not only were they expected to be at the beck and call of the party President, they would be routinely removed from their positions depending on the whims of the high command.

Sonia Gandhi's change of tack may have been prompted by the recognition that it was easier to use the chief ministers as pin-up boys and girls than to rejuvenate the entire party apparatus. On the other hand, it may have been prompted by a genuine desire to decentralise the party. Either way, the effects were the same—the geriatrics were effectively marginalised and a new lot of leaders was projected as the party's future. However, the outcome of the December 2003 assembly polls came as a setback to this strategy—the party had performed terribly in Madhya Pradesh under the leadership of Digvijay Singh who was the state's Chief Minister for 10 years and had also lost out in Rajasthan where Gehlot was Chief Minister for five years. In Chhattisgarh, a state that had been in existence for barely three years, Ajit Jogi too had to eat humble pie as the BJP romped home to victory.

Groping for a Strategy

Events in late 2002 and early 2003 revealed very starkly how devoid of a coherent strategy the Congress has been in its attempts to counter the aggressive Hindutva campaign of the Sangh Parivar. The best illustration of this was in Gujarat, during the campaign for the state assembly elections of December 2002. Shortly before the elections were formally notified, the Congress replaced the President of the state unit, Amarsinh Chaudhary, with Shankersinh Vaghela, a former BJP Chief Minister of the state and someone who had been an RSS activist for most of his political career. Vaghela had quit the BJP after factional fights in the party (see the chapter on the BJP) and formed his own party, the Rashtriya Janata Party (RJP) in 1995, that was later merged with the Congress.

The appointment of Vaghela as the Gujarat Congress Chief disappointed all those who had seen the Gujarat elections as a crucial battle between the aggressive Hindutva of Chief Minister Narendra Modi and the VHP, and secularism. It appeared likely that the Congress would not be confronting the BJP's aggressive Hindutva head-on. This suspicion was further strengthened when another former RSS activist was nominated to contest against Modi for the assembly elections. Any doubts that remained were settled by the tone and tenor of the Congress campaign. Individuals and organisations close to Vaghela—including a group of *sadhus* (ascetics)—attacked the Modi government for not having done enough to completely eliminate cow slaughter in the state. The fact that an issue that had traditionally been raked up by the Sangh Parivar was now being used by people working for Vaghela, if not at his behest, spoke volumes about the so-called 'soft' Hindutva strategy adopted by the Congress.

The Congress predictably denied the charge made by secularists that it was following a soft Hindutva policy, but Modi remarked at more than one election meeting that the people of Gujarat were known for their willingness to pay a couple of rupees more to buy 'the real thing' rather than settle for an imitation product. 'Don't buy copycat products', he exhorted the crowds, drawing appreciative chuckles and applause.

The election results showed just how miserably the Congress strategy had fared. The BJP romped home with a two-thirds majority. In the introspection meetings that followed within the

Congress, there were some leaders who blamed the soft Hindutva strategy for the debacle. Officially, however, the party concluded that the Gujarat election results were a consequence of a severely communally polarised society that had been brought about on account of the post-Godhra violence and not because the Congress had adopted a faulty campaign strategy to woo the electorate of Gujarat.

The diffidence about taking on the Hindutva campaign was also evident in the Congress' response to the assembly elections in Jammu & Kashmir, which had taken place in October 2002, just two months before the Gujarat elections. The National Conference, which had been in power till the elections, finished as the single-largest party in the newly elected assembly with 28 seats, but was well short of 41, the number needed for a majority. The Congress with 21 MLAs finished second. The next biggest party in the assembly was the People's Democratic Party (PDP) led by Mufti Mohammad Sayeed, a former Congressman who had also served as Union Home Minister in V.P. Singh's government in 1989–90. The PDP won in 15 constituencies, while the BJP, which had eight MLAs in the outgoing assembly, managed to retain just one seat.

The indecisive nature of the mandate in the elections meant that no single party could form a government. It was also clear that the electorate of the state had voted against the National Conference. The obvious combination to form a government in the state, therefore, was an alliance between the PDP and the Congress supported by independent MLAs and MLAs belonging to smaller political parties (including the Panther's Party and the CPI[M]). There was, however, a more ticklish issue that had to be resolved. Which of the two parties would be the senior partner in the alliance and whose representative would become the Chief Minister? It might appear obvious that the Congress as the larger party should have had the privilege of leading the government. But, the regional composition of the seats won by the Congress and the PDP posed a problem. While the Congress had won a majority of its seats in the Hindu-dominated Jammu region, almost all of the PDP's MLAs had been elected from the Muslim-dominated Kashmir Valley.

Why should this have posed a problem? The answer lies in the turbulent history of insurgency in the Valley. Secessionists have had some influence in Kashmir ever since its accession to the Indian

Union in 1948. But from 1989 the secessionist demand gathered momentum and turned violent, especially in the Kashmir Valley. Most analysts agree that the perception that elections in the state have repeatedly been rigged by the ruling party contributed to fuelling the insurgency and the violence. This is why Prime Minister Vajpayee and Chief Election Commissioner J.M. Lyngdoh repeatedly assured the people of the Valley that the 2002 elections would be 'free and fair', a promise that was by and large fulfilled when the elections did take place. As a matter of fact, Lyngdoh alleged after the elections that the NC had tried to manipulate the government machinery to influence voter behaviour, but its attempts had been foiled by the EC, a charge that Farooq Abdullah predictably vehemently denied.

The October 2002 elections were, therefore, seen as the first genuine chance the people of the Valley had had in a long time to exercise their franchise. The positive impact of a credible election, it was feared, would be offset if the people of the Valley did not have their representative as chief minister, Mufti and his daughter argued. To be fair to them, this was a view that most neutral observers also shared. The Congress, however, was reluctant to concede the post of chief minister to a smaller party.

The Congress' reluctance to concede the Chief Minister's post to the PDP was not merely a reaction of a 'big brother' to his smaller sibling. In the Jammu region, campaigners of the Congress party (including Ghulam Nabi Azad) had categorically stated that if the Congress performed well in Jammu, there was every reason to break with tradition and have a person from this region as Chief Minister. (The state of Jammu & Kashmir comprises three distinct ethno-religious regions, Jammu, the Kashmir Valley and Ladakh–Leh: the state's Chief Minister has always been an individual from the Valley.) The Congress also appeared to be concerned about the BJP accusing it of 'appeasing' the minority community (in Gujarat) if it conceded the Chief Minister's post to a person from the Valley instead of an individual from the Jammu region, even if both contenders were in this case Muslim. The Congress leadership dilly-dallied for over a fortnight before it eventually agreed to Mufti becoming the next Chief Minister of Jammu & Kashmir.

The ambivalence of the Congress' approach towards Hindutva was evident once again in early 2003, when Madhya Pradesh Chief

Minister Digvijay Singh suddenly raised the issue of cow slaughter. Singh was at pains to portray himself as a devotee and protector of the cow and the BJP as negligent on this issue. The MP Chief Minister went to the extent of publicly drinking cow's urine and vouching for its therapeutic qualities. He then accused the BJP of being insincere in its campaign against cow slaughter. If, he argued, the BJP was really keen about banning cow slaughter, what prevented it from enacting an all-India law on the issue.

The BJP was quick to pounce on this 'challenge'. In April 2003, during a discussion on a non-official—private member's—Bill in Parliament calling for a national ban on cow slaughter, Minister for Parliamentary Affairs Sushma Swaraj embarrassed the Congress, which opposed the Bill. The Minister recalled what had been stated in the Lok Sabha by Shivraj Patil, a senior Congress MP and former Speaker in support of a national ban on cow slaughter. Patil was left sheepishly admitting that he could not recall what he had earlier said on the subject.

Hindutva is not the only issue on which the Congress has of late been somewhat ambivalent. Economic policy is another area in which the party's rhetoric has been perceived to be inconsistent. There have been deep divisions within the party on the ideological thrust of the economic reforms programme, including the issue of privatising public sector undertakings. While there is a more detailed discussion of this topic in the chapter on the economy, it is worth pointing out here that there has been a marked leftward shift in the party's rhetoric in 2003. Indira Gandhi's *garibi hatao* has been resurrected as: *Congress ka haath, garib ke saath* ('the Congress' hand is with the poor', a reference to the election symbol of the party which is an open palm). The actual practice of Congress governments in the state has, however, not mirrored this shift in the rhetoric.

Given the absence of a coherent ideology, either political or economic, can the Congress regain its past glory and form a government on its own? That is a rather remote possibility. Can the party then head a coalition that would replace the NDA after the 14th general elections? That is a possibility that cannot entirely be ruled out.

Chapter 3

Caste in Stone

Politics of the Hindi Heartland

Political parties with a base only in specific regions or states have been around for as long as India has been independent. Such parties would typically appeal to the narrow, parochial sentiments of the people of a particular part of the country or even of a specific section of people within that geographical area—emphasising regional over national loyalties and stressing affiliation to caste, religion and language. The omnibus label of 'regional party', however, could be misleading in many cases. It would be worthwhile to make a distinction between parties that consciously appeal to a regional identity and those that seek to appeal to people over a wider geographical area, but have in practice been unable to exert their influence beyond one or two states.

For instance, the DMK and the AIADMK are by definition not even seeking to appeal to voters in the north, east or west of the country, since these populaces would not qualify as 'Dravidian'. In fact, these parties are apparently not even interested in extending their support base very much beyond the Tamil-speaking areas, which include Tamil Nadu, Pondicherry and a few pockets in neighbouring Karnataka. The Samajwadi Party, on the other hand, appeals to a constituency that is largely caste-based (though, of late, it is trying to reach out beyond this constituency). The fact that support for the SP has remained, by and large, confined to Uttar Pradesh is not on account of the party's unwillingness to spread its wings to other parts of the country, to states like Maharashtra for example. The same considerations hold good for the Rashtriya Janata Dal, which has been unable to find too many supporters outside Bihar, not for want of trying.

There are a number of examples of political parties that have defined themselves in terms of a particular region or ethnic group. In that sense, the term 'regional' is appropriate to describe a wide and diverse range of political parties which would include the Telugu Desam Party (TDP) in Andhra Pradesh, the Shiromani Akali Dal (SAD) in Punjab, what was once the Tamil Maanila Congress (TMC) in Tamil Nadu, the Asom Gana Parishad (AGP) in Assam, and the Haryana Vikas Party (HVP) in Haryana. In another category would come parties like the Biju Janata Dal (BJD) in Orissa, the National Conference (NC) in Jammu & Kashmir, and the Trinamool Congress in West Bengal—all these three parties apparently do not appeal to people belonging to a certain region but have, in fact, not even attempted to go beyond the particular state in which they originated. Then there are parties like the Bahujan Samaj Party (BSP)—like the SP and the RJD—that are often considered 'regional' but in fact would like to spread their support base across a number of states. Into this group would also fall the Shiv Sena (which is based mainly in Maharashtra) and the Nationalist Congress Party that broke away from the Indian National Congress in 1999 but had a presence mainly in Maharashtra and Meghalaya (thanks to the influence of two of its stalwarts, Sharad Pawar and P.A. Sangma) before it split.

The fact that some of these parties are by definition regional while others do not quite fit the tag is no coincidence. This distinction stems from the factors that have contributed to the emergence and growth of each of them. The Hindi heartland—in particular the states of Uttar Pradesh, Madhya Pradesh and Bihar—has witnessed the phenomenon of 'Mandalisation' since August 1990. The Mandal commission had advocated reservation of 27 per cent of all government jobs for the OBCs. The decision sparked off a sharp polarisation along caste lines in many states in north India. Parties like the SP and the RJD (both of which did not exist at that time and were part of the undivided Janata Dal) have been the main beneficiaries of this polarisation, emerging as champions of the OBCs.

This was possible because while the two biggest national parties—the Congress and the BJP—did not overtly oppose the implementation of the Mandal Commission's recommendations, restricting their official criticism to the manner in which V.P. Singh had attempted to implement the Commission's suggestions, it was hardly a secret that the bulk of the leadership of both the Congress and the BJP was unhappy with the decision. The violent protests by upper-caste students all over north India that followed the decision were widely believed to have had the tacit support of both the Congress and the BJP. In this highly charged atmosphere, only parties that were willing to aggressively play the caste card could hope to win the loyalty of the OBCs. V. P. Singh's Janata Dal—of which the SP and the RJD are offshoots—was the only major political force that adopted such an aggressive posture.

The BSP too has, from its very inception, defined itself as a party of the dalits and other oppressed castes. Its origins lie in the All India Backward (SC, ST, OBC) and Minority Communities Employees' Federation (BAMCEF), an organisation of government employees led by Kanshi Ram when he was himself a government employee. It is hardly surprising, therefore, that the BSP's vision is not confined to any specific state or region.

Many supporters of the BJP and the Congress often disparagingly dismiss the communist parties too as regional parties, pointing out that their influence is largely restricted to the states of West Bengal, Kerala and Tripura, though they may have enclaves of influence in various other states. This is not factually inaccurate, though the two communist parties have had their representatives elected to the legislatures of most states in India barring Gujarat and a few of the smaller states. Nevertheless, it would be incorrect to club the left even with parties like the SP or the RJD, which claim a national vision but are restricted to a couple of states. This is because, unlike the SP or the RJD, which are targeting specific caste or community groups, the left's appeal is not sectarian in nature.

Parties like the TDP and the AGP, in contrast to the caste-based formations of northern India, have emerged by exploiting the apprehensions of domination by Delhi. They are manifestations of what academics would refer to as sub-national aspirations. By the very nature of their sub-national character, they cannot afford to broaden their support base for fear of losing their core section of followers. The Dravidian parties may seem to fit into the category of caste-based formations. After all, their origins lie in the anti-Brahmin movements led by the Justice Party in British-ruled India. Yet, the fact is that the process of social churning that has been witnessed in north India since the 1990s had taken place in south India more than half a century earlier. From the 1960s, therefore, the Dravidian movement has acquired an increasingly regional flavour rather than a caste identity. So much so that the unchallenged leader of the AIADMK, J. Jayalalithaa is herself a Brahmin. To that extent, the DMK and the AIADMK are more akin to the TDP or the AGP today than to the SP, the BSP or the RJD.

Like the regional parties, the left too has made an issue of the centralised and unitary nature of the Indian state and of the 'discrimination' faced by states ruled by it. The communist parties have repeatedly alleged that the Union government has starved states like West Bengal, Tripura and Kerala of funds for development for partisan political reasons. The left had till the 1980s also often taken a lead in organising conclaves of state governments to demand a more federal fiscal structure and a more de-centralised polity. (More on this in the chapter on the left.)

The supporters of the BJP and the Congress have often sought to portray the so-called regional parties as having narrow, partisan interests. The leaders of these parties have been described as 'myopic' individuals who have not been able to transcend the confines of their state. Thus, sections of the BJP and the Congress have argued that the interests of the country as a whole cannot be safe in the hands of leaders of these regional political formations. However, such a coloured view cannot be substantiated, as such leaders have time and again displayed a capacity to look at issues from a wide perspective. On the contrary, it is the failure of the 'national' political parties to address the aspirations of large sections of the population that has contributed in no small measure to the emergence and growth of regional parties. The fact that Indira Gandhi, sitting in New Delhi, whimsically and contemptuously changed successive Chief Ministers in Andhra Pradesh was taken advantage of by N.T. Rama Rao, founder of the TDP. He was able to successfully use injured 'Telugu pride' to such effect that the TDP swept the first state assembly election it ever contested.

More importantly, the decline in the fortunes of the Congress and the inability of the BJP or the communist parties to fill the vacuum created by this decline resulted in the growing influence of smaller parties. It also meant that no single party was any longer able to win a majority in the Lok Sabha. As a result, the smaller parties have often been able to exert an influence on the government disproportionate to their numerical strength. The clout that the AIADMK led by Jayalalithaa wielded in the second Vajpayee government and the manner in which the TDP led by Chandrababu Naidu was often able to have its way with—some would say arm-twist—the third Vajpayee government are clinching evidence of the growing importance of smaller parties in national politics.

The Samajwadi Party and the Bahujan Samaj Party: Caste Assertion in Uttar Pradesh

The course of politics in Uttar Pradesh in the last decade to an extent represents a microcosm of what is happening in Indian politics as a whole. Arguably, no other state has seen as rapid a fragmentation of the society and the polity as UP has since the beginning of the 1990s. Nor, for that matter, have the BJP and the Congress become as weak anywhere else as they have in UP. Understandably, the fragmentation in the largest state, accounting for more than a sixth of the country's population, has not been on linguistic or ethnic lines, but along the lines of caste and commu-nity. This polarisation of UP society along caste lines has resulted in the rise of two strong regional parties, the BSP and the SP, both of which have enjoyed power in the state, in alliance with each other and separately with the support of other parties. At the same time, the polarisation has led to the marginalisation in UP of the once-powerful Congress, which, despite a modest resurgence in the 1999 Parliamentary elections, has been relegated to an also-ran in the politics of the state. The BJP, on the other hand, through astute management of caste equations, had become the strongest of all the parties in the state, that is, till the results of the assembly elections of February 2002 gave it a severe jolt. In those elections, the BJP finished third behind the SP and the BSP.

The process of social churning in UP is far from over. Caste equations and correlations are fast changing and how they move will remain the key determinant of the course of politics in the state in the foreseeable future. It is not surprising, therefore, that the 1990s in UP saw political alliances that proved extremely shortlived and fragile. A single-party majority has not been thrown up in the state since 1991.

The rapid rise of overtly caste-based parties in UP was clearly precipitated by the decision of V.P. Singh's government to imple-ment the recommendations of the Mandal Commission. While this led to an immediate and violent backlash among the upper castes in the state, as in some others, it also helped to a large extent in consolidating the OBCs, who are estimated to account for over a third of the state's population. Simultaneously, the process of dalit consolidation behind the BSP also gathered steam. Though neither the OBCs nor the dalits completely switched allegiances to any one party, the magnitude of the consolidation of these two vote banks was sufficient to create new viable political forces that could play a major role in the politics of UP.

By the time of the state assembly elections in 1993, though, a series of political developments, including some emanating from the national capital, had repercussions in UP which left the Janata Dal in no position to capitalise on this consolidation. On the contrary, it was the Samajwadi Party, a breakaway group of the Janata Dal, which cashed in on the benefits of the Mandal programme. The events that led to this denouement began with the BJP's *rath yatra* to Ayodhya in 1990, as part of an agitation to 'grab' the Babri masjid from the Muslims and build a temple dedicated to Lord Rama. This was really part of a calculated strategy to create a communal polarisation across the country and in UP in particular. The BJP believed, rightly as subsequent events proved, that such a polarisation would work to its advantage in electoral politics.

Mulayam Singh Yadav, who was then the Janata Dal Chief Minister of UP, cracked down on the agitators ruthlessly. While this led to his being accused of running a police state and derogatorily dubbed 'mullah Mulayam' by the BJP, it also ensured that he won the loyalty of the Muslims who, till that stage, had by and large been voting for the Congress. This switch on the part of the Muslim community was to prove crucial in determining the new equations in UP. Yadav also had the support of the bulk of his community, the Yadavs, who account for about 10 per cent of the state's population. The Mandal programme also meant that the Janata Dal had the support of substantial sections of other OBC castes. However, some of the most backward castes among the OBCs were not too enamoured of the Mandal plank, convinced as they were that it would yield benefits only to the relatively advantaged sections among the OBCs. This conviction and the successful mobilisation of these sections by the BJP through the emotive Ram temple issue also won the BJP the support of a major chunk of the OBCs.

Despite this, however, the Janata Dal at this stage could reasonably hope to command over a third of the popular vote in the state, with almost the entire Muslim community and the bulk of the OBCs as also a section of the dalits backing it. In a four-cornered fight with the BJP, the Congress and the BSP, that should have been sufficient to bring it back to power. This was, however, not to happen. When V.P. Singh's government fell in November 1990 within a year of coming to power, the Janata Dal itself split. While in most other parts of the country the bulk of the Janata Dal remained in the parent party, in UP a substantial chunk, led by Yadav, joined the breakaway Samajwadi Janata Party headed by Chandra Shekhar, who replaced V.P. Singh as Prime Minister with the support of the Congress. The only major leader of the Janata Dal in UP who remained with the parent party was Ajit Singh, the son of former Prime Minister Charan Singh, who was the unquestioned leader of the Jats of western UP and Haryana in his time. While the US-educated Ajit Singh, who had worked in an American computer firm before taking to politics, was not a patch on his father as a political leader, old loyalties meant that the Jats, a powerful peasant community in the grain bowl of western UP, continued to support the Janata Dal.

The split in the Janata Dal meant that Yadav's government, which was always in a minority, now became even more precariously perched, entirely dependent on Congress support for its survival. Since the Congress was supporting the SJP government in New Delhi, it also extended its support to the government in UP. Soon after the Congress withdrew support to the Chandra Shekhar government in March 1991, however, the clamour to pull down Yadav's government grew within the upper caste-dominated Congress in UP. This was partly triggered by the feeling that Yadav's aggressive championing of the OBC cause could alienate upper-caste supporters of the Congress, who could consider the BJP a better option, and partly by the fear that Yadav's continuing in power could further cement his already strong roots among the Muslim community. The Congress' central leadership, with Prime Minister Narasimha Rao at the helm, resisted such pressures for some time, but ultimately succumbed, precipitating midterm elections to the assembly in 1991.

As was to be expected, the vertical split in the Janata Dal's support base ensured an easy victory for the BJP, which won 221 seats in the 425-member assembly. Apart from the emotive appeal of the Ram temple issue and the split in the Janata Dal vote, another key factor in the BJP's win was its projection of Kalyan Singh, a leader who belonged to the Lodh community (part of the OBCs), as the party's Chief Ministerial candidate. For the first time, the BJP, a party that had traditionally been dominated by the upper castes, was projecting someone from an intermediate caste as its main leader. This helped the BJP win over a sizeable section of non-Yadav OBC votes, in particular those of the Lodhs and Kurmis, who, like the Yadavs, are among the relatively better-off sections of the OBCs with many among them being middle peasants. As was to happen later in neighbouring Bihar, the attempt by Yadav leaders to monopolise the benefits of the Mandal platform alienated other sections of the relatively powerful among the OBCs. As later in Bihar, so also in UP in 1991, this rift within the ranks of the OBCs worked to the advantage of the BJP.

The BJP government in UP, however, lasted just over a year, before being dismissed (along with three other BJP-led state governments) by the Union government in December 1992 for having aided and abetted the demolition of the Babri masjid. There followed a nearly year-long spell of President's rule before fresh elections to the UP state assembly were held in November 1993.

By this time, Mulayam Singh Yadav had floated his own party, the Samajwadi Party, though he continued to have an alliance with Chandra Shekhar's SJP. Political commentators writing before the elections foresaw an easy victory for the BJP despite the tie-up between the SP and the BSP. This was largely based on the assumption that the old Janata Dal base would still be vertically split between the parent party and the SP. As it turned out, this did not happen. Yadav's credentials among the Muslims and in his own community stood him in good stead. The SP–BSP alliance and the BJP emerged as the largest groups with 176 members each in the 425-member state assembly, though short of a majority by about 37 seats. The Janata Dal managed to win just 27 seats and the Congress a mere 29 seats, by far the lowest number of MLAs it had ever had in the UP assembly. Given the composition of the assembly, both the Janata Dal and the Congress, as also the four MLAs from the left parties, had little choice but to support the Yadav-led SP–BSP government to keep the BJP out of power. The change in the vote shares of the various parties and groups in these elections was a clear indicator of the changing patterns in UP politics. While the Congress lost about 2.4 per cent of the vote from the 1991 elections, the BJP and the BSP gained about 2 per cent each. The major loser was the Janata Dal, whose share of the vote dropped from 18.8 per cent in 1991 to 12.2 per cent in 1993, most of this loss being picked up by the SP, which, in its earlier incarnation, had won 12.5 per cent of the votes in 1991, but now managed 18 per cent.

The violent incidents inside the state assembly on the first day that it met were later seen as symbolic of the new-found confidence among sections that had traditionally been at the lower rungs of the social hierarchy. The predictable jibes between the BJP MLAs on the one hand, and the SP–BSP MLAs on the other, soon degenerated into ugly brawls in which microphone stands were uprooted from their tables and used as weapons, while paperweights were used as missiles. Several MLAs, most of them from the BJP, were injured in the fracas and were taken to hospitals for first aid. Scenes of BJP MLAs crouching behind the assembly benches while their SP–BSP counterparts attacked were seen on national television that night and have remained imprinted in the memories of those who saw the episode as a powerful symbol of changing caste equations in the state. Even those who interpreted the unruly scenes in the UP assembly as the beginning of the state descending into a phase of anarchy, chaos and criminalisation of politics, reluctantly agreed that the days of upper-caste domination of the state's politics were on the way out, if not over.

The SP–BSP alliance, though heralded as the first real consolidation of the oppressed sections of UP society, was beset with internal contradictions from its very inception. With the benefit of hindsight, it can be argued that the alliance never had the potential for longevity given the ground realities of caste equations in UP. While the BSP's support base was almost entirely confined to the dalits (and in particular to the Jatavs or Chamars, who are traditionally in occupations connected with leather and hides), the SP's stronghold was among the relatively affluent sections of the OBCs, particularly the Yadavs. The Yadavs, thanks to tenancy reforms ushered in by Congress governments since independence, had become a prominent land-owning community, like many of the other relatively prosperous OBC communities—the Kurmis, the Lodhs and the Koeris, to name a few. The bulk of the dalits in the rural areas, on the other hand, were agricultural labourers with little or, more often, no land. It was hardly surprising, therefore, that there should be a fierce hostility between these two communities, which were constantly pitted against each other in real life. The alliance between the SP and the BSP was, to that extent, an attempt to impose from above a coalescing of forces that were inherently opposed to each other and had conflicting interests.

The bickering between these two alliance partners continued, but remained within manageable proportions for the best part of the next year-and-a-half. The BSP's two most prominent leaders, Kanshi Ram and Mayawati, throughout this period used public platforms to drive home the point that while Yadav was the Chief Minister and commanded the support of a larger number of MLAs than their party, he would ignore the BSP's strength at his own peril. Despite these tensions, however, Yadav used his tenure as CM to further buttress his claims of being the champion of the OBCs in the state. One of the key instruments used was his decision in 2000 to extend the reservation for OBCs in government jobs to the hill districts of the state, now Uttaranchal.

These districts of western UP had for long witnessed a movement for a separate state—proposed to be called Uttarakhand—and the attempt to foist OBC reservations in an area which had virtually no OBC population added fuel to the fire. Of all the districts of what was then UP, the territory of the proposed Uttarakhand was the most upper-caste dominated, with Brahmins and Rajputs constituting the majority of the population. While the dalits too had a significant presence, though less than in the plains, the OBCs were conspicuous by their absence. The attempt to introduce reservations in these areas was, therefore, viewed as just another instance of people from the plains trying to exploit the hill folk. The Uttarakhand agitation visibly gained impetus and a call was made for a mass rally in Delhi to press for the demand for a separate state and to protest against the reservation policy.

The state administration decided to do its best to prevent the agitators from reaching Delhi, and on October 2, 1994, the anniversary of Mahatma Gandhi's birth, busloads of Uttarakhand supporters were stopped on their way to Delhi and brutally beaten by the police near Muzzafarnagar in the plains. Some of the women in the group were allegedly raped by policemen. While this incident shocked the country and gave the Uttarakhand movement a profile that it did not have nationally till that stage, political observers also saw it as a cynical ploy by Yadav to gain support among the OBCs in the plains at the expense of unpopularity in an area of the state in which he had no political stake.

The period of Yadav's government was also characterised by deep-rooted suspicion within the BSP that he was trying to engineer a split in the BSP's ranks, particularly among the Muslim and non-dalit MLAs of the party, to further consolidate his position. The apprehension, as later events proved, was not entirely misplaced. Matters came to a head in the elections to the panchayats and *zila parishads* held in May 1995.

In these elections, the SP was seen as having used muscle power not just to defeat the BJP and Congress candidates, but also BSP candidates in several areas. Many instances of SP workers voting for Janata Dal candidates to defeat BSP aspirants were witnessed in the state. This proved the proverbial last straw for the BSP, which was already finding it difficult to justify the alliance among its cadre and support base, which felt that Yadav's tenure as Chief Minister had only further emboldened their Yadav oppressors in the rural areas. The BSP withdrew its ministers and its support from the Mulayam Singh Yadav government in June 1995, with the BJP's Murli Manohar Joshi, who later became the party's President and a Union Cabinet Minister, actively egging the BSP on to part ways with Yadav.

On June 2, 1995, the day after the BSP withdrew support to Yadav's government, the state guest house in Lucknow was witness to scenes that were testimony to all the acrimony between the erstwhile partners, the SP and the BSP. Thousands of SP activists patrolled the streets outside the guest house where Mayawati was staying at the time, and virtually kept her under house arrest while Yadav and his lieutenants worked on weaning away some of the BSP's legislators to ensure that his government would survive. Sensing an opportunity to build ties with the BSP, the BJP 'rescued' Mayawati from the guest house. Once out, Mayawati insisted that the SP activists had been sent specifically to physically eliminate her, while Mulayam protested that they had merely been 'protecting' her from those who might be incensed at the BSP's 'betrayal'. Even ignoring these exaggerated claims, there is no denying the fact that the fateful day has left as indelible a mark on UP politics as the violence in the UP assembly the first time it met during the SP–BSP government's tenure. Ever since that fateful day, the SP and the BSP have been sworn enemies. The BSP has since then fought an election in alliance with the Congress, it has formed governments with the help of the BJP, but it has refused to have anything to do with the SP.

Despite the rift between the SP and the BSP, over the second half of the 1990s and the first couple of years of the new millennium, both parties have managed to consolidate their electoral base in UP, relegating the BJP and the Congress to third and fourth positions respectively. Interestingly, while the BSP has used its brief stints in power to great effect in its strategy to woo new sections to its fold, the SP has thrived despite having been out of power in the state throughout this period.

The BSP has made no bones about the fact that it has no compunctions about aligning with anybody in its attempts to come to power. It has, in the last decade, made alliances with the SP, the Congress and the BJP at different points of time in UP. On none of these occasions has there been any attempt to justify the alliance on ideological grounds. As far as the BSP is concerned, all of these parties are *manuvadi* (which can be loosely translated as serving the upper castes) and there is fundamentally no difference between them. The BSP states quite clearly that it merely uses these *manuvadi* parties to further the interests of the dalits. In this sense, the BSP is quite unique in Indian politics. No other party is as brazenly contemptuous of the need to cover up opportunism with an ideological fig-leaf.

The BSP is perhaps also the only party to publicly favour unstable governments. Mayawati and Kanshi Ram have said several times that they prefer a *majboor sarkar* (a dependent government) to a *mazboot sarkar* (a strong and stable government). Their rationale is fairly simple: only a government dependent on them for survival will be forced to listen to the voice of the dalits; one that is stable would ignore them as most governments have done. Stable governments, the argument goes, are in the interests of the elite and those in favour of the status quo, not those who wish to change society for the better.

While Mayawati's stints in power in UP have been characterised by an imperious style that has antagonised her coalition partners and large sections of the state's bureaucracy, apart from her political opponents, she does seem to have been successful in using power to consolidate the BSP's vote bank among the dalits.

The mainstream English—and vernacular—media have built a stereotype of Mayawati as a whimsical, crude, crass, domineering Chief Minister who throws her weight around and terrorises anybody who dares to oppose her. Interestingly, these same attributes are seen to be her strengths by her supporters. But for the terror she evokes in the state administration, her supporters argue, the upper-caste dominated bureaucracy would have remained unsympathetic and callous towards the dalits. These supporters are quick to cite instances of the difference her presence has made to their lives. Said one dalit at a village near Hapur in western UP: 'In the old days, if we went to the police station to complain about our women being molested by some upper-caste males, not only would no case be registered, the officer-in-charge would probably abuse us and perhaps even beat us up, accusing us of bringing false charges against respectable citizens. We would not even be allowed to sit on the bench in the police station, we would have to squat on the floor. After *behen* [sister] Mayawati came to power, that has changed. The police will now register a case, even if nothing much happens thereafter. We are at least treated with respect. The policeman knows that if word reaches Mayawati that he has illtreated dalits or refused to register their complaints, there'll be hell to pay.'

Unlike most other parties in coalition situations, the BSP has also shown that it is quite willing to antagonise even sections that support its partners in the alliance. The rationale seems to be that the BSP's need is less than the partner's need to keep the coalition going. This has been true of the BSP's alliance with the SP, in which Kanshi Ram and Mayawati were not afraid of publicly and repeatedly proclaiming the SP's dependence on them and threatening to pull down Mulayam Singh Yadav's government if he did not heed their word. It has also been true of the BSP's alliances with the BJP on more than one occasion. The BSP seems to take the attitude that it will pursue its agenda and if the partner does not like some elements of the agenda, so be it.

The most recent (2003) manifestation of this attitude was the way in which Mayawati confronted Raja Bhaiyya. She was well aware that large sections of the BJP, which was supporting her government, were against his arrest and his being charged under the POTA. However, she was also aware that the BJP central leadership would do its best to prevent the disgruntled BJP MLAs from destabilising her government. Many others in her position might not have thought the gamble worthwhile, but she did. The arrest of Raja Bhaiyya triggered off a reaction that did, for some time, threaten the survival of Mayawati's government, but she had gambled right. The BJP's top leadership, including Vajpayee and Advani, intervened to ensure that the dissident MLAs fell in line.

Unlike the BSP, the SP has made a virtue of the necessity of remaining in Opposition since 1995. While the BJP was in power in the state, it positioned itself as the only party that had the intent and the strength to present a credible opposition. The Congress was evidently too weak to play this role and the SP was keen to drive home the point, particularly among Muslims, that the BSP could not be depended upon to oppose the BJP since it had in the past had an alliance with that party. This campaign does seem to have ensured that the bulk of the Muslims of UP have remained loyal to the SP, though Muslims in specific constituencies have voted for the Congress or the BSP, where these parties have been perceived as best placed to defeat the BJP.

When Kalyan Singh was expelled from the BJP, the SP promptly took up cudgels on his behalf and even had a tacit understanding with him during the February 2002 assembly elections. This was despite the fact that Kalyan Singh was one of those accused of conspiring to demolish the Babri masjid at a time when he was the Chief Minister. One of the factors that ultimately led to Kalyan Singh's expulsion from the BJP was the fact that he had publicly accused Vajpayee of having 'cheated' his supporters by promising to build a Ram temple if the BJP came to power and then having forgotten about the promise. Logically, one would expect that Kalyan's projecting himself as the real Ram *bhakt* (devotee) while Yadav was seen as the strongest opponent of the Ram temple agitation led by the Sangh Parivar should have made it impossible for them to make common cause. Yet, it was widely acknowledged that Kalyan Singh's Rashtriya Kranti Party and the SP had an implicit electoral understanding. Both sides, understandably, preferred to play up their OBC identity rather than focus on their respective positions on the Ayodhya *mandir–masjid* (temple versus mosque) controversy. (As already mentioned, Kalyan Singh later returned to the BJP's fold.)

After the 2002 assembly elections, with the BJP in decline in UP, the SP switched tack to portray itself as the only credible opposition to the BSP and Mayawati. In the Raja Bhaiyya incident, for instance, the SP was quick to cash in on the disillusionment with the BJP among the Thakurs. Amar Singh, the SP's General Secretary, who is himself a Thakur, was projected as a *Thakur kulbhushan* (an ornament of the Thakur or Rajput clan) at a public rally organised by the members of his caste. The message was loud and clear: Rajputs had been loyal to the BJP for close to a decade, but had been badly let down by the party. It was time they switched allegiance to the SP.

Dramatic events in August 2003 led to the ouster of Mayawati and to Mulayam Singh Yadav being sworn in as Chief Minister for the third time in his political career. There was hardly any indication of the impending changes when Mayawati hinted to the media on August 24 that she would give them 'spicy news' the next day, when the BSP was scheduled to hold a public rally in Lucknow. The papers the next morning were rife with speculation that the BSP leader might be preparing for a break with the BJP and for a snap poll in the state. The speculation was not misplaced. On August 25, Mayawati held a Cabinet meeting barely an hour before the rally in which—she later claimed—it was decided that the government would recommend dissolution of the assembly and the holding of fresh elections. The BJP disputed her claim.

The provocation for this decision came from a standoff between Mayawati and the BJP on the Taj Mahal issue that had been brewing for a couple of months. What had transpired was that work on a project to develop a commercial corridor near the Taj had begun without obtaining the necessary approval of particular departments of the Union government—these included the Ministry of Culture and the Ministry of Environment and Forests. The matter came to light after media reports highlighted how the area around the Taj—declared as a World Heritage Site by UNESCO—was going to be disfigured. A public interest petition was also lodged. Subsequently, the Union government clarified that it had not sanctioned the project and sought the state government's explanation on who was responsible for approving the commencement of work on such a project. Mayawati flatly denied that she had approved the project and, in fact, called for the resignation of Jagmohan, Union Minister for Culture and Tourism.

What was till that stage a minor fracas between coalition partners, spun out of control after the Supreme Court ordered the CBI to inquire into who was responsible for sanctioning the project. Mayawati was humiliated when forced by the BJP to withdraw her demand for Jagmohan's resignation. The CBI then started interrogating various officials in the UP government to find out the truth. What is significant is that Mayawati decided to part ways with the BJP a day after the CBI interrogated her confidante, the state's Environment Minister Nazimuddin Siddiqui.

After the BJP–BSP alliance broke, both sides freely traded charges against each other. Mayawati accused the BJP of putting pressure on her to tinker with the legal cases on the Babri masjid demolition in which Advani, Joshi and Uma Bharati, among others, had been named as accused. BJP loyalists on the other hand claimed that Mayawati was on the defensive because the CBI investigation would ultimately rest at her doorstep.

While there was a dispute between the BJP and the BSP about whether Mayawati had first recommended dissolution of the assembly or whether the BJP had withdrawn its support to the BSP, the fact is that the BJP Parliamentary Board met in New Delhi on August 27 and decided that the party would play the role of Opposition in the state. On August 28, UP Governor Vishnu Kant Shastri formally asked Mulayam Singh Yadav to present him with a list of MLAs who would support his claim to becoming Chief Minister. The SP provided the governor with a list of 205 out of 405 MLAs, including MLAs belonging to the Congress, the RLD, Kalyan Singh's RKP and sundry small parties (including the ABCD, or the Akhil Bharatiya Congress Dal). Interestingly, the list also included 14 MLAs from the BSP. The list was enough to convince Shastri that Yadav should be invited to form a government, though the actual trial of strength would take place on the floor of the assembly two weeks later.

What went on behind the scenes after Mayawati's dramatic announcement that she had sought the dissolution of the assembly highlighted quite clearly how desperate the BJP's position in UP had become. It was quite apparent that the BJP did not under any circumstances want an immediate election in UP. The only way of avoiding an election was to allow the SP to form a government. The BJP, therefore, let it be known that it would not try and prevent Yadav from forming the government in Lucknow. This was quite a remarkable turnaround for a party that had repeatedly aligned itself with the BSP in the past for the sole reason of ensuring that the SP could *not* form a government in the state.

What had changed in 2003? For starters, the BJP's rank and file—and a substantial section of its upper-caste leadership—had realised that the alliance with the BSP was steadily eroding the party's support base. At the same time, it needed time for the 'taint' of its association with the BSP to be washed away from public memory before any elections. An SP government in Lucknow, therefore, suited the party admirably. It would, the BJP hoped, give the party some breathing space and hopefully ensure that any anti-incumbency sentiment would work against the SP rather than the BJP because of its association with the BSP. Finally, with an SP government, the BJP could hope to turn the political battle in the state into one between itself and the SP, pushing the BSP off centrestage.

This was important for the BJP because, over the last decade, the BSP and the SP had, willy-nilly—or perhaps deliberately—emerged as the two parties with the sharpest contradictions in UP politics. In the process of fighting their battles, neither set too much store by ideological niceties. But the fact that they managed to dictate the terms of political confrontations in the state meant that first the Congress and then increasingly the BJP were getting marginalised in India's most populous state.

Bihar: Can the 'Worst' State Show the Way?

During the 1950s and even during much of the 1960s, Bihar was considered to be one of the best-administered states in the country. However, through the 1970s, 1980s and the 1990s, this image plummeted precipitously. The state acquired the reputation of being one of the most backward in India, backward in just about every respect—certainly in terms of social and economic indicators. It is said that Bihar symbolises the existence of a 'Fourth World' in a Third World country.

Bihar is the one state where feudal feelings are perhaps most evident, where caste sentiments determine the course of politics, and where the economic divide has resulted in active Naxalite groups espousing the cause of poor and landless labourers fighting periodic pitched battles against 'armies' comprising members of upper castes and representatives of landlords. Bihar is also a state where corruption has become more than a fact of everyday life; it is a state where corruption is so endemic that myths and legends have been woven around the phenomenon.

In the middle of the 1970s, Bihar became the focal point of a political and social movement aimed at *sampoorna kranti* or 'total revolution', spearheaded by Jayaprakash Narayan (JP). The movement that had begun in Gujarat and had spread rapidly across the country acquired such momentum in Bihar that Indira Gandhi placed many leaders of the movement behind bars before declaring Emergency in June 1975. The fact that Bihar remains the only state in India in which individuals who had cut their teeth in the Janata Party and later the Janata Dal continue to dominate the course of politics, is undoubtedly an important legacy of the JP movement.

But the existence of a strong anti-Congress political formation dates back to 1967. That was the year in which the Congress for the first time saw its hold on power slipping in many states in India, particularly in northern India. The Samyukta Vidhayak Dal government that came to power in Bihar in 1967 saw the left and the right coming together for the first time to prevent the formation of a Congress government in the state. The socialists, the communists and the BJS made common cause. Given the obvious political differences between these groups, it is hardly surprising that there followed a period of considerable instability, with chief ministers enjoying brief stints punctuated by the frequent imposition of President's rule. Between 1968 and 1980, President's rule was imposed in Bihar on as many as five occasions. Between March 1967 and June 1980, chief ministers were sworn in on no less than 15 occasions in Patna. No chief minister lasted even two years in this phase, Karpoori Thakur's 22-month-long tenure from June 1977 to April 1979 being the longest.

Karpoori Thakur's espousal of the interests of the intermediate castes was to leave a lasting legacy, though the Congress remained in power through almost all of the 1980s. Thakur had forged a coalition of backward and intermediate castes including the numerically significant Yadav community and made this social coalition the pivot of his anti-Congress political platform. This was quite akin to what happened in neighbouring Uttar Pradesh, where leaders like the socialist Ram Manohar Lohia and Charan Singh had built a similar caste-based coalition.

After the V.P. Singh government implemented the recommendations of the Mandal Commission, the Janata Dal was able to tap into this hitherto dormant political base both in UP and in Bihar. In both states, the Congress—which lost power in 1989—has since been relegated to an also-ran in the electoral race. In Bihar, as in UP, the Congress has seen its erstwhile supporters from the upper castes shifting allegiance to the BJP, which these sections feel is better placed to confront the growing political clout of the intermediate castes and protect their interests. Again, as in UP, in Bihar too a single party has been unable to garner the support of all of the intermediate and lower castes. Just as in UP, with the SP and the BSP competing to occupy this political space, in Bihar also the RJD and the Samata Party both claim to be the true representatives of the 'downtrodden'. Interestingly, in both states, this fragmentation in the ranks of the middle and lower castes has not worked to the advantage of either the Congress or the BJP. Politics in Bihar (after Jharkhand was carved out) is dominated by the confrontation between the RJD and the Samata Party, with the Congress and BJP being reduced to lesser partners of these two antagonists.

While Bihar was still undivided, it was not quite as obvious that the BJP and the Congress were not powerful forces in the state's electoral battleground. In the 1999 Lok Sabha elections, for instance, the BJP won 23 of the 54 seats in the state, more than any other party. However, 11 of these 23 seats came from the 14 that were subsequently carved out to form Jharkhand. Further, many of the remaining 12 seats that the party won in central and northern Bihar (which constitute the truncated Bihar) could not have been won without the support of the Samata Party and the Janata Dal (United), the BJP's allies. Similarly, the Congress won three of the 54 seats in undivided Bihar in the 1999 elections, but two of these were in what became Jharkhand. The bulk of the 40 seats that now remain in Bihar, therefore, were won by the RJD and the Samata Party, neither of which won any seats in Jharkhand. The division of Bihar has, therefore, made a dramatic difference to electoral politics in the state. The RJD, which has never managed to win a majority on its own in the state after the 1989 assembly elections, can now hope to make a credible bid for power on its own. The Samata Party which, since its inception, was compelled to play second fiddle to the BJP, can now assert its dominance in the alliance.

Again, there is a parallel with the situation in Uttar Pradesh. In UP too, Uttaranchal was an area in which neither the SP nor the BSP had a meaningful presence, while the BJP and the Congress were the two dominant parties. Thus, the separation of Uttaranchal undoubtedly helped the SP and the BSP in Uttar Pradesh, while hurting the BJP and the Congress. The difference, however, is that while Uttaranchal accounted for just five of the 85 seats in undivided UP, Jharkhand had a considerably bigger share of the Lok Sabha constituencies that formed undivided Bihar. Clearly, therefore, the impact of the division of the state is greater in Bihar than in UP.

It would be interesting to see how the division of Bihar would change caste-based political affiliations in the state. In undivided Bihar, the upper castes had the choice of supporting either the BJP or the Congress, and in recent years, had opted for the former. Now that they have been relatively marginalised in the state, upper-caste voters could conclude that going along with the BJP may not be an effective strategy to make their presence felt. Such voters could be confronted with having to choose between two parties, the RJD or the Samata Party, both of which espouse the cause of the intermediate and lower castes. In Tamil Nadu, those belonging to the upper castes found that their votes would be 'wasted' if they did not support either of the two Dravidian parties. In UP as well, upper-caste voters increasingly have to choose between the SP and BSP since both the BJP and the Congress have become weak in the state. Will a similar voting pattern be replicated in Bihar? The possibility certainly exists. If such a situation indeed takes place, as the Tamil Nadu experience has indicated, the sectarian, caste-based character of the RJD and the Samata Party could undergo a gradual change. These regional parties would necessarily have to broaden their appeal if they are to attract voters from different social strata—as the BSP and the SP have already begun to do in UP.

Laloo Prasad Yadav, who was a student leader during the JP movement in the mid-1970s, became Chief Minister of Bihar in February 1990, less than three months after V.P. Singh became Prime Minister in December 1989. Despite the nation-wide anti-Congress wave in the 1989 Lok Sabha elections, which was still in evidence during the February 1990 assembly elections in Bihar, the Janata Dal did not actually obtain a majority on its own or even come close to doing so. In the 324-member assembly, the JD's tally was only 123. It was with the support of the BJP (39 seats), the CPI (23 seats), the JMM (19 seats) and the CPI(M) (six seats) that Laloo was able to form the government in Patna. Having formed the government, he lost little time in trying to reduce his dependence on these allies. He engineered defections from the BJP, the JMM and the Indian People's Front (IPF), one of the few Naxalite groups that participated in electoral politics, to increase his strength in the assembly. It was this strategy that enabled Laloo to survive in office even after the BJP withdrew its support to his government following the arrest of L.K. Advani in Bihar in October that year.

This episode helped Laloo acquire a national profile. Advani's nation-wide *rath yatra* was halted at Samastipur in Bihar and he was 'jailed' in a government bungalow at Masanjore near the Maithon dam. The incident sparked off riots in neighbouring UP with protesting BJP supporters going on the rampage and targeting the Muslim community, but Bihar remained peaceful. This did not go unnoticed. The same Bihar had in October 1989 witnessed one of the worst riots in its history, when over a thousand people were killed in Hindu–Muslim clashes in Bhagalpur. The arrest of Advani and the state administration's determination to prevent any communal backlash helped Laloo consolidate the support of the Muslims. Along with his own Yadav community, this gave him a formidable electoral base to build on. At this early stage in his political career, Laloo also had with him prominent leaders of the Kurmi and dalit communities in Nitish Kumar and Ram Vilas Paswan, who were to later break away from him.

By the time the Bihar assembly elections of 1995 were held, the JD under Laloo had strengthened its position considerably. The party secured a slim majority on its own, winning 167 of the 324 assembly seats. With its allies from the left, the CPI (26) and CPI(M) (six), the JD had control of 199 seats. The BJP, which was the next biggest party in the state assembly, won just 41 seats, while the fledgling Samata Party had a mere seven seats in the new assembly. The Congress too had been reduced to 29 seats.

Ironically, having survived a full term as Chief Minister without having a majority in the state assembly, Laloo could not complete his second term when he *did* have a majority. Barely a year after his second stint as Chief Minister, the 'fodder scam' hit the headlines. The Comptroller and Auditor General (CAG) had found that hundreds of crores of rupees from the state's coffers had been siphoned off under the pretext of being used to provide fodder for cattle. The period to which the audit pertained included Laloo's first term as Chief Minister as well as that of his predecessor Dr. Jagannath Mishra. The BJP demanded Laloo's resignation, alleging that he was not just morally responsible for the scam, but one of those directly involved and among the biggest beneficiaries of the funds siphoned off government coffers. The party demanded an inquiry into the scandal by the CBI and urged the Union government, then headed by Rao, to grant permission for such an inquiry, which was acceded. The investigations were spearheaded by U.N. Biswas, who was the CBI's Joint Director (east) based in Kolkata. Whereas one section perceived Biswas as a maverick police officer who was incorruptible, dogged and unafraid of politicians in power, others saw him as a publicity seeker and even as a closet sympathiser of the Hindutva ideology to explain his zealousness in pursuing the cases against Laloo.

At the end of July 1997, after the CBI had decided to prosecute both Chief Minister Laloo and former Chief Minister Mishra, Laloo was arrested for the first time. He remained in jail for more than 100 days before he was released in December that year. Over the next four years, Laloo was to be jailed on four more occasions. However, well before he was actually arrested and imprisoned, Laloo had been forced to resign as Chief Minister after the CBI filed a chargesheet against him. By this time, there was a United Front government in power in New Delhi with H.D. Deve Gowda as Prime Minister. The sequence of events can be summarised thus: The BJP and its allies had been demanding Laloo's resignation on the ground that he was a Chief Minister against whom corruption charges had been levelled that were being probed by the CBI. If he remained in office, he could influence the course of the investigations and misuse his position to tamper with evidence, it was argued. On the other hand, the UF government—of which the Janata Dal was the biggest constituent—contended that an elected chief minister should not be forced to resign merely because certain unsubstantiated allegations had been made against him. Not even a formal chargesheet had been issued against him, it was pointed out. When the CBI actually chargesheeted Laloo, the Janata Dal as well as the rest of the UF were in a quandary. They clearly found that it was becoming increasingly difficult to continue defending Laloo. They advised him to put in his papers, which he was unwilling to consider.

It was at this juncture that the Janata Dal split. The party was to elect a new president on July 6, 1997. Laloo and his supporters announced that they would be boycotting the elections and instead organised a parallel meeting on July 5 at which the Rashtriya Janata Dal was formed and Laloo was voted as its first President. Sharad Yadav was elected President of the Janata Dal. Given the split in the JD, the Bihar Governor A.R. Kidwai asked Laloo to seek a fresh vote of confidence in the state assembly. On July 15, Chief Minister Laloo won the vote of confidence with the support of two factions of the JMM (one led by Shibu Soren and the other by Kishan Marandi) and 14 independent MLAs. The Congress was in an uncomfortable situation. It did not wish to be seen as supporting a 'corrupt' chief minister and at the same time did not want to go along with the BJP. It therefore abstained from voting during the confidence motion in the assembly. On July 17, the United Front in New Delhi realised that the RJD could no longer be a part of the UF so long as Laloo was the head of the RJD. Eight days later, on July 25, Laloo finally resigned as Chief Minister after the designated CBI court issued an arrest warrant against him. The same day, Laloo got the RJD MLAs to ratify his decision to nominate his wife, Rabri Devi as his successor. She thus became the first woman Chief Minister of Bihar.

Why did Laloo decide to resign only after he realised that the CBI had issued a warrant of arrest against him and not earlier? It seemed that Laloo wished to ensure that his nominee—in this case, his wife—would succeed him as chief minister rather than wait for a situation where he would be behind bars and a party colleague who could later become his rival would be elected by the MLAs of the RJD. The sheer cynicism of the move shocked quite a few people, including many who were not hostile to him. After all, till she became Chief Minister, Rabri Devi had been a home-maker looking after their nine children. She had never contested an election in her life or even participated in any political activity worth mentioning. Neither Rabri Devi nor Laloo made any bones about the fact that he would continue as the de-facto Chief Minister of the state. Even those sympathetic to Laloo felt that he had gone too far in taking the support of his party's MLAs for granted and that Rabri Devi would not be able to survive the mandatory vote of confidence that any new chief minister would necessarily have to seek. Three days later, on July 28, the Rabri Devi government won a vote of confidence in the Bihar assembly.

The very next day, the CBI ordered Laloo's arrest. Laloo surrendered before the CBI court in Patna and he was remanded to judicial custody. Before his arrest, the CBI's Biswas reportedly asked the court to seek the intervention of the Army, fearing a violent backlash from Laloo's supporters. This was a completely unprecedented situation. Law and order is meant to be a state subject and the state government has to decide how this is to be maintained. Laloo was to later argue that this was yet another clear instance of Biswas over-stepping his authority and attempting to paint him black. He claimed that the fact that nothing much happened when he was arrested went to show how Biswas had sought to malign him by raising the bogey of RJD hoodlums wreaking violence on the streets of Patna.

In 1999, Rabri Devi survived an attempt made by the NDA government in New Delhi to dismiss her government by invoking Article 356. By this time, Kidwai had been replaced as Bihar's Governor by Sunder Singh Bhandari, a member of the RSS and a former Vice President of the BJP. The incident that prompted the NDA government to invoke the controversial provisions of Article 356 was the massacre of 12 dalits by members of an upper-caste 'army' at Narayanpur village in Jehanabad district. Governor Bhandari, in his report to New Delhi, had suggested that there had been a complete breakdown of the working of the constitutional machinery in the state. On February 12, two days after the Jehanabad massacre, the Union government dismissed the Rabri Devi government. It had two months' time to have this decision ratified by both houses of Parliament. After dithering for some time on what position it should take, the Congress decided to oppose the government's resolution authorising President's rule in Bihar. Some of the BJP's allies in the NDA, like the TDP and the Shiromani Akali Dal, were uncomfortable about supporting the use of Article 356 to dismiss an elected state government, but they eventually fell in line.

In the Lok Sabha where the NDA had a clear majority, the government was able to get the resolution imposing President's rule in Bihar passed quite easily on February 26. The problem arose in getting the resolution adopted by the Rajya Sabha in which the NDA was in a minority. The BJP believed the Congress could be persuaded to change its stance since the party's state unit was clearly opposed to the idea of bailing out the Rabri Devi government, so much so that as many as 40 members of the party's local executive had put in their papers in protest against the decision of the Congress central leadership to oppose President's rule. Sonia Gandhi too had earlier been rather critical of the RJD government in the state. On March 7, Prime Minister Vajpayee spent 45 minutes with Sonia Gandhi trying to persuade her to make her party change its position on opposing the imposition of President's rule in Bihar, ostensibly on the ground that it would be in the 'national interest' to do so. It was reported at that time that Vajpayee had even offered to replace Governor Bhandari with a person 'more acceptable' to the Congress as part of a quid pro quo if the Congress was willing to vote in favour of the government's resolution in the Rajya Sabha. Sonia Gandhi refused to oblige Vajpayee.

At this juncture, two points of view emerged within the NDA. One, espoused by the Samata Party and sections within the BJP, was that the government should indefinitely postpone the voting in the Rajya Sabha on the issue and thereby allow the Article 356 notification to automatically lapse after the two-month deadline for its ratification expired on April 12. The other viewpoint was that since it had become apparent that the NDA government would not be successful in continuing with President's rule in Bihar, it should accept defeat gracefully, revoke the notification and allow Rabri Devi to resume office as Chief Minister. Such a position, this section argued, would save the Vajpayee government the embarrassment of its resolution being defeated in the Rajya Sabha while, at the same time, allowing the NDA to take the moral high ground by accusing the Congress of being guilty of 'double standards' by opposing the RJD government and also by not allowing its dismissal. Eventually, the latter view prevailed and on March 8, Home Minister L.K. Advani announced in the Lok Sabha that the Cabinet had decided to revoke the imposition of President's rule in Bihar.

Soon after Rabri Devi resumed office as Chief Minister, Governor Bhandari decided to quit. Since he had evidently been a prime mover in the attempt to unseat Rabri Devi, her return to power was clearly a loss of face for Bhandari. However, the BJP did not want to convey the impression that he had been sacked. He was, therefore, promptly appointed Governor of Gujarat. The man who replaced him at the Raj Bhavan in Patna was Vinod Chandra Pande, a former bureaucrat, who had risen to prominence as Revenue

Secretary in the Rajiv Gandhi government and later as Cabinet Secretary in the V.P. Singh government.

Many political analysts saw the Congress' decision to oppose the dismissal of the Rabri Devi government as a 'blunder' on par with Sonia's ill-considered boast just a month later—in April 1999—that she had the support of 272 Lok Sabha MPs for her bid to become Prime Minister after the Vajpayee government lost a vote of confidence. The results in Bihar of the September–October 1999 general elections seemed to bear out this analysis. The NDA won 41 of the 54 Lok Sabha seats in Bihar, the BJP winning 23, the JD(U)—which included the Samata Party—getting 17, and the Shiv Sena winning one seat. In contrast, the RJD won just seven seats and the Congress four. The BJP and the JD(U) were ecstatic. Their decision to dismiss the Rabri Devi government had been ratified by the people of Bihar, they claimed, and the Congress' decision to stick by the RJD had been rejected.

The euphoria was not to last very long. In the state assembly elections of February 2000—barely four months after the Lok Sabha elections—the RJD once again emerged as the single-largest party. The party won 124 seats in the 324-member assembly on its own. Along with the Congress and the CPI(M), which had fought the elections as its allies, it could count on the support of 149 MLAs in the new house. The NDA, on the other hand, could muster only 122 MLAs from within its own ranks, the BJP having won 67 seats, while the Samata Party and the JD(U)—which were by this time once again two separate parties—won 34 seats and 21 seats respectively. Yet, what was clear was that neither of the two pre-election alliances had a majority in the newly elected assembly.

Both sides started frantically hunting for possible supporters among the 53 MLAs who were part of neither front. Here again, the RJD had an advantage over the NDA. Various left parties—like the CPI, the CPI(ML)-Liberation and the Marxist Coordination Committee—accounted for 12 of the 53 seats. While they had their reservations about the RJD and Laloo, there was little doubt that the NDA was for them the bigger enemy and when it came to the crunch, they would not allow an NDA government to be formed in Patna. The only other big blocks that could be wooed by either side were the JMM (12 MLAs) and the independents (20 MLAs, many of them with criminal backgrounds who had in fact contested and won the elections while in jail). The RJD soon announced that it had secured the support of the JMM and that it was, therefore, just two short of the 163 required to muster a majority. The NDA, which had nominated Nitish Kumar as its Chief Ministerial aspirant—despite the Samata Party being a junior partner in the alliance—predictably rubbished the claim and presented its own counter-claim. Nitish's bid for Chief Minister, they asserted, had the support of 146 MLAs. Further, they maintained that this was more than the RJD could muster, since not all the Congress MLAs would actually support Rabri Devi's bid to become Chief Minister for a second term. As has become the norm in such situations, both sides presented lists of 'supporters' to the Governor.

Governor Pande—for reasons best known to him—decided to swear in Nitish Kumar as the next Chief Minister of Bihar on March 4, 2000. The RJD protested, arguing that the Governor was only encouraging horse-trading since parties and individuals who accounted for at least 173 seats in the 324-member assembly had gone on record to say that they would not support an NDA government in Bihar. Neutral observers could not help but agree with this contention. Pande asserted that his intentions were above board and in an attempt to prove that his motives were honourable he gave Nitish Kumar only 10 days to seek and win a vote of confidence in the assembly. The NDA's power brokers got into the act. The 20 independent MLAs were aggressively wooed. Those of them who were in jail informally elected Suraj Bhan their leader. Suraj Bhan, who was accused in as many as 26 cases, told reporters that his group had decided to support the NDA 'to give a new direction to development in the state'.

Despite such brazen attempts at garnering support, it was becoming clearer each day that Nitish Kumar would find it extremely difficult, if not impossible, to win the vote of confidence. The first effective trial of strength was to take place even before the formal vote of confidence. The Speaker of the new assembly was to be elected on March 9. The RJD-led alliance proposed the name of Sadanand Singh, a Congress leader, for the post. The voting to elect the Speaker, the alliance asserted, would nail Nitish's claims to having the support of a majority of MLAs in the assembly. That the NDA was also aware of this became clear when it announced that it would not put up its own candidate—ostensibly because it wanted a consensus—for the post of Speaker. The game was almost over by then. The next day, on March 10, Nitish resigned after two-and-a-half hours of the debate on his motion of confidence, without waiting for the debate to conclude and the assembly to vote. The second brief interlude in the 11-year-old Laloo–Rabri reign had lasted less than a week.

The Samata Party: Tripping on Egos

The Samata Party—and later the Janata Dal (United)—perhaps best illustrates how Laloo's near-instant success in dominating Bihar's politics also became his biggest weakness. The Janata Dal in Bihar at the end of the 1980s and in the early 1990s was certainly a party with no dearth of leaders. Apart from Laloo himself, there were George Fernandes, Nitish Kumar, Ram Vilas Paswan and Sharad Yadav, each of whom could in varying degrees lay claim to having acquired a national profile. Of these, George Fernandes and Sharad Yadav were not strictly speaking Biharis—the former being a Mangalorean and the latter a native of Madhya Pradesh—but both had made Bihar their political home.

When Laloo became Chief Minister of Bihar in 1990, he was definitely a relative newcomer to the big stage of politics compared to these stalwarts. Yet, within a couple of years it was clear to everybody that the undisputed leader of the Janata Dal in Bihar was Laloo. It also became increasingly clear that despite the presence of Nitish Kumar and Paswan in the party's leadership, neither the Kurmis nor the dalits could hope to break the stranglehold of the Yadavs on the levers of power in Patna under Laloo's regime. Laloo was also not averse to periodically 'reminding' George Fernandes that he remained a leader in Bihar only at Laloo's mercy. He also made it clear to Nitish and Paswan that while he did not grudge them their share of the limelight in New Delhi, they would be well advised to play second fiddle to him in Bihar. The repeated rebuffs eventually proved too much for Fernandes and Nitish to stomach. In 1994, the two left the Janata Dal to float the Samata Party and immediately launched a virulent campaign against the 'misrule' of Laloo's government.

As yet, however, the two Samata Party leaders were not willing to consider an alliance either with the Congress—against which party Fernandes had fought throughout his political career—or with the BJP, which they continued to see as a communal outfit. In the 1995 state assembly elections, therefore, the Samata Party was on its own, and—as we have seen—made a rather pathetic debut in electoral politics. This soon convinced the party that the BJP's communalism was a 'lesser evil' in Bihar than Laloo's so-called 'jungle raj' and caste-based politics. Thus, by the time the 1996 Lok Sabha elections took place, the Samata Party had struck an alliance with the BJP in Bihar. The alliance was not spectacularly successful, but it did help the Samata Party win its first Lok Sabha seats—six from Bihar and one each from Uttar Pradesh and Orissa.

Since then, the Samata Party has grown considerably to become the main rival to the RJD in Bihar after the state was divided. It has become the nucleus around which political and social forces hostile to Laloo's Yadav–Muslim combine have gathered. There is a parallel in this with what had happened in Uttar Pradesh, though there are important differences as well. The social support base of the RJD in Bihar, like that of the SP in UP, is largely among the Yadavs and the Muslims. Like in UP, in Bihar too the BJP succeeded in preventing this base from expanding further to include all the non-Yadav OBCs. The difference, however, is that while in UP the BJP was able to achieve this by projecting a non-Yadav OBC leader—Kalyan Singh, who belongs to the Lodh community—from within its own ranks, in Bihar it had to depend on the Samata Party to split the pan-OBC coalition that Laloo was attempting to build. Another similarity between the political situation prevailing in UP and Bihar in terms of caste equations is the manner in which dalit leaders like Mayawati and Paswan have managed to deny the SP and the RJD—as well as the BJP and the Congress—substantial sections of the votes of their community.

Unlike the SP in Uttar Pradesh, however, Laloo started off with the support of powerful non-Yadav OBC castes like the Kurmis—he was, of course, a part of the Janata Dal at the time. He also had the support of the dalits, which again was something that the SP did not have to a significant extent at any stage. In that sense, it would perhaps be fair to say that Laloo has contributed in substantial measure to the alienation of these castes from his party and has squandered more opportunities than Mulayam ever had to widen and expand his support base across different caste groups.

Politics in Bihar, of course, is substantially different from that in UP in at least one major aspect: The presence of 'armies' and

Naxalites who are outside the electoral process, but who are nevertheless an important and integral part of politics in the state. While the Naxalites, as Marxists, are ideologically not motivated by caste factors, there is little doubt that the bulk of their sympathisers come from those at the lower end of the caste hierarchy. This is not surprising given the fact that their focus on agrarian issues has pit the Naxalites constantly against the big land-owners of Bihar and in favour of the agricultural labourers. Since the upper castes and Yadavs dominate big landholdings in Bihar and agricultural labourers in the state are predominantly dalits and other lower castes, there is a considerable intermeshing of caste and class in the battles between the Ranvir Sena—the private army of upper-caste landlords—and Naxalite groups like the People's War Group (PWG) and the Maoist Communist Centre (MCC).

To return to the Samata Party in Bihar, ego clashes among its leaders have from time to time conveyed the impression that the party could break up. Besides the existence of two factions allegedly owing allegiance to George Fernandes and Nitish Kumar, the party's MPs and MLAs have often issued statements in their 'personal' capacity, which have run contrary to the official party position. For instance, the former spokesperson of the party Shambhu Srivastwa was extremely critical of the failure of the Gujarat government to control the communal riots in the state. He stopped short of asking for what the Opposition to the NDA had been demanding—the resignation of Modi. Srivastwa's statements were brushed aside as his 'personal' views and not those of the Samata Party. Subsequently, in May 2003, Srivastwa—a medical doctor by profession—quit his post and joined the Congress. Certain Samata Party representatives have also openly expressed their unhappiness with their party's leadership on account of the presence of former party General Secretary Jaya Jaitly who is close to George Fernandes.

Matters came to a head in June 2003 when Nitish Kumar submitted his resignation from the post of Railway Minister to Vajpayee on the grounds that it would be morally untenable for him to continue since his own party colleagues were accusing him of corruption in purchase contracts. The reference was to charges made against him by Samata Party MP Prabhunath Singh. While Singh has always had the reputation of being a maverick and a 'loose cannon', Nitish clearly believed that he had Fernandes' backing. Nitish specifically asked why no disciplinary action had been taken against Prabhunath Singh by the Party President George Fernandes. The resignation drama lasted three days, during which time speculation was rife about a possible split in the Samata Party with Fernandes and Nitish leading rival factions. As in the past, however, the storm soon blew over after Nitish was 'persuaded' to withdraw his resignation.

The Samata Party has by and large been confined to Bihar, despite the fact that it had MPs like Kalpnath Rai (who had been asked to quit his post as Food Minister in the Narasimha Rao government for alleged acts of corruption) from neighbouring Uttar Pradesh and Bhakta Charan Das (formerly of the Janata Dal) from Orissa. The party, however, surprised many by obtaining the allegiance of a number of MLAs from Manipur. This state has witnessed rapid changes in government and its MLAs have acquired notoriety for the frequency with which they have switched political parties. In the run-up to assembly elections to the state in February 2002, a group of MLAs from Manipur decided to support the Samata Party and even took on the BJP (with which it was in alliance in New Delhi) to destabilise the state government in Imphal. It was not as if the Samata Party had had a support base in Manipur for a long time; it was merely that a group of MLAs from the state found the Samata Party a convenient platform on which they could come together.

What follows are thumbnail sketches of some of these important politicians from Bihar.

Laloo Prasad Yadav

In less than a decade-and-a-half, Laloo Prasad Yadav has risen from being a virtual nonentity, even in his native Bihar, to arguably one of the best-known political leaders in India. True, Laloo had been a member of the Lok Sabha as early as 1977, when the Janata Party made a clean sweep of all 54 seats in Bihar riding a wave of popular anger against the Emergency which had ended barely three months before the elections were held. Yet, hardly anybody outside his constituency had heard of Laloo in this period. In fact, he had not even been a member of the Bihar assembly prior to contesting the Lok Sabha elections. Today, he

symbolises the very essence of Bihar for most Indians like nobody else ever has.

Laloo's beginning in politics was in the JP movement in the
mid-1970s. He was at that time—in 1973–74—the President of the
Patna University Students' Union. There's a story about a specific
incident during those days that could well be apocryphal. The
story goes that on the day of a much-publicised rally to be addressed by JP in Patna, the police cracked down with teargas and
lathi charges to ensure that many of those who wanted to participate in the rally would not be able to do so. That evening, Laloo
himself called up newspaper offices to announce grandly that
'Laloo Yadav has been arrested'. Many of the journalists contacted
were puzzled by this piece of information and wanted to know
who Laloo Yadav was. At which point Laloo is said to have expressed shock at their ignorance of such an important student
leader. The story may well be untrue, but if it sounds plausible it
is because Laloo remains to this day a man who knows how to
stay in the news and hog the headlines, whether for the right reasons or for the wrong ones.

Despite his carefully cultivated image of being a rustic buf-
foon, Laloo has certainly been one of the most media-savvy politicians in India. He has never ducked questions or refused a re-
quest from a journalist for an interview, no matter how big or small
the publication or organisation the journalist represents. His clever
one-liners have not merely spawned a series of jokes but have
also been the delight of television journalists looking for a sound
byte and a godsend for headline writers. For example, on the day
the RJD was formed in July 1997, Laloo had appeared on a TV news
programme where the anchor patronisingly remarked that his
party could at best hope to be described as a regional party. Pat
came the reply without batting an eyelid: 'Regional party? RJD is
the original party'. Of course, this was not a just a play on words.
In his characteristic style, Laloo had used humour to drive home
the message that his party would be the one to matter in Bihar,
not the parent Janata Dal.

Humour has been an important weapon in Laloo's armoury.
He has used it to disarm aggressive critics—whether inside a TV
studio or on the floor of the Bihar assembly or in Parliament. He
has also used it to great effect in attacking his opponents. While
most other 'secular' leaders prefer to angrily rave and rant at the

Sangh Parivar's activities, Laloo more often than not resorts to ridiculing them. For instance, at a public rally he made fun of Murli Manohar Joshi—who was then the BJP President—for getting knocked down by police personnel using water cannons during a demonstration near Parliament during the tenure of the Narasimha Rao government. He referred to Joshi 'keeling over like a sick pup' under the impact of a 'shower' and wondered aloud how such a leadership could claim to provide an alternative to the Congress. Most other politicians would have considered his choice of words 'unparliamentary' if not downright vulgar, but the guffaws that followed from the thousands assembled near the Red Fort left little room for doubt that his gag had gone down well with the crowd. His penchant for referring to the Chief Secretary of Bihar as *bade babu*—a term more commonly used to describe a head clerk—was another instance of his deliberate use of ridicule. It certainly wasn't considered offensive or rude behaviour by millions of people who did not think too highly of a bureaucracy that they perceived as an institution that only harassed them. At the same time, it also served to tell the Chief Secretary—and hence the rest of the bureaucracy—who the real boss was.

The choice of language and idiom is decidedly rustic, but undoubtedly deliberately so. Laloo realises only too well that the more he is berated by the English media for being a boor, the easier it is for him to project himself as a man of the people, one who doesn't mind talking bluntly. Unlike many others, who might prefer to play down their humble beginnings, Laloo goes out of his way to keep reinforcing the fact that he is from a family of cowherds and had lived for many years in the quarters given to his brother as a government peon. While other politicians from northern India will spend Holi paying visits to other bigwigs or receiving guests at home and exchanging sweets, Laloo can be seen on the evening news drenched in coloured water and playing the *dholak* with gay abandon. It is not uncommon to find TV footage of Laloo talking to journalists wearing a sleeveless *ganji* (vest) and *dhoti*. Most other politicians would dread the thought of appearing in public dressed so informally, but for Laloo it is just one more opportunity to tell his supporters that he remains one of them, not a leader who has become so big as to live like the hoi polloi.

Laloo also knows, perhaps better than any other Indian politician, the public relations value of being able to laugh at oneself.

Thus, when asked about the incongruity of his government preaching the virtues of small families when he himself is a father of nine children—two sons and seven daughters—Laloo just chuckles. Similarly, when asked whether Rabri Devi is merely a de-jure Chief Minister and he is the man who really calls the shots, Laloo grins and says that Rabri is a good Indian wife and like all good Indian wives takes her husband's word as her command. The candour is disarming, as Laloo knows only too well. His whacky sense of humour is also evident from the fact that he named one of his daughters Misa—the acronym for Maintenance of Internal Security Act (MISA) that was misused by Indira Gandhi during the Emergency—because she was born while he was imprisoned under that Act. Another of Laloo's daughters is named Jalebi, a popular sweet.

It would be foolish, however, to view Laloo as merely a person with a sense of humour and as a good communicator. As he has revealed on more occasions than one, he is no simpleton when it comes to high-stake political battles. The ease with which he has managed to engineer defections from other parties—those friendly to him as well as those hostile to him—and keep his governments and Rabri Devi's governments afloat even when they were in a minority in the assembly is testimony to his consummate skills in the murky numbers game that has come to dominate many of India's legislatures. An equally telling indicator of his political acumen was the manner in which he transformed Jagannath Mishra, a former Congress Chief Minister of Bihar, from one of the biggest leaders in the state to someone who was seen as Laloo's lackey even by his own party colleagues.

Laloo has also shown a better appreciation of the compulsions of coalition politics than many other Indian politicians, especially the dictum that there are no permanent friends or enemies in politics. When the RJD was formed in 1997, he was ostracised by many of his own former colleagues in the JD, as well as erstwhile allies in the United Front. In such a situation, many politicians would have become bitter and borne a grudge, but not Laloo, who has displayed a spirit of magnanimity. In this respect, he presents a sharp contrast to another Yadav leader, Mulayam Singh Yadav, who has never forgotten his brushes with his political rivals or opponents, be these in the Congress party (Sonia Gandhi's alleged disrespect towards Amar Singh before she staked her claim to form the Union government in April 1999), or the Bahujan Samaj Party (the Lucknow guest house incident involving the attack on Mayawati by goons allegedly owing allegiance to the Samajwadi Party).

At the same time, Laloo also suffers from a weakness common to many Indian politicians. He has been unable to resist the temptation of flaunting his riches and his power. Thus, his daughter Misa's wedding was celebrated with much pomp and splendour that stood out starkly in an economically backward state. It was reported that his cohorts coerced car dealers to part with their brand-new vehicles for a short period to ensure that the wedding guests could travel in style.

Laloo has also been quite brazen about the manner in which he has patronised criminals and goons. Mohammed Shahabuddin, the RJD MP from Siwan in northern Bihar is notorious in the area as a 'don' who has been accused of engineering the murder of several people including Chandrashekhar, a former President of the students' union at Jawaharlal Nehru University in New Delhi, for daring to organise political opposition to him as part of a Naxalite group. Laloo's own brothers-in-law, Sadhu Yadav and Subhash Yadav, are a law unto themselves in the state and, as in the case of Shahabuddin, the local administration and the police have never taken any action against their strong-arm tactics. To be fair to Laloo, however, it is not as if he is the only politician in Bihar—or indeed in India—to patronise criminals and musclemen. Yet, Laloo and subsequently Rabri Devi have been unable to prevent Bihar from being seen as the most lawless of India's states.

The Samata Party first referred to the RJD's reign as 'jungle raj', an accusation that has subsequently been echoed by many others, including the BJP, the Congress and the CPI, not to mention the media. Laloo once attempted to laugh this away by quoting from a hit Hindi film song of the 1970s—*Chahe koi mujhe junglee kahe, kahne do ji kahta rahe, hum pyaar ke toofanon mein ghire hain, hum pyaar karen* (loosely translated, 'I don't care if anybody calls me a savage, I'm caught up in a whirlwind of love, I just continue to love'). However, when *India Today* magazine organised a conclave in New Delhi and disclosed the results of a survey that ranked Bihar at the bottom of the list of all Indian states in terms of various socio-economic criteria, Laloo got Rabri Devi to walk out of the conclave in protest. Laloo himself stayed on, since he was one of the speakers. In his speech, he argued that Bihar's economic backwardness was due to the discriminatory attitude that New Delhi had adopted towards Bihar since it was ruled by a party hostile to the BJP. Laloo hasn't always bothered to seriously respond to the charge that economic development has been a casualty under the RJD. For instance, there is this story—once again perhaps apocryphal—about a villager complaining to Laloo that the road passing through the village had been potholed for years without anybody bothering to repair it. Laloo is said to have replied that smooth roads would only help those with fancy cars and would actually be a threat to the children and cattle in the village, who might be run over by speeding vehicles.

In his otherwise successful political career, Laloo has once had to face an embarrassing defeat. This was during the 1999 Lok Sabha elections, which Laloo contested from Madhepura, considered a stronghold of the Yadavs and hence of the RJD supremo. The contest was particularly important for Laloo because the man opposing him as the NDA's candidate was his erstwhile colleague in the Janata Dal, Sharad Yadav. Laloo boasted that he would prove Sharad Yadav a mere paper tiger and a person without a mass base. Sharad Yadav, on the other hand, asserted that he would prove he was a taller leader of the Yadavs in Bihar than Laloo. As the campaign progressed, it was evident that the contest would be closer than initially expected. Nevertheless, few people expected Laloo to lose. So much so, that immediately after the polling was over, Sharad Yadav demanded a re-poll alleging massive rigging by RJD supporters. When the Election Commission refused to yield to the demand, Sharad Yadav alleged bias and announced that he would fast unto death unless a re-poll was ordered. The EC went ahead with the counting and Sharad Yadav was ultimately left facing the comic situation of wildly cheering supporters informing him that he could break his fast, since he had won in an election that he had earlier insisted had been rigged!

Nitish Kumar

The two tallest leaders of the Samata Party, Nitish Kumar and George Fernandes, come from different backgrounds, the only common thread being their espousal of the socialist cause. Born in 1951, Nitish cut his political teeth in the JP movement—he was held under the notorious MISA in 1974 and was also jailed during the Emergency. Despite his claims to the contrary, his support base was confined largely to the Kurmis, an intermediate caste that is powerful in his Lok Sabha constituency, Barh. He became an MLA for the first time in 1985, and in 1987 became the President of the Yuva Lok Dal in Bihar. In 1989, when the Janata Dal was formed, he became the Secretary General of the party's Bihar unit. The same year, he was elected to the Lok Sabha for the first time. He has been re-elected on four subsequent occasions from the same Parliamentary constituency.

Nitish Kumar's first stint as Union minister in the V.P. Singh government was a short one—from April to October 1990—when he served as Minister of State for Agriculture. He became all-India General Secretary of the Janata Dal in 1991. He was appointed to the important post of Railway Minister in the second Vajpayee government in 1998. He moved to the Ministry of Surface Transport, then to the Agriculture Ministry. He moved back to the Rail Bhavan in March 2001 after Mamata Banerjee resigned as Railway Minister, holding additional charge of the Railway Ministry while continuing as Agriculture Minister. In July that year, he was relieved of the Agriculture portfolio when Ajit Singh took over as Agriculture Minister. From March 1998 onwards, he has continuously served in the Union Cabinet holding some portfolio or the other, barring the brief period between March 3, 2001—when he had to resign as Union minister to be sworn in as Chief Minister of Bihar—and March 20 when he rejoined the Union government.

One of the most controversial decisions taken by Nitish Kumar as Railway Minister was to reorganise the different railway 'zones' in the country. He decided to break the erstwhile Eastern Railways into three parts, including a large chunk that went into a newly created zone called the East Central Railways headquartered at Hajipur in Bihar. This move, although accompanied by less controversial decisions to create six more railway zones, was opposed by each and every political party in neighbouring West Bengal while being supported by every party in Bihar. Thus, while the CPI(M) and the RJD would act together on many national issues, the two parties found each other on opposite sides of the debate to create the new railway zone. Similarly, the Trinamool Congress headed by Nitish Kumar's predecessor in Rail Bhavan, Mamata Banerjee, staunchly opposed the move to trifurcate the Eastern Railways although both the Trinamool Congress and the

Samata Party were constituents of the NDA. Such indeed were the curious compulsions of coalition politics. At one stage, Mamata had issued veiled threats to quit the NDA unless Vajpayee reversed Nitish's decision but that did not happen. Nitish, on his part, pointed out that the decision to create new railway zones had been taken when Ram Vilas Paswan was Railway Minister and that this decision had not been reversed during Mamata's tenure as head of the Railway Ministry.

The other controversial decision taken by Nitish Kumar was his move to build an 'extension' of an existing railway line to make it run through three Parliamentary constituencies: his own (Barh), that of his party colleague and Union Defence Minister George Fernandes (Nalanda), and that of Union Minister Dr. C.P. Thakur (Patna). The existing railway line, approved by the Planning Commission, currently runs between Fatuah and Islampur. Without obtaining fresh approval from the Planning Commission, Nitish Kumar carried out what was euphemistically described as a 'material modification' to the railway line to ensure that it would now run 123 kilometres from Neora to Daniama, Biharsharif, Barbigha and on to Sheikhpura. Since Neora and Sheikhpura are already connected, the 'modified' railway line is slated to run more or less parallel to an existing railway line. Nitish claimed that he was within his rights as Union Railway Minister to 'modify' the railway line by incurring an additional expenditure of Rs. 255 crore not included in the annual Railway Budget, but his political opponents (as well as estranged MPs belonging to the Samata Party) argued that the Railway Minister had 'abused' his authority to benefit his constituents and those of his colleagues and allies.

Nitish Kumar had earned compliments in February 2002 when his Railway Budget had taken the politically difficult decision to increase passenger fares. His predecessor Mamata Banerjee had not increased passenger fares for two years in succession—a move that was described as 'populist'. In February 2003, however, faced with a 4 per cent drop in passenger earnings, Nitish Kumar took a leaf out of Mamata's book and chose not to touch passenger fares.

George Fernandes

If Nitish Kumar's term as Railway Minister was reasonably controversial, the political career of George Fernandes is replete with so many twists and turns that it is a difficult task to unravel the ideological contradictions that are apparent in his complex personality. Born in 1930 to a poor Christian couple from South Kanara district of the Mangalore region of Karnataka, in his youth Fernandes was sent to a seminary by his father to become a Catholic priest. Not only did he choose not to pursue his theological studies, he became a confirmed socialist after a meeting with Ram Manohar Lohia. The man who would have been a priest became instead a firebrand labour leader and a 'younger brother' of socialist ideologue Madhu Limaye. In 1967, he captured national attention when he beat S.K. Patil—a senior Congress leader—to enter the Lok Sabha for the first time from a Mumbai constituency. Four years later, however, he had to eat humble pie when he not only lost in the 1971 general elections, but forfeited his deposit as the Congress rode the electoral wave generated by the euphoria of the war that year and the creation of Bangladesh. An angry Fernandes swore he would never again contest from Mumbai. He has stuck to that pledge.

He gained national prominence once again in 1974 when, as President of the All India Railwaymen's Federation, he spearheaded the longest-ever strike by workers in the Indian Railways. In fact, the strike was one of the important factors that prompted the imposition of the Emergency. During the strike, he was charged with sedition and attempting to destabilise the Indian state by, among other things, planting dynamite allegedly to blow up railway tracks in what came to be known as the Baroda Dynamite Case. He was jailed towards the fag end of the Emergency and was still in prison when the general elections were conducted in March 1977. He won from Muzaffarpur in Bihar by about 3.5 lakh votes, one of the largest margins of victory at that juncture. Since then, Bihar has served as Fernandes' political home although he has also contested from Bangalore.

As Industry Minister in Morarji Desai's government, George acquired international fame when he decided to throw out two giant multinational corporations from India, Coca-Cola and IBM (formerly International Business Machines), for not adhering to the provisions of the Foreign Exchange Regulation Act (FERA). Yet, during the same period, Fernandes was also accused of unduly favouring the German multinational Siemens by 'forcing' the Indian public sector engineering company, Bharat Heavy Electricals

Limited (BHEL), to enter into a technical collaboration agreement with the German firm. Even though Fernandes insists till today that he remains a socialist at heart, he has become the blue-eyed boy not only of Vajpayee and Advani but also the RSS and organisations affiliated to it. In fact, Fernandes is the only non-RSS, non-Hindu political leader to have featured on the cover of *Panchajanya*. Asked to explain the contradiction between his personal economic ideology and the policies followed by the Vajpayee government, he argues that Narasimha Rao had surrendered India's economic sovereignty to the World Trade Organisation and that successor governments have no choice but to continue along the same path.

Many years earlier, in July 1979, when the Morarji Desai government was teetering on the brink of collapse, Fernandes had made an impassioned speech in the Lok Sabha defending the government during a vote of confidence. Within days, however, he had switched sides and became an equally vociferous supporter of Charan Singh, Desai's rival who deposed him as Prime Minister with the support of the Congress. When asked to explain his sudden turnaround, Fernandes claimed that he was not aware at the time that he was making the speech in Parliament, that many of his close political associates like Madhu Limaye and Biju Patnaik had already decided to ditch Morarji Desai and support Charan Singh instead. When he subsequently learnt about this, he says he was left with the choice of either falling out with his associates or eating his own words. He says he chose the latter, knowing that it was bound to adversely affect his personal credibility.

His ideological somersaults have not been confined to the economic and political spheres. While he was in jail in 1974, he had stayed up all night to write a long diatribe against Indira Gandhi's decision to conduct nuclear tests at Pokhran. 'Should any government discuss such a proposition [meaning, building nuclear weapons] seriously without first taking steps to provide all citizens of the country with food, clothes, shelter, pure drinking water, education and a chance to live a life befitting human beings, such a government can be called nothing but criminal,' Fernandes wrote (in what was later published as a booklet) while describing talk of building a nuclear bomb as so much 'bombast'. Twenty-four years later, after the Vajpayee government had conducted nuclear tests in May 1998, as Union Defence Minister George

Fernandes was to remark that he was proud of the achievements of Indian scientists in making India a nuclear weapons state. His explanation for his about-turn was that there is one aspect of national life that comes above everything else—and that is national security.

One consistent aspect of Fernandes' worldview through the many metamorphoses he has undergone is his dislike for China. At the time of the Pokharan II blasts, he had reportedly stated that India's nuclear programme should not be seen as being aimed primarily against Pakistan and that China was a larger and perhaps more dangerous 'enemy' in India's neighbourhood. After his remarks raised a hue and cry in diplomatic circles, Fernandes clarified that this view had been stated in successive annual reports brought out by India's Ministry of Defence. But Fernandes' views on China may now be undergoing a change following his visit to Beijing as Union Defence Minister in May 2003.

The change in Fernandes' position on civil liberties has not been any less dramatic than the volte face in his views on nuclear disarmament. As a man who has been associated with Amnesty International and the People's Union of Civil Liberties (PUCL), Fernandes had a history of opposing all 'draconian' laws. In fact, he had once stated in Parliament that the only purpose served by laws like TADA was to suppress legitimate trade union activity at the behest of influential business groups. Yet, Fernandes had no compunctions supporting the enactment of POTA. Still, these apparent ideological contradictions pale into insignificance when one considers how Fernandes' views on the communal character of the BJP and the RSS have changed over the years.

Till 1996, Fernandes had consistently opposed the Sangh Parivar. As a matter of fact, an important reason why the Janata Party split in 1979 was his insistence that the two ministers in the Morarji Desai government belonging to the erstwhile Bharatiya Jana Sangh—that is, Foreign Minister Vajpayee and Information and Broadcasting Minister Advani—should give up their 'dual' allegiances since they continued to be members of the RSS although their party (the BJS) had formally merged with the Janata Party. After his decision to ally the Samata Party with the BJP in 1996, George Fernandes was attacked time and again and reminded of his speeches and statements against the BJP and the RSS following the demolition of the Babri masjid in December

1992. Interestingly, even at this stage, Fernandes and his party did not question the characterisation of the RSS and the BJP as communal organisations. They merely argued that in the specific context of Bihar, casteism and corruption were bigger and more immediate dangers than communalism. They had, the argument went, joined hands with the lesser evil to defeat the bigger one.

In the years since then, Fernandes has changed his position even further. Today, he insists that the RSS and the BJP are transformed from what they once were and are no longer communal. The very fact that he—a Christian—has been given such a high position in the BJP-led government and treated with great respect by the RSS and its front organisations is illustrative of how they have changed, he asserts. Perhaps the most telling indicator of how much Fernandes' view of the RSS and BJP has changed over the years is the fact that the Samata Party has remained silent even when other allies of the BJP in the NDA have kicked up a fuss about the big brother trying to 'impose' its agenda on the NDA. Whether it was the Gujarat riots of 2002, the murder of Australian missionary Graham Staines in 2000, or the controversy over the VHP's Ayodhya agitation, the one 'secular' ally of the BJP that has steadfastly refused to criticise the BJP or even the VHP is Fernandes' Samata Party. As a matter of fact, even when individual leaders of the Samata Party like former spokesperson Shambhu Srivastwa had expressed their dissatisfaction with the communal agenda of the Sangh Parivar, the party was quick to dissociate itself from such views.

As Defence Minister, Fernandes took great pains to project an image of being the soldier's man. More than any other minister, he has repeatedly visited *jawans* at the military base located on top of the Siachen glacier—the world's highest battleground and one of the coldest. The same individual who had participated in innumerable anti-war demonstrations all over the world did not find it incongruous to transform himself into an ardent advocate of India's military might. One of his most controversial decisions as Defence Minister was his removal of Chief of Naval Staff Admiral Vishnu Bhagwat. The decision strained relations between the bureaucracy and the military establishment as never before. But Vajpayee and Advani stood steadfastly behind Fernandes on this occasion, as they have on most other occasions. As a matter of fact, as convenor of the NDA, he has revelled in his role as the

Prime Minister's trouble-shooter—rushing to Chennai to placate a recalcitrant Jayalalithaa during the second Vajpayee government, to keeping in regular touch with a sulking Mamata Banerjee.

Usually clad in a cotton *kurta* and *pyjama*, 'socialist' George Fernandes' 'clean' image took a beating like never before when tehelka.com, a news and current affairs website, produced secretly-recorded videotapes in which Fernandes' companion and Samata Party General Secretary Jaya Jaitly was heard discussing defence deals with two journalists posing as arms dealers. What made matters worse was that the videotape had been recorded in Fernandes' official residence. The Tehelka tapes also contained recordings of conversations with the then treasurer of the Samata Party R.K. Jain (who was promptly sacked), bragging about how he could swing defence contracts because of his proximity to Fernandes. The Defence Minister's explanation of how a man like Jain could become party treasurer was not particularly convincing. Soon after the Tehelka tapes (that also depicted the then BJP president Bangaru Laxman receiving wads of currency notes) were made public in March 2001, Fernandes put in his papers. He had insisted that he wanted to resign before he actually did but that Vajpayee did not wish to accept his resignation letter.

The government appointed a one-man inquiry commission headed by a retired judge of the Supreme Court to inquire into the revelations made in the Tehelka tapes, but well before the commission could arrive at a conclusion Fernandes was reinducted into the Union Cabinet later that year. Soon thereafter, in December, the Comptroller and Auditor General of India published a report alleging that the Indian Army had purchased coffins from the US for those killed during the Kargil war at highly inflated prices. The coffins had arrived well after the conflagration was over. The scandal, dubbed 'Coffingate', also dented Fernandes' image as a 'clean' minister who took care to uphold the interests of ordinary soldiers. After he returned to the Cabinet, the entire Opposition took a decision not to recognise Fernandes as Defence Minister and boycotted proceedings of Parliament that involved interacting with him. This decision was broken as late as May 2003 by a few Congress MPs including Jagmeet Singh Brar—who went on to apologise for his actions but was nevertheless reprimanded and removed from his position as party whip. Other Congress MPs who had violated the party's directive to boycott Fernandes in

Parliament included Madhya Pradesh Chief Minister Digvijay Singh's brother Laxman Singh and former Union minister K.P. Singhdeo.

Ram Vilas Paswan

When Ram Vilas Paswan first entered parliamentary politics in 1977, he seemed to be a politician with a bright future. He made his presence felt in the first Lok Sabha elections he contested from Hajipur, setting a new record for the highest margin of victory in any Lok Sabha constituency up to that point—4.24 lakh votes. He was to subsequently break his own record by winning from the same constituency in 1989 by 5.05 lakh votes, a record later broken by Narasimha Rao when he won from Nandyal in Andhra Pradesh by over 6 lakh votes in a by-election.

By the late 1980s, Paswan had not only made a habit of winning Lok Sabha elections by huge margins, he had also acquired a profile well beyond his constituency or even his state. He had started being recognised as an important leader of the dalits even in areas like western Uttar Pradesh and the outskirts of Delhi. So much so that the Dalit Panthers—an organisation floated by some of Paswan's supporters—were able to organise fairly impressive rallies in western UP. The extent of Paswan's fan following can be gauged from one of the slogans often raised at these rallies: *Upar aasmaan, neeche Paswan* (there's the sky above and on the earth there's Paswan). Analysts saw in him the first dalit leader after Jagjivan Ram (who was also from Bihar) to have a support base extending across a wide swathe of the Hindi heartland.

Right up to the mid-1990s, Paswan remained on a steadily climbing political career graph. In 1988, he became the General Secretary of the newly formed Janata Dal and a Secretary of the National Front that the JD had forged with the left parties and some regional parties. When the National Front led by V.P. Singh came to power in 1989, Paswan—who was barely 43 at the time— became a Cabinet Minister handling the Labour and Welfare portfolios. When the United Front came to power in 1996, Paswan not only got the prestigious Railways portfolio, he was also designated the leader of the Lok Sabha. This unusual situation of the Prime Minister not being the leader of the lower house came about because both H.D. Deve Gowda and I.K. Gujral, his successor as Prime Minister, were members of the Rajya Sabha and not the Lok Sabha.

Even if the position came to Paswan partly by default, it was an indication of his political stature.

Since then, Paswan's career seems to have stagnated, while his politics have been perceived as crassly opportunist. By the time of the 1998 elections, the Janata Dal in Bihar had badly disintegrated. Having survived the exit of people like George Fernandes and Nitish Kumar to form the Samata Party in 1994, the Janata Dal in 1998 was struggling to cope with the serious damage done by Laloo Yadav's decision to split the party and form the RJD in 1997. In 1998, therefore, Paswan and Sharad Yadav were the only leaders of any consequence in the JD in Bihar and of these Sharad Yadav was hardly a person with a huge mass base in the state. Not surprisingly, the JD fared very poorly in the 1998 Lok Sabha elections in Bihar. Though Paswan comfortably retained his own seat, no other candidate of the JD won from Bihar. Paswan could, however, draw some consolation from the fact that his party had polled close to 9 per cent of the total votes despite having fought on its own.

When the second Vajpayee government faced its crucial vote of confidence in April 1999, after the AIADMK had withdrawn support, Paswan was among those who spoke strongly against the 'communal' BJP and voted against the government. Yet, when the 1999 Lok Sabha elections were held barely six months later, the JD led by Paswan and Sharad Yadav had made common cause with the NDA and formally joined the Front. Like the Samata Party, Paswan was now rather unconvincingly trying to argue that his alliance with the BJP was not opportunistic but based on the principle of fighting corruption and jungle raj in Bihar.

Paswan's ability to attract as much as 9 per cent of votes in Bihar may have amounted to little in the 1998 elections, but in 1999, this proved a decisive advantage for the NDA against the RJD–Congress–Left alliance. The NDA won as many as 40 of the 54 seats in Bihar. The Samata Party and the Janata Dal, which had fought under the common symbol of the Janata Dal (United), won 16 seats. The RJD was reduced to just seven seats. Paswan's reward for his role in bringing about this scenario came in the form of the coveted Telecommunications portfolio in the Union Cabinet.

As Telecommunications Minister, Paswan lost much of his earlier image as a dynamic leader. Instead, he came to be seen as a man more interested in doling out favours to cronies by setting up various official bodies to accommodate them. Speculation also started mounting about whether it was just a coincidence that some of his policy decisions as Minister suited the business interests of powerful industrial houses.

In September 2001, Paswan was ultimately relieved of the Telecom portfolio in the face of mounting criticism by the media and others. He was assigned the Coal and Mines portfolio, which was seen as a distinct demotion from his earlier job. Already smarting under this 'insult', Paswan realised that his future within the NDA was dim when the BJP formed a coalition government with the BSP in Uttar Pradesh in March 2002. It was clear to most observers that BSP leader Mayawati would use her new-found clout with the BJP to try and cut Paswan to size. Given the fact that Paswan, like Mayawati, is a dalit leader, the latter was keen to ensure that Paswan's political stature did not reach a point where he could become a threat to her mass base in UP or become a rival dalit leader at the national level.

However, Paswan could not be seen to be exiting the NDA because of a political or ego clash with another dalit leader. He, therefore, needed a credible reason for his exit. The communal riots in Gujarat provided him with just the excuse he was looking for. He joined various other allies of the BJP in asking for the resignation of Gujarat Chief Minister Narendra Modi for his dubious role in the manner in which the state government dealt with the riots, but unlike the others quit the NDA in April 2003 when the BJP refused to sack Modi.

Paswan has formed his own party, the Lok Jan Shakti Party. As the 1998 and 1999 Lok Sabha elections have taught him, he can be a formidable force in Bihar as part of an alliance, but can hope to win very little contesting without any allies. It is a foregone conclusion, therefore, that Paswan will have to forge alliances with other parties in Bihar. Which way he turns is another matter.

Chapter 4

Small is Beautiful

Rooted in Region

The Telugu Desam Party: NTR, the Populist; Chandrababu Naidu, the Opportunist

Andhra Pradesh, formed in 1953 out of the Telugu-speaking areas of the erstwhile Madras province, is the largest of the four states of south India. For nearly three decades after the state came into existence, it was ruled by the Congress party. Between November 1956 and January 1983, the month Nandamuri Taraka Rama Rao (better known as NTR) was first sworn in as Chief Minister, the state had seen eight Congress chief ministers and one governor. One Chief Minister, Bhavanam Venkatram, remained in his position for only seven months.

Venting his anger against the Congress headed by Indira Gandhi, NTR, who founded the Telugu Desam Party (TDP) after having acted in some 300 films, wrote the following in the first manifesto of the party that he drafted: 'The 35 years of Congress misrule has created such a mess that the Telugus have to hang their heads in shame. Despite the overwhelming majority of the ruling party in the state assembly, political instability has become the order of the day. The enthronement of four and the dethronement of three chief ministers within the span of five years is an indication of the sorry state of affairs. The elected representatives of the people have become mere pawns....'.

The way the Congress functioned under both Indira Gandhi and Rajiv Gandhi was to a great extent responsible for NTR's meteoric rise to power and his successful projection of himself and his party as upholders of the 'self-respect' of the Telugu-speaking people. Former President Neelam Sanjiva Reddy ruled Andhra Pradesh as Chief Minister from November 1956 till June 1964, after whom K. Brahmananda Reddy ascended the seat of power in Hyderabad. He was rudely removed by the Congress high command in September 1971 to make way for P.V. Narasimha Rao, who eventually went on to become India's first Prime Minister from the south in June 1991. During successive Congress governments, all important decisions in the state—including the transfer of middle-level officials—were referred to New Delhi. In fact, the Congress in Andhra Pradesh was deeply divided into at least three major factions led by Narasimha Rao, M. Chenna Reddy and T. Anjaiah (all of whom served as CMs at different points of time).

Another factor that surely must have contributed to the Andhra Pradesh electorate's disenchantment with New Delhi was the fact that under Congress rule and even thereafter, Andhra Pradesh remained the least developed of the four southern states. A study conducted by the Planning Commission had estimated that the state had slipped from 8th position in 1961 to 14th position in 1978. Though the literacy rate in the state went up from under 30 per cent in 1981 to just over 45 per cent 10 years later, Andhra Pradesh still lagged behind other southern states in most respects.

Besides exploiting the resentment born out of slow economic development, NTR was also able to channelise the attempt by the Kammas (whose standing in Andhra Pradesh is not dissimilar to that of the Yadavs in UP or Bihar) to grab the reins of power from the Brahmins and the Reddys who had traditionally dominated Andhra Pradesh politics. The dominance of the Reddy community can be gauged from the fact that approximately one out of four members of the legislative assembly belonged to this caste.

In the 1983 assembly elections, the newly formed TDP swept to power winning 203 seats out of the 294 seats in the assembly with over 46 per cent of the popular vote. The Congress won only 60 seats despite retaining more than one-third of the total votes cast. NTR stormed to power as Chief Minister within barely nine months of having formed his own political party. The TDP was the main Opposition party in the 8th Lok Sabha (1984–89) during Rajiv Gandhi's tenure as Prime Minister and the party joined the National Front led by V.P. Singh after he became Prime Minister in December 1989.

There are a number of similarities between the TDP and parties like the DMK and the AIADMK in Tamil Nadu. One was the whipping up of sub-national sentiments. The second related to the fact that like NTR, almost all the important leaders of the DMK and the AIADMK have been associated with films. NTR's was a household name in Andhra and having spent all his life in show-business, he excelled in using all forms of media to project himself as the saviour of Telugu pride, a just ruler who was a *sanyasi* (ascetic) as well. He portrayed himself as someone who desired nothing but the welfare of the poor, having accumulated enough riches of his own thanks to his flourishing career in cinema. He played out on celluloid the characters of Krishna, Karna, Bhishma, Rama—just about everybody's favourite Hindu mythological figures.

As a political leader, NTR traversed the length and breadth of his state in an adorned vehicle he called the *Chaitanya ratham* (Chaitanya's chariot) long before L.K. Advani's *rath yatra* aboard a similar vehicle. Above all, NTR assured voters that they would get rice for Rs. 2 a kg through the ration shops and children in schools would be provided free mid-day meals. Like Tamil Nadu's Dravidian parties, NTR asserted time and again that the Union of India had discriminated against states like Andhra Pradesh. Right through the early 1980s, NTR aligned himself and his party with all those who supported his theme of the economic neglect of the states by the central government in New Delhi. Yet, the public rhetoric of NTR was different in one important respect from that of the Dravidian parties. He never brought up the issue of secession from the Union. On the contrary, NTR said he wanted to integrate Andhra Pradesh with the Indian nation. At the same time, he also stood for local autonomy.

The Congress used every trick at its command to oust NTR's party from power in Andhra Pradesh. In fact, NTR was elected to his post no less than four times in 11 years, first in January 1983, then in September 1984, again in March 1985 and for the fourth and last time, in December 1994. On each occasion the Congress tried to remove him, he emerged stronger. But there was one problem with the charismatic NTR: his populism was not entirely sustainable in economic terms. The Rs. 2-a-kilo rice scheme as well as the mid-day meal scheme drained the state's exchequer. The TDP lost the assembly elections in March 1989 and the party's vote share came down by almost 10 per cent to under 37 per cent—the

TDP had 74 MLAs against 181 owing allegiance to the Congress in the legislative assembly.

The TDP under NTR was, however, able to bounce back five years later in the November 1994 elections winning a record 213 seats in the 292-member assembly. NTR's charisma faded somewhat towards the end of his life and his fourth and last term as Chief Minister. A widower, his decision to marry his official biographer Lakshmi Parvathi was disapproved of by many, notably his son-in-law N. Chandrababu Naidu with whom his relationship was often strained. Naidu made no secret of the fact that he was most unhappy that NTR, by then over the age of 70, had chosen to marry a once-married woman who was then half his age. And, he was upset by NTR's opposition to his own marriage to his eldest daughter. Even if NTR's mass appeal was on the wane at that time, his death on account of a heart attack while in office, on January 18, 1996, ensured that he would remain a martyr in the minds of many in Andhra Pradesh.

NTR was succeeded as Chief Minister by his astute 45-year-old son-in-law. Chandrababu Naidu (or Babu as he is often called) apparently lacked his father-in-law's appeal but he turned out to be a durable politician. By the turn of the century, in a period of less than five years, Naidu had acquired a high profile in India and abroad. He became one of the country's best-known Chief Ministers the world over thanks to his propagation of the virtues of information technology and his self-projected image as the Chief Executive Officer of Andhra Pradesh. Naidu has evidently come a long way from the days when he was known as an activist of the Youth Congress. Public memory is short and few remember Naidu as the person who had stood staunchly behind Sanjay Gandhi well after the infamous 19-month Emergency.

Born on April 20, 1950 in Naravaripally in Chittoor district, Chandrababu Naidu became an MLA for the first time in 1978 from the Chandragiri constituency from the same district on a Congress ticket. He served for a while as Director of the state's Small Industries Development Corporation. He even served as a Minister in the state government headed by K. Vijayabhaskar Reddy. Between 1980 and 1983, he held various portfolios in the state government including Archives, Cinematography, Technical Education, Animal Husbandry, Dairy Development, Public Libraries and Minor Irrigation. He also served as head of a state government body (Karshak Parishad) looking after farmers' interests, before he quit the Congress and joined the recently founded TDP. He initially served as General Secretary of the party. In 1989, Naidu was elected from Kuppam and was re-elected in 1994 from the same constituency by a handsome margin of around 57,000 votes. Thereafter, he was entrusted with the crucial portfolio of Finance and Revenue by NTR.

Naidu and Lakshmi Parvathi perceived each other as competitors for NTR's attention and Naidu was not averse to hijacking the party and splitting it to quash Lakshmi Parvathi's political ambitions. A month after NTR's death, in February 1996, Lakshmi Parvathi bitterly complained in an interview to a journalist: 'I will not sleep till I teach Naidu a lesson' (*Outlook*, March 13, 1996). She—like NTR's son Haribabu, who later parted ways with Naidu in 1998—proved no match at all for Naidu's masterly political skills. Both were eventually consigned to oblivion and remained outside the public eye.

Naidu's political stature rose really rapidly after he became the Convenor of the centre-left United Front, the 13-party coalition that came to power in New Delhi in the wake of the May 1996 general elections. After the fall of the UF government headed by I.K. Gujral and after the outcome of the February 1998 elections (that saw the second Vajpayee government comprising the NDA coming to power) became known, the computer-savvy politician from Andhra Pradesh demonstrated his astute abilities yet again. He dropped the United Front like a proverbial hot potato and instructed the 12 MPs belonging to the TDP in the 12th Lok Sabha to abstain from voting against the second Vajpayee government in the motion of confidence adopted by the Lok Sabha. For his support, which was critical for the new government to survive, Vajpayee appointed Naidu's nominee, G.M.C. Balayogi as the Speaker of the Lok Sabha—in fact, Balayogi became the first (and thus far, the only) dalit to hold this important post. (Balayogi died on March 3, 2002 in a helicopter crash.)

A former Congressman himself, Naidu persuasively argued that the very existence of the TDP depended on it continuing to oppose the Congress. Naidu's opportunism paid him rich political dividends. Although he realised that he risked alienating nearly 20 per cent of the voters of his state—mainly Muslims and Christians—he took a calculated risk and aligned the TDP with the BJP after ditching the communists. In the September–October 1999 Lok Sabha elections that were conducted simultaneously with the assembly elections in Andhra Pradesh, the TDP was able to return to power albeit with a reduced majority. The Congress improved its performance but not enough to threaten Naidu's government.

The media has often painted Naidu as the most 'forward-looking' among India's Chief Ministers. He too has been adept at managing the media and his visit to the US to meet, among others, Bill Gates, was widely publicised. He has successfully sought to place Hyderabad on the 'netlas' of the world and set up a high-profile educational institution, the Indian School of Business. He has also headed the first state government in India that successfully obtained a huge Rs. 2,200 crore loan from the World Bank despite the economic sanctions imposed against India in the immediate aftermath of the nuclear tests conducted by the Vajpayee government in May 1998.

Unlike his one-time mentor and father-in-law, Naidu has apparently shunned the economic populism that was associated with NTR. He has cut subsidies by increasing power tariffs, water rates and bus fares. The state government has reduced subsidies on the distribution of rice and increased taxes on professionals and traders. While Naidu says he wants to make Andhra Pradesh the fastest-growing and economically most advanced state in India, he, more than anyone else, surely knows he has a long way to go. Like many other states, the Andhra Pradesh government remains steeped in debt and teeters periodically on the brink of bankruptcy. Even as Hyderabad glitters and glows and promises to match Bangalore as the infotech capital of the country, if not the world, the rural population in the state remains vulnerable to epidemics and penurious farmers commit suicide when they are unable to repay loans. Extremist groups, including the People's War (earlier the People's War Group), a Naxalite outfit, continue to indulge in acts of violence with impunity. Naxalite groups are active in many parts of the state, including Telengana, which has a long history of violent insurgency from the pre-independence period when peasants rose in arms against the Nizam of Hyderabad's mercenaries as well as the British.

Naidu, like other Chief Ministers of Andhra Pradesh, has equivocated on the issue of dealing with the Naxalites. Attempts at initiating a dialogue with the People's War have been interspersed with periods in which the state government cracks down hard on the Naxalites and the latter respond similarly. During one such phase, in October 2003, Naidu came perilously close to being assassinated by a landmine planted along a route he was travelling. The mine exploded as his car passed over it, killing his driver and seriously injuring one of his ministers who was travelling with him. Naidu himself suffered relatively minor injuries. His subsequent decision to call for early elections to the state assembly was perceived as an attempt to cash in on the 'sympathy' factor.

While asking for enhanced central financial assistance to tackle the activities of Naxalite groups in Andhra Pradesh, Naidu has strongly opposed the Vajpayee government's position on carving out smaller states from big ones. He certainly does not want Telengana to become a separate state. Naidu and the TDP have also opposed the position of the BJP hardliners on the Ayodhya issue. As recently as August 3, 2003, Naidu reiterated his party's position that it was in favour of the Supreme Court resolving the dispute over the construction of the Ram temple. Earlier, in February 2003, he had reportedly said exactly the same thing during his meetings in New Delhi with BJP leaders, including Vajpayee and Advani.

Naidu has time and again affirmed the TDP's support for the BJP-led NDA government but emphasised that its support is contingent on the government sticking to the Common Minimum Programme of the NDA. For instance, a resolution passed by the party's *mahanadu* (or convention) held at Tirupati in May 2002 stated that the TDP would 'not continue its support blindly' if the BJP introduced its own agenda which was different from the agenda of the NDA.

While occasionally asserting its 'independence' from the BJP on issues like Ayodhya and while underlining the fact that the TDP is not a part of the government or the NDA, Naidu has not been averse to arm-twisting the Union government to ensure that more funds flow from New Delhi to Hyderabad. He successfully lobbied with the Vajpayee government to ensure that more money was given to the state for various natural calamities and to ensure that the public sector Food Corporation of India procured large quantities of rice from farmers in the state. The state government was at the forefront while representing before the Eleventh Finance Commission that it should not be 'discriminated' against for having 'performed' well—that is, by bringing down the rate of growth of population and by improving education and health care facilities in the state. The TDP was also among the political parties that had vehemently opposed the decision of the then Finance Minister Yashwant Sinha to increase the officially administered prices of fertilisers in his budget speech delivered in February 2002.

On one occasion it appeared as if the ideological rift between the TDP and the NDA government would widen. This was during the communal riots in Gujarat between March and May 2002. Less than six weeks after the communal riots had begun in Gujarat, on April 11, 2002, the TDP formally called for the ouster of Narendra Modi. At a meeting of the politbureau of the TDP—the only common aspect of the communist parties and the TDP is the name of their highest decision-making bodies—the party adopted a resolution asking the BJP for an immediate change in leadership in Gujarat. The TDP was severely critical of Modi's administration and leadership and said the Gujarat government had 'failed miserably' in discharging its responsibilities in an impartial and effective manner. The party was also critical of the state government not providing adequate relief to the victims of the communal riots. It said that there had been 'erosion of public confidence' because of the Gujarat government's failure to provide 'just governance' and that it was important at that juncture for the state to provide a 'healing touch'. Asserting that secularism was one of the 'fundamental tenets' of the TDP, the party resolution did not stop at criticising the Modi government but added that the communal riots in Gujarat had 'tarnished India's image' as a liberal, modern and secular society.

It was reported in newspapers that Naidu had been told in confidence by Vajpayee that Modi would be replaced in Gujarat and it was this 'assurance' that emboldened the TDP to attack the BJP, using the kind of strong language that it did, language that would normally have been associated with a party of the Opposition and not an ally of the ruling coalition. It was further claimed that Vajpayee's statement at the Goa conclave of the BJP in support of Narendra Modi came as a surprise to Naidu. While it is difficult to verify if there is any grain of truth in these speculative reports in the media, what is a fact is that the 28 MPs of the TDP abstained from voting in the Lok Sabha on May 1, 2002 after a

16-hour debate during which the Opposition unsuccessfully sought to pass a motion castigating the government for the communal riots in Gujarat.

Even on the eve of the Gujarat assembly elections that took place in December 2002 in a communally charged atmosphere, on November 17 the TDP publicly backed the order of the Election Commission banning religious rallies from being held in Gujarat. The party categorically stated: 'religion and politics should not be mixed'. Naidu, presumably with an eye towards the Muslim voter, would periodically seek to underline his party's secular character and would emphasise the fact that the TDP was only supporting the BJP-led NDA government 'from outside', that the party was not a part of the coalition government and that it was not interested in the perquisites of power. The TDP was also at the forefront of the protests in Parliament over the issue of imposing a ban on cow slaughter. Naidu reportedly told Vajpayee that not only was the issue not part of the NDA's agenda, it certainly could not be considered a priority for the country.

What Naidu's supporters claimed was his 'independent' position was predictably perceived by his political opponents as a hypocritical stand. Like NTR, Naidu has travelled extensively across Andhra Pradesh and has sought to temper his pro-rich image (played up by his political opponents) by initiating schemes like the Janmabhoomi scheme: a programme of community participation to build projects in rural areas. His critics complain that Naidu's policies have widened the gap between the rich and the poor, that he is too opportunistic to be a reliable ally, and that he believes in no ideology other than the ideology of power. His supporters, on the other hand, have contended that more than most other Indian politicians, Naidu has understood the importance of modern technology and its potential to radically change the lives of the majority of Indians, especially those living in rural areas. He is a zealous economic liberaliser pleading for higher inflows of foreign investment in the poorest state in south India. Will the real Chandrababu Naidu stand up?

Friend or Foe?—Changing Equations in Tamil Nadu

Tamil Nadu can lay claim to at least one unique feature in Indian politics—it is the only state in which no national party has ever been in power in the last three-and-a-half decades, to be precise, since 1967. Nothing can illustrate the lasting impact of the Dravidian movement in the state better than this simple fact. Yet, ironically, each of the several pillars on which that movement was built has been dismantled by parties that are offshoots of that very same Dravidian movement. The pillars of the movement were anti-Brahminism, an antipathy to the north of India and its pre-dominant language, Hindi, atheism, rationalism—none of these is in evidence today in the inheritors of the Dravidian movement, so much so that Jayalalithaa of the AIADMK is herself a Brahmin. Also, her government has been one jump ahead of even the BJP in pushing through a law ostensibly aimed at checking forcible reli-gious conversions. As for the hostility to the north, both the DMK and the AIADMK have, since 1998, had alliances with the BJP, a party that was till a few years back almost entirely confined to north India and was seen as the most ardent champion of a uni-tary nation in which the hegemony of Hindus and Hindi was taken as an evident truth.

Tamil Nadu had more political parties represented in the 13th Lok Sabha than any other Indian state. The 39 MPs that the state sent to the Lok Sabha in the 1999 general elections belonged to as many as eight political parties. (West Bengal had representatives of seven parties in the Lok Sabha.) In the 1998 elections, there were nine parties representing these 39 Lok Sabha constituencies in Tamil Nadu. Despite this proliferation of parties, the state has not had a coalition government since its inception. Even when alliances have won assembly elections, it has invariably been the case that the leading party in the winning alliance has secured a majority of the assembly seats on its own, enabling it to form a government without having to accommodate the junior partners.

Till as late as 1998, the only national parties with any presence in Tamil Nadu were the Congress, the CPI and the CPI(M). The BJP had not won even a state assembly seat, let alone a Lok Sabha constituency in the state. Even the three national parties that did have a presence in the state were in no position to contest on their own and had to align themselves to one of the two main Dravidian parties—the DMK or the AIADMK—to be able to make any head-way in terms of winning a sizeable number of seats in either the assembly or the Lok Sabha. In 1998, Jayalalithaa surprised every-body by tying up with the BJP for the Lok Sabha elections. Political pundits, opinion polls and exit polls all suggested that the experiment would be a failure. The results proved all of them completely wrong, with the AIADMK-led alliance winning 36 of the 39 seats in the state. Besides the AIADMK and the BJP, the coalition included a clutch of smaller parties—many of which had come into being only in the 1990s—like the Marumalarchi Dravida Munnetra Kazhagam (MDMK), the Pattali Makkal Katchi (PMK), the Tamizhaga Rajiv Congress (TRC) and the Janata Party. The BJP had finally managed to register its presence in India's southernmost state and as subsequent events indicated, it was there to stay. Even today, the BJP would be hard put to win a single seat on its own strength, but since the 1998 general elections the party has made a significant breakthrough—it is no longer considered an 'untouchable' in Tamil Nadu politics.

The reasons for the dominance of the AIADMK and the DMK in Tamil Nadu politics since 1967 lie in a socio-political movement whose origins can be traced back to the Justice Party formed in 1916 in what was then the Madras Presidency of the British Raj. The Justice Party was formed by P. Thyagarayar as a platform for the area's non-Brahmin social elite. In the first general elections in British India held in 1920, the Justice Party won a landslide victory in the Madras Presidency, bagging 63 of the 98 seats. It remained in power in the provincial government for the next 17 years, advocating 'social justice and equality' for all segments of society. E.V. Ramaswamy Naicker (EVR), who was a member of the Indian National Congress, found himself agreeing with the ideology of the Justice Party. He joined the party and started the Non-Brahmin Self-Respect Movement in 1925. In 1944, by which time Naicker was the leader of the party, he renamed the party the Dravida Kazhagam (the Dravidian Federation) and demanded the establishment of an independent state called Dravidasthan. The Dravidian movement had begun.

To the anti-Brahmin thrust of the Justice Party was now added an ideology that defined itself in racial terms. The Brahmins—and the people of north India—were identified with the Aryans, who were invaders, while the non-Brahmins were portrayed as Dravidians and the true descendents of those who had built the Indus Valley civilisation. So virulent was the Justice Party's opposition to 'the north' and its leaders, that the party saw August 15, 1947 as a 'black day', a day on which the British rulers while leaving

Small is Beautiful | 231

the country had left them at the mercy of the north. The Justice Party had demanded that if India were to be granted independence, the south should be carved out as a separate Dravidasthan.

The antipathy to 'Aryans' also extended to hostility to their religion—Hinduism—which was seen as a religion that had sanctified caste oppression, by the Brahmins in particular. Thus, the Dravida Kazhagam campaigned actively against religion, indeed even against the concept of God. The most prominent religious texts of the Hindus—the Ramayana and the Gita—were denounced as part of an Aryan conspiracy to enslave the Dravidians. The DK also launched a campaign for *sua-maryadai kalyanam* (self-respect marriages), which were weddings bereft of any of the Sankritised rituals and hence, of Hindu priests. This again was an attempt to deny the Brahmin any pride of place in the everyday lives of people.

The next plank of the Dravidian movement was a logical corollary of these moves. Language became the central focus of the movement. Tamil was eulogised as the oldest 'living' language in the world and the most 'evolved' of all languages, while Sanskrit and Hindi were presented as impositions by the aggressors from the north. It was this, in fact, that provided the real cutting edge for the Dravidian movement in electoral politics. The Congress, being an all-India party, could hardly have accepted such a hardline linguistic stance. As the party governing India, it was also committed to the attempt to make Hindi a link language nationally. It could, perhaps, have shown greater sensitivity towards the suspicions of the Tamils about the attempts to 'impose' Hindi, but it seems to have failed to understand the depth of feelings on this issue.

The language issue was to become the catalyst that precipitated the decline of the Congress in Tamil Nadu and the ascendance of the Dravidian parties. But before that could happen, EVR himself had lost the leadership of the movement. A group of young DK leaders, led by C.N. Annadurai and including Muthuvel Karunanidhi (both were to later become Chief Ministers of the state) left the party over personal differences with EVR. They formed the Dravida Munnetra Kazhagam (DMK) in 1949 which remains to this day one of the two main Dravidian parties in Tamil Nadu.

The first anti-Hindi agitation was launched by EVR in 1952, but it was the agitations of 1965 and 1968 that really assumed a mass character. Both were spearheaded by the DMK. In 1965, the Congress was still in power at the centre and in what was then the state of Madras. Its government in Madras cracked down on the agitation, arresting thousands of agitators. This played no small part in the DMK's victory in the 1967 assembly elections—one in which Congress leader K. Kamaraj had boasted that he would win without having to get up from bed. As soon as it came to power, with 'Anna' as the Chief Minister, the DMK government released all those jailed for the anti-Hindi agitation. The very next year, in 1968, another massive agitation against the centre's attempts to impose Hindi was launched, this time with a sympathetic government running the state. The DMK warned the Congress government in New Delhi that any attempt to impose Hindi would only strengthen the demand for a separate Dravida Nadu (the land of the Dravidians). A group of students leading the anti-Hindi agitation told Prime Minister Indira Gandhi when she met them that she should choose between Hindi and the unity of the nation.

An interesting paradox of Tamil Nadu politics is the fact that in a state in which language has been the major political issue, at least three important political personalities trace their origins from outside the state. M.G. Ramachandran, or MGR as he was popularly called, whose iconic status remains unchallenged, was a Malayalee of Sri Lankan origin. Jayalalithaa, though a Tamil, comes from a family of Brahmins from Mysore. Finally, Rajnikanth is a Marathi who spent the early part of his adult life as a bus conductor in Bangalore before moving to Madras and Tamil films. Throughout MGR's tenure as Chief Minister, the DMK cadre would try to make an issue of the fact that he was not a Tamil, though the leadership would never publicly raise the issue. Yet, the campaign cut no ice with the electorate. Equally, the AIADMK cadre's attempts to counter this by insinuating that Karunanidhi himself was actually a Telugu and not a Tamil left the voters cold.

Having ridden to power on the strength of a movement that was explicitly anti-Brahmin, anti-religion and anti-north, the DMK gradually diluted each of these agendas. This process picked up pace after the formation of the AIADMK in 1972, when MGR broke away from the DMK. He preferred to focus on projecting the image of the AIADMK as a party of the downtrodden. The groundwork for this had, ironically, already been done by his erstwhile mentor M. Karunanidhi, who had written the scripts for most of the films that MGR had starred in. As a conscious political strategy that has perhaps no parallel anywhere in the world, the DMK had systematically used the medium of cinema to project its leaders and its message. MGR had been the prime vehicle for this strategy. In film after film, he appeared either as someone from the working classes or as a benefactor of the working classes—fishermen, rickshaw pullers, landless labourers and so on. Karunanidhi's acknowledged prowess in writing powerful scripts had ensured that MGR was seen as a 'messiah of the people' even before he floated his own political party.

MGR made the most of this image both as the leader of a political party and as Chief Minister of Tamil Nadu after 1977. He also made a conscious effort to specifically target women as a vote bank, coining the term *tai kulam* (literally, the family of mothers) while referring to them. Arguably the single-most important measure he undertook as Chief Minister was to introduce the mid-day meal scheme in the state. Under the scheme, every child who attended primary school was entitled to a meal in school at the expense of the state. There were additional incentives for girl children in particular. The idea was to provide an economic incentive for poor families to send their children to school rather than to work for a living. To begin with, most economic commentators were aghast at the scheme, derogatorily describing it as 'populist' and arguing that it would place an unsustainable burden on the state's coffers. More than a decade later, even the World Bank, one of the most virulent critics of the mid-day meal scheme when it was introduced, was forced to admit that it had indeed been a major success and more and more states sought to emulate the scheme.

There were other schemes as well that buttressed MGR's image as a messiah of the masses. One scheme was to motorise rickshaws in Chennai (as the city of Madras came to be called) which did away with almost all the physical labour involved in plying such vehicles. The other scheme was to construct *pucca* houses for fisherfolk. These schemes became so popular that MGR came to be known as *puratchi thalaivar* (revolutionary leader) and the AIADMK was to stay in power from 1977 to 1989. Many outside Tamil Nadu have simplistically perceived MGR's popularity to be primarily a consequence of his popularity as a film personality. The reality was clearly more complex.

MGR's tenure also saw an interesting innovation being brought into the manner in which electoral alliances were struck. After the creation of the AIADMK, the politics of Tamil Nadu had followed a pattern—the Congress, which by this time had acknowledged that it could not come to power on its own in Tamil Nadu, realised that it could play a decisive role by aligning with either the DMK or the AIADMK. The two Dravidian parties also recognised that the Congress could tilt the electoral balance even if it couldn't do very much on its own. MGR, however, carried this logic a step further. In 1984, when general elections and state assembly elections were held simultaneously, the AIADMK agreed to let the Congress contest as many as 26 of the 39 Lok Sabha constituencies in Tamil Nadu. In the assembly elections, however, the Congress contested only 72 of the 234 seats, while AIADMK candidates contested from as many as 155 constituencies.

This was a radically different approach from what had been practiced all over India till then. Traditionally, the share of seats contested by alliance partners remained more or less the same irrespective of which level of government the elections were for, and would depend on the relative strength of the partners. What MGR's 'two-third, one-third' formula sought to formalise was the understanding that while the Congress was undoubtedly the only partner in the alliance making a bid for power in New Delhi, in the state the AIADMK would be the one that would form the government if the alliance was voted to power. In effect, MGR was telling Rajiv Gandhi, the then Prime Minister and leader of the Congress, 'you keep New Delhi, but leave Madras to me'.

The formula may not have become a precursor for coalition arrangements in other parts of the country, but it was a significant acknowledgement by both the Congress and the AIADMK of their relative strengths and weaknesses. The Tamil Nadu electorate had in 1980 played its part in bringing about this recognition. That year, roughly four months had separated the Lok Sabha elections that saw Indira Gandhi returning to power and the state assembly elections. In both the elections, the Congress was in alliance with the DMK, while the AIADMK contested with the left parties as partners. The Congress–DMK alliance swept the Lok Sabha seats, winning in 37 of the state's 39 constituencies. Just three months later, the same alliance fared miserably in the assembly elections, winning just 68 of the 234 seats, while the AIADMK-led alliance won in 156, or two-thirds of the assembly constituencies.

By the time of the 1984 elections, Jayalalithaa was already one of the most important leaders of the AIADMK. Her rise in the party structure had been meteoric thanks to the patronage of MGR. Jayalalithaa formally joined the AIADMK only in June 1982, but the following year MGR made her the party's propaganda secretary. The move was stiffly resisted by senior AIADMK leaders, but MGR refused to budge. As propaganda secretary, Jayalalithaa was increasingly calling the shots in the absence of MGR, who was often bed-ridden or hospitalised. The victory in the 1984 assembly elections, in which Jayalalithaa was the main campaigner, further strengthened her position in the party.

When MGR ultimately died of a prolonged illness in 1987, the battle for succession in the AIADMK had boiled down to MGR's widow Janaki Ramachandran and Jayalalithaa. Senior AIADMK leaders recognised that they could not take on Jayalalithaa on their own, since MGR in his lifetime had made it amply clear that he saw her as his second-in-command. In Janaki, however, they thought they had found a person who could make the most of the 'sympathy wave' that was bound to follow MGR's death. Jayalalithaa was not willing to give up her claims to the MGR legacy without a fight. She tried to portray herself as the Chief Mourner at MGR's funeral, fighting to clamber on to the vehicle carrying his body, only to be rudely pushed away by party leaders who felt they no longer had to play second fiddle to her. Janaki became Chief Minister and leader of the AIADMK legislature party, while Jayalalithaa was left out in the cold.

The unsavoury infighting that followed saw the Election Commission 'freezing' the AIADMK's election symbol of 'two leaves'. The resultant confusion helped the DMK come to power in the 1989 elections, winning 155 of the 234 assembly seats. Both factions of the AIADMK—the AIADMK(JR) and the AIADMK(JL)—were humiliated. Despite the humiliation, however, Jayalalithaa had scored an important political point. While the Janaki faction managed to win just one assembly seat, the Jayalalithaa faction won 27. The debate over which of the two women in MGR's life was his political heir had been settled.

Jayalalithaa emerged as the undisputed leader of the AIADMK, with her supporters anointing her *puratchi thalaivi* in an obvious allusion to the sobriquet conferred on MGR. Janaki faded into oblivion and most other AIADMK leaders who had supported her swallowed their pride and pleaded with Jayalalithaa to let them back into the party. Most importantly, the party had got back its election symbol, the two leaves by which voters all over the state recognised the AIADMK candidate on the ballot papers. The impact was immediate. In the Lok Sabha elections of December 1989, the AIADMK–Congress alliance made an almost clean sweep, winning all but one of the 39 seats in the state. The AIADMK itself won all the 11 seats it contested.

In the 1991 assembly elections, the party's performance was even more impressive. This time, the AIADMK–Congress alliance won in 224 of the state's 234 assembly constituencies, a performance that has not been bettered before or since by any alliance in Tamil Nadu. The DMK was left with just two MLAs in the new assembly, one of them the deposed Chief Minister, M. Karunanidhi.

The period since then has seen fairly dramatic developments in Tamil Nadu politics. Jayalalithaa's first term as Chief Minister saw her adopt an imperious style of functioning that has now become her trademark. Stories abound of how even senior ministers and party leaders would not be allowed to sit at the same level as 'amma' on a dais during public meetings. They would also publicly touch her feet and make it a point to sing praises of the *puratchi thalaivi* at every opportunity. The state's bureaucracy too learned how not to offend the Chief Minister in any way, since she could be extremely humiliating. Jayalalithaa was also perceived as a corrupt leader, one who used power to confer undue favours on those close to her, including, above all, Sasikala Natarajan, a woman who had almost overnight become her close confidante and was seen as an extra-constitutional authority in the state. A southern industrialist, Rajarathinam, who emerged as a take-over tycoon out of the blue, was also seen as a frontman for Jayalalithaa.

The incident that did most damage to Jayalalithaa's reputation, however, was the marriage of Sasikala's son in 1995. The streets of Chennai through which the wedding procession was to pass were decorated in a manner reminiscent of royal weddings of yore. Plantain trees in hundreds were cut down in various parts of the state and planted along the route of the procession and the state machinery was blatantly used for the organisation of the lavish ceremony. Many residents of Chennai who witnessed the extravaganza first-hand were shocked at the pomp and show, but the DMK made sure this sense of shock was not confined to

Chennai alone. Sun TV, the most popular private TV channel in the state and one that was owned by DMK leader the late Murasoli Maran's family, spared no effort in ensuring that the pictures of this outrageous splurge reached every corner of the state.

As the 1996 Lok Sabha and state assembly elections drew near, it was becoming increasingly clear that Jayalalithaa's charisma had begun to fade and the people were disillusioned with her government and fed up with her autocratic and corrupt ways. The Congress leadership in the state, having seen the writing on the wall, tried to persuade the central leadership of the party that striking an alliance with the AIADMK for the elections would prove suicidal. P.V. Narasimha Rao, who was then Prime Minister and Party President, however, insisted on an electoral pact with Jayalalithaa. This led to a revolt in the state unit, with almost the entire local leadership quitting the Congress to form the Tamil Maanila Congress (TMC). The TMC then struck an alliance with the DMK. In the assembly elections that followed, the DMK–TMC alliance romped to victory, winning 212 of the 234 seats. Tamil Nadu had rejected Jayalalithaa almost as decisively as it had voted her to power just five years earlier.

Among the first things the DMK government (the TMC did not join the government, but supported it from outside) did after assuming power was to get the state administration to institute a slew of corruption cases against Jayalalithaa, charging her with impropriety in land allotments, import of coal, foreign exchange transactions and so on. Special courts were set up to deal with these cases on the grounds that they involved the larger public interest and could not be allowed to proceed at the languid pace at which cases normally proceed in India's logjammed judicial system. At the behest of the DMK government, police officials raided her residence at Poes Garden. The media was treated to detailed accounts of the number of sarees she possessed, not to mention pairs of shoes and jewellery. These were also shown on the Sun channel and she was sought to be derogatorily portrayed as an Indian version of Imelda Marcos, the late Filipino dictator's wife with a reputation for a fondness for the good things in life.

Jayalalithaa was arrested and put in jail. This, as later events proved, was an error of judgement on the part of the DMK government. As with Indira Gandhi in the immediate aftermath of the Emergency, public anger against Jayalalithaa soon turned to sympathy for a woman who was seen as being hounded by her political opponents. Jayalalithaa contributed to this by portraying herself as a defenceless woman who was being made to suffer in jail like an ordinary criminal as part of a politically motivated witch-hunt. However, she also realised that mere public sympathy would not be enough to undo the damage that the cases against her could do. For that, she would need access to the levers of power.

In 1998, she took the plunge by striking an alliance with the BJP and a host of smaller parties that had sprung up in the state during the mid-1990s. Most analysts and political pundits were dismissive of this alliance. The BJP, it was pointed out, was rather weak in the state, having won an assembly seat in Tamil Nadu for the first time in 1996. The other partners in the AIADMK-led alliance included fledgling regional parties like the PMK, the MDMK and the TRC, none of which were expected to make a major contribution to the cause of the alliance. Opinion polls and exit polls conducted before and during the 1998 Lok Sabha elections seemed to bear out the prognostication of political analysts that the AIADMK-led alliance would not perform well. The results, as already mentioned, proved the pollsters and the pundits completely wrong.

In retrospect, a series of bomb blasts in Coimbatore on February 14, 1998, the day L.K. Advani was to address an election meeting in that city, appear to have played a significant role in catalysing the switch in voter preference towards the AIADMK and the BJP. The blasts, which were the handiwork of an organisation of Muslim fundamentalists, served the AIADMK–BJP alliance at two different levels. At one level, they helped the BJP polarise voters along communal lines not only in Coimbatore, but also in other parts of the state where it had had till that stage a marginal presence. At another level, it helped the alliance portray the DMK government as being inept and reluctant to deal with the menace of terrorism.

The AIADMK with 18 MPs turned out to be the single-largest ally of the BJP in the second Vajpayee government that came to power in New Delhi in March 1998. Jayalalithaa used her clout from the word go—she delayed providing a formal letter of support to the Vajpayee government till almost the final hour. Then, she demanded that her nominees (including Dr. Subramaniam Swamy of the Janata Party who had, ironically, earlier been responsible for instituting a number of criminal cases against her) be allocated key portfolios in the Union government. As a matter of fact, she even demanded that Dr. Swamy be made Finance Minister, a demand that was rejected by Vajpayee and his supporters (including Jaswant Singh who had gone to Chennai to negotiate with Jayalalithaa). The AIADMK General Secretary did, however, succeed in having her party's MPs as Union Law Minister and Minister of State for Finance.

What became evident in no time at all was that these Ministers had a single-point agenda: to ensure that the criminal cases against their leader were either dropped or placed in cold storage. Minister of State for Finance, R.K. Kumar, who was in charge of Revenue, Banking and Insurance, did his bit for his leader by transferring a number of income tax officers. However, Jayalalithaa asked him to resign in May 1998. The ostensible reason was that his health was rather poor. It was another matter that speculation was rife that the real reason for his removal was that Jayalalithaa felt he hadn't done what she had expected of him. Another AIADMK leader, K.M.R. Janarthanan, who was earlier Minister of State for Personnel and Grievances in the Vajpayee government, later got Kumar's job in the Finance Ministry. Another AIADMK Minister, Sedapatti Muttiah, who held the Surface Transport portfolio, had to quit within weeks of his becoming Minister for different reasons—a court hearing the corruption cases against AIADMK leaders passed strictures against Muttiah for allegedly acquiring assets disproportionate to his known sources of income.

Law Minister M. Thambidurai transferred large numbers of legal officers in Tamil Nadu. Jayalalithaa's supporters wanted to transfer some of the criminal cases pending against her from the special courts in Chennai to the Supreme Court in New Delhi. The gameplan was to try and ensure that the state government would not remain the prosecuting authority. Jayalalithaa's lawyers also sought to convince the apex court of the country that the criminal cases against her had been politically motivated and should, therefore, be dropped and the special courts be disbanded.

The Supreme Court did not accept the AIADMK's plea that the cases against Jayalalithaa should be moved from Chennai to New

Delhi. She and her supporters then stepped up their demands for the dismissal of the Karunanidhi-led DMK government in Tamil Nadu under Article 356 of the Constitution of India. The Coimbatore blasts and the DMK's alleged softness towards the perpetrators of that crime were presented as the reason for invoking Article 356. Vajpayee and other senior leaders of the Union government refused to play ball. Having always protested against the misuse of Article 356 by Union governments led by the Congress, they argued, they could not now turn around and apply the same constitutional provision on the flimsiest of excuses to dismiss a democratically elected state government. The friction between the BJP and the AIADMK that was to ultimately result in the fall of Vajpayee's government in April 1999 had reached a critical point.

The dispute between Tamil Nadu and Karnataka over the sharing of the waters of the River Cauvery (also spelt Kaveri) became another issue on which the Vajpayee government found itself facing pressure from Jayalalithaa. For the BJP, the issue was decidedly ticklish. On the one hand, Karnataka was a state in which the BJP had made significant inroads in recent years. The party also believed it could split the ruling Janata Dal in Karnataka and further enhance its presence in the state. The Vajpayee government could not, therefore, adopt a stand on the sensitive issue of apportioning the waters of the Cauvery (especially during the summer months) that would be seen to be against Karnataka's interests. On the other hand, taking a position that was entirely supportive of Karnataka would nip in the bud any prospects the BJP had of making headway in Tamil Nadu, a state in which the party had only just managed to register its presence. Jayalalithaa also spotted in the controversy an opportunity to embarrass an ally who had refused to give in to all her demands, while simultaneously scoring political points against her main political opponent in the state, the DMK and its Chief Minister M. Karunanidhi. She, therefore, adopted a hardline stance, accusing the centre of being deliberately partisan towards Karnataka and the DMK state government of not doing enough to protect the interests of the farmers of Tamil Nadu's Cauvery delta.

Jayalalithaa also took exception to the dismissal of Chief of the Navy, Admiral Vishnu Bhagwat. This was a clear sign that the AIADMK leader was increasingly distancing herself from the

Vajpayee government, since Fernandes had often acted as an emissary between the Prime Minister and her, and was seen as having a better rapport with her than many others in the Vajpayee government.

It was a matter of time before the rapidly deteriorating relationship between the AIADMK and the BJP finally fell apart. Matters came to a head in April 1998, ultimately leading to the fall of the government. However, Jayalalithaa's gameplan did not succeed fully. The Congress' attempt to form an alternative government failed. The AIADMK supremo did not have the friendly government in New Delhi that she had so desperately tried to bring about. The criminal cases instituted against her continued to do the rounds of courtrooms.

In the September–October 1999 Lok Sabha elections, political alliances in Tamil Nadu had changed drastically from what they were a year earlier. The BJP was now in an alliance with the DMK, as were smaller parties like the PMK, the MDMK and the TRC. The TMC, earlier the DMK's partner, refused to have anything to do with an alliance that included the BJP. On the other hand, the Congress and the left parties being in alliance with the AIADMK meant that the TMC could not be part of that front either. After all, the very existence of the TMC was due to the fact that its leaders had left the Congress because of its tie-up with the AIADMK. Thus, the TMC was left out in the cold, having to contest more or less on its own, though it had an alliance with the Puthizha Tamizhagam (PT), a party that was trying to build itself as a representative of the dalits, much like the BSP in Uttar Pradesh.

The results of the 1999 elections in Tamil Nadu were not quite as decisive as had been the trend in the state. The DMK-led NDA won 26 of the 39 seats, but the AIADMK-led alliance also managed to win 13 seats. The TMC, not surprisingly, drew a blank. In 2000, Jayalalithaa became the first Chief Minister to be convicted and sentenced in a criminal case of corruption. The case involved allotment of land by a state government undertaking, the Tamil Nadu Small Industries Corporation (TANSI), allegedly at throwaway prices, to a company associated with the Chief Minister. Jayalalithaa's lawyers appealed against the special court's decision in the High Court but before the court decided on the appeal, assembly elections were notified to take place in May 2001. It was generally believed that the AIADMK would be able to defeat the

DMK in the elections. Jayalalithaa becoming the next Chief Minister of Tamil Nadu seemed an almost foregone conclusion. She filed her nomination as a contestant from four separate constituencies—Krishnagiri, Pudukottai, Andipatti and Bhuvanagiri—but her nomination papers were rejected in all four constituencies.

In Krishnagiri and Andipatti, her nomination papers were rejected on the ground that she had been convicted in a criminal case and hence could not contest elections under Section 8(3) of the Representation of People Act, 1951. Jayalalithaa's lawyers argued that since she had filed an appeal against her conviction in a higher court, she should be allowed to contest the elections. The returning officer of the constituency from where she had filed her nomination, on the other hand, ruled that as a convicted individual she was not eligible to contest the elections under the provisions of the Act. The fact that she had filed an appeal against her conviction, the returning officers pointed out, did not imply that the conviction was no longer valid. In Bhuvanagiri and Pudukottai, the returning officers rejected her nomination on the ground that Section 37(7)(b) of the Act prohibited a person from contesting elections from more than two constituencies simultaneously.

The dispute on Section 8(3) went to the Supreme Court, which stated that during an election, the ruling of the returning officer was final. Any appeal against the officer's order could be made only after the elections had been concluded. Jayalalithaa was thus unable to contest the assembly elections that saw the AIADMK emerging as the ruling party—the party on its own won 132 seats and with its allies (the Congress, the left parties and the PMK) won 173 seats in the 234-member assembly. Jayalalithaa was sworn in as Chief Minister because the law provided for a person who was not an elected member of the assembly to become a Chief Minister provided such a person was elected to the assembly within a period of six months. The decision of Tamil Nadu Governor Fatima Beevi to swear Jayalalithaa in as Chief Minister despite her conviction drew a lot of flak not just from the DMK and the BJP, but also from several legal luminaries and political leaders. The critics pointed out that as the first woman to become a judge of the Supreme Court, Beevi should have known better than to interpret the law in the manner in which she did. So much so, that the Governor was eventually asked by the Union government to put in her papers. However, Jayalalithaa continued as Chief Minister even after Beevi was replaced.

Jayalalithaa nevertheless needed to get elected to the state assembly by November 2001, when the six-month deadline would run out. Unfortunately for her, the High Court did not decide on her appeal against her conviction in the TANSI land case by that time. Jayalalithaa appealed to the Supreme Court to ask the High Court to expedite its decision, but the highest court of the land refused to intervene. Hence, she had no choice but to step down as Chief Minister. The question upper-most in the minds of most political analysts was, whom would she nominate to act as stand-in Chief Minister. In her characteristically imperious style, Jayalalithaa deliberately chose O. Panneerselvam, a first-time MLA to succeed her. Not only was Panneerselvam too junior to harbour any ambitions of his own, he was also a 'dependable' stand-in because he was a protégé of T.T.V. Dinakaran, the nephew of Jayalalithaa's confidante Sasikala and a member of the Lok Sabha.

Soon thereafter, the Chennai High Court upheld Jayalalithaa's appeal against her conviction in the TANSI land case, thereby clearing the way for her to become Chief Minister once again. She was subsequently elected to the assembly from Andipatti. Soon after she returned as Chief Minister in March 2002, Jayalalithaa left nobody in doubt that the DMK and others in the Opposition would have to pay for the 'wrongs' done to her during the DMK's stint in power. A slew of corruption cases were filed against Karunanidhi and some of those who had been ministers in his government. Officials who were seen as close to the DMK were transferred en masse. The extent to which Jayalalithaa's quest for 'revenge' would go became clear when policemen arrested Karunanidhi from his home in the middle of the night. The DMK alleged that the septuagenarian leader had been manhandled by policemen and Sun TV repeatedly broadcast shots of Karunanidhi being bodily lifted to the waiting police vehicle while crying out for help. Karunanidhi would not spend too much time in jail, but the drama had made its point—Jayalalithaa would not pull punches in her battle against the DMK and its top leadership.

Any doubts on this score were settled when the AIADMK used its majority in the assembly to push through legislation which prohibited the same person from being a member of the legislative assembly and holding the post of mayor at the same time. It was no secret that the law was aimed specifically at M.K. Stalin, Karunanidhi's son and heir apparent. Stalin was at that time Mayor of Chennai as well as an MLA. Despite the passage of the law, Stalin refused to resign from either post. He was then disqualified from holding the post of Mayor.

Subsequently, in July 2002, the Tamil Nadu government threw another bombshell when it had V. Gopalaswamy (who prefers to be known as Vaiko) arrested under POTA on the ground that he had made speeches supportive of the banned LTTE. The MDMK leader had been among the most vociferous in supporting the enactment of POTA, in particular arguing strongly in Parliament that it had enough safeguards to prevent its misuse for partisan political purposes. (Vaiko was released from jail on bail a year-and-a-half later in February 2004.)

At the time of Karunanidhi's arrest, together with two of his party colleagues who were central ministers, the Union Law Minister Arun Jaitley had argued that a grave constitutional impropriety had been committed. A state government, he insisted, could not arrest central ministers without the permission of the Union government. The governor of Tamil Nadu was asked for a report on the law and order situation in the state, the underlying threat being that the central government could invoke the provisions of Article 356 to dismiss the state government. When Vaiko was arrested, on the other hand, the BJP restricted itself to making statements to the effect that the use of POTA may have been inappropriate in this case. The reason for the strangely subdued tone of the protest was not very hard to find. Jayalalithaa had by the time of Vaiko's arrest started making overtures to the BJP, clearly indicating that she was willing to forget the acrimony of the past and build new bridges with the Vajpayee government.

The message became increasingly louder thereafter. One of the clearest signals was when Jayalalithaa, during a press conference in Delhi, 'volunteered' the information that she was against Sonia Gandhi becoming Prime Minister because she was born an Italian. Considering that the press conference was taking place after a meeting convened by the Prime Minister to discuss the Cauvery waters dispute between Tamil Nadu and Karnataka, Jayalalithaa's unsolicited comment on the Congress President's Italian origins acquired considerable political significance. In December 2002, Jayalalithaa was the only Chief Minister whose party was not a member of the NDA to be invited to the swearing-in ceremony of Gujarat Chief Minister Narendra

Modi and the only one to attend it. The AIADMK supremo also gladdened the BJP by enacting a law in Tamil Nadu ostensibly aimed at preventing 'forcible' religious conversions. Modi approvingly cited Tamil Nadu's example and promised to follow suit by enacting a similar law in Gujarat.

While these moves by Jayalalithaa were signs of a growing closeness between the AIADMK and the Vajpayee government, they were also a telling indicator of how drastically 'Dravidian' politics had changed over time. The AIADMK today is indistinguishable in its ideology (and to a large extent so is the DMK) from any of the other mainstream parties in India. The anti-Brahminical thrust, the shunning of ritual and religion, the demonisation of the north of India are at best fast-fading memories.

This perhaps also explains the fragmentation in Tamil Nadu's polity in recent years. The reasons for the formation of each of the many new parties in the state may vary, but ideology certainly doesn't appear to be the motive force. The MDMK, for instance, was formed because Vaiko, who was one of the most prominent young leaders in the DMK, could see that the rise of Stalin under Karunanidhi's patronage made his progress within the party hierarchy extremely unlikely. The PMK arose as a party restricted to espousing the cause of the Vanniyars, an intermediate caste group accounting for a significant part of the population in some of the northern districts of Tamil Nadu. The PT has emerged as a party specifically focusing on dalits, though it is yet to make much headway. In the heyday of the Dravidian movement, these were all groups who saw their aspirations find expression within the Dravidian fold.

At the same time as these small groups have been breaking away, the DMK and the AIADMK have been trying to extend their influence beyond their traditional vote banks to groups like the Brahmins. Interestingly, the beginning of a similar phenomenon is discernible in the caste-polarised polity of states like Uttar Pradesh and Bihar, where the SP, BSP and RJD are all attempting to woo voters from the upper castes as well.

Biju Janata Dal: Naveen Patnaik's Political Initiation

Any account of the Biju Janata Dal (BJD)—named after the late Biju Patnaik, political stalwart of Orissa, freedom fighter, Chief

Minister, daredevil pilot and Union Steel Minister, among other things—has to begin with his second son Naveen Patnaik. Naveen Patnaik was by any reckoning the most unlikely successor to Biju Patnaik. It seems the first person who was chosen to succeed Biju-babu was his eldest son, Prem, a businessman with interests in the paper industry. He refused. Gita Mehta, Biju Patnaik's only daughter, is married to publisher Sonny Mehta and divides her time between New York, London and Delhi. She was also said to be not particularly keen on becoming a politician and, almost by default, the mantle of Biju-babu's political legacy fell on his younger, unmarried son, Naveen.

To many who had known Naveen, his decision to leave the rarefied comfort of his Aurangzeb Road house in New Delhi for Aska, a dusty township north-west of Behrampore (the closest airport, Bhubaneshwar, is a three-hour drive away) to contest the Lok Sabha elections came as a bit of a surprise. Till 1997, Naveen Patnaik was better known for his parties than his party work, for his connections with socialites than his socialist ideology. Naveen's friends were among the rich and the famous, his social and intellectual pursuits more jet-set cosmopolitan than grassroots provincial. His friends and acquaintances include Rolling Stone Mick Jagger whom he met in 1970, Martand Singh of INTACH (Indian National Trust for Art and Cultural Heritage) and the Rajmata of Jaipur, to name just a few. Jagger and Jerry Hall had invited him to stay at their chateau in France. Yet, Naveen Patnaik invariably claims he is appalled by the appellation of 'socialite' tagged on to him.

Admittedly, Naveen Patnaik had no experience of either politics or social work. Until his election in 1997, he had never visited Aska, although he does remember going once in the 1960s to a neighbouring town, Chhattarpur, for a Congress party session that his father was attending. When he contested the by-election for the Aska Parliamentary seat in June 1997, he could barely speak his mother tongue and his campaign speech comprised a single sentence—'Mothers, sisters and brothers please vote for me'—delivered in hastily-learnt Oriya. This limitation hardly affected the electoral verdict. He won by a huge margin of some 76,000 votes and became an MP in the 11th Lok Sabha. His political rivals attributed his victory to feudal instincts running deep among the electorate and the so-called 'sympathy factor'. Naveen Patnaik himself cited the love of the people of his constituency for his father as a major factor in his electoral success.

Within six months of Naveen Patnaik's election as MP from Aska, on December 15, 1997, the Janata Dal in Orissa split: 29 out of 43 legislators left the party to form a new political entity under the stewardship of Naveen Patnaik. The chief architect of the rebellion was Dilip Ray, who had served as Union Minister of State for Food Processing in the United Front government. The split was justified on the ground that it had become 'impossible' for the new group to cohabit with the United Front in Delhi, which was then being supported by the Congress, whereas the group was staunchly opposed to the Congress in the state. Soon thereafter, the Biju Janata Dal (BJD) came into being as an independent electoral entity. Two of the four MPs of the JD in Orissa joined the new party and the BJD went on to form an alliance in the state with the BJP that had, incidentally, not won a single seat in Orissa in the 1996 Lok Sabha elections.

As for his party's alliance with the BJP, Naveen Patnaik said his principal aim was to fortify anti-Congress forces in Orissa. He told *Frontline* magazine that the voters of Orissa had 'rejected the corrupt Congress Government'. He added, 'Ours is a secular party. We have built up an alliance with the BJP with the primary objective of removing the corrupt Congress from power in the state.' The victory of BJD candidates, he said, had 'vindicated our contention that our party is the real inheritor' of Biju Patnaik's legacy. He said the BJD had entered into a seat-sharing adjustment with the BJP but did not necessarily agree with every aspect of the BJP's agenda: An objective reading of the politics of Orissa would suggest that the BJD had recognised the writing on the wall and was acting before it was too late.

The BJP had been a growing political force in the state, though it had not yet reached a stage where its presence could be electorally felt. There was a growing feeling within the erstwhile Janata Dal in Orissa that the BJP's growing influence was eroding its vote base to a level where the Congress might become invincible. The tie-up with the BJP was thus an attempt to consolidate the anti-Congress vote. For the BJP too the alliance made sense. While it might over time have dislodged the Janata Dal or its successor as the main challenge to the Congress in Orissa, here was an opportunity to fast-forward the process.

In the 1998 elections, Naveen Patnaik was re-elected to the Lok Sabha from Aska. Out of the 21 seats from Orissa, the BJD obtained nine, the BJP seven while the Congress was left with the remaining five seats. The rise of the BJD–BJP combine in Orissa saw the simultaneous decimation of the Janata Dal and its left allies together with the decline of the Congress. Enfeebled by the December 1997 split, the JD saw a large-scale desertion of party workers and suffered a funds crunch. The party's sole star candidate, former Union Minister for Tourism and Parliamentary Affairs Srikant Jena, finished third in Kendrapara, a key coastal constituency that was hitherto considered a 'safe' seat for the JD. Jena secured only 91,565 votes against the BJD candidate's 2.82 lakh votes, while the Congress came a close second with 2.74 lakh votes.

If the JD was wiped out, the Congress was severely battered. Having won 17 of the 21 Parliamentary seats in the state in 1996, the Congress was swept aside by an anti-incumbency wave. Only twice in the past had the Congress fared worse—in 1977, when it won four seats, and in 1989, when it won three. Three campaign tours by Sonia Gandhi did not have much of an impact in electoral terms. The BJP won its first Parliamentary seats from Orissa in 1998 when it won seven of the nine seats it contested, mainly from western and northern Orissa. The BJD won nine of the 12 seats it contested and most of these were in coastal Orissa. Significantly, the BJD–BJP combine made inroads into Congress strongholds in constituencies with a high proportion of tribals and dalits.

Congress leaders in Orissa claimed that the outcome of the 1998 Lok Sabha elections was not a referendum on the performance of the state government and J.B. Patnaik dismissed calls for his resignation. Some Congress leaders, however, admitted in private that a strong anti-establishment mood combined with the Janata Dal's obliteration led to a consolidation of BJD–BJP votes. Others blamed the infighting in the Congress. Dissident leaders claimed that the party fared badly because voters were disenchanted with J.B. Patnaik's alleged misrule and nepotism: they pointed to the fact that his wife, son-in-law and relatives all held positions of power.

After the poor performance of the Congress in the Lok Sabha elections, in February 1999, the party's leadership decided to replace J.B. Patnaik as Chief Minister with a tribal, Giridhar Gamang, who had earlier served as Union minister. (Patnaik, incidentally, was one of the longest-serving Chief Ministers in the country, having headed the state government for 13 years over three terms.) The position of the Congress in Orissa continued to deteriorate rapidly. In the September–October 1999 Lok Sabha elections, the BJD–BJP combine won 19 out of the 21 Parliamentary seats in the state—the Congress was left with only two MPs from Orissa.

In the assembly elections of February 2000, the BJD–BJP combine wrested power from the Congress in Orissa by forming the government in Bhubaneswar. On March 5, 2000, Naveen Patnaik was sworn in as the new Chief Minister of the state—the date of the swearing-in is significant as it is the birth anniversary of the late Biju Patnaik. Capitalising on the strong anti-incumbency sentiments prevailing in the state, the BJD–BJP combine secured a two-thirds majority in the 147-member assembly, virtually repeating its performance in the 1999 Lok Sabha elections. The BJD contested 84 assembly seats and won 68; the BJP won 38 of the 63 seats it contested. The Congress, which had 81 members in the earlier assembly, suffered a serious setback winning only 26 seats. The BJD–BJP coalition won most of the seats in western and southern Orissa.

Within the BJD, however, Naveen Patnaik has perpetually been kept on his toes by internal rivalry and squabbles. In most cases, the challenge to his leadership or his decisions has come from a group of leaders who were perceived as being very close to Biju Patnaik while he was alive and who clearly resent Naveen Patnaik's attempts to sideline them and gain unquestioned command over the BJD. These individuals include Bijoy Mohapatra, Nalini Mohanty and Dilip Ray. Thus far, Naveen Patnaik has been successful in warding off challenges to him from within the BJD. He has even been able to expel these three leaders without the party splitting down the middle, as seemed possible at one stage. One reason for his success, it appears, is the fact that he has taken on his detractors within the party sequentially rather than at one go. Another could be the fact that most BJD politicians would face a TINA (There Is No Alternative) factor. If they were to leave the BJD, their only option would be to either join hands with the Congress, a party they have opposed throughout their political careers, or risk facing marginalisation in the state's politics. Whatever the reason, the BJD has survived more or less intact under Patnaik. Whether his marginalisation—and in some cases expulsion—of senior leaders costs the BJD dear at the hustings remains to be seen.

Patnaik has also periodically had to deal with friction between his party and its ally, the BJP. For instance, in October 2001, a problem arose for his government following a sudden spurt in the influx of refugees from Bangladesh following the assumption of power by the Bangladesh National Party (BNP) government in Dhaka. There were tensions between Bangladeshi refugees and local tribals in the Raigada district. The tribals claimed the state government was not evicting illegal migrants from their lands. In November, there were clashes between tribals and Bengali settlers and three tribals died in police firing. There were also instances of deportation of alleged infiltrators from Bangladesh who were accused of spying and gathering sensitive information on defence installations like the missile testing range at Chandipur in Balasore district. The state government's Welfare Minister Mangala Kisan said that after thorough investigations, a number of Bangladeshi citizens had been booked under the Foreigners Act. He told the state assembly that a total number of 2,854 infiltrators had been identified in the districts of Sambalpur, Bhadrak, Jagatsinghpur, Malkangiri, Kendrapara and Nabarangpur, and that 392 of them had been deported to Bangladesh with the help of the Union government.

These developments caused a strain in relations between the BJD and the BJP. Spokespersons of both parties attacked each other at public press conferences. While a section of the state's BJP leaders took up cudgels on behalf of the Bengali-speaking settlers in Raigada, the BJD in turn accused its coalition partner of double standards. BJD Secretary General Dr. Damodar Rout pointed out that while the BJP had been agitating for deportation of infiltrators from Assam and West Bengal, it was opposing their deportation from Orissa. BJP spokesperson Raj Kishore Das and party MP Anadi Sahu, however, claimed after the party's two-day state executive committee meeting that the Bengali-speaking individuals being deported were refugees who had come to the state in the 1960s and were not infiltrators. Political analysts saw the tensions between the two coalition partners as a consequence of the fact that while the BJP had a support base among the Bangladeshi refugees and settlers, the BJD had the support of tribals who lived in the same areas in Orissa's Nabarangpur and Malkangiri districts.

On March 16, 2002, activists of the Vishwa Hindu Parishad and Bajrang Dal stormed the Orissa assembly building, smashing the window-panes of the Chief Minister's office. The VHP and Bajrang Dal goons ransacked the assembly complex, protesting against remarks allegedly made against the two organisations by certain MLAs. The protesters, including a number of women, had been agitating outside the main gate of the assembly. Subsequently, some of them managed to get past two police cordons, entered the assembly building complex and went on a spree of destruction shouting 'Jai Shri Ram' and 'Naveen Patnaik *murdabad*'. Sporting head-bands bearing the names of the VHP and the Bajrang Dal, the protesters hurled stones, broke flower pots, tore out name plates of ministers in the assembly library complex, and pulled out fire extinguishers from the walls and hurled them into the garden. The mayhem continued for roughly 20 minutes. The protesters could have wreaked more havoc but were prevented from entering the lobby of the assembly by security personnel who had by then bolted the doors.

Besides checking dissension within his party and the alliance, Naveen Patnaik has a long way to go before he is able to improve the economic condition of the majority of the people living in Orissa. The state has been and remains one of the most backward in the country, as the starvation deaths in the state in 2001 so starkly highlighted. What does not help is that, perhaps on account of his upbringing and his association with the well-off, Naveen Patnaik continues to be perceived as a member of the elite and an individual who has remained aloof from the people of his pathetically poor state.

Trinamool Congress: Mamata the Maverick

To talk about the Trinamool Congress party in West Bengal without talking about its colourful leader Mamata Banerjee is almost impossible. Born on January 5, 1955, to lower-middle class parents, the late Promileswar Banerjee and Gayatri Banerjee, Mamata was the second of eight children, six sons and two daughters. While she has preferred to remain single, her brothers are all married and run small businesses of their own. Her father had opposed British rule as a supporter of the Congress party. He died soon after Mamata completed her school-leaving examinations.

After joining Jogamaya Devi College in Kolkata, she started a unit of the Chhatra Parishad (the students' wing of the Congress party) to confront the existing students' union and the communist parties. Mamata became an active supporter of the Congress when the violent Naxalite movement (of left extremists) was at its height during the late 1960s and early 1970s.

Right through her childhood and youth, Mamata had to struggle hard to overcome economic hardship—she presumably got used to a spartan lifestyle at that stage of her life, a lifestyle that she would flaunt many years later as a Union Minister in New Delhi. During her years in college, she earned around Rs. 150 a month giving tuition to four or five school-going children. Besides, she did all kinds of odd jobs so that she could complete her studies without imposing any additional financial burden on her family. She worked as a part-time assistant in a state government milk depot earning Rs. 60 a month. She also worked as a part-time teacher in several local schools and was reportedly even instrumental in founding a school.

It was in the mid-1970s that Mamata found a supporter and mentor in Subrata Mukherjee, who was a Minister in Siddhartha Shankar Ray's cabinet and also a leader of the Chhatra Parishad. As President of the South Calcutta (Kolkata) District Congress Committee, Subrata Mukherjee displayed faith in Mamata's political skills and made her Secretary of the committee, a position she held from 1978 to 1981. Through the 1970s, she also held the posts of General Secretary, Mahila Congress(I), West Bengal. Subrata Mukherjee then entrusted her with overseeing accommodation arrangements for Rajiv Gandhi at the plenary session of the All India Congress Committee held in Calcutta in 1983. This, incidentally, was the last AICC session presided over by Indira Gandhi who was then Prime Minister and Congress President while Rajiv Gandhi was one of the General Secretaries of the party. Mamata's work evidently did not escape the attention of Rajiv Gandhi for when her name was proposed as the Congress candidate for the Lok Sabha seat at Jadavpur (in south Kolkata) in 1984, he was quick to recollect her name and promptly gave the green signal.

That year, two Congress stalwarts from West Bengal, Professor Debi Prasad Chattopadhyay (who had served as a Union Minister in Indira Gandhi's government) and Saugata Roy, had both refused to contest from Jadavpur, which was considered to be a stronghold of the Marxists. Subrata Mukherjee proposed Mamata Banerjee's name and she ended up creating history in the first election she contested. Mamata was elected to the 8th Lok Sabha by defeating CPI(M) stalwart, Somnath Chatterjee, by a margin of nearly 20,000 votes.

From the mid-1980s onwards, Mamata held a number of positions in New Delhi while continuing to maintain close contact with her supporters in Kolkata. By 1990, she had become President of the Youth Congress in West Bengal. On August 16 that year, she survived what she claimed was a near-fatal attack on her by goons supporting the CPI(M). The following year, in May 1991, she was re-elected to the 10th Lok Sabha for a second term. Between 1991 and 1993, for the first time, she served as a Union Minister in New Delhi in the P.V. Narasimha Rao government.

In the April–May 1996 elections, she was elected yet again to the Lok Sabha. The ensuing months saw her party, the Congress, supporting the centre-left coalition government of the United Front. The fact that the UF government was supported by the CPI(M) made Mamata most uncomfortable. After all, her fight in West Bengal was first and foremost against the ruling Left Front in the state. By this time, she had begun openly rebelling against the official leadership of the Congress in West Bengal—the party in the state was at that time being headed by Somen Mitra. Mamata was also very unhappy with the central leadership of the party for ignoring her claim to become the head of the party in West Bengal.

In September 1997, after a four-month-long agitation, she floated a formation called the Trinamool Congress (or the Grassroots Congress) after accusing the official leadership of the Congress in the state of being ineffective and acting as if it was the 'B Team' of the CPI(M)-led ruling Left Front. The then President of the Congress, Sitaram Kesri, finally expelled Mamata Banerjee from the Congress in December 1997 for allegedly splitting the party's West Bengal unit. The Trinamool Congress then became a political entity.

By the time the March–April 1998 general elections took place, it was clear to most that Mamata was ready to jump ship and would be throwing her weight behind the BJP-led National Democratic Alliance (NDA) formation. Sure enough, after she was elected to the Lok Sabha for the fourth time and after Vajpayee was sworn in as Prime Minister for the second time, Mamata Banerjee was elevated to the highest official post she had ever held, that of Union Minister for Railways, heading the second largest railway system in the world.

The first Railway Budget presented by Mamata Banerjee in late February 2000 was described by all as 'populist': she took the decision to not increase passenger fares and increased freight rates only moderately. She was especially generous towards her own state. Eleven railway projects in West Bengal that had been in limbo for a decade-and-a-half were all revived and money sanctioned for land acquisition.

Mamata's second Railway Budget for 2001–2002 presented in February 2001 turned out to be an even more blatantly populist exercise than her first budget. This time, she clearly had an eye on the elections to the West Bengal assembly scheduled for May that year. She chose to ignore all advice given to her about the need to take hard decisions to improve the financial health of the Indian Railways. In an unabashed bid to woo her constituents, she announced a slew of new projects for West Bengal, including seven of the 24 new trains that she proposed to start. She left her political opponents in the Left Front government in West Bengal completely dumbfounded—they could not criticise her budget for the new trains would clearly benefit the state. (The left had been arguing for years that the Union government in New Delhi had neglected West Bengal by denying it new projects, including new railway lines.)

If people in West Bengal cutting across political lines were happy with Mamata Banerjee's Railway Budget for 2001–2002, those in other states were rather vocal in expressing their dissatisfaction. No railway minister is able to satisfy the demands of all states, but this time round there were unusually loud protests from MPs belonging to Bihar, Andhra Pradesh, Karnataka, and particularly, Orissa. The protests from Orissa MPs were rather embarrassing for the Vajpayee government. The Biju Janata Dal, together with the BJP, was not only ruling Orissa but the party was a part of the NDA coalition in New Delhi. BJD MPs registered their protest against the Railway Budget by walking out of the Lok Sabha after claiming that they were being given 'step-motherly' treatment.

Mamata Banerjee was roundly criticised by the media for her populism. But she remained unfazed. After all, she was convinced her actions would be supported by the people of the country—not excluding, of course, the voters from her own state. But weeks before the assembly elections took place in West Bengal, two extremely significant developments took place. The first and most important development was Mamata's decision to switch sides—she chose to ditch the BJP-led NDA in March 2001 and go along with the Congress—a party she had earlier derogatorily referred to as the 'B team' of the CPI(M) in West Bengal. She quit her post as Union Minister for Railways and her party, the Trinamool Congress, left the NDA coalition.

The stated reason for her decision to resign from the Union government was Prime Minister Vajpayee's apparent reluctance to accept the resignation of Defence Minister George Fernandes who was then in the dock following the tehelka.com episode. The real reason for Mamata quitting the NDA government was, of course, quite different. She wanted to improve her party's electoral prospects by aligning the Trinamool Congress with its parent party, i.e., the Congress, by forming a *mahajot* or grand alliance against the CPI(M)-led Left Front. And this was simply because she felt (rightly so) that West Bengal's Muslim voters would stay away from the Trinamool Congress as long as it was closely associated with the BJP.

The second important development that considerably weakened Mamata Banerjee and the Trinamool Congress days before the elections was the revolt that took place within the ranks of her own party. This revolt was led by Ajit Panja. He was the only politician other than Mamata in the Trinamool Congress who had had a long career in politics. As a matter of fact, Panja had held positions in the Union government and been around in Congress politics much longer than Mamata. On April 17, 2001, Panja publicly aired his differences with Mamata Banerjee at the Kolkata Press Club. Panja, a co-founder of the Trinamool Congress, said he could not go along with Mamata's decision to align with the Congress and ditch the BJP-led NDA alliance before the West Bengal assembly elections. Though a tearful Panja said he had taken a principled position, cynics claimed he was most reluctant to give up his post as Minister of State, External Affairs, in the Vajpayee government—a post with considerable perks and opportunities to travel all over the world.

The Congress–Trinamool Congress combine, which had been cobbled together barely a month before the last date of filing nominations, failed to defeat the CPI(M)-led Left Front in the assembly elections held on May 10. On the contrary, the ruling Left Front improved its position by bucking anti-incumbency sentiments and successively romped home. The electoral victory of the left in West Bengal was the sixth consecutive one since 1977—a record of sorts not only in India but perhaps anywhere in the world. Many voters in the state clearly perceived Mamata as a maverick, an impulsive and unreliable individual heading a team that would not have been able to offer better governance in the state. She had been going hammer and tongs at the Left Front government for its alleged failure to maintain law and order—especially after a series of violent incidents in Midnapur district where Trinamool Congress sympathisers were reportedly killed by left supporters.

Despite Mamata Banerjee's shrill criticism of the Left Front, her charges clearly failed to influence the pattern of voting in the state. It was not merely the infighting within the ranks of her party that adversely affected her credibility as a political leader, but the local units of the BJP seized the opportunity to play spoiler. The other factor that worked in favour of the Left Front was the image of Chief Minister Buddhadeb Bhattacharjee, who is a good 30 years younger than his predecessor Jyoti Basu. During the election campaign, Bhattacharjee had cleverly refrained from personal attacks on Mamata and he was successful to an extent in winning back the support of the middle-classes in urban and semi-urban areas in the state—sections of the electorate that had become staunchly anti-left. The Chief Minister's 'new left' image evidently went down well with the voters. He was seen as a communist who was not only willing to acknowledge the mistakes made by the CPI(M) in the past, but was also willing to mend the ways of his party's cadres to make them more responsive to the aspirations of the people of the state.

The Left Front improved its position in the 294-member West Bengal assembly from 189 seats to 200 seats. Even the most ardent supporters of the left were unwilling to predict such a convincing victory. In the earlier assembly elections held in 1996, the undivided Congress had obtained 85 seats. On this occasion, the Trinamool Congress–Congress alliance could win only one extra seat. The poor performance of the Trinamool Congress–Congress combination shocked Mamata. She had, after all, confidently predicted an electoral defeat for the Left Front and at least on this occasion, she knew that her standard complaint that the Left Front's victory was on account of 'scientific rigging' of elections would sound like a lame excuse.

After the assembly elections were declared, Mamata Banerjee went into a deep sulk. She held the Election Commission of India, the central government as well as the 'machinations and manipulations' of the Left Front responsible for her party's performance. Her criticism of the Election Commission appeared to be an instance of the referee being blamed for the defeat of one's team. Asked why she had chosen to align her party with the Congress during the assembly polls, she claimed: 'We had waited for the BJP for a seat adjustment, but they rejected it. Since the Left Front had so many parties in its fold, we too wanted to have a front. So, we had to go along with other parties to fight the left.'

Her explanations did not sound convincing. Mamata then decided to act against Ajit Panja by stripping him of all official positions in the party. On May 21, Panja was reduced to becoming an ordinary primary member of the party. Panja had earlier held the positions of Chairman of the party's West Bengal unit and a member of the All India Trinamool Congress Working Committee. Panja remained unrepentant and continued to criticise Mamata's decision to quit the NDA and go along with the Congress. (During the election campaign, Panja had shared a platform with Prime Minister Vajpayee at a rally near Kolkata.) Panja told all who were willing to listen that he was the only 'real' leader in the party and that Mamata Banerjee's style of functioning was 'undemocratic'.

While the assembly elections debacle did not lead to any real questioning of Mamata Banerjee's authority in the party, there was growing criticism of what was seen as a tendency on her part to take hasty and impulsive decisions. Though all talk of a split in the party was quelled, there were reports that Panja might attempt to woo two of the party's nine MPs away from Mamata. On August 28, 2000, the former Union minister and founder-member of the Trinamool Congress was formally suspended from the party.

A day before she removed Ajit Panja from the Trinamool Congress, on August 27, 2001, Mamata indicated that her party's alliance with the Congress was over. She said the Congress had been more of a burden than an asset for the Trinamool Congress during the West Bengal elections. Mamata and her Trinamool Congress were back with the NDA. She sought to emphasise that her party's support was being extended to Prime Minister Vajpayee and his government but that this did not imply that the Trinamool Congress would automatically have an understanding with the state unit of the BJP. There was a touch of irony in the fact that it was none other than Prime Minister Vajpayee's trouble-shooter, Defence Minister and NDA convenor, George Fernandes, who persuaded the alliance to readmit Mamata Banerjee.

She justified her re-entry by saying her party had left the NDA on the Tehelka issue and that the Prime Minister had subsequently accepted all the demands she had made on the issue. She also claimed that the Trinamool Congress would give 'issue-based' support to the Vajpayee government, a fact that she pointed out had been clearly mentioned in the party's election manifesto. Despite disagreements with the BJP-led alliance, Banerjee maintained that the NDA was a 'natural ally' of her party.

Mamata Banerjee's morale touched a new low after four of her party legislators voted in favour of a rival candidate in the Rajya Sabha elections. Then, in March 2002, an important party leader Debi Prasad Pal quit the Trinamool Congress and returned to the Congress. These two incidents exposed the fragility of the party leadership. While the Congress candidate for the Rajya Sabha, Arjun Sengupta, failed to get elected and the Trinamool Congress candidate, Dinesh Trivedi, did, the cross-voting exposed the dissensions that continued within Mamata's party.

Her relations with the BJP as well as the NDA had been turbulent and continued to be so. As early as October 1998, during the second Vajpayee government, Mamata went on record stating that she and her party were unhappy with the agenda to 'saffronise' education as devised by Human Resources Development Minister Murli Manohar Joshi. Then, in October 2000, Mamata Banerjee and Ajit Panja put in their papers protesting against the government's decision to hike the prices of petroleum products. Mamata claimed she had not been consulted on the decision. She withdrew her resignation only after Prime Minister Vajpayee sent her a fax saying he would personally look into the issue after he returned to Delhi following surgery of his knees. The prices of petroleum products were not rolled back and Mamata and Panja continued in their positions.

Much later, during the communal carnage that took place in Gujarat in April and May 2002, she repeatedly sided with the government's opponents by calling for the removal of Narendra Modi. She also demanded a 'comprehensive relief package' for the victims of the carnage and urged that an all-party peace march take place to restore the confidence of minorities in the state. At the same time, she could not resist taking pot-shots at the West Bengal government. In the Lok Sabha, she claimed that the violence that had occurred in both Gujarat and West Bengal was tantamount to state-sponsored terrorism while urging the Union government to intervene and put a stop to this kind of 'barbarism'. Yet, curiously, despite demanding the removal of Narendra Modi, when it came to voting in the Lok Sabha, she and MPs from her party voted in favour of the Vajpayee government.

Earlier, MPs belonging to the Trinamool Congress deliberately absented themselves during the discussion in Parliament on POTO and also abstained from voting in favour of the Ordinance. Mamata Banerjee said she and her party could not support POTO since the Trinamool Congress had opposed a similar act, POCA, or Prevention of Crime Act, that had been enacted by the West Bengal government. She claimed that both POTO (that later became POTA) and POCA would be misused by the authorities to harass the political opponents of those in power, both in New Delhi and in Kolkata.

Besides POTO, the Trinamool Congress also expressed serious reservations about the Union government's proposal to amend the Industrial Disputes Act by permitting employers to lay-off or retrench workers in industrial units employing up to 1,000 employees without obtaining the prior approval of the concerned government authorities. Describing the decision to amend the Act as 'dangerous' for employees, Mamata Banerjee said such decisions should be arrived at only after wide-ranging consultations had taken place among all political parties in the NDA.

In late May 2003, Vajpayee decided to reshuffle his Council of Ministers and it was widely believed that the Trinamool Congress would once again find representation in the Union government. There was speculation about the portfolio that would be allotted to Mamata since Nitish Kumar was well ensconced in the post of Railway Minister and it seemed unlikely that he would be removed. Media reports suggested that Mamata might be made Agriculture

Minister. What transpired thereafter turned out to be a bit of an anti-climax. On the evening of May 24, 2003, the day before the reshuffle, Mamata reportedly spoke to Vajpayee and BJP president Venkaiah Naidu and told them not to induct any representative of her party in the government. She told her party colleagues in Kolkata that the Trinamool leader in the Lok Sabha, her one-time confidante Sudip Bandopadhyaya, had been lobbying hard with Deputy Prime Minister L.K. Advani and was expecting to be made minister. She told members of her party's working committee that Sudip was proving to be a 'risk to the unity' of the Trinamool Congress.

Just as the manner in which Mamata fell out with Sudip seemed inexplicable to many, the way in which she buried the hatchet with Ajit Panja was equally unexpected. Nearly two years after he had been suspended from the Trinamool Congress, Panja's suspension was formally revoked in July 2003. There was no explanation as to how the person who had publicly trashed his party leader had again endeared himself to her.

Mamata's long wait to become a minister in the Cabinet finally ended in September 2003, but in the most bizarre fashion. While she was made a Cabinet Minister, Vajpayee refused to succumb to her demand that she be given the Railways portfolio. With Mamata also refusing to settle for any other portfolio, the stand-off meant that she remained a Minister without portfolio till January 2004, when she finally accepted the portfolio of Coal and Mines.

Mamata Banerjee's unpredictable behaviour has not exactly endeared her to her current political allies and has made potential partners circumspect about aligning with her.

Asom Gana Parishad: Co-opted rebels

Assam is by far the biggest of the seven states, or 'seven sisters', of the north-eastern part of India. The north-east is separated from the rest of the country by a narrow 'chicken's neck' in West Bengal, but more than the geographical separation, the people of north-east India have for long felt alienated from the country's mainstream. Questions relating to sub-nationalism and regional identity, illegal immigration and violent separatist movements have dominated the political discourse surrounding Assam and the north-east for more than half a century.

Till December 1985, nine out of the 10 individuals who served as Chief Ministers of Assam belonged to the Congress party; the exception was Golap Chandra Borbora of the Janata Party who was Chief Minister between March 1978 and September 1979. From the late 1970s, a series of agitations against the state government as well as the Union government spearheaded by the All Assam Students' Union (AASU) paralysed the working of the state for long periods. President's rule was imposed in Assam on no less than three occasions in December 1979, June 1981 and March 1982. In the 1980 general elections, polls were not conducted in 12 out of the 14 Lok Sabha constituencies in the state. In December 1985, nearly one year after the 1984 general elections had taken place, the voters of Assam exercised their franchise. Again in 1989, the Lok Sabha elections did not take place in Assam.

Until recently, many political observers believed that national parties like the Congress and BJP had lost most of their influence in Assam. The 13th general elections, however, proved such a perception wrong. Not only did the electoral fortunes of the Congress revive, the BJP too performed better than it ever had in the state. The outcome of the 12th and the 13th general elections delivered rude shocks to the former student leaders of AASU who had gone on to form the Asom Gana Parishad (AGP) after the 1985 accord with the Rajiv Gandhi government in New Delhi and had come to power in the state. During both the 1998 and 1999 elections, the AGP could not win a single Lok Sabha seat in Assam. The Congress, as already mentioned, had played a dominant role in the state. It was only in the 1985 Lok Sabha elections in Assam that the vote share of the Congress dipped below the 45 per cent mark. Between 1985 and 1991, the share of the Congress in the total votes polled in the state went up from below 24 per cent to over 28 per cent in both the Lok Sabha and assembly elections. Thus, the improved performance of the Congress in the 12th and 13th general elections was not entirely surprising.

What was unexpected was the emergence of the BJP as the main opposition party to the Congress by sidelining the AGP. Since the 1980s, the BJP started recording its presence in Assam. Within the party, individuals like L.K. Advani and former General Secretary K.N. Govindacharya could sense that the state would one day become a fertile ground for the BJP's brand of politics. There were two important reasons for this perception. Assam has a long international border with Bangladesh which has been traditionally difficult to police. Even if the BJP was branded a communal party by its political opponents, a substantial section of the upper-caste Hindus in Assam had been wary of the BJP. This section saw the party as one that was supported by Marwari traders: the alien 'exploiters' of the people of Assam.

Initially, the BJP was perceived to be soft on Hindu immigrants and hard on Muslim immigrants. This policy did not, however, elicit the sympathies of those sections of the ruling elite in the state who were more fearful of the alleged domination of Bengalis (both Hindus and Muslims) in Assam. The apprehension that the original inhabitants of Assam could become a 'minority' in their own state and that their own culture and tradition would be submerged by waves of immigration fashioned the reactions of many sections of Assamese society (from the peasantry to the middle- and upper-classes) which supported the AASU-led agitation against 'foreigners' in the state in the late 1970s and early 1980s.

By the time the Assam accord was thrashed out in 1985, large sections had become completely disillusioned with the Congress. Following an all-party meeting convened when Rajiv Gandhi was Prime Minister, Parliament passed the Illegal Migrants (Determination by Tribunal) Act or the IMDT Act. The accord was aimed at disenfranchising illegal immigrants who had settled in Assam in the period between 1965 and1971, the year in which Bangladesh became an independent nation-state. After the erstwhile AASU leaders formed the AGP, which came to power in 1985, many in Assam believed the accord would be fully implemented. The AGP was also expected to try and resolve the problems of unemployment and lack of industrial development in the state, issues which the party's leaders had themselves raised as student leaders.

It did not take very long for the realisation to sink in that the process of detecting and deporting illegal immigrants was easier said than done. The biggest 'constraint' of the Act was that the onus of proving that a person was a foreigner rested with those who made the complaint. Much to the dissatisfaction of the AGP, the party's leaders realised that the state government as well as its supporters would at best be able to identify a few hundred thousand 'illegal immigrants' and that it would be next to impossible to deport even these individuals to Bangladesh. Not only was the AGP government unable to tackle the issue of 'foreigners' effectively, the party's leaders proved to be as inefficient, corrupt and fractious as those belonging to the Congress. Far from setting up employment generation schemes, the erstwhile students' leaders fell out with one another, the most significant being the parting of ways between Chief Minister Prafulla Kumar Mahanta and his one-time associate-turned-bitter-rival Bhrigu Kumar Phukan.

As the AGP weakened, the Congress was able to return to power in the May–June 1991 elections winning 66 out of the 126 seats in the state assembly. In the same election, the AGP's vote share nearly halved from 35 per cent in 1985 to under 18 per cent in 1991; the number of the party's MLAs shrank from 65 to 19. Unhappy with the AGP's poor track record in power, sections within the party started breaking off and one radical group formed the United Liberation Front of Asom (ULFA), which proclaimed the need for a violent secessionist movement. The ULFA claimed that the only way the problems of Assam could be resolved was if the state ceded from the Indian Union.

Taking a cue from the first AASU-led agitation and the rise of the ULFA, militant organisations were formed by sections of other important tribal groups in Assam, like the Bodos and the Karbis. The ULFA attracted, and continues to attract, considerable notoriety because it is running a 'parallel' administration in large parts of Assam by levying 'taxes' and eliminating 'collaborators'. The ULFA and its sympathisers have been responsible for innumerable hit-and-run killings in remote areas of Assam and many government officials and owners of tea gardens have had no alternative but to pay the 'dues' demanded by the militants to 'protect' themselves and their family members. The problem reached such a stage that the Mahanta government in 1997 even accused officials employed by Tata Tea, which is part of one of the biggest corporate groups in the country, of collaborating with militants by arranging for the medical expenses incurred by their supporters in Mumbai hospitals.

The electoral debacle of 1991 seemed to convince the AGP that it would be unwise to confront the Congress entirely on its own. Thus, by the time the 1996 assembly elections took place, the AGP had cobbled together an alliance that included the left, in particular the CPI. The strategy worked with the AGP-led alliance returning to power. The AGP itself won 59 seats, a little short of a majority, against 19 seats in 1991 and 65 in 1985. The Congress was reduced to 34 seats against 66 in 1991 and 25 in 1985, while the BJP, which had 10 seats in the outgoing assembly, managed to win only four seats this time round. The 1996 assembly elections saw a sizeable section of the minority Muslim community voting for the first time for AGP candidates—as many as 10 Muslim MLAs were elected to the assembly on AGP tickets against 12 Muslim MLAs belonging to the Congress.

The alliance between the AGP and the left meant that when the United Front was being formed in New Delhi in May 1996, it was a foregone conclusion that it would be a part of the UF. The AGP formally remained with the UF right up to the 1999 Lok Sabha elections. However, there was evident strain within the Front, with the left parties in Assam refusing to back the AGP in the 1999 elections, accusing the party of having a tacit understanding with the BJP against the Congress. The AGP repeatedly denied the existence of any such unwritten pact, but it was a widely held perception that it fielded weak candidates in some Lok Sabha constituencies to let the BJP emerge as the main challenger to the Congress in these constituencies.

In 1999, the BJP managed to win two of the state's 14 Lok Sabha seats—the prestigious Guwahati seat and Nowgong. Bijoya Chakraborty, who won from Guwahati, went on to become a Minister in the Vajpayee government. AGP chief Mahanta's remark that 'one of our own' had become a minister confirmed the perception that the AGP and the BJP had come closer together. (Chakraborty was AGP MP in the Rajya Sabha between 1986 and 1992.) Whereas the BJP's vote share had jumped from less than 0.4 per cent in the 1985 Lok Sabha elections to 33 per cent in the 1999 elections, the AGP's share of the total votes cast had crashed to less than 17 per cent by 1999.

In 2000, Advani complimented Mahanta for his handling of the situation after ULFA militants attacked Hindi-speaking settlers in Assam. And while there were murmurs of dissent within the AGP about the party's growing proximity to the BJP, it was not until as late as April 2001 that the AGP formally became a part of the NDA on the eve of the assembly elections in the state. By then, the Muslim minority in Assam had become alienated from the AGP because (among other things) of the party's demand to scrap the IMDT Act and because it had come close to the BJP. The AGP–BJP electoral alliance, however, proved to be a political disaster for the erstwhile student leaders of AASU who had been easily co-opted by the establishment thanks to their evident love for all the pomp and pelf that came with being in power.

Prime Minister Vajpayee and Advani campaigned for the AGP in Assam. In the run-up to the elections, Vajpayee made a controversial statement that the Union government would consider providing work permits to illegal immigrants from Bangladesh. But this statement evidently did not have much of an impact on the electorate of Assam, nor did the accusation by the BJP that the Congress was hand-in-glove with ULFA militants. While both the BJP and the AGP harped on the issue of illegal immigration from Bangladesh, the statistics issued by the Census Commission of India indicated that for the first time in a century, the rate of growth of population in Assam (at around 1.6 per cent per year between 1991 and 2001) was lower than the average rate of growth of the population in the country as a whole (roughly 1.8 per cent per annum). The demand for the repeal of the IMDT Act turned out to be a less emotive issue than had been presumed by the AGP and the BJP.

The 2001 assembly elections saw the AGP obtaining only 20 seats in the 126-member assembly against the 59 seats it had held in the outgoing assembly. The Congress obtained a majority on its own with 71 seats, more than double the 34 seats it had won in the 1996 assembly elections. On May 18 that year, Tarun Gogoi became the new Chief Minister of Assam and since then, little or nothing has been heard about the AGP–BJP alliance in the state.

Thus, over the course of its brief history, the AGP has tried to stick it out on its own in Assam politics, has flirted with the left—which was totally opposed to the AASU movement—and then with the BJP. A priori, an alliance with the BJP seemed the most viable, since the two parties share a common base—both deriving their support essentially from within the Asom community. Ironically, this is the strategy that proved the least fruitful. Where the AGP goes from here remains to be seen. What is certain though is that a party that arose out of a movement projecting itself as a challenge to mainstream politics has today become completely co-opted in that same mainstream. There is little to distinguish the AGP of 2003 from any other party in the state, though positions on individual issues may differ from party to party.

Dramatic developments in December 2003 might well have a bearing on the fortunes of not just the AGP, but also the BJP and the Congress in Assam. In that month, the Royal Army of Bhutan, which shares a border with Assam, launched a massive offensive against ULFA camps located in Bhutan. The operation was quite successful in closing down the camps and in flushing out some important ULFA leaders. New Delhi was quite obviously pleased at this development and repeatedly tried to drive home the point that other neighbours like Bangladesh and Pakistan should follow the example set by Bhutan.

The significance of this development for the politics of Assam is that the BJP would obviously try to take credit for New Delhi's success in persuading Bhutan to cooperate. If the ULFA's ability to operate in Assam is indeed seriously affected by the Bhutanese army's operation, the BJP would like to derive political mileage from the fact that its government was instrumental in solving a problem that successive Congress and AGP governments had been unable to tackle. If the electorate in Assam responds to this campaign, the BJP could make a serious bid to emerge as the Opposition to the Congress in the state.

National Conference: Keeping New Delhi Happy

The history of the Jammu & Kashmir National Conference, more commonly known as the National Conference, is quite intimately and inextricably linked with the history of the state itself and it is not surprising that the NC today is quite radically different in character from the one that was founded by Sheikh Mohammed Abdullah in 1939. Jammu & Kashmir is at the core of India's tensions with Pakistan and hence has attracted considerable international attention. Moreover, the politics of Jammu & Kashmir is intimately linked to the question of how the state's relationship with the rest of India is to be defined.

When India gained independence from British rule in August 1947, Jammu & Kashmir was not a part of the territory agreed upon as part of the new Indian Union. Like other princely states, Jammu & Kashmir too subsequently joined the Union. The process of its integration into India, however, was quite different from other princely states. To begin with, J&K was unique among the princely states in the fact that a Hindu king ruled it though the vast majority of his subjects were Muslims. Also, unlike in most other princely states, the king, Maharaja Hari Singh, had not decided to join either India or Pakistan.

Things changed dramatically in October that year, when Pakistan first prevented the movement of essential supplies to J&K

and then actively encouraged armed tribesmen to enter Kashmir. Hari Singh, apprehensive of Pakistan's intentions, sought India's help in countering the offensive. The Indian government made it clear that it would come to Hari Singh's defence only if he were willing to join the Indian Union. On October 26, 1947, Hari Singh, with little choice in the matter, signed the instrument of accession, which was no different from those signed by almost 500 other erstwhile rulers of princely states. The very next day, Indian troops arrived in Kashmir to combat the Pakistani troops that had come in on the heels of the tribesmen.

On January 1, 1948, Prime Minister Nehru declared a unilateral ceasefire and India filed a complaint with the United Nations against Pakistan for invading Kashmir. At this point, Pakistan occupied about two-fifths of the original area of J&K while India was in control of the remaining three-fifths. Over the next 55 years, that has not substantially changed, though the Line of Control has been marginally altered in the course of the two wars—1965 and 1971—India has fought since then. United Nations resolutions pending since 1948 have made no difference to the situation on the ground or been able to make India and Pakistan reach a final settlement on the Kashmir issue.

The partitioning of Kashmir may not have been accompanied by the kind of violence and bloodshed that was witnessed in Punjab, or Bengal, but it continues to rankle much more than the splitting up of these two states. This is not surprising. In both Punjab and Bengal, the partition was along communal lines. Thus, the phenomenon of families being separated by international borders is not quite as widespread in Kashmir, where Kashmiri Muslims inhabit both sides of the border. Also, from the Pakistani point of view, J&K remains the most obvious challenge to the 'two nation theory' (the theory which held that Muslims and Hindus in India were two separate nations, on the basis of which the Mulsim League demanded partition and got it).

This perhaps explains more than anything else why Kashmir's relationship with India—or with Pakistan—remains a live political issue. This is the context that has defined the politics of the NC and indeed of other parties in the Kashmir region of J&K. The NC from the very beginning, therefore, has sought to strike an aggressively pro-autonomy posture while also distancing itself from those demanding secession of J&K from India. In fact, till 1969, Sheikh Abdullah had led a formation called the Plebiscite Front which continued to demand a plebiscite to determine the will of the people of the state—whether they wanted to stay with India or not—that Nehru had offered at the UN. India continued to argue that a plebiscite could not be held as long as Pakistan occupied part of the territory.

It was only after the 'Kashmir Accord' was reached between Sheikh Abdullah and Indira Gandhi in 1975 that the former gave up the demand for a plebiscite, disbanded the Plebiscite Front and rejoined the NC. This was to be the beginning of an era of cosy relationships between the NC and whichever party happened to be in power in New Delhi. The NC continued to pay lip service to the state's autonomy, but did not really put up any resistance to J&K being treated like any other state in India.

Periodically, under pressure from competing groups in Kashmir, the NC has gone through the motions of demanding that the relationship between the state and New Delhi should go back to the pre-1953 arrangement, when J&K had its own prime minister, constitution and flag and New Delhi's writ ran in the state only in matters of finance, defence and communications. In fact, right up till 1965, J&K continued to have a prime minister and a president instead of a chief minister and a governor. However, this has been perceived as mere posturing not just in New Delhi, but also in Kashmir itself.

To return to the NC's penchant for staying on the right side of the government of India, what had only been a matter of practice from 1975 to 1998 was elevated to the status of principle when Dr. Farooq Abdullah, who was then Chief Minister of J&K and the president of the NC, declared that the NC would always support the government in New Delhi. He sought to justify this 'principle' on two grounds, one applicable not just to J&K and the other specific to his state. He argued that those who ran governments in India's smaller states had no option but to build bridges with the party in power at the centre, since they were heavily dependent on the Union government for financial assistance. Further, he added, in the specific case of J&K, the menace of terrorism made it imperative that Srinagar and New Delhi pull along well.

Critics of the NC view the process of its 'co-option' rather differently. They point out that J&K is the recipient of generous transfers of funds. In per capita terms, the residents of J&K have received more money from New Delhi than people living in any other state in India barring one, that is Arunachal Pradesh. Yet, ironically, the people of J&K as well as its politicians complain—and rightly so—that the state remains economically underdeveloped and dependent on a few industries such as tourism, handicrafts and horticulture. The NC's critics, therefore, claim that the bulk of the money that comes to the state gets siphoned off by the ruling elite—including politicians and bureaucrats. Thus, local politicians have a vested interest in maintaining cordial relations with whoever is in power in New Delhi to ensure that the flow of funds does not abate.

But, if the NC has run such a thoroughly corrupt administration, what explains the fact that it has managed to remain the dominant political party in J&K and has repeatedly come back to power, till it was deposed by an alliance of Mufti Mohammed Sayeed's People's Democratic Party and the Congress in the October 2002 elections? Part of the explanation lies in the early history of NC rule in J&K. Arguably the most crucial step taken by the NC in these early years was the implementation in 1950 of some of the most radical land reforms ever seen in India. This step meant that lakhs of ordinary peasants, who had till that stage been working on people's lands, became the owners of the land they tilled. This certainly contributed to the NC acquiring a sizeable popular base.

The NC's hold on power, however, hasn't always remained secure for such laudable reasons. Few today dispute the fact that the NC had—particularly in the 1980s—been a major beneficiary of systematically rigged elections in the states. In fact, most commentators on Kashmir acknowledge that rigged elections have been a major—perhaps even the single-most important—factor in alienating large sections of the people of Kashmir and making them disillusioned with Indian democracy. Governments in New Delhi and pliant Election Commissions either connived in this subversion of the electoral process or at least looked the other way. The reason seems to have been the belief that the NC was the only political party that could keep J&K with India and that allowing its rivals in Kashmir to come to power would have strengthened the secessionists.

Even the 1996 elections, which were held after a prolonged spell of President's Rule in J&K, were widely perceived as rigged with widespread allegations of Indian security forces coercing voters to vote and in some cases to vote for the NC. The official figures suggest that almost 54 per cent of eligible voters voted in these elections. But groups like the All Party Hurriyat Conference—a united front of motley groups including some demanding *azadi* (freedom) and others in favour of joining Pakistan—insist that these are highly exaggerated figures and that barely 10 per cent of the electorate actually voted.

Many would also argue that it was precisely because the 2002 elections were widely recognised as being by and large free and fair that the NC finally lost power. Whether or not that is entirely true, it has thrown up a new coalition in Srinagar—the PDP–Congress coalition. Whether the PDP is able to redefine the politics of Kashmir or—like the NC—discredits itself as another pet of New Delhi remains to be seen.

What has changed is the NC's relationship with New Delhi. In July 2003, NC President Omar Abdullah announced that his party was pulling out of the NDA and its government. Omar admitted that the decision was long overdue and that the NC should have exited from the NDA when the communal carnage in Gujarat was on. He publicly apologised for the NC's silence during that period and was also candid enough to admit that instead of being seen as a party representing Kashmir in New Delhi, the NC had over time come to be perceived in the Valley as New Delhi's representative in the state.

What explained the dramatic shift in the NC's attitude towards those in power in the national capital? Omar Abdullah and his party would have liked people to believe that it was a genuine case of introspection leading to correction. What many believed, however, was that there was a rather more mundane explanation for the parting of ways between the NC and the Vajpayee government. According to those who held this view, the NC had been trying to persuade the BJP to accept Dr. Farooq Abdullah as the NDA's candidate for Vice President of India or—failing that—to make him a minister in the Vajpayee cabinet. It is when these attempts came a cropper that the NC suddenly discovered the evils of the BJP, argue the cynics.

Whatever the real reasons for the NC's leaving the NDA, there is little doubt that the decision was welcomed both by people in the Kashmir Valley and by Opposition parties. Rallies addressed by Omar Abdullah in the days immediately following his announcement reportedly drew huge crowds and he was also soon attending Opposition conclaves.

Shiromani Akali Dal: Comfortable in Coalitions

The Shiromani Akali Dal (SAD)—or rather one of its predecessors, the Akali Party—has the distinction of being the dominant party in the first non-Congress government ever to be formed in independent India. That was the government headed by Gian Singh Rarewala formed in April 1952 in the erstwhile PEPSU (Patiala and East Punjab States Union). Rarewala was himself not a member of the Akali Party at the time, but an independent MLA. The Akalis, however, were the single-largest group in the United Front headed by Rarewala. The Congress had emerged as the largest party in the 60-member PEPSU assembly after the 1951 elections, but with 26 MLAs was just short of the halfway mark. The Akalis, who had won 19 seats, cobbled together the United Front with the help of independent MLAs and the CPI. Ironically, Rarewala was to later join the Congress in 1956 and become a minister in Pratap Singh Kairon's cabinet in 1957, before again joining the Akalis in 1969, who had by now renamed themselves the Shiromani Akali Dal.

From that historic beginning in 1951 to date, the Akalis have periodically been part of coalitions, both in Punjab and in New Delhi, and have maintained a consistently anti-Congress stance.

The Akalis did not start as a political party or even a political movement. On the contrary, the SAD traces its origins to an organisation set up primarily for religious reform within the Sikh community. This forerunner of today's SAD was the Gurudwara Sewak Dal, formed in December 1920 to raise and train volunteers for what came to be known as the Gurudwara Reform Movement. The primary objective of the movement was to break the stranglehold of the *mahants* (priests) on gurudwaras since they had acquired a reputation for corruption and misuse of their position for personal gratification. The Gurudwara Sewak Dal was renamed the Akali Dal in 1921 and SAD the following year.

Though it started primarily as a religious reform organisation, the SAD even in its early days had sections that felt it needed to play a larger role—whether in India's struggle for independence or in the revolts of the peasantry. The embryo of a political party thus existed even in those early days. As it has evolved, the SAD has remained a party almost solely of Sikhs, but one that provides expression to Sikh consciousness in all aspects of society, not just religion. It is important to recognise also that despite being a party with an explicitly Sikh character, the SAD has never been perceived as a communal organisation or one that discriminates against non-Sikhs in matters of state. Its secular credentials have never seriously been in doubt, though it was not till as late as 1995 that the party permitted non-Sikhs to become members.

Because of the part-religious, part-political character of the SAD, Akali politics has traditionally revolved round more than one power centre, unlike with most other Indian parties. The party president, the leader of the legislative wing and the head of the Shiromani Gurudwara Prabandhak Committee (SGPC)—a body that is ostensibly purely religious and responsible for the management of gurudwaras—have all been part of the same loose organisation, but on occasions at loggerheads with one another. It has been said of the Akalis that they tend to unite when out of power, but resort to factional feuds when in power.

There is merit in this apparently sweeping statement given the number of occasions on which governments in Punjab led by the Akali Dal have fallen because of internal strife. For instance, between March 1967 and March 1970, the state had three different chief ministers—all from the Akali Dal—and a brief spell of President's Rule in between. Again, when Surjit Singh Barnala became Chief Minister in September 1985, he lasted less than two years before he was pulled down by intra-party fights leading to the imposition of President's Rule in May 1987, which continued for nearly five years till February 1992. This was to become the longest spell of President's Rule in the state, since it also coincided with the period when Sikh militancy was at its peak.

Interestingly, one man has been involved in each of these episodes of factional fighting, either as the incumbent chief minister facing dissidence or as the man leading the revolt against the chief minister. He is Parkash Singh Badal, who has proved to be the greatest survivor in Punjab politics, having served as Chief Minister of the state on three occasions. The fact that these occasions have been as far apart as 1970, 1977 and 1997 is a testimony to Badal's tenacity through the ups and downs of electoral politics.

Badal is arguably also the man primarily responsible for the Akali Dal being perceived as the natural party of the Jat Sikh peasantry in Punjab. This is no small achievement considering that till the 1960s, the SAD was a party largely under the leadership of urban Sikhs and the Sikh farmers by and large voted for the Congress in elections to the state assembly and Parliament. Of course, the process of the farmers moving out of the Congress fold has been a general phenomenon in north India and not just in Punjab, but Badal's aggressive championing of issues that appealed to the farmers—like free power, higher support prices and subsidised fertilisers—certainly helped hasten the process and ensured that farmers disillusioned with the Congress gravitated towards the SAD.

The events of the late 1970s and the first half of the 1980s further alienated large sections of Sikhs—and not just those in rural areas—from the Congress. In retrospect it can be said that the Congress paid the price for trying to be too clever by half. The rise of militancy in Punjab might have happened even without the Congress covertly playing along, but there is little doubt that Giani Zail Singh, who was Chief Minister from March 1972 to June 1977 and later became President of India, tacitly encouraged the growth of leaders like Jarnail Singh Bhindranwale. The idea apparently was that Bhindranwale, with his militant espousal of the Sikh cause, would provide an alternative centre of power in Sikh politics and hence reduce the Akali Dal's support base. The growing clout of Bhindranwale could also be expected to heighten tensions within the Akali Dal, between the faction led by Badal and the one led by Gurcharan Singh Tohra and Jagdev Singh Talwandi.

The plan worked up to a point. Bhindranwale did rapidly become a cult figure in Sikh politics. Akali leaders were clearly apprehensive of losing many of their supporters to him, but finding it hard to match his militant rhetoric, which was increasingly acquiring secessionist tones. The more moderate Akali stance—which was to demand greater autonomy for Punjab and indeed all states—did not quite have the same appeal. The problem, however, was that having tacitly supported Bhindranwale while he took on the Akalis, Zail Singh and his mentor Indira Gandhi found that they could not put the genie back into the bottle once he had served his purpose.

By the beginning of the 1980s, Bhindranwale was no longer just a leader of a relatively insignificant group called the Damdami Taksal. He had acquired the halo of a saint and was called Sant

Jarnail Singh Bhindranwale. He not only called upon Sikhs to take up arms against the Indian state, he also preached the virtues of abstinence. His puritanical and spartan lifestyle combined with his militant rhetoric proved the perfect magnet for thousands of unemployed youth. Bhindranwale's group started gaining control over many important gurudwaras in Punjab and the Akal Takht located in the Golden Temple complex at Amritsar—said to be the holiest shrine of the Sikhs—became the de-facto headquarters of Bhindranwale and his supporters.

By 1984, the Akal Takht was a hotbed of militant activity and a place where huge quantities of arms were stocked. In June that year, Indira Gandhi took a step that few—including Bhindranwale—believed she would dare take. On June 6, 1984, the Indian Army stormed the Akal Takht using tanks and infantry to flush out Bhindranwale and his men. Bhindranwale died in the fighting, as did many of his men, but the Army could not achieve its objective without inflicting considerable damage on the Akal Takht. The incident shocked even those Sikhs who had no love lost for Bhindranwale. Their holiest shrine, they felt, had been desecrated by Indira. The government tried in vain to argue that it was really Bhindranwale who had desecrated the Akal Takht by using a place of worship as a base for subversive activities.

What followed was Indira Gandhi's assassination on October 31 which in turn sparked off one of the worst communal genocides India has ever witnessed. The repercussions for the Congress were severe, both in Punjab and in Delhi. In Delhi, large sections of the Sikhs had traditionally been Congress voters and in fact the only Sikh political leaders in Delhi were those in the Congress. Following the storming of the Akal Takht, however, the community switched en masse to the BJP, a fact that decisively changed the electoral arithmetic in the national capital. The Congress had to wait till 1999 before it could outdo the BJP in elections in Delhi, whether for the Lok Sabha, the assembly or the local bodies.

Similarly, in the 1985 elections in Punjab after 1984, the Akali Dal romped home to victory. Again, as with the BJP in Delhi, this was not so much because of its popularity as on account of the perception that it was the only credible alternative to the Congress. The Akalis, despite the victory, were in disarray in the state. Throughout the period of militancy, the Akalis had been marginalised in Punjab, unable to decide whether they should adopt a stance sympathetic to the militants or take a firm position against them. Whatever little political resistance was being offered to the militants came from smaller parties like the CPI, whose leader Satpal Dang was nationally recognised as one who was bravely opposing militancy on the ground.

Just before the 1985 elections, however, the Akalis had made a serious bid to get back into the thick of Punjab politics. The Congress, now led by Rajiv Gandhi in New Delhi, was desperately seeking ways of dealing with the problem of militancy in Punjab. The Akalis were equally looking for ways to remain relevant in the politics of the state. The accord signed between Rajiv Gandhi and Sant Harcharan Singh Longowal, the Akali Dal President, was a result of this convergence of necessities between the two traditional rivals in Punjab politics. The accord sought to convey the impression that it was addressing most of the genuine concerns of Punjab and the Sikhs. Thus, it provided for Chandigarh—which was a Union Territory that served as the capital for both Punjab and neighbouring Haryana—to be transferred to Punjab. It also stipulated that any river-water sharing arrangement involving Punjab, Haryana and Rajasthan would ensure that Punjab's farmers did not get less water than they were already getting.

The accord was denounced as a 'surrender' of Punjab's interests by the militants. The crucial question of autonomy of the state, they pointed out, had not been adequately addressed. The Anandpur Sahib Resolution—a document asking for greater autonomy, and which got its name from the place at which the meeting in which it was adopted was held—had, the hardliners argued, been effectively consigned to the dust heap since the accord merely said that it would be 'referred to the Sarkari Commission' which was dealing with centre–state relations.

Longowal was assassinated in August 1985, even as the campaign for the September 1985 assembly elections were on. The transfer of Chandigarh to Punjab, which should have taken place on January 26, 1986 according to the Rajiv–Longowal accord never did take place. The much-touted accord had effectively been buried within months of its being signed. The militants could adopt a 'we told you so' attitude, while the Akali Dal was left desperately trying to defend its 'surrender'. With the imposition of President's Rule in 1987, politics in Punjab took a back seat and so did the Akali Dal. The confrontation between the administration—in particular the police—and the militants took centrestage. As so often happens in such situations, innocents were often caught in the crossfire, literally and metaphorically. While the police was cracking down on those suspected of being sympathetic to the militants, the militants too were terrorising innocent people into providing them shelter and money.

Ultimately, as the militants gradually lost their ideological edge and were increasingly seen as extortionists, as incidents of women being molested and even raped by them grew, Sikh militancy in Punjab lost its support base. Combined with strong-arm tactics by the police, led by K.P.S. Gill, this helped bring militancy under control by the beginning of the 1990s.

When the P.V. Narasimha Rao government announced its decision to hold elections to the state assembly in 1992, almost every party except the Congress protested saying the situation on the ground was hardly conducive to the conduct of a free and fair poll. True, militancy had been considerably reduced from its peak, but it remained a serious problem. Rao, however, got a pliant Election Commission to hold the elections despite the protests. The Akali Dal boycotted the elections and appealed to people not to participate in them. Whether because of this appeal or because of fear, the turnout in the 1992 elections was 20 per cent, the lowest Punjab has ever witnessed. Despite this, the political process in Punjab had unmistakably resumed.

The Akalis, who had been drifting aimlessly till this stage found once again that they had been given an emotive issue by default. Since the Congress was identified with the excesses of the police during the militancy years, the Akalis were the obvious rallying point for those demanding action against police officers who had exceeded their brief and made innocents suffer. In the next elections in 1997, therefore, it came as no surprise that the Akali Dal emerged as a comfortable winner.

At this stage, the Akali Dal was still a constituent of the United Front government in New Delhi. However, with the collapse of the UF in 1998, the Akalis had to look for other options in Punjab. In the 1998 Lok Sabha elections, therefore, the Akali Dal became the first of the UF constituents to join the BJP-led alliance. The two partners complemented each other remarkably well. While the Akali Dal had a strong base in rural Punjab and among the Sikhs, the BJP was almost entirely a party of the Hindus in Punjab's urban centres. Predictably, the alliance won the overwhelming majority (11) of Punjab's 13 Lok Sabha seats in 1998.

Since then, the Akali Dal has stuck to the NDA despite occasional friction with the BJP. It has not managed to replicate the success of 1998, with the Congress winning nine of the 13 Lok Sabha seats in 1999 and then going on to win the state assembly elections in 2001. This is not to suggest that the relationship between the two parties has always been smooth. In fact, on one occasion in 2000, the Akali Dal came close to snapping its ties with the NDA over the creation of Uttaranchal. The bone of contention was the district of Udham Singh Nagar, in the 'terai' region of Uttar Pradesh, which was dominated by rich Sikh farmers who had settled in what was once marshland but has now been transformed into a fertile grain and sugarcane cultivating area. The Sikh farmers of Udham Singh Nagar were averse to the idea of their district being made part of Uttaranchal. The Akali Dal championed their cause, threatening to withdraw support to the Vajpayee government unless the map of Uttaranchal was redrawn to exclude Udham Singh Nagar. Eventually, the matter was sorted out, but for a while the threat seemed serious.

Similarly, the Akali Dal has been at the forefront in opposing moves by New Delhi to hike fertiliser prices or keep the minimum support prices for procurement of grain by official agencies in check. It has—with support from other 'pro-farmer' parties like Ajit Singh's RLD and Om Prakash Chautala's INLD—successively resisted such moves. The most obvious instances were in 1998, when the then Finance Minister Yashwant Sinha announced in his budget that urea prices would be hiked, but had to beat a hasty retreat within days. Similarly, Jaswant Singh tried in his budget of 2003–2004 to raise fertiliser prices by barely 2–3 per cent. Once again, the Akali Dal and like-minded parties were able to force a rollback.

Despite such periodic tensions, there is little reason to believe that the BJP–Akali Dal tie-up will disintegrate soon. The Akali Dal has a long history of coalition politics and is unlikely to overlook the fact that the BJP remains a useful ally in taking on the Congress in Punjab. More importantly, there is hardly any other party in Punjab that could prove even a partial substitute for losing the BJP's support base. The CPI, which once had a reasonably strong base in the state, is too emaciated a force today to be a major ally and the BSP cannot ally with the Akalis since their support bases—the lower-caste Sikhs and the Jat Sikhs, respectively—are at logger-heads with each other.

INLD and RLD: Fathers and Sons

The names of both the Indian National Lok Dal led by Om Prakash Chautala and the Rashtriya Lok Dal headed by Ajit Singh would literally imply that the two political parties have a 'national' char-acter. But the fact is that the INLD and the RLD, both offshoots of the Bharatiya Lok Dal (BLD), are confined to specific geographi-cal areas—the INLD to Haryana and the RLD to western Uttar Pradesh. Unlike the BLD that in its heyday in the 1970s had a base almost through all of the Hindi heartland—from Haryana to Bihar—the INLD and the RLD have not been able to expand their political influence beyond areas where Jat farmers comprise a substantial portion of the population. In fact, curiously, these two political parties have relatively little influence over the Jat com-munity based in Rajasthan, which borders Haryana.

Another common factor binding these two parties is the fact that their leaders are both sons of prominent political personalities—Ajit Singh is the son of former Prime Minister Chaudhary Charan Singh while Chautala's father was Chaudhary Devi Lal, who served as Deputy Prime Minister in V.P. Singh's government in 1989–1990. Yet another common aspect of the working of the INLD and the RLD has been the utterly opportunistic manner in which they have formed and broken alliances with other political parties.

Like their fathers, Ajit Singh and Chautala have relied prima-rily on projecting themselves as champions of the interests of farmers to garner votes. Of the two, Chautala has been the more successful in taking over the mantle from his father, while Ajit Singh's stature as a leader has never come close to matching his father's. At the height of his popularity, Charan Singh was not only the undisputed leader of the Jats of both western UP and Haryana, but had also successfully cobbled together a caste-based social coalition popularly referred to in Uttar Pradesh by the acronym AJGAR, standing for Ahirs (Yadavs), Jats, Gujjars and Rajputs. He had also emerged as a leader of the intermediate castes in other parts of the Hindi heartland. In contrast, Ajit Singh has struggled to even keep his hold over the Jats of western UP secure. So much so that in the 1998 Lok Sabha elections, he was himself defeated by Som Pal from Baghpat, the constituency that had been his father's pocket borough and had elected Ajit Singh himself on four occasions prior to 1989.

To be fair to Ajit Singh, the comparison with Chautala is perhaps unduly harsh on him. Singh could legitimately argue that the number of Lok Sabha constituencies in which the RLD has influence and a real chance of winning is significantly larger than those in which the INLD is a serious contender. The RLD can claim considerable influence in at least 14 seats in UP, whereas the INLD cannot realistically lay claim to any influence outside the 10 Lok Sabha seats in Haryana. While this is true to a great extent, unfortunately for Ajit Singh, the 14 constituencies in which his party wields influence are part of a state that had 85 Lok Sabha seats before it was bifurcated and even today has 80 seats. Thus, while the INLD has the ability to come to power in Haryana, the RLD can at best hope to be a minor partner in any alliance that rules Uttar Pradesh.

This could well explain the RLD's periodic attempts to raise the demand for a separate 'Harit Pradesh' (green state) to be carved out of Uttar Pradesh, comprising 22 of the state's western districts. This demand was also raised by the INLD in the 2002 state assembly elections, when it was trying to establish an independent presence in UP, without much success. Though neither Chautala nor Singh can seriously believe that they will make a serious impact in each other's territories, both sides keep up the apparent battle to inherit the legacy of Charan Singh. This has given rise to animosity between the two, which they have made no secret of.

Thus, for instance, when Ajit Singh—in one of his many flip-flops—decided to join the NDA in 2001 after having contested the 1999 Lok Sabha elections in alliance with the Congress, Chautala publicly threatened that he would quit the NDA if Ajit Singh were made a member of Vajpayee's cabinet. Eventually, when in July 2001 Ajit Singh became Union Agriculture Minister, Chautala was left sulking. There was precious little he could do, apart from 'clarifying' that he had never questioned the Prime Minister's prerogative to appoint anyone he liked as a member of his cabinet.

However, in the February 2002 assembly elections in UP, Chautala saw an opportunity to do some damage to the RLD's prospects. He put up candidates in more than 100 constituencies in western UP, knowing full well that none of them had even a reasonable chance of getting elected. The idea was to split the Jat vote in these constituencies, thereby sabotaging the prospects of victory for some of the RLD's candidates. Throughout the campaign, Chautala also concentrated his attack on Ajit Singh, accusing him of having betrayed the cause of Harit Pradesh once he had secured a ministerial berth. The beneficiaries of the rivalry between the INLD and the RLD—which were both members of the NDA—turned out to be the SP and the BSP.

Chautala's apparent indignation at Ajit Singh's opportunism was quite hypocritical to say the least. The Haryana leader has himself shifted political allegiances with alacrity in an expedient manner. For instance, the INLD had been a part of the United Front government that was in power from June 1996 to February 1998. In the Lok Sabha elections that followed, the party contested the polls as part of the UF with its main rivals in Haryana being the Congress led by Bhajan Lal and the Haryana Vikas Party (HVP) led by former Congress Chief Minister, Bansi Lal, in alliance with the BJP. When the results were announced, the INLD had won four out of the state's 10 seats and its ally the BSP (which was not part of the UF but had tied up with the INLD in Haryana) had secured one seat. The BJP won two of the remaining five seats, the Congress winning three. The HVP could not win a single seat.

What followed was opportunism at its worst. Since the BJP-led alliance had not secured a majority in the Lok Sabha, it was left hunting for potential new allies. The constituents of the UF, which had performed quite poorly in the 1998 elections, became obvious targets. The INLD was just one of the many parties in the UF which was wooed by the BJP to support its government in New Delhi. Like the DMK, the TDP and the NC, the INLD too decided it wanted a piece of the national cake. But that was not all. Having joined the BJP at the national level, the INLD set about ensuring that the quid pro quo was complete. In 1999, the BJP—which had partnered the HVP in the 1996 assembly elections and joined the coalition government in the state—withdrew its support to Chief Minister Bansi Lal, precipitating the fall of his government. It then extended support to Chautala to form the next government. The flimsy pretext of the BJP being dissatisfied with the Bansi Lal government's performance fooled nobody.

Described in his official curriculum vitae as a 'computer expert' educated at the Indian Institute of Technology, Kharagpur and the

Illinois Institute of Technology, Chicago, Ajit Singh had worked in the American computer industry for 15 years before entering the hurly-burly of politics in India's Hindi heartland. Like Chautala, Ajit Singh too has excelled at switching allegiances to be on the right side of whoever happens to be in power in New Delhi. When the Janata Dal was in power between 1989 and 1991, Singh was in the JD. When the Narasimha Rao government was struggling to win a vote of confidence in the Lok Sabha in 1994, Rao found Ajit Singh willing to bail him out. The price the Jat leader extracted for his support in a time of need was a berth in the Union Cabinet. In February 1995, Ajit Singh became Cabinet Minister for Food in the Rao government. When the UF came to power in 1996, Ajit Singh was again on the winning side and was made a Cabinet Minister yet again. Finally, in 2001, he joined the Vajpayee government, despite the fact that he had contested the 1999 Lok Sabha elections in alliance with the Congress.

Despite all these flip-flops—or perhaps because of them—Ajit Singh has failed to outflank his *bete noire* in Uttar Pradesh politics, Mulayam Singh Yadav. Until the fall of the V.P. Singh government in November 1990, Ajit Singh had tried to better Mulayam Singh Yadav while remaining in the same party, the Janata Dal. Since then, he has been part of virtually every possible political formation or combination. However, while he has remained a leader in only one region of UP, Mulayam has grown in stature to become one of the state's most important leaders and perhaps even a national leader of sorts.

Chautala, who has been sworn in as Chief Minister of Haryana no less than five times (in December 1989, July 1990, March 1991, July 1999 and March 2000), had a rather controversial first term as Chief Minister that began on December 2, 1989, after his father Devi Lal was designated Deputy Prime Minister in the V.P. Singh government. At the time he was sworn in as Chief Minister, Chautala was a member of the Rajya Sabha and he was required to win an assembly election. He chose to contest a by-election in February 1990 from the Meham constituency against a popular Congress candidate Anand Singh Dangi (who was once Chautala's colleague in the Congress but had later become a bitter rival).

During the election, senior policemen who were stationed at Mokhra Madina village claimed they were attacked by a mob that included Dangi's supporters. Subsequently, three persons died in police firing and another was killed in a separate incident. The Meham by-election was countermanded in the wake of allegations by Dangi and others to the effect that state government officers and policemen had rigged the polls to ensure Chautala's victory. After elections were conducted again, Chautala was declared the winner. A commission of inquiry was later instituted by the Punjab and Haryana High Court and criminal cases were registered against police officers present during the Meham incident after Bhajan Lal of the Congress party became Haryana's Chief Minister in 1991. While neither Chautala nor any Haryana police officer was formally indicted for what had taken place, the stigma of the 'mayhem in Meham' remained with him for many years.

Chautala's attempts at portraying himself as a farmer-leader too have not always been successful. His most significant setback in this regard came in 2002, when his erstwhile ally, Mahendar Singh Tikait, the leader of the pro-farmer Bharatiya Kisan Union (BKU), led an agitation against Chautala's government in Haryana on the issue of electricity dues. Tikait charged Chautala with going back on his election promise of waiving all past arrears. With the state government taking a tough stand, the agitation took a violent turn resulting in policemen being taken hostage by farmers. Thereafter, the police fired on protesting farmers. While the issue has since died down, it has dented Chautala's pro-farmer image to some extent. To his credit, however, unlike Ajit Singh, Chautala has not remained content merely projecting a unidimensional image of himself as a farmer-leader. He has assiduously tried to create an image of himself as a dynamic chief minister who is keen on implementing economic reforms; one who is determined to make Haryana one of the country's most industrialised and technologically advanced states. Whether he succeeds in this attempt and whether this can pay electoral dividends to him and the INLD remains to be seen.

As for Ajit Singh, he quit the Vajpayee government in a huff in May 2003 when he heard that he would be removed from his position as Union Agriculture Minister and replaced by Rajnath Singh, former BJP Chief Minister of UP. Soon thereafter, he met Congress President Sonia Gandhi and Samajwadi Party Chief Mulayam Singh and said he was willing to support them to topple the Mayawati government regime in UP.

Ajit Singh asked his party's 14 MLAs, including five ministers, to resign from the state government and herded them away from the heat of Lucknow to more pleasant climes, first to Pachmarhi and then to Srinagar, so that they would not be 'tempted' to defect. At least one MLA did not oblige Ajit Singh. Mayawati, who was at that time on a tour outside the country, was not particularly perturbed by Ajit Singh's 'threat' to topple her government together with the SP and the Congress—she realised that despite the departure of the RLD MLAs, there was not much of a danger of her government getting destabilised. Meanwhile, Ajit Singh continues to contemplate his future political strategy with his political friends-turned-enemies-turned-friends again.

Shiv Sena: Riding the Hindutva Tiger

It would be difficult to find any political leader of significance anywhere in the world who openly praises Adolf Hitler for his 'nationalism'. The founder leader of the Shiv Sena, a right-wing political party with a base in Maharashtra, specifically Mumbai, Balasaheb Thackeray (pronounced Thaak-re), former cartoonist, is one person who remains unabashed and uninhibited in his adulation for the German dictator.

The Shiv Sena, it is believed, was used by textile mill owners of Mumbai to counter the left trade unions in the commercial capital through the 1960s and 1970s. The Sena's strident rhetoric against 'outsiders'—people who were not natives of Maharashtra—and in favour of 'sons of the soil' was a very useful tool in dividing the workers, large sections of whom were migrants from states like Tamil Nadu, Bihar and eastern Uttar Pradesh. The Sena in its early years was also not averse to using brute force to break up strikes.

While the Sena cut its political teeth in the movement for including the Dharwar and Belgaum districts of adjoining Karnataka in Maharashtra, it is not surprising, therefore, that it first consolidated its strength in the city of Mumbai and surrounding industrial areas like Thane. Having tasted considerable success in breaking the back of the left trade unions, it then went on to capture many of the unions and hence establish a base for electoral conquests in the future.

The first major electoral success for the Shiv Sena—which uses a snarling tiger as its party symbol—came when it won the Bombay Municipal Corporation elections in 1968, barely two years after the party formally came into existence on June 19, 1966. The Sena owed its victory in part to dissension within the Congress, in particular to the confrontation between the Bombay Pradesh Congress Committee (BPCC) and the Maharashtra Pradesh Congress Committee (MPCC). The two Congress committees were bitterly opposed to each other because of the contradictory stands they had taken on an extremely emotive issue: the creation of the state of Maharashtra from the erstwhile Bombay Presidency. While the BPCC, dominated by the city's industrial and trading elite, was against the idea of Bombay being part of Maharashtra, the MPCC, which was dominated by the rural elite of what is today western Maharashtra, had argued for Bombay being part of the new state.

This conflict within the ranks of the Congress certainly helped the Shiv Sena in the elections for the Bombay Municipal Corporation. But, it wasn't just a victory by default. The Sena's virulent campaign against the *lungi walas*—a disparaging sartorial term used to describe those from the southern states of India—also played a significant part. Migrants from the south, particularly from Tamil Nadu, had a considerable share in white-collar jobs in Bombay and the Sena's demand that these jobs should go to native Maharashtrians found an echo among the Maharashtrian middle-class, given the context of rising unemployment. The Sena chose to attack restaurants run by south Indians to highlight its opposition to 'outsiders'.

Despite this early success, the Sena remained essentially a party confined to Mumbai and some neighbouring smaller industrial towns till the mid-1980s. Through the late 1960s, the 1970s and the early 1980s, the Sena experimented with various alliances, without succeeding in making a major impact on the politics of Maharashtra. According to Praveen Swamy (*Frontline*, May 26, 2001):

> It is also instructive to note that opportunistic alliances have been a second key element of Sena strategy. Many of its collaborators have been improbable allies. It fought the 1973 Mumbai municipal elections, for example, in alliance with the pro-Dalit Republican Party of India, and then had its candidate elected as Mayor in a deal with the Muslim League, the socialists, the Congress (O), and both the BPCC and the MPCC; all these were wooed and in turn courted the Sena. The only consistent element in Sena politics was its hostile anti-communism, a project that had the gleeful

support of both factions of the Congress. Through the 1970s, Sena gangs repeatedly attacked leading communist trade union leaders, and in 1973 were responsible for the murder of popular Parel MLA Krishna Desai. It was only in 1984, with the Sena discredited as a criminal mafia and in electoral decline, that Thackeray sought alliances with the Hindu Right, first forming the Hindu Mahasangh, and then allying with the BJP.

The period since 1984 has seen the Sena acquiring the image that has now come to stay—as a rabidly anti-Muslim organisation and one that believes in violence as a means of getting its point of view accepted. Thus, the Shiv Sena proudly took credit for the fact that its supporters actively participated in the demolition of the Babri mosque. It has also been at the forefront of the campaign to oust 'illegal' Bangladeshi migrants from Mumbai and other parts of the country. While the issue is ostensibly one of national sovereignty and preserving the sanctity of international borders, the Sena's interest in it clearly stems from the fact that the Bangladeshi migrants also happen to be Muslims.

For six years, between December 1995 and December 2001, Thackeray had in fact been disenfranchised because he had been held guilty of delivering speeches and writing articles that were considered communally inflammatory. During the hearing of this criminal case (which was upheld by the Supreme Court), there was a marked contrast between Thackeray's conciliatory attitude in court and his public belligerence.

While the BJP–Shiv Sena government was in power in Maharashtra, it spared no effort to prevent the smooth functioning of the Justice B.N. Sri Krishna Commission of inquiry. The commission's report had categorically blamed the Sena for fomenting the violence that had been largely targeted against Muslims, though it was also critical of the failure of the state government to quickly contain the violence that left over 1,000 killed and many more injured and rendered homeless. At the time of the riots, the Maharashtra government was headed by Congress Chief Minister Sudhakar Rao Naik, who was not exactly on the best of terms with fellow Congress leader from Maharashtra, Sharad Pawar (who was then Union Defence Minister in the Narasimha Rao government).

The BJP–Sena government stalled the presentation of the Sri Krishna Commission report in the state assembly for as long as it possibly could. And not surprisingly, the state government headed by Manohar Joshi (who went on to become Union Minister for Heavy Industry and Public Enterprises and subsequently, Speaker of the Lok Sabha) chose to reject the report's findings and not accept most of its recommendations that called for punitive legal action against Sena supporters allegedly responsible for the communal carnage—the likes of which had never been witnessed in Mumbai and did much to tarnish the cosmopolitan image of a city that is considered by many to be the bastion of capitalism in India.

In September–October 1999, during the state assembly elections—which were held simultaneously with the Lok Sabha elections—the Congress claimed during its campaign that it would properly implement the recommendations of the Sri Krishna Commission if it were voted to power. Eventually, the Congress came to power in the state by forming a coalition government with the Nationalist Congress Party headed by Vilasrao Deshmukh but this government did not do much to follow up its election campaign promises. At one stage in July 2000 it appeared as if the Congress–NCP government would initiate stern action against Thackeray when state Home Minister Chhagan Bhujbal (a former Shiv Sainik himself who had broken away from Thackeray) indicated that the police might arrest his former mentor.

As soon as this seemed possible, the Shiv Sena threatened that violence would rock Mumbai if Thackeray were arrested. In New Delhi, the Shiv Sena ministers in the Union government—besides Joshi, such ministers included Minister for Chemicals and Fertilizers Suresh Prabhu and Minister of State for Finance Balasaheb Vikhe Patil—decided to resign from the government in protest and stayed away from work for nearly a week demanding that Prime Minister Vajpayee intervene to prevent Thackeray's arrest in Mumbai.

What was eventually enacted was a damp squib, with Thackeray being released within minutes of being 'arrested'. Several observers felt that the Congress–NCP government had simply lost its nerve and sought a face-saving way out of the mess. Whether that is true or not, this was not the first time that Thackeray had successfully dared his opponents to arrest him. At the height of the communal riots in December 1992–January 1993, when calls for Thackeray's arrest were mounting and the Naik government seemed to be toying with the idea, the Sena had threatened that blood would flow on the streets of Mumbai if 'Balasaheb' was placed behind bars. Not only was Thackeray not arrested, the Mumbai police actually went round town announcing from loud-speakers mounted on police jeeps that 'rumours' about the impending arrest of the Shiv Sena chief were false. The police later justified this action on the ground that it was necessary to diffuse tension in the city to prevent the law and order situation from getting completely out of hand.

There is a section of opinion that argues that Thackeray is just an overgrown bully and that like all bullies he is essentially a coward. Those who subscribe to this view point out that after the bomb blasts of March 1993, including one very close to Thackeray's residence and another near the Sena headquarters, there was no further communal violence in Mumbai. Hence, they argue, the state government should call Thackeray's bluff and arrest him without fear of the consequences. Whatever the merits of this hypothesis, it has not been put to test.

Since 1984, the Sena and the BJP have remained affiliated to each other and Sena supremo Thackeray has not found it necessary to go along with any other political party, in contrast to the Sena's fast-changing alliances in the past. The Sena, despite its ideological affinity with the BJP, however, has not always supported the larger party. It has periodically sought to distinguish itself as the more 'radical' of the Hindutva parties. Just as the BJP has time and again accused the Congress of 'appeasing minorities', the Sena has been critical of the BJP for its alleged appeasement of 'secularists'. One of the more obvious attempts by the Sena to portray itself as the more radical Hindutva party was in 2002, when Thackeray grandly announced that his party would form 'suicide squads' of Hindus to counter the suicide squads of the Kashmiri militants. Not surprisingly, nothing has since been heard of such Hindu suicide squads, but Thackeray had derived the limited mileage that he sought.

The tensions within the Sena–BJP alliance in Maharashtra were most evident after they lost power in 1999. In mid-2000, at a time when Thackeray was besieged by criminal cases filed against him, BJP leader Gopinath Munde (who was earlier Deputy Chief Minister in the Manohar Joshi government and is the brother-in-law of Pramod Mahajan) converted a public rally by the BJP into a

Sena-bashing session. He accused the Sena of being selective in its use of Hindutva and claimed that the BJP was more faithful to the ideology, sticking with it even through difficult times. Relations between the two allies deteriorated quite sharply after this incident and the BJP even suggested that it would contest elections for local bodies in Maharashtra—held in September that year—without the Sena as a partner. Bickering within the Sena–BJP alliance became so endemic that there was even speculation on whether the BJP was attempting to topple the Vilasrao Deshmukh government by forging an alliance with the NCP rather than the Sena.

This, of course, did not happen, and the Sena and BJP soon mended fences, but the alliance has never been free of tension and jockeying for position in the state. Not surprisingly, this has had its impact on the coalition in New Delhi as well, with the Sena often going public with its criticism of the Vajpayee government on different issues. On several occasions, for instance, Thackeray has sought to rubbish the government's peace talks with Pakistan, arguing that the only way to settle the India–Pakistan dispute was to teach Pakistan a military lesson by forcibly occupying Pakistan Occupied Kashmir. The Shiv Sena chief even went to the extent of opposing cricket matches between the two neighbouring countries. In January 1999, a relatively unknown Sena supporter in the capital went as far as digging up the cricket pitch and filling up the holes with oil in New Delhi's Feroz Shah Kotla stadium in the middle of the night to prevent the test match that was scheduled to start the following day. The Sena has also opposed performances by Pakistani artistes like the popular ghazal singer Mehdi Hasan and were also allegedly responsible for an attack on film star Dilip Kumar's residence after he was awarded the Nishan-e-Pakistan— the highest civilian award of the government of Pakistan.

Another occasion on which the Sena openly attacked the Vajpayee government was in early 2001, when editorials written by Thackeray in the *Saamna* were scathing in their reference to Brajesh Mishra, Principal Secretary to the Prime Minister and the government's National Security Advisor. The editorials suggested what many believed: that Mishra had acquired power way beyond what was desirable and that his competence also left much to be desired. The editorials came at a time when several in the media were already questioning the 'extra-constitutional' nature of the clout wielded by a coterie in the Prime Minister's Office (PMO) led by Mishra and including Nand Kishore Singh, a career bureaucrat who had retired but was an Officer on Special Duty (OSD) in the PMO. Thackeray also questioned the clout of Prime Minister Vajpayee's foster son-in-law Ranjan Bhattacharya. The attack on the PMO from one of the BJP's closest and biggest allies was particularly embarrassing.

Sanjay Nirupam, a Sena MP perceived as being a young firebrand who enjoys the confidence of Thackeray, initiated another of the periodic spats between the BJP and the Sena in 2002, when he attacked Disinvestment Minister Arun Shourie in Parliament for the manner in which a public sector hotel, the Centaur Hotel at Juhu near Mumbai airport, had been privatised. Nirupam joined the Opposition in attacking the government for irregularities in the deal and even hinted that Shourie was personally involved in the alleged irregularities and that the Minister had swung the deal to favour a friend, a charge that Shourie denied. Ultimately, the controversy died down, but it did underline once again that the BJP could not take the Sena for granted.

Nirupam had on at least one other occasion in the past embarrassed the Vajpayee government after the former Chairman of the Unit Trust of India, P.S. Subramanyam, had been arrested by the CBI for alleged financial misdemeanours. Nirupam created a furore when he released documents that indicated that the Prime Minister's foster son-in-law Ranjan Bhattacharya and N.K. Singh had been calling Subramanyam frequently on his mobile telephone. Singh later sought to justify the calls he had made to the disgraced UTI Chairman by describing them as 'routine'.

Thackeray also has not been averse to occasionally establishing that 'he is the boss' in the relationship between the two pro-Hindutva parties. For example, Suresh Prabhu, who had managed to earn a reputation for himself as a dynamic Union Power Minister during a fairly short stint, was suddenly asked to put in his papers by the Sena chief. Thackeray had ostensibly decided that Prabhu was needed for party work in Maharashtra, though the political grapevine suggested that the move was prompted by Thackeray's feeling that Prabhu was not doing enough for the Sena in the Union government. Vajpayee and other senior BJP leaders were quite evidently upset at Prabhu's being pulled out of the government, but Thackeray not only stuck to his decision, but also ensured that the man replacing Prabhu in the power ministry would be another Sainik, Ananth Geethe.

The Sena's 'cultural policing' has also proved an embarrassment for the BJP on several occasions. For instance, the Sena decided to 'enforce' a self-proclaimed ban on the film *Fire* directed by Mira Nair on the grounds that it depicted two Indian women in a lesbian relationship that was supposed to be against Indian culture. Earlier, during the tenure of the Sena–BJP government in Maharashtra, its Culture Minister, Pramod Navalkar, a Sainik, had earned a dubious reputation for moral policing, raving and ranting against couples dating and pubs.

Despite all the embarrassment and the periodic friction, what has kept the BJP firmly wedded to the Sena in Maharashtra for close to two decades? Part of the reason of course lies in the fact that the ideological affinity between the two parties is strong enough to offset minor—or at times even major—irritants. But the bonding is not all ideological. The BJP is also acutely aware of the fact that the Sena has over the years acquired a strong base in a section of Maharashtrian society that is electorally crucial—the upper-caste Marathas. The Maratha community had traditionally been loyal to the Congress, and the BJP—or its forerunner the BJS—had never succeeded in making a dent in this section. The Sena, on the other hand, has managed to woo large sections of the Marathas. In fact, studies have shown that in Maharashtra today, the NCP and the Sena are the two parties that contend for the bulk of the Maratha vote, with the Congress left to mop up the crumbs. The OBCs constitute another section into which the Sena has made significant inroads and the BJP has not. For the BJP, therefore, the Sena's base serves as the ideal complement to its own electoral base in the state.

In December 2003, however, there were signs that the BJP was making a serious attempt to widen its options in Maharashtra by roping in the NCP (as detailed in an earlier chapter). Had the attempt succeeded, the BJP's bargaining position vis-a-vis the Shiv Sena would have dramatically improved. Not only would the NCP have brought into the NDA's kitty additional Maratha votes, it would also have left the Congress on its own. All indications at the time of writing, however, were that the NCP was only talking to the BJP to build its own bargaining strength against the Congress.

Chapter 5
Left Parties
Caged Birds?

The left parties in Indian politics—the two communist parties, the Revolutionary Socialist Party (RSP) and the All India Forward Bloc—have arguably had more experience with coalitions than any other political group in India. Not only have these parties been running the state government in West Bengal for almost 27 years since 1977—a record by itself—they also have a similar formation in Tripura and (with the exception of the Forward Bloc) in Kerala. It is another matter that the left has not had quite the same degree of success in either of these two states, though the Left Front in Tripura has lost a state assembly election only once since 1977.

A key difference between Kerala and the other two states in which the left is a major political force is the fact that the Front in Kerala includes parties that do not subscribe to a leftist ideology, which is why it is called the Left Democratic Front (LDF), rather than merely the LF. It is also a fact worth noting that neither West Bengal nor Kerala or Tripura has ever had a single-party government since the left first came to power in each. In Kerala, this has meant that the state has not had a single-party government since 1957, when the E.M.S. Namboodiripad government became the first elected communist government in the world. In Tripura, on the one occasion that the left lost power, in 1988, it was a coalition of the Congress and the Tripura Upajati Juba Samiti (TUJS)—a party with a base confined largely to the tribals in the state—that formed the government under Sudhir Ranjan Majumdar.

What is interesting is that this absence of single-party rule has not been because no party has been able to win a majority of the seats in the assembly. On the contrary, the CPI(M) has in every state assembly election in West Bengal since 1977 won a comfortable majority on its own. This holds true in Tripura too (barring 1988). Since the Left Fronts in West Bengal and Tripura as also the LDF in Kerala have been pre-poll alliances, it might seem only natural that the governments formed after the election should be coalition governments, even if one of the partners is able to muster a majority on its own. However, it is not uncommon in Indian politics to find the dominant partner in a pre-election alliance ultimately forming a single-party government if it has a majority on its own in the state assembly. For instance, while the TDP and the BJP fought the 1999 Andhra Pradesh assembly elections as an alliance, the BJP was not invited to join the TDP government headed by Chandrababu Naidu after the elections. The same was true in Haryana, where the INLD–BJP pre-poll alliance won comfortably, but the INLD formed the government on its own since it had a majority. More recently, in 2001, the AIADMK in Tamil Nadu had a pre-poll alliance with the Congress and the left parties for the assembly election, but after the elections, formed the government entirely on its own. The fact that the CPI(M) has not adopted this attitude towards its junior partners in the Fronts in West Bengal and Tripura suggests that its attitude towards coalitions is somewhat different from most other parties in India.

This is also borne out by the fact that the Left Front has lasted without a break ever since it was formed in 1977 and—more importantly—that it is not merely an electoral alliance. The Front also functions jointly as an opposition group within Parliament and in various agitational activities throughout India. In particular, the Left Front has had coordinated protests against the economic reforms programme launched in 1991 and sustained by successive governments in New Delhi ever since. The coordination between the left parties extends also to their mass organisations—thus the student organisations affiliated to the various left parties periodically organise joint rallies in New Delhi and in state capitals in support of their demands. Similarly, rallies and demonstrations by the left trade unions too have more often than not been a joint effort. Thus, unlike almost all other coalitions in the Indian context, the Left Front has functioned as a broad ideological coalition that is not limited to electoral politics. The only other alliance that comes close to achieving such unified functioning is the one between the Shiv Sena and the BJP in Maharashtra. However, while the two partners do share a close ideological affinity, their joint activities are kept to a minimum and generally restricted to the electoral arena.

The different approach that the left parties have towards coalitions and coalition politics is not really surprising, given the ideologies of these parties, in particular the two communist parties. The CPI(M) for instance, believes that its immediate task is the building of a 'people's democratic front' to usher in people's democracy—an intermediate stage in the ultimate goal of building a socialist society. This is something that is written into the party's programme—a document that lays down the long-term vision of the CPI(M) as distinct from election manifestoes, which espouse limited tactical objectives applicable in a given situation. The party believes that for people's democracy to be built, a broad coalition of various classes will have to be built against landlords and representatives of monopoly capital—which are the classes the party characterises as the ruling classes. Thus, the programme of the CPI(M) itself envisions the party playing only a leading—or vanguard, to use Marxist jargon—role in a broader coalition. With some differences on exactly which classes constitute the ruling classes and hence what kind of coalition needs to be built, the CPI too shares this understanding that it can only lead a social coalition to bring about a revolution in India. Since both parties see themselves as representing the working classes, it follows from their strategic vision that the coalition to be built with other classes will involve parties that represent the interests of these classes.

Most of the writing on the left parties, in the mainstream media and elsewhere, has tended to overlook this fact. As a result, it has not been sufficiently highlighted that unlike the other parties in Indian politics, the left has pursued coalitions as an objective rather than merely accepting them as a necessary evil thrown up by a polity that is increasingly getting fragmented. Thus, the political resolution discussed and adopted at every congress (held roughly once in three years) of the two communist parties invariably has a section on left unity and on how much progress has been made towards cementing this unity and towards broadening it to include forces outside the left fold. In fact, the focus on building a 'left and democratic' coalition has been such that recent party congresses of the CPI(M) have had to take note of the fact that the party's independent activities have tended to be over-shadowed by its joint efforts with other parties.

None of this is to suggest that the relationship between the various partners in the Left Fronts in West Bengal and Tripura and the LDF in Kerala has been free of acrimony. As with any other alliance, there has been a fair amount of bickering, particularly by the junior partners in the Fronts, who perceive the CPI(M) as acting like a 'big brother' and being insensitive to their concerns and interests. In West Bengal, for instance, there have been occasions when the RSP and the Forward Bloc have held out veiled threats of leaving the Left Front if the CPI(M) did not desist from its 'authoritarian' ways. The Forward Bloc, in fact, underwent a split in the early 1990s when one section walked out of the party, accusing the other of subjugating the party's interests to those of the CPI(M). Typically, the bickering between the partners has tended to peak around election time, when the issue of which partner would contest from which constituency heightens differences and raises tempers. Nevertheless, the friction between the constituents of the Left Front has never seriously threatened its survival.

At a national level, the fissures within the Left Front came to the forefront like never before in April 1999 just after the second Vajpayee government lost a vote of confidence and Congress President Sonia Gandhi decided to stake a claim to form an alternative government. Her efforts were scuttled largely because the Samajwadi Party chose not to support her as a likely Prime Minister heading an anti-NDA coalition. Together with the SP, two of the largest constituents of the Left Front after the CPI(M) and CPI decided to make common cause with the SP—these were the Forward Bloc and the RSP. The leaders of these two parties were evidently uncomfortable supporting a government headed by Sonia Gandhi. Despite attempts by individuals like Harkishen Singh Surjeet, General Secretary of the CPI(M), to persuade MPs and leaders of the Forward Bloc and the RSP to support a Congress-led coalition headed by Sonia Gandhi, the two smaller left parties stood their ground.

Some would argue that the survival of the Left Fronts in West Bengal and Tripura and the LDF in Kerala is entirely because of the overwhelming dominance of the CPI(M) in all of them. The others in the Fronts, they would argue, know that their political survival depends on remaining part of the Front and that they would be committing political *hara kiri* by trying to contest on their own. There is certainly an element of truth in this analysis. However, it would be facile to explain the continued cohesion of the left purely in terms of political pragmatism. To understand why, a look at the electoral arithmetic of West Bengal or Kerala would suffice. While the Left Front has had an uninterrupted period of close to 27 years in power in West Bengal, the dominance of the Left Front in the state's politics is overstated by the number of seats that the Front has won in every election after 1977.

If one were to look at just the number of seats won, the Left Front has consistently won a two-thirds majority in the 294-member assembly. However, if we take a look at the vote shares the picture appears quite different. The most dramatic illustration is provided by the 1987 assembly elections. The Left Front won in 242 of the 294 constituencies, with the CPI(M) alone winning 187 seats, while the Congress won only 40 seats. In terms of vote share, however, the Congress won 41.8 per cent of the votes against the CPI(M)'s 39.3 per cent, while the CPI, Forward Bloc and RSP put together won 11.6 per cent of the votes. Had the CPI(M)'s partners in the Front deserted it and joined the Congress instead, the result would probably have been a sweep for the Congress-led alliance. This is even more evident in the context of Kerala, where many state assembly constituencies are often won or lost by a few hundred votes. The shift of a single party, however minor, from one alliance to the other could therefore decisively alter the verdict of the electorate. That the Left Fronts and the LDF have more or less held firm despite this suggests that ideological affinity between the partners has played at least as important a role as political pragmatism.

Ideological affinity apart, the Left Fronts in West Bengal and Tripura have consciously built an institutional mechanism to ensure that the Front stays together and that there is a platform apart from the state government in which the various constituents of the Front have the opportunity to discuss issues and sort out differences between themselves. This institutional mechanism is in the form of regular meetings of representatives of the parties constituting the Front. It is not a coincidence that the convenors of the Left Front have always been individuals who are not part of the state government. As a matter of deliberate policy, the distinction has always been maintained between the Front per se and the government run by it. Typically, in West Bengal, the secretary of the state unit of the CPI(M) has been the Convenor of the Front. At its inception, the Convenor of the Front, Promode Dasgupta—or PDG as he was popularly known—was perceived as being as powerful as Chief Minister Jyoti Basu. Also as a matter of conscious policy, PDG was projected as first among equals in party and Front matters, while Jyoti Basu was seen as the undisputed leader of the government.

In more recent years, however, this separation between the Front and the government in West Bengal has become somewhat more blurred. Whether this is because CPI(M) state secretaries after PDG did not have quite the same stature as Jyoti Basu or because the state government increasingly became the focus of the CPI(M)'s activities in the state is a moot question. The answer, as often, probably lies somewhere in between. What is more relevant to the larger national context, however, is that this mechanism of a formal coordinating body of a coalition was subsequently picked up by the United Front when it came to power in New Delhi and then the NDA.

Prior to the UF, there had been five non-Congress coalition governments formed in New Delhi. None of them had any formal mechanism for discussion and policy formulation among the partners of the coalition. The UF became the first Union government in which a party from the left—the CPI—joined the government. That may well explain the fact that it was the first time a coordination committee of the Front was formed. It was also the first time that a coalition forming a Union government formally adopted a Common Minimum Programme acceptable to its constituents. The model was later replicated by the NDA, which adopted an 'agenda for governance'. To the extent that formal mechanisms for consultations among partners and clearly-spelt-out programmes for the government indicate a maturing of coalition politics, the left can justifiably lay claim to having made a significant contribution to the evolution of coalitions in India, particularly at the national level.

Despite its success in setting a model for others to follow in terms of what the BJP today calls 'coalition dharma', the left has remained a fringe player in national politics, unable to make its impact felt in terms of influencing policy. Since 1977, the left has supported five governments in New Delhi—the ones led by Morarji

Desai (1977), Charan Singh (1979), V.P. Singh (1989), H.D. Deve Gowda (1996) and I.K. Gujral (1997). One section of the left—the CPI—was part of the last two governments. Yet, on none of these occasions has the policy of the government made any concessions to the left. The impotence of the left in this respect was most obvious during the tenure of the two UF governments in the late 1990s. The left was avowedly against the processes of economic liberalisation and globalisation launched by the previous Narasimha Rao government. Yet, neither the Common Minimum Programme of the UF nor the actions of its governments showed the slightest concession to this position. On the contrary, P. Chidambaram, who was Finance Minister in both the UF governments, was hailed as one of the most enthusiastic liberalisers India has seen.

Ironically, on the one occasion on which the left was able to stall a reform measure during the UF's tenure, it was not because Chidambaram or others in the government yielded to its persuasion; it was the result of unexpected support from the main opposition party, the BJP. This was when the Finance Minister was trying to push a bill through Parliament to open up the insurance sector to private firms, both Indian and foreign. Despite vehement opposition from the left, including the CPI, which was part of the government, Chidambaram decided to go ahead because he had obtained informal assurances from both the BJP and the Congress that they would support the bill. Ultimately the BJP reneged on its informal commitment to Chidambaram, on the plea that the insurance sector should be opened up in stages—allowing only the Indian private sector in during the first stage.

The inability to influence policy—particularly economic policy—is not inexplicable. It has been a consequence of the fact that the left's support to governments in New Delhi has, unlike its formation of coalitions in the states, been driven by political compulsion rather than choice. Thus, the support extended by the CPI(M) to the Janata Party governments of the late 1970s was a result of the desire to prevent the 'authoritarian' Indira Gandhi and Congress from returning to power. Having identified the Congress as the biggest enemy and recognising that the CPI(M) on its own was in no position to counter the Congress, except in the three states of West Bengal, Tripura and Kerala, the party had no choice but to support the Janata Party governments. (The CPI at this stage was still of the opinion that the Congress under Indira Gandhi should be supported since it was fighting the right-wing RSS.) Similarly, in 1989, it was the same desire to keep the Congress—still seen as the main enemy—out of power that forced the left to align itself with the V.P. Singh-led Janata Dal.

While the formation of the V.P. Singh government has often been portrayed as an occasion on which the left and the right in Indian politics came together to keep out the Congress, the reality is more complex. The fact is that the left throughout the 1989 Lok Sabha election campaign attacked both the Congress and the BJP, refused to share a platform with the BJP, and repeatedly exhorted V.P. Singh not to have any arrangement with the right-wing party. In states like Bihar, where both the left and the BJP had some electoral presence, they fought elections against each other. While both were aligned to the Janata Dal, they were openly hostile to each other.

By the time of the 1996 Lok Sabha elections, the growing influence of the BJP had convinced the left that it was at least as big an enemy as the Congress. Hence, when the UF and its government were formed, the left's stated objective was to keep both the Congress and the BJP out of power. On each of these occasions, the immediate political objective was perceived as being of such over-riding importance that the left was prepared to sacrifice its economic agenda to achieve the more urgent political goal. Since those running the government were also aware of the overarching importance of the political objective for the left, they knew only too well that the left's ability to bargain in terms of policy measures was limited if not totally absent.

It is the same awareness of a lack of bargaining power in terms of policy that ultimately led to the CPI(M)'s decision not to join the UF government in June 1996—a decision that was later famously described as a 'historic blunder' by Jyoti Basu, the man who was the UF's first choice to become Prime Minister. It remains the only occasion on which the representative of a party has been offered the post but had to refuse because his own party voted against accepting the offer. The decision was by no means easy. It was also not the unanimous view of the party leadership. In fact, when, after a meeting of the UF constituents suggested that Jyoti Basu be made Prime Minister, the CPI(M)'s politbureau decided by a majority decision to accept the offer. However, the party's central committee—which under the party's constitution is the highest decision-making body between two party congresses—reversed the politbureau's decision, again by a split decision, leaving the door open for H.D. Deve Gowda to become the Prime Minister.

The decision continues to remain controversial with the CPI(M)'s leadership and cadre divided on whether it was right or wrong. Those in favour of the decision argue that the manner in which the UF government functioned and the fact that it collapsed after 18 months bears out the proposition that being party to it would have done the CPI(M) no good. Those against the decision argue that Jyoti Basu as Prime Minister could have run a much more successful government than either Deve Gowda or Gujral and that the CPI(M) would have been able to significantly influence policy. Even in a worst-case scenario, they add, the party would at least have acquired a national profile and could have broken out of its image of being confined largely to three states. While the debate has not been clinched, it increasingly looks likely that the CPI(M) will not repeat its 'historic blunder', given another chance. Whether such a chance will be available in the foreseeable future is, of course, another matter.

If there is one issue that has troubled the left parties—in particular the two communist parties—more than any other throughout their history, it has been their inability to make their presence felt in the Hindi heartland: the states of Uttar Pradesh, Bihar and Madhya Pradesh. Not only are these states electorally crucial (between them, before each was bifurcated in 2000, they accounted for 179 of the Lok Sabha's 543 seats), any political movement would have to recognise that it cannot acquire a truly all-India character without having a foothold in the Indo-Gangetic plains, which have dominated the politics of the country.

Between the two communist parties, the CPI has over the years had a stronger base in the Hindi heartland than the CPI(M), which is by far the more dominant of the two communist parties in most other parts of the country. Yet, even at its best, the CPI has had only a modest influence in Bihar, present-day Jharkhand and Uttaranchal, a marginal presence in Uttar Pradesh and not even a token presence in Madhya Pradesh or present-day Chhattisgarh. For the CPI(M) too, Bihar has presented more reason for hope than any of the other parts of this region, though its strength in each of the states has consistently been much less than the CPI's.

Interestingly, the weakness of the left parties in the electoral arena in the Hindi belt does not necessarily extend to their mass organisations. The CPI-affiliated All India Trade Union Congress (AITUC) and the CPI(M)-affiliated Centre of Indian Trade Unions (CITU), for instance, are among the strongest unions in this region, as indeed in the rest of the country. Yet, the same workers who opt for these unions are quite reluctant to extend their support to the electoral battle when it comes to bargaining for their economic rights.

One of the reasons most commonly cited for the failure of the CPI and the CPI(M) to make a breakthrough in the Hindi belt has been the inability of the communists to fully comprehend and come to terms with the caste phenomenon. With their emphasis on class, this view would suggest that the communists have simply not recognised that caste is a much stronger motivating force in the Hindi belt and a decidedly better platform for political mobilisation. This is a view that is not merely confined to outsiders analysing the communist movement. The late Indrajit Gupta, one of the foremost leaders of the CPI for over four decades, shared this view. In a personal interview a few months before he died, Gupta 'admitted' that the left had seriously underestimated the influence of the caste system in Indian politics in general and in the Hindi belt in particular. This, he felt, was one of the key reasons for the left's failure to grow beyond the narrow confines of West Bengal, Kerala and Tripura.

Gupta said:

> Exploitation of one caste by another was never a big factor in our minds. But in a Hindu society, I find this is the dominant thing...much more than class. We have a working class in the big industrial centres where we were the dominant force among the workers, particularly at the trade union level. Big strikes were taking place. We were leading those strikes. But when it came to elections, the same worker who was carrying a red flag on his shoulders in order to get a higher salary or a bonus...would look towards his own caste.... This disrupted the unity of the class completely. But I don't think the communists, the Marxists in this country paid sufficient attention or made a proper study of this phenomenon.... This thing [caste] is so deeply rooted in our psyche, this Manusmriti, this Chaturvarna, to get out of it will take a thousand years.

There is indeed some merit in the argument that the communist parties have failed to understand the importance of caste in the

Hindi heartland or have at least underestimated its hold on the people. However, to see this as the sole or even the main reason for the failure of the left to make inroads in this region might be to over-simplify a complex reality. There could be other historical reasons for the weakness of the left in this region. For instance, it is the Hindi belt in which the 'socialist' parties have traditionally had a significant presence. Thus, if one considers the left-of-centre space in Indian politics, it might with some justification be argued that while the communist parties faced little or no challenge for this space in the southern states and in West Bengal and Tripura, they had to face the challenge of the Samajwadis in the Hindi heartland. Leaders like Ram Manohar Lohia and Acharya Narendra Dev were definitely a formidable challenge. Of course, it is also true that Samajwadi politics right from its inception has had caste overtones and this could be a factor in its gaining greater success than the communist parties.

Another factor in the weakness of the left could be the manner in which the two major splits in the communist movement took place in 1964 and 1967. When a section of the CPI broke away in 1964 to form the CPI(M), in most other parts of the country the bulk of the undivided party's support base and some of the key figures in its middle-level leadership were part of the breakaway faction. As history subsequently proved, it was the breakaway CPI(M) which was to become the more dynamic of the two communist parties and the one that would grow faster, while the parent CPI was clearly on a downhill slope. The fact that most of the communist leadership in states like Bihar and Uttar Pradesh remained with the CPI may also, therefore, have contributed to the gradual demise of the mainstream left parties in this region.

Once again, when the CPI(M) in turn split in 1967, with the breakaway group forming the CPI(ML), which was to lead what came to be known as the Naxalite movement, the Hindi heartland again saw a larger proportion of the cadre and leadership joining the CPI(ML) than in many other parts of the country. Thus, both in 1964 and in 1967, the CPI(M) was at the losing end of the split in the Hindi heartland. To what extent this has had an effect on the growth of the communist parties as a whole in the Hindi region is a moot question.

As later events have shown, the CPI in Bihar—and to a lesser extent in UP—was soon beset with caste-based factionalism (ironical considering that the party has been accused of not understanding caste as a phenomenon) and hence became easy prey for the likes of Laloo Prasad Yadav and Mulayam Singh Yadav when they emerged as caste-based leaders in their own right. Both in Bihar and in UP, the CPI was split by the two Yadav chieftains, with a section joining the SP in Uttar Pradesh and the then Janata Dal in Bihar. The desertion of Mitrasen Yadav in UP was particularly embarrassing for the party since it had always been proud of the fact that he (as a CPI leader) had managed to win the Faizabad Lok Sabha seat, which included Ayodhya, at the peak of the BJP–VHP movement for the construction of the Ram temple. The CPI(M) too has not been entirely free of caste-based factionalism in Bihar, though the virus may be less virulent than in the CPI.

In the context of the weakness of the left in the Hindi heartland, it must also be recognised that while the mainstream left parties may have failed to make much headway, the extreme left has had a consistent—and growing—strength in rural Bihar and Jharkhand. This has happened despite repeated splits and mergers in the CPI(ML) since it was formed in 1967. Briefly, in the late 1980s and early 1990s, it appeared that the ultra-left in Bihar could even emerge as a credible electoral force, when the Indian People's Front (IPF) made significant inroads in some districts of central Bihar. However, it turned out to be a false promise and the IPF, which metamorphosed into the CPI(ML)-Liberation, subsequently lost steam. As with the CPI, it also had to face the embarrassment of some of its elected representatives switching to Laloo Yadav's RJD.

Outside the electoral arena, however, the extreme left has significantly expanded its influence in central Bihar and in Jharkhand, through groups like the Maoist Communist Centre (MCC) and the People's War Group (PWG). These groups are able to strike at police stations and other symbols of state authority with impressive regularity, and in parts of Jharkhand in particular their writ seems to run at least as much as the elected government's. The extent of their influence is such that political commentators and intelligence sources have on more than one occasion pointed out that all the way from Nepal in the north through Bihar, Jharkhand and Chhattisgrah, to Telengana in northern Andhra Pradesh, there is a huge swathe of land that faces a 'Maoist menace'.

The growth of the extreme left could also provide some pointers to why the more moderate sections of the left have been unable to make serious headway beyond the states of West Bengal, Kerala and Tripura. Arguably one major factor has been the tendency of the left to 'tail' one of the established parties in each state in order to defeat whichever party it views as the biggest enemy in a given context. Thus, the left has tailed one or the other of the Dravidian parties in Tamil Nadu for most of the period since 1967, initially on the grounds that defeating the Congress was the priority and in more recent years with the objective of keeping the NDA at bay. Similar considerations have meant that the left has latched on to the RJD in Bihar and the SP in Uttar Pradesh, the Akali Dal in Punjab (before the Akalis joined the NDA), and so on. As a result, any chance that the left might have had of establishing its distinct identity, it can be convincingly argued, has been lost. In fact, even where the left historically had a presence, it lost out to regional parties. The most telling example of this is in Andhra Pradesh. In the elections held in 1952, when the state was part of the Madras Presidency, the undivided CPI had emerged as the single-largest party ahead of the Congress. Today, the two communist parties put together would be hard-pressed to win more than a couple of Lok Sabha seats in Andhra Pradesh on their own.

In Power in the States

The Left Front may have failed to make an impact on policy, particularly economic policy, at the national level, even when it has supported governments in New Delhi, but in the states where it has been in power, the story is somewhat different. While Tripura being a small state has escaped national attention more often than not, the left's successes in implementing at least parts of its agenda in West Bengal and Kerala have often been commented upon. What is particularly significant is that the 'Kerala model' of development, initiated by the E.M.S. Namboodiripad government of 1957, has not only been widely commented upon, it has by and large been adopted by most governments that have followed in the state. Thus, the left has influenced policy in Kerala not only when in power, but also when it has been out of power. In West Bengal, of course, there is no way of knowing whether this pattern would be repeated, since the left hasn't lost power since it assumed office in 1977 after two brief stints in the late-1960s.

What is clear, however, is the fact that the left-led governments in West Bengal and Kerala have been unable to sufficiently distinguish themselves from 'pro-reform' state governments since the process of pro-market economic reforms was initiated in India in 1991. While the left has been a virulent critic of the liberalisation and globalisation programme, its practice has not been markedly different from the Congress government of S.M. Krishna in Karnataka or the TDP government of Chandrababu Naidu in Andhra Pradesh.

Like other state governments, those led by the left have also sought to attract foreign investment and even privatised ailing state-owned enterprises (though they have tried to couch privatisation as 'partnership' with the private sector). It is not surprising, therefore, that most commentators see the left's attack on the reforms either as part of a more general trend of parties being anti-reform when they are in opposition and pro-reform when in office, or as a case of serving vested interests like those of the trade unions. The left's response to such criticism has been to argue that state governments are constrained in terms of economic policy by what New Delhi decides and can only tinker at the margins. While this may be true to some extent, it is not a position that the left has been able to successfully present to commentators or to the public at large.

Prior to the reforms, on the other hand, the left was successful in demarcating its economic agenda from those of others. This was particularly true of the early years of left-led governments in Kerala and West Bengal. The Namboodiripad governments of 1957 and 1967, for instance, initiated radical land reforms of the sort never seen anywhere in India before, except in Jammu & Kashmir under the National Conference. These governments were also responsible for setting up what remains, to date, the only universal Public Distribution System (PDS) in the country.

A slight digression is necessary at this point to explain the significance of this move. The responsibility for running the PDS in India is shared jointly by the Union and state governments. While New Delhi is responsible for centralised procurement for the PDS and for passing on the grain, sugar, etc. procured or obtained through levies to the states, the states bear the responsibility of actually distributing material under the PDS to the populace. As a result, the actual coverage of the PDS varies widely across states. Kerala has the distinction of being the only state with a PDS that reaches every resident of the state. Also, Kerala's PDS distributes through its chain of fair price shops several items—like soap, detergent, etc.—that are not part of the centrally determined list of items to be made available under the PDS.

Kerala's record in health care too is remarkable in comparison to other states in India. The Human Development Report 2003 of the United Nations Development Programme (UNDP) states: 'The state of Kerala, India, has health indicators similar to those of the United States—despite a per capita income 99% lower and annual spending on health of just $28 a person.' By any yardstick, this is a considerable achievement, particularly considering that Kerala is not even among the most prosperous Indian states.

As already mentioned, the fact that the left has repeatedly lost and regained power in Kerala has not undone the radical measures it has taken while in office. The land reforms, which ensured the abolishing of landlordism and the distribution of small land holdings to millions of agricultural labourers who were till that stage landless are arguably major factors in Kerala having significantly better social indicators than any other Indian state. The land reforms and the universal nature of the PDS also go some distance towards explaining the fact that Kerala has significantly lower poverty ratios than many other states with much higher per capita incomes.

In more recent years, the left in Kerala has also been at the forefront of initiating genuine decentralisation of the planning process down to the level of the village panchayat. Again, as with earlier radical measures taken by the left in the state, decentralisation has proved irreversible even after the left lost power in the state assembly elections in 2001.

In West Bengal too the Left Front to begin with followed an economic policy that had elements quite distinct from the policies that had been followed by earlier governments. In particular, the very first Left Front government that came to power after the 1977 assembly elections initiated a radical programme called Operation Barga that dramatically altered agrarian relations in rural West Bengal. In essence, the scheme institutionalised the rights of sharecroppers tilling land formally owned by others, often absentee landlords. Such was the effect of this move in terms of empowering millions of relatively poor farmers that the CPI(M)'s hold on the Bengal countryside has remained unshakeable to this day, over a quarter of a century after Operation Barga was launched. The same Left Front government also initiated land reforms on a scale never before seen in the eastern state.

The Left Front in West Bengal can also legitimately claim credit for making panchayati raj a reality, more than in most other states in India, though the extent of decentralisation may not quite match up to what has been achieved in Kerala. Some of the left's other pet initiatives have been less successful. In particular, the attempt to make Bangla the mandatory medium of instruction in primary education proved a failure and public pressure from parents who felt that their children were losing out to those educated in English-medium schools in other states ultimately forced the government to abandon this plan after having experimented with it for more than two decades.

Other key problem areas for the Left Front government in West Bengal have been its perceived neglect of Kolkata and other major urban centres as well as its inability to overcome the state's image of being prone to labour unrest. The net result is that the left, despite ruling West Bengal for more than 26 years, remains much weaker in the towns and cities than in the rural areas. The Left Front has consistently argued that the 'de-industrialisation' of Bengal—the most industrialised of India's provinces when the country became independent—is a consequence of the stepmotherly treatment meted out to the state by hostile governments in New Delhi, whether these governments have been run by the Congress or by the BJP. For instance, they point out, central public sector undertakings have stopped investing in the state. Also, New Delhi has always fixed royalties on minerals at inordinately low levels, thereby effectively subsidising the rest of the country at the expense of mineral-rich states like West Bengal.

This is a complaint that other mineral-rich states like Bihar, Jharkhand, Chhattisgarh, Madhya Pradesh, Assam and Orissa have also echoed on several occasions. Similarly, they argue that a now-defunct 'freight equalisation' scheme—under which coal and steel were made available throughout the country at the same price from the 1960s and 1970s to the 1990s—undermined the locational advantages that states with abundant coal, iron ore and limestone reserves would otherwise have enjoyed.

There is certainly a grain of truth in these complaints. However, it cannot seriously be denied that the major reason why industries fled West Bengal through the 1970s and 1980s was political. In the first half of the 1970s, the violent nature of politics in the state—with the Congress, the CPI(M) and the Naxalites fighting each other on the streets and in the villages—was enough to scare business away. After the Left Front came to power in 1977, the violence gradually abated, but replacing the old scare was a new one: the fear of labour militancy backed by a state government favourably inclined towards the unions. The phase of militant trade unionism in West Bengal dated back to the 1960s and peaked between 1967 and 1969, the two years which saw the formation of two United Front governments in the state, both dominated by the CPI(M).

Since the beginning of the 1990s, the CPI(M) has consciously tried to get out of this 'image trap'. Leaders like Somnath Chatterjee have periodically travelled abroad to try and woo investors, attempting to convince them with facts and figures that labour unrest in West Bengal is no worse than anywhere else in India. These attempts have had, at best, limited success. However, after Budhdhadev Bhattacharjee replaced the octagenarian Jyoti Basu as Chief Minister in 2001, there has been a perceptible improvement in the manner in which Indian industry looks at West Bengal. The fact that the power situation in the state is significantly better than it was in the 1970s has also helped. Ironically, one of the key reasons why the power situation improved from the mid-1990s onwards is because de-industrialisation meant that demand for power did not grow at the pace at which it would otherwise have done.

The Left and the Congress: A Love-Hate Relationship

Virtually right through the first five decades since the country became independent, the left has participated in coalition politics with the specific purpose of keeping the Congress out of power, whether at the level of the states or at the Union. What has been described as 'pathological' anti-Congressism dominated the psyche of communist leaders simply because these individuals looked at the Congress as representing the interests of the big bourgeoisie and the capitalist class. The notable exception was in the early 1970s, when the CPI had supported Indira Gandhi's government. The party was clearly impressed by her 'socialist' image, and even during the initial phase of the Emergency period in 1975–1977, the CPI supported her regime although the bigger CPI(M) remained steadfastly opposed to the Congress. Eventually, the CPI agreed that its support to the Emergency had been a mistake.

Anti-Congress sentiments in the left remained strong even when the CPI decided to participate in a Union government for the first and (so far) only time, namely the United Front government headed first by Deve Gowda and then Gujral. The CPI's representative in the government was one of its senior-most and tallest leaders, Indrajit Gupta, a veteran of Parliamentary debates. As a matter of fact, before he became Union Minister for Home Affairs in the Deve Gowda government, he was the senior-most member of the Lok Sabha as a result of which he served as protem Speaker when the lower house of Parliament assembled in May 1996 to elect P.A. Sangma (then of the Congress) as Speaker. Despite Gupta's long innings as a politician and despite the fact that the UF government was dependent on support from the Congress to remain in power, Gupta could not resist making jibes against the Congress while he was Home Minister.

Gupta had stated that if the Congress decided to withdraw support to the UF, they would offend the public at large and might provoke people to throw *chappals* (slippers) at them (Congress leaders). Leaders of the Congress, including its then President Sitaram Kesri, made no secret of their deep displeasure at Gupta's remarks. In one of his last interviews to the present authors, he conceded that his comments were 'indiscreet'. The Congress, it may be recalled, changed the first Prime Minister in the UF government Deve Gowda within eight months and replaced him with Gujral. The Congress then went on to withdraw its support to his government roughly a year later.

After the BJP-led NDA government came to power in 1998, the two communist parties and the left as a whole started coming closer to the Congress. Although the two relatively small left parties, the All India Forward Bloc and the Revolutionary Socialist Party, went along with the Samajwadi Party in not supporting Sonia Gandhi's candidature as Prime Minister after the second Vajpayee government lost a vote of confidence in April 1999, the left as an ideological grouping was clear that the Congress was the 'lesser evil' when compared to the BJP. Whereas the left agreed that there was little to distinguish between the economic policies followed by the two largest political parties in the country, unlike the BJP the Congress was not considered 'communal'.

In the run-up to the 14th general elections, the left finds itself in a dilemma at the time of writing. While it would like to ensure that the anti-NDA vote does not get divided, it does not want to push possible allies like the SP and the NCP into the NDA camp by forcing them to choose between the Congress and the NDA. As a result, it finds itself becoming the fulcrum of a non-Congress 'secular' platform. What the ultimate denouement of this secular front will be remains to be seen.

Chapter 6

Friends in Need

Are Coalitions Inherently Unstable?

The present phase of coalition governments at the level of the Union has thrown up a wide-ranging debate on what the nature of coalitions must be and what characteristics they should have if they are to prove long-lasting and stable. In particular, there have been suggestions that coalitions formed before elections are likely to be more stable than those cobbled together after the elections. Ideological cohesion within the parties of a coalition has also been seen by many as a reasonable guarantor of its longevity. Another proposition that has been put forward is that 'outside support', that is, political parties supporting a government on the floor of the legislature but not participating in it, tends to be a destabilising factor. Finally, it has been suggested by the BJP, among others, that if one constituent in a coalition is dominant in terms of size, such a coalition would last longer than one in which there are several small partners. It would be worth examining each of these propositions in light of the actual experience with coalitions in India.

In the context of the Union government in New Delhi, experiments in coalitions began only in 1977 with the Janata Party government headed by Morarji Desai; this was followed more than 12 years later when the V.P. Singh government was sworn in in 1989. However, in the states, coalition governments have existed from the time the very first elections were held in independent India in 1952. While at first sight there may seem to be very little in common between the manner in which coalitions in the states and those at the centre have worked, there are nevertheless enough common features to make a study of coalitions in the states a worthwhile exercise. The early experiments with coalition politics in various states threw up methods and results that were not very different from what we are witnessing at the centre. The fact that today there do exist some stable coalition governments, notably in West Bengal, Tripura, Kerala and Maharashtra, suggests that there has been a process of learning which could be cut short at an all-India level if relevant lessons are drawn from history. This chapter traces the experience of coalitions at the level of the Union government and in the states. As will become evident, many apparently obvious guarantors of stable coalitions have not actually proved to be so.

Coalitions at the Centre

While the first real coalition at the level of the Union government had to wait till 1977, three decades after independence, there was already, in 1969, a government led by a Congress that no longer had a majority in the lower house of Parliament. The situation arose thanks to a split in the Congress, which, in turn, was the culmination of a power struggle within the party, accelerated by the electoral setbacks during the 4th general elections of 1967. In the elections, the Congress was swept out of power in as many as nine states—Punjab, Haryana, Uttar Pradesh, Bihar, Madhya Pradesh, West Bengal, Orissa, Madras and Kerala. The extent of the damage to the Congress' hold over political power was brought out in a telling comment which became popular at the time: for the first time since independence, one could travel from West Pakistan to East Pakistan without once entering a state ruled by the grand old party of the Indian freedom movement.

The debacle aggravated factional fights within the Congress and heightened tensions between powerful party organisers and Indira Gandhi, the then Prime Minister. It also found expression in strong disagreements over some radical economic policies advocated by her, particularly from more conservative Congress leaders like Morarji Desai. This ultimately led to a split in the Congress which robbed the party of 62 Lok Sabha MPs, reducing it to a minority in November 1969.

For the first time, therefore, the ruling party in New Delhi did not have a majority of Lok Sabha MPs. Indira Gandhi's government, however, survived because of the support extended to it by the DMK, the Communist Party of India, the Akali Dal, the Muslim League and some independents. Thus, this was also the first occasion when the concept of 'outside support' was put into practice at the level of the Union government, though, as we shall see later, similar experiments had already been tried out in some states. The tenure of the minority government came to an end in December 1970, when Indira Gandhi herself chose to recommend dissolution of the Lok Sabha and the holding of fresh elections. This too was unprecedented and the 4th Lok Sabha became the first to have not completed its full five-year term.

If Indira Gandhi's minority government between November 1969 and December 1970 is disregarded, the first real attempt at a coalition government at the level of the Union was made in 1977 when the Janata Party came to power. The party was itself a coalition of several pre-poll allies who had come together on the issue of opposition to the Emergency.

The alliance that contested the March 1977 elections announced by Indira Gandhi after she suddenly lifted the Emergency comprised various political streams. In terms of its ideological moorings, the alliance can be broken up into four broad streams—those who had been in the Congress but had left the party at some point, the socialists, the right-wing Bharatiya Jana Sangh (or today's Bharatiya Janata Party), and a section of the left, notably the CPI(M) and some other smaller parties which, unlike the CPI, had consistently opposed the imposition of the Emergency.

Within the group of former Congressmen were people like Jagjivan Ram and Hemvati Nandan Bahuguna, who had been influential leaders within the Congress but had quit shortly before the elections on an anti-Emergency platform to form the Congress for Democracy (CFD). Then there were those who had been part of the erstwhile Congress (O), which was formed in 1969 when the Congress split thanks to a struggle for supremacy between Indira Gandhi's supporters and others in the organisation. During the Emergency, many of these leaders had been part of Jayaprakash Narayan's movement. One of these, Morarji Desai, ultimately emerged as the consensus choice to head the Janata Party government. A third constituent from among those who had once been within the Congress was the party led by Charan Singh, who was to later replace Desai as Prime Minister. Singh had, after quitting the Congress in 1967, floated his own party, the Bharatiya

Kranti Dal, later renamed the Bharatiya Lok Dal (BLD). Charan Singh had cultivated the peasantry, notably the Jats of western Uttar Pradesh and Haryana, as his core political base.

Among the non-Congress streams within the anti-Emergency alliance were the socialists—followers of Ram Manohar Lohia and Acharya Narendra Dev—George Fernandes, Madhu Dandavate and Madhu Limaye being among the more prominent leaders of this group. Another stream was the BJS whose association with the RSS was to become the bone of contention within the Janata Party leading to the fall of its government. Finally, there was the CPI(M) and smaller left parties. The Janata Party that was formed after the 1977 elections and which assumed office was a coalescing of these various streams, barring the left.

After a little over two years, the contradictions within the Janata Party reached a climax with the non-Jana Sangh components of what was essentially a coalition disguised as one party insisting that those from the Jana Sangh must choose between loyalty to the RSS and loyalty to the party. Ironically, the 'dual membership' issue as it came to be known was raised most vehemently by leaders like George Fernandes of the socialist stream, who are today among the staunchest allies of the BJP. With the leaders of the BJS, among them Atal Bihari Vajpayee (who was External Affairs Minister in the Desai Cabinet) and L.K. Advani (who was Information and Broadcasting Minister) refusing to give up their allegiance to the RSS, the Janata Party ultimately split and Morarji Desai's government was reduced to a minority in the Lok Sabha.

The Congress stepped in to prop up Charan Singh as Prime Minister, with the left supporting him, but this proved to be India's most shortlived government, that is, till the 13-day Vajpayee government in mid-1996. The Congress, which clearly sensed a rising tide of popular support, thanks largely to what was perceived as a disappointing performance by the Janata Party government, decided to withdraw support to Charan Singh. Having held the post between July 28, 1979 and January 14, 1980, Charan Singh remains the only Prime Minister in India never to have faced Parliament, leave alone proving his government's strength on the floor of the Lok Sabha.

The first major attempt at a coalition at the centre thus came to an end within two-and-a-half years of its inception with the Janata Party having disintegrated and the Congress sweeping back to power in the general elections held in January 1980, making admirable tactical use of skyrocketing onion prices and the popular disillusionment with a government that was seen as being too busy settling internal squabbles to govern. (Nearly two decades later, in November 1998, the price of onions again became a major political issue which benefited the Congress in assembly elections held in Rajasthan, Madhya Pradesh and Delhi.)

An interesting fact to be noted here is that despite the Janata Party alliance being essentially anti-Congress and drawing sustenance from diverse ideological groups, both the Prime Ministers thrown up by the coalition were from among those who had earlier been with the Congress. This was a pattern that was repeated in subsequent anti-Congress coalitions too, which is why Vajpayee was seen as the first truly non-Congress Indian Prime Minister. That former Congressmen should have led anti-Congress coalition governments is perhaps not as strange as it may seem, given the rainbow nature of these coalitions (with right and left groups supporting them). Under the circumstances, it is perhaps understandable that the only acceptable compromise solutions would have to emanate from the centrist political space. Since the Congress had a virtual monopoly of that space till the mid-1960s, it is not surprising that the compromises needed to form coalitions should have repeatedly been settled by placing former Congressmen at the helm of power.

The next coalition government at the Union level (though in a strict sense it was more a minority government supported by a coalition) was formed in December 1989 by the Janata Dal led by V.P. Singh, another former Congressman. In fact, Singh was Finance Minister and then Defence Minister in Rajiv Gandhi's Cabinet till he fell out on the issue of corruption in high places (including the scandals involving Swedish armaments manufacturer Bofors and the German submarine producer HDW). He went on to form the Jan Morcha, which later merged into the Janata Dal. The Janata Dal experiment had one very interesting feature—while both the BJP and the left extended support to it from outside, there was no arrangement before or after the elections between these two 'props' of the Janata Dal government. During the elections, the Janata Dal had a separate electoral understanding with both the BJP and the left who contested against each other.

After the 1989 elections, the Congress emerged as the single-largest party in the Lok Sabha but was short by over 75 seats of the required majority. (As it has turned out, the 1989 elections were the first of five successive general elections which have not yielded any one party a majority in the Lok Sabha.) The Janata Dal, with its mutually antagonistic allies, had a comfortable majority, but since neither of its two allies was willing to share power with the other, it was left to run the government on its own with 'outside support'. Barring the brief tenure of the Charan Singh government, this was the first occasion when the ruling party on its own had less than one-third of the Lok Sabha seats.

The V.P. Singh government proved shortlived, once again thanks to a standoff with the BJP. Its 10-month long tenure proved a truly eventful chapter in Indian political history with major upheavals. The first of these was caused by the government's decision to implement the recommendations of the Mandal Commission. With the anti-Mandal agitation having already set the tone for tension between the BJP and the Janata Dal, it was now the turn of the BJP to up the ante. It did so by launching the Ayodhya movement.

The upper-caste Hindu outrage at the V.P. Singh government's decision to implement the Mandal Commission report was effectively channelised by the BJP in the Ramjanambhoomi agitation. Party President L.K. Advani led his famous *rath yatra* across the country, and as communal clashes dotted the points on the map through which it travelled, there were growing demands for the government to stop its march. Posed against this was the BJP's threat that it would withdraw support if any such measure were undertaken. Even as the Singh government pondered its options, the Janata Dal governments in Bihar and Uttar Pradesh took strong measures. The government of Bihar, headed by Laloo Prasad Yadav, arrested Advani in Samastipur and stopped the progress of the *rath* to its ultimate destination, Ayodhya. In Uttar Pradesh, Chief Minister Mulayam Singh Yadav ordered a crackdown on those gathering in Ayodhya to welcome Advani. What followed was police action in which several died in firing and thousands were jailed.

The BJP then called for the dismissal of the Mulayam Singh Yadav government in Uttar Pradesh, failing which it threatened to withdraw support to Singh's government in New Delhi. With Singh sticking to his stand that he would rather lose power than compromise on the issue of safeguarding secularism and the rule of law, the BJP ultimately withdrew support and Singh lost a vote of confidence in the Lok Sabha in November 1990. For the second time in a decade, an attempt to form a non-Congress coalition government at the centre had failed because of contradictions between the right-wing BJP and the others.

As in 1979, the fall of the coalition government in November 1990 was followed by a breakaway group of the Janata Dal forming a government with outside support from the Congress. The group, which called itself the Janata Dal (Samajwadi) and was led by another former Congressman, Chandra Shekhar, had just 57 MPs in the Lok Sabha, all the others supporting it from outside. The JD(S)—which was to later split into the Samajwadi Janata Party led by Chandra Shekhar and the Samajwadi Party headed by Mulayam Singh Yadav—thus became by far the smallest party to have headed a Union government. As with Charan Singh, so also with Chandra Shekhar, the Congress withdrew support within months on the flimsiest of pretexts. The plea given was that the Prime Minister had ordered police surveillance on Congress leaders including Rajiv Gandhi and thus betrayed their trust, a charge that was never proved.

Shortlived as the tenure of the Chandra Shekhar government was, the Congress found time to pressurise it into taking certain decisions that were to have an impact on the future course of Indian politics. One such decision was the dismissal of the state government of Tamil Nadu headed by M. Karunanidhi of the DMK. While Karunanidhi's government was clearly dismissed to serve the interests of the Congress and its ally in Tamil Nadu, the AIADMK, the ostensible reason for the dismissal, under the much-abused Article 356 of the Constitution, was the local government's allegedly poor track record in countering the activities of the militant LTTE. (The same plea was to be used seven years later in 1998 by the Congress to pull down another government in New Delhi, that is, the United Front government headed by I.K. Gujral.)

The Governor of the state at that time, Surjit Singh Barnala, a veteran Akali Dal leader and former Chief Minister of Punjab, refused to play along with the wishes of the central government, preferring to resign rather than submit a report that would suit the Chandra Shekhar government's gameplan. This cemented a relationship between the DMK and the Akalis, both parties that have consistently argued for a more federal structure in India. The relationship between the two regional parties later proved useful to the BJP, but that's a different story.

The elections that followed in May–June 1991 again threw up a minority government with the Congress failing to secure a majority despite the sympathy generated for the party in the second half of the polling after Rajiv Gandhi's assassination on May 21 after one round of polling had taken place. The Congress government headed by P.V. Narasimha Rao managed to last its full term and in fact secure a majority in the Lok Sabha thanks to defections and parties switching sides, one such switch becoming the subject of a case of alleged bribery of MPs to vote for the government (which is detailed in the following chapter).

After the May 1996 elections, which followed the end of Narasimha Rao's tenure, India saw four coalition governments come into being and fall in less than three years. The first of these four coalition governments was formed by the BJP in May 1996 and lasted just 13 days before the Prime Minister designate, Vajpayee, resigned after it became clear that he would lose the vote of confidence. Unlike in 1998, the BJP was unable to win over a single major party to support its government despite having been given the chance by the President on the grounds that it was the single-largest party in the Lok Sabha. Its support was thus limited to its pre-poll allies like the Akali Dal in Punjab and the Shiv Sena in Maharashtra.

This was followed by the United Front government headed by H.D. Deve Gowda and supported by the Congress. The United Front was a post-election formation and consisted of 13 parties, many of which had alliances with some of the other constituents in individual states while contesting against other constituents. The single-largest party in the Front was the Janata Dal with 44 Lok Sabha MPs, drawn mainly from Bihar, Karnataka and Orissa. The second biggest was the CPI(M). The other parties of the Left Front, the CPI, the RSP and the Forward Bloc, were also constituents of the Front. Among the others were several regional parties with bases in one state each like the Telugu Desam Party (TDP) in Andhra Pradesh, the Samajwadi Party in Uttar Pradesh, the DMK in Tamil Nadu, the Asom Gana Parishad (AGP) in Assam, and the National Conference (NC) in Jammu & Kashmir.

With the UF making it clear that it would support neither a BJP-led nor a Congress-led government, nor even accept a sharing of power with the Congress, the onus was on the Congress to support a UF government without participating in it, which it did.

The CPI(M) too stuck to its earlier stand of not participating in a government at the centre, a stand which provoked heated debate within and outside the party. While the RSP and the Forward Bloc also adopted a similar stance, the CPI became the only constituent of the left to participate in the government. The result was that the two largest supporting parties—the Congress and the CPI(M)—were not part of the government.

There was, however, a distinction between the nature of support being offered from 'outside' by the non-CPI left and the Congress. While the former was not part of the government, it was part of the United Front, which had institutions like the Steering Committee, the Core Committee and the Coordination Committee to discuss issues and provide direction to the government. This was another novel step in coalition politics, the first time that parties joined a ruling coalition with formal institutions, but stayed out of government. The Congress, on the other hand, was neither in the government nor in the United Front. Its support was, to that extent, more along the conventional lines of outside support practised by the party on numerous occasions in the states and at the centre in the past.

Given the nature of the United Front, it was hardly surprising that there should be differences and in some cases even conflicts of interest among the partners. In particular, inter-state disputes were thorny, particularly the manner in which Karnataka and Tamil Nadu were to share the Cauvery waters, which remained a hotly contested question despite the fact that the governments in both states were run by UF constituents—the DMK in Tamil Nadu and the Janata Dal in Karnataka. Similarly, Andhra Pradesh and Karnataka had an ongoing dispute over the height of the Almatti dam that at one stage looked like snowballing into a major problem for the UF with the Janata Dal government of Karnataka and the TDP-led Andhra Pradesh government at loggerheads. The fact that the Prime Minister was, in both these cases, from one of the states involved could have contributed to heightening hostility, but to the credit of Deve Gowda and the UF it must be said that though the issues were not resolved, they were not allowed to get out of hand either.

Predictably though, it was the Congress that was to queer the pitch for the UF government, this time on an even flimsier pretext, as detailed earlier. While Kesri's explanation for pulling down the Deve Gowda government clearly did not convince anybody, it provided the basis for another Congress-supported UF government to assume office. Inder Kumar Gujral thus came to head the third of four successive coalitions, none of which lasted more than 13 months. As we have seen, his government too was to be shortlived.

In the elections of February–March 1998 that followed, it was fairly clear to analysts, voters and pollsters alike that the possibility of any party getting a majority in the Lok Sabha was remote. The result of that very widely held perception was a significant step forward in coalition politics in India. For the first time, the BJP decided to forge electoral alliances with as many regional parties as possible in a bid to capture power. Prior to these elections, both the BJP and the Congress had preferred to contest the bulk of Lok Sabha seats on their own and restrict alliances to a minimum in those states where they would otherwise be at a clear disadvantage.

For the 1998 elections, the BJP secured tie-ups with as many as 13 big and small regional parties spread over nine major Indian states, which between them account for 334 of the 543 Lok Sabha seats. Its partners were the Akali Dal in Punjab, the Haryana Vikas Party in Haryana, the Samata Party in Bihar and Uttar Pradesh, the Trinamool Congress in West Bengal, the Biju Janata Dal in Orissa, the Shiv Sena in Maharashtra, the Lok Shakti in Karnataka, the TDP (Lakshmi Parvathi) in Andhra Pradesh, and five parties in Tamil Nadu—the AIADMK, the Pattali Makkal Katchi (PMK), the Marumalarchi Dravida Munnetra Kazhagam (MDMK), the Tamizhaga Rajiv Congress (TRC) and the Janata Party. There were several factors that dictated this coalitional strategy from a party that had always been a proponent of a unitary India and a strong centre, positions that would normally be a restraint on any large-scale alliances with regional parties.

One major factor was the perception that no party would be able to form a government on its own. Added to this was the BJP's own experience of its attempt to form a government which collapsed within 13 days without any fresh allies emerging after the elections. This helped in convincing the party that the only way of breaking its isolation within the political class was to build alliances *before* the elections rather than seeking them *after* the polls. A third factor was the recognition that the party had acquired the image of being confined to the north and west of the country and therefore not being well-placed to run a government in New Delhi.

The BJP knew it had to shed this image of not being a pan-Indian party and could not do so on its own.

A crucial fourth factor lay in the party's electoral track record in many of the states where it sought alliances. Of the nine states in which it roped in regional partners, it had never won a single seat in Tamil Nadu or Orissa, which between them have 60 seats in the Lok Sabha. In West Bengal, which has 42 seats, it had not won a seat after 1952. In Andhra Pradesh, which also has 42 seats, it had only twice in 11 general elections won just one seat. In Punjab (14 seats), the party had last won a seat in 1962. In Haryana (10 seats), after failing to register a win in elections since 1977, it had won four seats in 1996 thanks to its tie-up with the HVP. In Karnataka, while the party had registered its first wins in 1991 and increased the tally from four to six in 1996, it was still a minor presence in a state that sends 28 MPs to the Lok Sabha. Thus, the BJP faced the prospect of winning no more than a handful of the 195 seats that these seven states have between them if it chose to go alone in the polls.

In Bihar, while the BJP had a significant presence and could bank on winning some seats on its own, the addition of the Samata Party's votes could prove decisive in a severely polarised state. Given the fact that Bihar then had as many as 54 Lok Sabha seats, the alliance was crucial to the BJP's prospects of forming the next government. The Samata Party's contribution to its vote base in UP would, of course, be very much less, but even a couple of extra MPs in a hung Parliament could mean the difference between being in government and sitting in Opposition. Indeed, the events as they unfolded proved the BJP's calculations right.

The BJP did emerge as the single-largest party in the 12th Lok Sabha, but with just 182 seats it was well short of the halfway mark of 272. With its electoral allies, however, it had 258 seats, putting it within striking distance of the target. Even so, covering that relatively small distance appeared for about a week after the elections to be quite a task. Ultimately, it needed a break-up of the United Front on the issue of whether or not a Congress government should be supported, before the BJP could breathe easy. After President K.R. Narayanan was satisfied that the BJP, while still short of a majority, had the support of more MPs than any other formation, he invited Vajpayee to form the government and seek a vote of confidence. The rest, as they say, is history.

The drama was, however, far from over. Even as the BJP and its electoral allies met to chalk out a National Agenda for Governance on the basis of which the government would be run, a block of 27 MPs from Tamil Nadu, led by the AIADMK, started bargaining hard for ministerial berths and other concessions. The AIADMK with its 18 MPs was the single-largest ally of the BJP and commanded the allegiance of four other smaller allies from the state who between them had won another nine seats. This block delayed giving the letter of support to the Vajpayee government that had been demanded by the President to prima facie establish that it would have the requisite numbers in the Lok Sabha. Another ally, the Trinamool Congress, which had seven MPs, announced that it would support the government but not participate in it. Ultimately two of the smaller partners from Tamil Nadu, the MDMK and the PMK also took the same stand. The jitters that these developments caused in the BJP camp were somewhat eased by the indications from the National Conference and the TDP that they would abstain in the crucial vote of confidence. Another small party, which had contested the elections against the BJP alliance in Haryana, the INLD, promised the support of its four MPs to the Vajpayee government.

Even so, the numbers between the government and the Opposition were finely balanced. That necessitated a tacit understanding between the TDP and the government under which a TDP member was elected as the Speaker of the Lok Sabha in return for which the 11 other TDP MPs ultimately voted in favour of the government in the vote of confidence. Just how crucial the changed stances of the TDP, the NC and the INLD (all of whom had opposed the BJP and the Congress in the elections) were can be judged from the fact that the vote of confidence was ultimately won by 275 votes to 263 with the three NC members abstaining. Even at this early stage, one of the BJP's electoral allies, Subramaniam Swamy of the Janata Party, had decided not to vote in favour of the government. The BJP in turn had already jettisoned one of its allies, the TDP (Lakshmi Parvathi) in Andhra Pradesh, clearly because of the extreme hostility between the two TDPs. With Chandrababu Naidu's TDP having 12 Lok Sabha MPs and Lakshmi Parvathi's party having drawn a blank, the choice for the BJP was clear, even if cynical.

The alliance continued to appear unstable with one ally or the other at frequent intervals threatening to withdraw support or 'reconsider' its support to the government if its demands were not met. While the AIADMK has been projected by the BJP as the sole culprit in this respect, the reality is that the independent MP Buta Singh was the first to quit the alliance, followed by the INLD. The Akali Dal at one stage in mid-1998, months after the government was formed, had announced that it would reconsider its support to the government if its demand for keeping Udham Singh Nagar out of the proposed state of Uttaranchal was not met. The Trinamool Congress too at various stages showed signs of unease and on one occasion pulled out of the alliance coordination committee protesting that the Prime Minister was not acting adequately on issues like the rise in prices of essential commodities. The spectacle of senior ministers like George Fernandes, Jaswant Singh and Pramod Mahajan rushing around from New Delhi to Chennai and Kolkata in a bid to placate angry allies became a regular feature for most of the tenure of the second Vajpayee government.

Under the circumstances, it is hardly surprising that the government fell when it did. The AIADMK had always been seen as being on the verge of pulling out of the alliance and it finally did in April 1999. While the BJP has since attempted to portray this as the result of the party and the government refusing to accept the AIADMK's unreasonable demands, the facts suggest a different story. Several ministerial portfolios were widely believed to have been demanded by the AIADMK and granted and several bureaucratic transfers and postings were so convenient for Jayalalithaa that the obvious inferences were drawn. If anything, the public perception is that the BJP was more than willing to accommodate the AIADMK supremo's whims till she made one demand too many.

In the vote of confidence that followed the withdrawal of support by the AIADMK, the rest of the BJP-led alliance held together despite speculation that some of the allies, notably the Samata Party, the Biju Janata Dal and the Akali Dal, may be heading for a split with factions from these parties likely to move over to the Opposition camp. Further, the BJP managed to win back the support of the INLD reportedly on the assurance that some populist measures for farmers would be adopted if the government stayed in the saddle. It also found a new ally in the DMK, which could not countenance the prospect of being on the same side as its rival, the AIADMK, and was apprehensive that any future government with the AIADMK as a partner may well dismiss its state government in Tamil Nadu.

Thus, the fourth successive coalition government in just over two years met the same fate as the others before it, but in doing so ushered in a fresh round of political realignments. The realignments continued as the parties prepared for the polls. The most significant of these was the decision of the TDP to drop the veneer of 'equidistance' from the BJP and the Congress. It forged an alliance with the BJP for the simultaneous Lok Sabha and assembly polls, though it decided not to formally join the NDA. The alliance worked to the benefit of both the TDP and the BJP, the former winning 29 of the 42 Lok Sabha seats in the state and the latter improving its tally from five to seven seats. The TDP on its own also obtained a majority in the state assembly. That this performance was despite the Congress increasing its share of the votes in the state is a pointer to the manner in which Chandrababu Naidu understood the electoral arithmetic. Significantly, the TDP, which emerged as the BJP's single-biggest partner in the 13th Lok Sabha, chose not to join the government.

As in the case of the TDP in Andhra Pradesh, the DMK in Tamil Nadu cemented a formal electoral alliance with the BJP and its other allies. In the process, the tie-up between the DMK and the Tamil Maanila Congress had to be given a quiet burial, with the latter refusing to go along with the BJP. The TMC also made it clear that it would not be part of any alliance headed by Jayalalithaa. Since the Congress and the left parties in the state had already tied up with the AIADMK, the TMC had no option but to forge a 'third front' which included other smaller parties like the Puthizha Tamilagam (a party that appeals to the dalits of the state) and the Samajwadi Party. This front predictably failed to win any Lok Sabha seat.

Another significant political development took place in the Janata Dal. The party split down the middle, with one section led by party President Sharad Yadav choosing to join the NDA, while another led by former Prime Minister Deve Gowda refused to do so. Most of the senior leaders of the Janata Dal, including former Prime Minister I.K. Gujral, Ram Vilas Paswan, who had been part of several Union governments, and the then Karnataka Chief Minister J.H. Patel, were part of the Sharad Yadav group in the JD. This group merged with the Lok Shakti in Karnataka, headed by the late Rama Krishna Hegde, former Chief Minister and then Union Commerce Minister, and the Samata Party in Bihar, to form the Janata Dal (United). In effect, the JD(U) included practically the entire Bihar unit of the Janata Dal and a substantial section of the Karnataka unit, these being the only states in which the JD had influence. The formation of the JD(U) was yet another instance of the realignments that have periodically taken place within those who originally formed the Janata Dal in 1989. Both the Lok Shakti and the Samata Party were breakaway groups from the JD. Thus, while the formation of the JD(U) was at one level a consolidation of the Janata Dal, which had got scattered over time, what was interesting was that this consolidation was now in favour of the BJP rather than against it.

This consolidation certainly helped the NDA put up an impressive performance in Bihar, where the coalition won 41 of the 54 Lok Sabha seats. In Karnataka, on the other hand, the addition of Patel and his supporters to the NDA bandwagon seems to have damaged rather than helped the NDA's prospects. While the BJP-led alliance had won 16 of the 28 seats in the state in the 1998 elections, the tally came down to just 10 in 1999. Clearly, the anti-incumbency feeling against Patel's government had overshadowed any arithmetic advantage that may have accrued to the NDA. In fact, this was not an unanticipated situation. The BJP's state unit had consistently and vehemently opposed the proposed merger on the ground that the party would lose one of its key campaign issues—the non-performance of the Patel government—on the eve of the assembly elections. The BJP's central leadership too saw the merit in this argument, but went on to add that it had little choice in the matter, since the Samata Party and the Lok Shakti had made it clear that they would brook no opposition from the BJP to the formation of the JD(U). The central leadership, therefore, prevailed on the state unit to accept Patel into the NDA fold in the larger national interests of the coalition.

In Haryana too alliances changed rapidly in the build-up to the 13th general elections. The HVP, which was ruling the state with the support of the BJP at the time of the vote of confidence in the Lok Sabha, was very quickly jettisoned thereafter by the BJP. The BJP withdrew support to the HVP government, precipitating its collapse and instead joined hands with the INLD. The link with the INLD's position on the vote of confidence in Parliament was all too obvious. The INLD had announced just two days before the crucial vote that it would vote against the Vajpayee government and would prefer a non-BJP, non-Congress Prime Minister like Deve Gowda, ostensibly because he would promote the interests of farmers. By the time of the actual vote, though, the INLD had switched its support to the Vajpayee government. It was hardly surprising, therefore, that the BJP soon thereafter supported Chautala's claim to form the government in Haryana. In the Lok Sabha elections that followed, the two parties fought in alliance, while the HVP and the Congress fought separately to the detriment of both. The results were a complete sweep of the 10 Lok Sabha seats from the state for the BJP–INLD alliance.

New allies, however, were not the only factor working in favour of the BJP-led NDA in the build-up to the general elections. An equally important development was a split within the Congress when Sharad Pawar, P.A. Sangma and Tariq Anwar were expelled and formed their own party—the Nationalist Congress Party (NCP). While this had little or no impact in most parts of the country, it did radically alter political equations in Pawar's home state of Maharashtra. The NCP managed to win just six of the state's 48 Lok Sabha seats, but divided the traditional Congress votes sufficiently to allow the BJP–Shiv Sena alliance to win 28 seats and reduce the Congress tally to just 10. This was despite a considerable erosion in the BJP–Shiv Sena alliance's share of the vote which would have otherwise left the alliance with just a handful of seats from Maharashtra.

The process of political realignments did not end with the 1999 Lok Sabha elections. As with other regional parties, in the case of the NCP too the realities of state politics dictated the future course of action. In the simultaneous assembly and Lok Sabha elections in Maharashtra, the Congress emerged as the single-largest party with 75 MLAs in the 288-member assembly. The BJP–Shiv Sena alliance won 125 seats while the NCP obtained 58 seats. The NCP, despite its professed opposition to Sonia Gandhi's so-called ambitions to hold the post of the Prime Minister of India, realised that if it were to form a government in Maharashtra, the only way out was an alliance with the Congress. Which is precisely what happened, but only after much political drama which included attempts to woo the 12 independent MLAs and those belonging to smaller parties like the Peasants and Workers' Party (PWP), the Republican Party of India (RPI), the JD(S), the CPI(M) and the SP. Even government formation took inordinately long on account of wrangling over ministerial positions.

The merger of the Lok Shakti with the JD(U) in Karnataka also ran into some rough weather after Rama Krishna Hegde was excluded from the Union Cabinet after having served in the second Vajpayee government as Commerce Minister. Hegde later held George Fernandes primarily responsible for his exclusion from the Cabinet and expressed unhappiness that Fernandes and Vajpayee had not shown a senior leader like him the courtesy of giving him some inkling of his exclusion from the Cabinet. A bitter Hegde claimed that Vajpayee looked a 'picture of sadness' when he met him. 'It seemed he [Vajpayee] did something he should not have done,' Hegde claimed.

It is worth noting that these internal wrangles within the JD(U) were also influenced by the reality of state politics. The party had a strength of 21 MPs in the Lok Sabha, of which 18 were from Bihar and just three from Karnataka. The JD(U) was also a party with an unusually high proportion of political heavyweights. As a result, there were at least five obvious contenders for a Cabinet berth from the party—Fernandes, Paswan, Sharad Yadav, Nitish Kumar and Hegde. It was obvious that Vajpayee could not afford to make them all Cabinet ministers without risking resentment from other partners in the alliance. At least one of these worthies would have to be dropped. The fact that the axe ultimately fell on Hegde could have been determined by political expediency: assembly elections were due in Bihar in February 2000, whereas they had just been concluded in Karnataka, Hegde's home state. Any dissension within the ranks of the JD(U) in Bihar could cost the NDA dear in the assembly elections, while the immediate stakes were lower in Karnataka, where the alliance was now in opposition to a Congress government with a comfortable majority.

In Jammu & Kashmir, the National Conference continued with its unique transparently opportunist stance: it would fight elections on its own without becoming part of any alliance, but would unconditionally support New Delhi since the state depends heavily on the Union government for support in countering secessionist militants. As in 1998, therefore, the NC in 1999 contested all the six seats in Jammu & Kashmir, winning four of them, but had no compunctions in joining the NDA government when it was formed. Omar Abdullah once again became a junior minister in the third Vajpayee government.

A common feature of all these realignments in Indian politics was that they were responses to the compulsions of state politics. This is true of the new allies of the BJP—the TDP, the DMK, the JD(U) and the INLD—each of which had been forced into joining hands with the NDA to combat their respective principal opponents in state politics—the Congress for the TDP in Andhra Pradesh and the JD(U) in Karnataka, the AIADMK for the DMK in Tamil Nadu, the RJD for the JD(U) in Bihar and the HVP for the INLD in Haryana. It is equally true in the case of the NCP, which ultimately joined hands with the Congress in forming a government in Maharashtra.

Coalitions in the States

Despite the popular notion that coalition governments are a phenomenon of recent vintage in India, and that even in the states they do not date further back than the 4th general elections in 1967, the fact is that the first coalition government in India was formed as a result of the first-ever round of general elections held in 1952. That government was the one headed by the Akali Dal in what was then PEPSU (Patiala and East Punjab States' Union) and covered some parts of the existing states of Punjab, Haryana and Himachal Pradesh. In two other states, Madras (comprising most of today's Tamil Nadu, the Rayalaseema and coastal parts of Andhra Pradesh and the Malabar region of north Kerala) and Travancore–Cochin (South Kerala and parts of today's Tamil Nadu), the Congress formed governments with the support of minor parties after it failed to win a majority of seats in the assemblies in the 1952 elections.

In both these states, communist-led coalitions formed before the elections had emerged as the largest blocks in the assembly, though the Congress was the single-largest party. While the Congress under Jawaharlal Nehru was quite content to allow the Akalis to form the government in PEPSU, it was determined not to allow the communists to come to power in any state. The reasons for this were not purely whimsical. The CPI in the 1952 general elections had emerged as the most potent opposition force, constituting the largest non-Congress group in both the Rajya Sabha and the Lok Sabha. In addition, the CPI-led alliance was the single-largest block in the two southern states of Madras and Travancore–Cochin, as we have seen, and similar alliances were the major opposition in Hyderabad and West Bengal, while Tripura, which did not then have a legislature, had elected communist MPs from both its constituencies. Thus, unlike the Akali Dal, which was restricted to what is today Punjab, the CPI posed a threat to Congress dominance in large parts of south and east India.

In what has over the years become the norm, the Congress was invited by the Raj Pramukh in Travancore–Cochin and the Governor in Madras to form the government, on the ground that it was the single-largest party despite being in a minority. In Madras, the Congress was able to win the support of smaller caste-based groups and the Indian Union Muslim League. But, it had to accept one of their demands before it could do so: The new-found allies insisted that they would support the Congress only if C. Rajagopalachari, the first Indian to become Governor General of India, headed the government. Since Rajaji, as he is better known, was not a member of the state legislature, he was nominated to the Legislative Council by the Governor, thus setting another dubious precedent. That the Congress should have stooped so low even in those early days, which are still seen by many as the era of principled politics, is explained by one of Rajaji's statements spelling out his priorities in no uncertain terms. He said: 'communists are my enemy number one, I fight them from A to Z.'

Having successfully formed the government, the Congress then used it to consolidate its position in Madras. Rajaji had to quit within two years of becoming Chief Minister to be replaced by K. Kamaraj, another prominent Congress leader. However, a significant development in the interim ultimately consolidated the hold of the Congress on the Madras assembly. This was the carving out of the Telugu districts of the province to form a separate state (Andhra Pradesh) in 1953. Since these districts had elected large numbers of communists, their exit significantly reduced the communist strength in what remained of Madras, and thus helped the Congress.

What is more, even in the newly created Andhra Pradesh, the Congress was able to woo many of the non-communist groups in the CPI alliance to its side, including the leader of the alliance,

T. Prakasam of the Kisan Mazdoor Praja Party (KMPP). As a result, in the mid-term elections in the Andhra province that were held in 1955, the Congress was able to lead a non-communist coalition to a resounding victory. Within the short span of time between the first general elections and the second in 1957, therefore, the CPI was considerably reduced in strength in both parts of the erstwhile Madras province and the Congress correspondingly strengthened.

In Travancore–Cochin, A.J. John became the Congress Chief Minister in 1952 and won over several small opposition groups to support his government. Among these was the Tamil Nadu Congress of South Travancore, a party championing the cause of the Tamil-speaking ethnic majority in the southern parts of the province. E.M.S. Namboodiripad, the communist leader who was to later become the first elected communist head of a government in a Parliamentary democracy, had this to say about the alliances forged by John in Travancore–Cochin and Rajaji in Madras in his book, *The Communist Party in Kerala, Six Decades of Struggle and Advance*: 'The new combinations led by John and Rajagopalachari were, in other words, the forerunners of the anti-communist combination that was to appear in Kerala in a short time.' He also observed that Rajaji's attitude towards the communists 'was enthusiastically taken up by the Christian clergy in Travancore–Cochin, who organised the first anti-communist front in the country.'

Despite his attempts at consolidation, however, John lasted less than two years with factional and caste-based fights within his own party and the alliance forcing the dissolution of the assembly after the Tamil Nadu Congress withdrew support, reducing his government to a minority. This forced a mid-term election in 1954 in which the Congress was reduced to a minority and, unlike in 1952, the Opposition alliance had a clear majority in the assembly, despite the Catholic church for the first time openly campaigning and warning people against the 'danger of communism'. This alliance consisted of the Left Front (the communists, the Revolutionary Socialist Party and the Kerala Socialist Party), the Praja Socialist Party (PSP) and the Tamil Nadu Congress.

It was clear, therefore, that the Opposition alliance would be called upon to form the government. The Congress had other ideas. It made an offer to the PSP leader Pattom Thanu Pillai. If the PSP was ready to form a single-party government, the Congress suggested, it would be willing to support the government without sharing power. The PSP accepted the offer, breaking the electoral pact. Thus, with just 19 members in an assembly of over a hundred, the PSP formed the government. Ironically, as the largest of the parties that was not in the government, the Congress was officially recognised as the 'Opposition'. Within months, the PSP was split at the all-India level with the creation of the Socialist Party by Ram Manohar Lohia, which led to the split of the PSP in Travancore–Cochin too. The predictable result was the replacement of the 'single-party' PSP government by a Congress-led government with the support of the Tamil Nadu Congress.

Against this backdrop came a significant development in 1956 which prepared the ground for the election of a communist-led government a year later. This was the creation of the state of Kerala as part of the country-wide exercise in creating new linguistically homogenous states. The new state of Kerala consisted of most of Travancore–Cochin and the Malabar districts of Madras. The addition of Malabar to Travancore–Cochin came as a shot in the arm for the CPI and a jolt for the Congress. In the 1952 elections, the Congress had won just four of the 30 seats in this region while the CPI–KMPP alliance had won close to half the seats.

Historic as it was, therefore, the communist victory of 1957 in Kerala did not come as a surprise. The CPI on its own won 60 of the 126 assembly seats and with the support of many of the 14 independents elected was able to form a government headed by Namboodiripad in April 1957. In just over two years, however, this state government was to become the first of many victims over the years of Congress rule in New Delhi. On July 31, 1959, President Rajendra Prasad, acting on the advice of Nehru's Cabinet, dismissed the state government despite its having a majority in the assembly, ostensibly because it had lost the support of the people. The move is widely believed to have been the handiwork of Indira Gandhi and a precursor to the strong-arm tactics she herself adopted after she became Prime Minister.

In the mid-term elections that followed in February 1960, the Congress managed to cobble together an alliance with the PSP and the Muslim League (which it had described as a 'dead horse' in the previous elections) and get caste organisations like the Nair Service Society to back its alliance. The results were a resounding victory for the anti-CPI alliance, but the price paid by the Congress was reinstating the PSP's Pillai as Chief Minister. This was despite the fact that the Congress had 63 seats in the 126-member assembly while the PSP had just 20 MLAs. Kerala to date has not seen a single-party government (barring the first minority PSP government). Coalitions have become the norm, but unlike the early experiments of the 1950s and 1960s, they are now more stable and most state governments last their full term. The coalitions too, which had seen repeated realignments, have now crystalised with the CPI(M)-led Left and Democratic Front on one side of the divide and the Congress-led United Democratic Front on the other.

The first major wave of coalitions in the states came in 1967, when the Congress lost power in nine states, in some as a result of electoral defeats and in others because of defections from its own ranks. Those who replaced it were different in each of the states, but in each case it was an anti-Congress coalition that came to the fore, except in Tamil Nadu, where the DMK won an absolute majority in the assembly on its own and the Congress, as events proved, was never again to form a government in the state.

In Punjab, the various factions of the Akali Dal were the backbone of the coalition, headed by Gurnam Singh of the Sant Fateh Singh group. In Bihar, a Samyukta Vidhayak Dal—which translates as the combined legislators' group/party and was used as common nomenclature for the anti-Congress coalitions of 1967 in other parts of the Hindi belt too—was formed by the Socialist Party, the PSP, the Jana Sangh, the BKD, the Jan Kranti Dal (JKD) and the CPI. Mahamaya Prasad Singh of the JKD, which later merged with the BKD, was Bihar's first non-Congress Chief Minister. In West Bengal two opposition fronts, one led by the CPI(M) and the other by the Bangla Congress came together to form a United Front government led by Ajoy Mukherjee. In Kerala, a United Front headed by Namboodiripad assumed office. In Orissa, the Swatantra Party, largely comprised of members of the royal families of erstwhile princely states, joined hands with the Jana Congress, a breakaway group of the Congress headed by Hare Krishna Mahatab. R.N. Singh Deo of the Swatantra Party headed the coalition government.

In Madhya Pradesh, Uttar Pradesh and Haryana, the Congress initially formed the state governments, but was deposed from power within periods ranging from a week in Haryana to four months in Madhya Pradesh with defections from the Congress helping the Opposition alliance to come to power. In Haryana, the Congress had won a comfortable majority in the elections (48 out of 81 seats) but Chief Minister Bhagwat Dayal Sharma lasted barely a week before a big chunk of dissidents from the party led by Rao Birender Singh left and joined the Opposition. A United Front government was formed with Singh as the Chief Minister. In Uttar Pradesh, while the Congress failed to win a majority, it emerged as the single-largest party in the assembly and was therefore invited by the governor to form the government despite a well-publicised tussle for leadership between Chander Bhanu Gupta and Charan Singh. Gupta's government lasted for just three weeks and fell when Charan Singh with his followers formed the Bharatiya Kranti Dal and joined the Opposition ranks. The Opposition SVD alliance came to power with Charan Singh as the Chief Minister in April 1967.

In Madhya Pradesh, the Congress government led by D.P. Mishra was pulled down after four months following defections from the party. Among those who left the Congress and declared support to the Jana Sangh was Rajmata Vijay Raje Scindia of Gwalior. An SVD ministry, led by G.N. Singh and including Congress defectors, the Jana Sangh, the PSP and the Socialist Party, came to power.

Ironically, the trend of defections that had helped topple the Congress from many of these states soon worked in favour of the party with all the non-Congress state governments proving extremely unstable. In a little over a year the governments of Namboodiripad and C.N. Annadurai in Tamil Nadu were all that remained of the first major wave of non-Congress coalition governments. While in Madhya Pradesh the Congress had regained power with the support of defectors from the SVD, in Bihar, West Bengal and Punjab the Congress supported those who split the Opposition coalition's ranks. Ultimately even these did not last and President's Rule was declared in most of these states, bringing India's first major flirtation with coalitions to a dismal end. Subhash C. Kashyap, former Secretary General of the Lok Sabha, has calculated in his book, *The Politics of Power: Defections and State Politics in India,* that while 542 legislators had defected in all the Indian states in the decade 1957–67, the number of defectors in a single year after the 1967 elections alone was 438.

The fickle and unstable nature of coalitions in states continued for the next decade till the CPI(M)-led Left Front came to power in West Bengal and Tripura in 1977. In the interim, West Bengal itself had seen a second aborted attempt at a United Front government. Other states like Bihar, Gujarat and Uttar Pradesh had seen repeated attempts at forging coalition governments suffer the same fate.

In later years too, the attempts at forging a Samajwadi Party–Bahujan Samaj Party–Left coalition in Uttar Pradesh in the early 1990s did not last and the BSP's successive attempts at coalitions with the BJP too proved shortlived. In Bihar, the seemingly secure alliance between Laloo Prasad Yadav's government and the left was shattered after Yadav's own party at the time (the Janata Dal) demanded his resignation for corruption charges and the left supported the demand. As a result, the newly created RJD of Laloo Yadav fought the 1998 Lok Sabha elections on a different platform from the Janata Dal and the left parties. By the time of the 1999 Lok Sabha elections, however, the left had veered around to the view that there was no option but to support the RJD–Congress alliance. Ultimately, though, while the CPI(M) joined this alliance, the CPI went it alone after differences with the RJD on seat-sharing within the alliance.

The CPI(M)-led Left Front in West Bengal, however, has stood the test of time, surviving intact and holding on to power since 1977. In Tripura too, the Left Front has remained united even when it lost power, as in 1988. In Kerala, the LDF in its new form, in which it has shed the Indian National Muslim League and acquired the CPI as a stable partner, has remained more or less unchanged for about a decade-and-a-half now, whether in power or in the Opposition. One major factor in the stable composition of all these alliances is the fact that the left has remained united in its practice, even when there have been public disagreements over specific policies or tactics.

Another stable coalition to have emerged in recent years is that of the Shiv Sena and the BJP in Maharashtra. There have been differences within the alliance, particularly on issues relating to power sharing, with the BJP harbouring the resentment that the Shiv Sena acts like a big brother in state politics and the Sena accusing the BJP of adopting a similar attitude in national politics, but the two partners have not yet parted ways and do not seem likely to do so for the moment.

Conclusion

To return to the propositions that we said we would examine, it is quite clear that alliances made before the polls are not necessarily more stable than those that are struck after them. The Janata Party and Janata Dal experiments at the centre and several attempts in the states (like the Communist–PSP alliance in Travancore in the mid-1950s) severely undermine this proposition. Nor does experience bear out the contention that those who participate in governments are more reliable allies than those who support them from outside. The AIADMK was a part of the Vajpayee government as were the two factions of the Janata Party that ultimately fell apart in 1979. Instances of partners in government switching sides are numerous in state politics, particularly after the 1967 elections. Again, the size of the dominant partner in a coalition does not seem to provide any guarantees to its longevity (as is evident from the collapse of the V.P. Singh government in 1990).

The one proposition that seems to have been borne out by history is that ideological cohesion helps a coalition stay together. The Left Front governments as well as the Shiv Sena–BJP alliance are strong evidence of this. There is, however, a caveat to be added here. Mere unity of purpose in opposing a common enemy is not to be confused with ideological cohesion. Whether it was the anti-Congress combines of the 1950s, 1960s, 1970s and 1980s or the anti-BJP combines of recent years, the existence of the common enemy has proved a weak cementing force.

It would also be simplistic to view mere pronouncements of a common agenda as evidence of ideological cohesion. Whether it was the Common Minimum Programme of the United Front or the National Agenda for Governance of the second Vajpayee government, these documents could not hold the coalitions together. This can be put down to the fact that the documents contained little more than pious statements of intent, which would be hard for anyone to oppose, while leaving out contentious issues on which many of the partners have radically differing views.

The fact that many states have lived with coalition governments for decades indicates that the notion of the electorate getting disgusted with coalitions may be wishful thinking. This notion suffers from the limitation that it treats coalitions among political parties as an isolated phenomenon. The reality, however, is that in most states the current era of coalitions is only a reflection of the social churning that is taking place. As previously suppressed sections of the people seek to assert themselves, the correlation of forces is constantly changing.

However, the experience of the states does suggest that coalitions of political expediency could over time be replaced by those with an ideological cohesion. Therein lies hope, not of an end to the era of coalitions, but of the beginning of a phase of more meaningful and consensual coalitions.

Chapter 7

Friends in Deed

Can Coalitions Govern Effectively?

Have political coalitions led to better governance in India? This is not an easy question to answer, for the picture is complex. Everybody has her or his definition of what constitutes good governance, which would include a slew of issues or a wish list. One such list could run like this: lower incidence of corruption, greater transparency and accountability on the part of politicians and bureaucrats with fewer discretionary powers for them, greater federalism in the polity and economy, better distribution of the benefits of economic growth among the weaker sections, and empowerment of those social sections which were less privileged in the country's caste-based society. The list would go on to include removal of the factors responsible for the world's largest population of the poor and illiterate living in India. In this chapter, we look at whether coalition governments have been able to reduce corruption in the country. The answer to this question is: 'Perhaps, but we are not sure.' The second question is whether coalition governments have brought about a greater degree of federalism (or de-centralisation) in India's polity and economy. The answer to this question is an unequivocal: 'Yes'.

Some would argue that the fragmentation of the polity and the existence of coalition governments have brought about a slow and gradual process of cleansing. The fact that coalitions by their very nature involve a sharing of power between constituents makes it more difficult for any one constituent to misuse discretionary powers, this school of thought contends. Others would argue equally convincingly that the incidence of scams and scandals would continue to rise as politicians and bureaucrats scramble to make a fast buck in a situation in which instability convinces them that the loaves and fishes of office may be available only for a short period. Businessmen too may want to make the most of periods when politicians favourably inclined towards them are in office. While both arguments have some merit, the issue cannot be settled through theoretical discussions. The answer to this conundrum will have to emerge from actual experience and empirical evidence. Clearly, there is not enough evidence yet to reach any definite conclusions. However, there are some pointers to the shape of things to come.

Sections of the judiciary, the media and non-governmental organisations have responded in the last decade or so to the public revulsion against corruption and have become increasingly activist. Some of the high and mighty, including former Prime Minister Narasimha Rao, former Union Minister Sukh Ram, former Chief Ministers Laloo Prasad Yadav and J. Jayalalithaa, among others, have faced corruption charges in court and a few have even spent time behind bars. Predictably, all these individuals claimed that the criminal charges against them were 'politically motivated'.

The last three Prime Ministers of India who headed coalition governments, Atal Bihari Vajpayee, I.K. Gujral and H.D. Deve Gowda, have all claimed that the governments they headed have been relatively free of corruption. If the number of scams that have surfaced during the tenure of different Prime Ministers is any yardstick, Vajpayee's claim appears a little thin. Deve Gowda and Gujaral, on the other hand, can justifiably argue that no major scandals emerged during their tenure. The same claim can justifiably also be made by V.P. Singh who was Prime Minister in 1989–1990. In marked contrast are the regimes of all Congress Prime Ministers with the exception of Lal Bahadur Shastri (1964–1966).

There were, of course, charges of corruption levelled against particular ministers in the Janata Party government headed by Morarji Desai (1977–1979) and the brief period thereafter when Charan Singh became Prime Minister in 1979–1980. But there is no doubt that corruption struck deep roots in the Indian polity during successive regimes of Congress Prime Ministers when a single party dominated Parliament. From the tenure of Jawaharlal Nehru (1947–1964) to those of Indira Gandhi (1966–1977 and 1980–1984) and Rajiv Gandhi (1984–1989), the country's polity arguably became more and more corrupt over time.

One of the important reasons why the Congress under Rajiv Gandhi lost the 1989 general elections was the general perception among large sections of the electorate that he was corrupt. This perception was, of course, assiduously propagated by Rajiv Gandhi's estranged Finance Minister and Defence Minister V.P. Singh. While he highlighted the instances of alleged kickbacks paid by Swedish armaments producer Bofors and German submarine manufacturer HDW to persons close to Rajiv Gandhi during his election campaign in 1989, Singh himself was projected by the media as the new 'Mr Clean' (a term that was ironically first used in India to describe Rajiv Gandhi in his first few months as Prime Minister) who would clean up the country's corrupt system of the sleaze associated with raising political 'donations'. During the year he was Finance Minister in Rajiv Gandhi's government, V.P. Singh's hand-picked officials carried out raids on many of India's leading industrialists, some of whom were arrested for violating foreign exchange and taxation laws.

It can be argued that since most coalition governments in India have been unstable, the shorter tenures of such governments have ensured that there has been a big scramble among influential functionaries to make as much money as possible through underhand means in the shortest possible time. An example of this phenomenon was witnessed during the shortlived government of Chandra Shekhar who became Prime Minister after the fall of V.P. Singh's government in November 1990. Barely four months later, the Congress headed by Rajiv Gandhi withdrew support to this government. Chandra Shekhar resigned in early March 1991 and served in a caretaker capacity till the general elections were conducted later that year in May–June. During this period, there was a flurry of accusations of corruption against government ministers.

In the last few months of the Chandra Shekhar regime, the President R. Venkataraman had to repeatedly intervene to ensure that the government did not award major contracts or enter into large financial obligations. So widespread was the perception of this government being corrupt that when Chandra Shekhar's Samajwadi Janata Party put up posters in the next elections saying: *chaar mahine, banaam chaalis saal* (four months versus forty years) in an obvious attempt to compare the government's 'achievements' in four months with the Congress' 'failures' over four decades, the slogan was mischievously interpreted to mean that the functionaries of the Chandra Shekhar government had made as much money in four months as Congressmen had in forty years.

The five-year regime of P.V. Narasimha Rao (1991–1996) was a period marked by a phenomenal rise in allegations of corruption being aired against people in high places. Scandal after scandal, including the country's biggest financial fraud related to trading in securities and involving stockbrokers like Harshad Mehta, hit newspaper headlines month after month. No Indian Prime Minister has been personally faced with as many charges of corruption as Narasimha Rao was. Mehta had even alleged in an affidavit in February 1993 that he had personally delivered a large suitcase containing Rs. 67 lakh in currency notes to the Prime Minister's residence in November 1991, as part of a 'donation' of Rs. 1 crore to him. Mehta aired this allegation at a press conference in Mumbai in mid-June 1993. A month later, the 'minority' government led by Narasimha Rao faced a confidence motion in Parliament and the manner in which the vote was won became the subject of another scandal that led to a legal tangle in which allegations were levelled that particular MPs had been bribed to vote in favour of the government.

The phenomenon of 'judicial activism' became a prominent feature of public life in India during Narasimha Rao's government. After May 1996, the relatively weak Union governments that followed were all coalitions and the judiciary continued to assert itself to check acts of political corruption and abuse of power by the executive. The media too has played its role in exposing corruption. Even if coalition governments have been more transparent because of their very nature, coalition politics could have spawned new forms of corruption relating to opportunistic alliances.

Stories of 'bribes for votes' of MPs and 'horse-trading'—a peculiarly Indian term for engineering defections of political representatives—have been an integral part of India's political folklore since time immemorial. But it has always been a far more difficult task to prosecute and prove criminal charges against politicians in courts of law. Many politicians have been able to get away without punishment for their misdemeanours even when strong circumstantial evidence has existed. The law-enforcing agencies, including the country's premier police investigation body, the CBI, have a rather poor track record in successfully prosecuting errant politicians on charges of corruption. The fact that the CBI none-theless has greater credibility than other police departments is because it has more often filed charges against politicians and other powerful people than has the police (controlled by state departments).

Still, it can be confidently asserted that more politicians have been arrested—even if for short periods—in recent years than in the past and there is greater public awareness today of the nexus between politicians and criminals. At least two prominent former Chief Ministers, Laloo Prasad Yadav and J. Jayalalithaa, have had to spend time behind bars. Former Prime Minister Narasimha Rao was hauled up by a junior judge in the third quarter of 1996 and asked to personally appear and testify before a court of law in a cheating case involving an expatriate pickle-making business-man Lakubhai Pathak who had claimed that he had paid a sum of US$ 100,000 in 1983 to an acquaintance of Narasimha Rao, 'godman' Chandra Swami, for a government contract which never materialised. The court, of course, had to be relocated from Tis Hazari in north Delhi to the Union government's conference venue Vigyan Bhavan in the central part of the capital where adequate security arrangements befitting such dignitaries could be provided. More than eight years later, Rao was acquitted by the Delhi high court.

A more far-reaching legal dispute involving Narasimha Rao was what came to be known as the JMM bribery case. Rao had in July 1993 managed to convert the minority character of his gov-ernment to a majority one thanks to the support of a batch of MPs, including four members of the Jharkhand Mukti Morcha (JMM). The allegation against Rao was that he and his associates paid bribes to these MPs to induce them to vote in favour of a govern-ment that they had been opposed to till that stage.

Narasimha Rao clearly did not want to head a minority gov-ernment. Cynical as he evidently was, the way out was an amoral one, if the allegations were true. It was in the belief that every individual—be he a representative of the people or someone else—had a price for which he could be purchased. This was hardly the first time that defections or splits in political parties were being engineered, but Narasimha Rao probably thought he would be able to get away with it. And get away he did, managed to last his full term as Prime Minister. But the sca this episode left on the body politic of the country may not have healed if successor governments had not been coalitions and hence necessarily had to act in a far more transparent manner. Yet, the compulsions of coalition politics also saw politicians who had abused each other for years for their alleged acts of corruption, quietly burying the hatchet and striking opportunistic alliances to share power.

If Narasimha Rao survived five years as Prime Minister despite a host of corruption charges being levelled against him by his opponents, some of his erstwhile ministerial colleagues like former Communications Minister Sukh Ram managed to switch sides and align themselves with the BJP. Jayalalithaa, who claimed that the slew of corruption cases instituted against her by the DMK government were politically motivated, has changed her political partners periodically: from the Congress to the BJP, back to the Congress, and back to the BJP in February 2004. The BJP had for decades claimed that it was the 'cleanest' political party in the country, but the compulsions of coalition politics evidently compelled its leadership to strike various kinds of alliances with individuals and parties it had earlier opposed on the ground that they were tainted.

Corruption in India is, to a great extent, a consequence of the highly discretionary system of bureaucratic and political control over public finances, which provides the opportunity and means for illegal rent-seeking. But, an important motive for corruption in public life, which goes beyond individual greed, is the illegal manner in which election campaigns are funded. The Election Commission has laid down spending limits for candidates of political parties fighting local as well as national elections. Though these limits have gone up in recent years, many have argued that these are still unrealistically low. At one stage, it had been calculated that the official limit on spending would not be sufficient for a candidate to mail an ordinary postcard to each eligible voter in his or her Lok Sabha constituency. This is particularly true for large Lok Sabha constituencies like Outer Delhi, which has an electorate of over three million.

The contrary view, articulated among others by the late Indrajit Gupta of the CPI, is that such huge sums are not really required to conduct an effective election campaign for a few weeks. Any observer of the Indian political scene would vouch for the fact that much of the money spent on election campaigns is not 'legitimate'. A fair proportion is used for inducements like free country liquor, blankets, clothing and so on, distributed among the poorer sections within a constituency. Clearly, these are not accounted for in the expenditure statements that candidates have to submit to the Election Commission.

There is a point of view that suggests that coalition politics, because of its unstable nature, could reduce the amount of black money used in election campaigns. The argument runs as follows. Most of the illegal funds deployed by politicians for their election campaigns have to be raised from industrialists, traders and dishonest bureaucrats. Even if one assumes conservatively that Rs. three crore is used in each Lok Sabha constituency by all the candidates put together, this would require over Rs. 1,500 crore to be raised for each general election. Clearly, such a huge sum of money cannot be easily raised if elections are held at frequent intervals. At a meeting of the Confederation of Indian Industry organised after the Vajpayee government lost on April 17, 1999, prominent industrialist Rahul Bajaj made this amply clear by publicly stating that politicians should not realistically expect donations from industry to fight elections every year. The instability that has characterised most coalition governments in India could thus have an unexpected but positive fallout by reducing the role of black money in election campaigns.

However, there is a counter-argument which runs like this. If an MP or a minister is of the view that elections would most likely be held frequently and party finances may be strained, he might well be tempted to make as much money as possible while in office. Hence, frequent elections may not in fact reduce the quantum of black money in politics, but merely change the manner in which it is raised—through individuals rather than through parties.

While there are a variety of factors which are responsible for the high incidence of corruption in India, in the context of coalition politics what can be stated is that political compulsions have resulted in the BJP seeking and finding allies among politicians tainted by corruption charges. The party's association with Sukh Ram and Jayalalithaa is evidence of this fact. Still, one needs to emphasise what was stated at the beginning of this chapter: a coalition government is almost always likely to be more transparent than a government dominated by a single party and, to that extent, less corrupt. It is not as if there are no corrupt individuals in coalition governments: this would be an utterly ridiculous proposition. But the fact is that the system of internal checks and balances that is integral to coalitions generally ensures greater accountability and hence, diminishes somewhat the scope for corruption.

India's value system is complex and there are no absolute standards of morality, not in traditional texts nor in real life. People distinguish between the more corrupt and the less corrupt, the corrupt and efficient person and one who is both corrupt and inefficient. A typical expression of this sentiment would be that a particular person receives bribes and does not do the 'work'—such an individual is 'worse' than the one who has to be bribed to work. It is also not uncommon to hear people suggest that a corrupt person who works is better than an honest one who does not.

A person who is perceived to be corrupt by others can be voted to power by his constituents because he is seen to be responsive to their aspirations. Examples of such politicians abound in India: former Railway Minister A.B.A. Ghani Khan Chowdhury, the late Kalpnath Rai, Laloo Prasad Yadav, Sukh Ram and Jayalalithaa, to name just a few. This phenomenon may not be directly related to coalition politics. Yet, in the new era of coalition politics in India, even if sections of the electorate are rejecting politicians who are considered non-performing, the same voters are willing to be more tolerant towards corrupt politicians who are seen to be doing 'something' for their supporters, even if that 'something' may be the assertion of a social identity if not creation of jobs and implementation of welfare projects. This is a reflection of the sense of alienation that four decades of stable governments have engendered among large sections of the population.

While the impact of coalition governments on the extent and nature of corruption in public life may be debatable, there is little doubt that federalism in Indian politics has been strengthened by the composition of the last few governments. The tenure of the United Front government between June 1996 and February 1998 set the trend. For the first time in the country's political history, chief ministers of small and big states across the country were formally and overtly very much part of the decision-making process in New Delhi. The Inter-State Council, for instance, had become virtually defunct during Narasimha Rao's five-year regime and the UF made much of the fact that it was reviving this institution. The UF also had a formal panel of its chief ministers, who periodically met to chalk out the government's agenda and discuss contentious issues.

In the past, the Union government had often been accused of ignoring the aspirations of different states and regions. Centre–state economic relations were often under a lot of strain with regional leaders blaming New Delhi for being parsimonious in allocating and releasing funds to states. The Union government, in turn, would blame states for being profligate. These tensions, which would come to the fore at least once a year when the Planning Commission would finalise the annual plans of different states, subsided to a great extent during the UF government. The government's supporters would claim that for the first time in independent India, chief ministers of states across the length and breadth of the country would participate in formulating and shaping the entire nation's economic policies. While there is some basis to this claim, what complicated matters was the internal dissension among the constituents of the United Front over economic policies.

The NDA too has a coordination committee of its allies, although this body is seen as being less effective than the institutions of the UF in influencing the government's policies. Formal institutional arrangements are, however, not a necessary or a sufficient condition for greater representation being given to states in the political process and in economic decision-making. The attitude of the leadership also matters. The tenure of the NDA has confirmed the feeling that the growing importance of chief ministers and other 'regional' leaders was not a passing phenomenon that began and ended with the UF's brief stint in power. During the UF's tenure, Chandrababu Naidu (Andhra Pradesh), Farooq Abdullah (Jammu & Kashmir), M. Karunanidhi (Tamil Nadu), Jyoti Basu (West Bengal), E.K. Nayanar (Kerala), J.H. Patel (Karnataka), Dasarat Deb (Tripura), Prafulla Kumar Mahanta (Assam), and Laloo Prasad Yadav (Bihar) were Chief Ministers who all played an important role in national politics.

During the second Vajpayee government, besides Naidu and Abdullah who aligned with the BJP, influential CMs included Kalyan Singh (Uttar Pradesh), Parkash Singh Badal (Punjab), Bansi Lal

(Haryana), and Manohar Joshi (Maharashtra). Other influential regional leaders included Jayalalithaa (Tamil Nadu), Mamata Banerjee (West Bengal), Naveen Patnaik (Orissa), Ramakrishna Hegde (Karnataka), Balasaheb Thackeray (Maharashtra) and others. In the third Vajpayee government, the list changed somewhat. Karunanidhi replaced Jayalalithaa for the first two years while Chautala replaced Bansi Lal and Naveen Patnaik became Chief Minister. Despite these changes, though, what remains constant is the crucial role being played by leaders from virtually every major state in running the coalition.

So-called regional *satraps*, chief ministers or opposition leaders of particular states, are evidently exerting a greater influence on the working of the Union government in New Delhi in more ways than one. Historians could argue that the immediate post-independence period, specifically the tenure of Jawaharlal Nehru, saw regional leaders playing a crucial role in the formulation of various national policies. This trend declined both during Indira Gandhi's and Rajiv Gandhi's terms as Prime Minister. There are examples galore of how chief ministers were whimsically changed because of a diktat from Delhi. From May 1996 onwards, the trend of state leaders not being consulted by the Union government in policy formulation got reversed thanks to coalition governments.

The loosening of the reins of the unitary Indian state has certainly helped regional *satraps* gain greater access to power in New Delhi. At the same time, though, it has also strengthened long-standing demands for the creation of new states from existing ones. This has created a rather piquant situation. While the dominant partner in the NDA coalition, the BJP, conceded some of these demands in the belief that it would be able to win popular support in the areas that would constitute the new states, regional leaders were less than enthusiastic about such proposals since they believed the formation of new states would erode their political influence.

The Vajpayee government has successfully carved out three new states: Uttaranchal on November 9, 2000, Jharkhand on November 15 the same year, and Chhattisgarh on November 1. More interesting than the reactions from within these states were the apprehensions expressed by a key ally of the BJP, the TDP. The party opposed the creation of new states on the ground that this could trigger off similar demands elsewhere in the country—a fear that was well-founded since there has been a long-standing demand to carve out Telengana from TDP-ruled Andhra Pradesh. Similar demands for the creation of Vidharba from Maharashtra, Bodoland from Assam and Gorkhaland from West Bengal are reason enough for other regional leaders to also be wary. Advani sought to reassure the TDP on this count and Vajpayee too made public statements asserting that no further proposals for new states would be considered, but the TDP remained at variance with the BJP's stance on this issue.

In the past, the war with China in 1962 and the wars with Pakistan in 1965 and 1971 had resulted in Congress governments tilting the polity in favour of a relatively strong centre, a trend towards centralisation that culminated in the Emergency which ended Indira Gandhi's tenure. Thereafter, although Rajiv Gandhi headed a Congress government with a three-fourth majority in the lower house of Parliament from December 1984 for a period of five years, the Indian polity never became more centralised than it was during the Emergency. On the contrary, the forces at the periphery appear to have gained ground at the expense of those in favour of a stronger Union government. So much so that the BJP, once among the most vehement advocates of a unitary India and a 'strong centre', has now come to accept that coalitions are necessary to govern a country as large and as heterogeneous as India.

The past trend towards centralisation and concentration of power had also resulted in politicians from UP acquiring almost unquestioned dominance over national politics. Since power lay largely in the hands of the Prime Minister and since most Prime Ministers came from UP because of its sheer size, other states had relatively little say in influencing politics in New Delhi. K.M. Pannikar, in his dissenting note to the report of the States' Reorganisation Commission, had voiced fears of 'the dominance of Uttar Pradesh in all-India matters'. For at least three decades after Pannikar made these remarks in 1955, expression of such sentiments were not uncommon.

Barring Morarji Desai's tenure as Prime Minister in 1977–1978 and Gulzari Lal Nanda's two short stints that lasted only for weeks, till June 1991, all Indian Prime Ministers had originated from Uttar Pradesh: Jawaharlal Nehru, Lal Bahadur Shastri, Indira Gandhi,

Charan Singh, Rajiv Gandhi, V.P. Singh and Chandra Shekhar. Thereafter, of course, the next three Prime Ministers came from outside Uttar Pradesh: P.V. Narasimha Rao from Andhra Pradesh, H.D. Deve Gowda from Karnataka and I.K. Gujral from (undivided) Punjab. Once again, we are back to UP with the current Prime Minister A.B. Vajpayee. Despite the fact that Vajpayee is from UP, the trend towards decentralisation of power means that his tenure has not marked a return to the days when UP dominated national politics.

The point to note is that even as the Indian polity gets increasingly fragmented, sub-national and regional movements based on language would continue to exert themselves from time to time. Having agreed to the formation of Uttaranchal, Chhattisgarh and Jharkhand, the Vajpayee government had to cope with renewed demands for the formation of Vidharba (out of Maharashtra), Telengana (out of Andhra Pradesh), Kodagu (out of Karnataka), besides Ladakh and Leh (out of Jammu & Kashmir). The list could well become longer as the years go by. For instance, sections of the population of the Cachar and Karbi Anglong regions of Assam (which had been given the option of remaining with Assam or joining Meghalaya in 1972) want their own state.

Linguistic and cultural considerations have mattered—and will continue to matter—much more than administrative or economic factors as India's internal boundaries are redrawn. There are at least 33 languages in India spoken by more than a million people each. If linguistic considerations are to once again determine the redrawing of state boundaries, can an arbitrary line be drawn which says: 'so far and no further'? What is more, it is important to remember that none of the three new states of Uttaranchal, Chhattisgarh, and Jharkhand has been formed for linguistic reasons, all of them being part of Hindi-speaking areas, though there are many different local dialects. A larger number of states may in itself not be an undesirable phenomenon, particularly if, like coalition politics, it reflects the diversity of the country.

It can be argued with some conviction that most demands for new states in India are in fact expressions of a feeling of alienation or of being exploited by a strong Union or state government and of being denied the right to determine their own destinies. Given this context, a question logically follows: is a coalition government likely to aggravate such feelings or assuage them? There is reason to believe that coalition governments are more likely to be in tune with the aspirations of smaller social and ethnic groups and hence would be able to instil in them a greater sense of belonging to the Union while retaining their distinctive identities.

During Jawaharlal Nehru's tenure as Prime Minister, there were no formal arrangements of the kind that have come up during the tenure of the recent coalition governments. Yet, Nehru certainly involved leaders from different regions—C. Rajagopalachari from Tamil Nadu, Atulya Ghosh from West Bengal or Biju Patnaik from Orissa—in governing the country, arguably much more than any other Congress Prime Minister did. Therefore, if smaller states are to be periodically created and these are not to unleash divisive forces, then it is imperative that coalitional arrangements at the level of the Union government are sufficiently responsive to local aspirations. In the recent political discourse in the country, much has been made of the distinction between coalition governments dominated by a single party and those in which no single party dwarfs the others. It can be contended that the second kind of coalition government (the one in which no party is dominant) is more likely to accommodate diverse identities and interests.

The survival of India as a Union of states is in itself an amazing account of the art and science of political reconciliation and accommodation. As coalitions dominate the composition of the Union government, it is perhaps time to turn an old adage on its head: Divided we stand.

Chapter 8

Illusion of Consensus

Economic policies pursued by coalition governments should presumably be different from those devised by governments that are led by, or comprise, a single political party. A coalition government by definition includes a number of political parties or groups, big and small; therefore economic policies of such a government should under most circumstances not only reflect the diversity and heterogeneity of their combination, but also be the outcome of a consensus among the constituents. But this has not always been the case in India.

A claim is often made that currently there is considerable consensus among contending political parties in India on the broad direction of economic policies that have been followed by various Union governments since June 1991 when economic reforms were introduced by Finance Minister Manmohan Singh in the Narasimha Rao government. This claim is, however, difficult to substantiate. There is quite a lot of confusion in the NDA government on the thrust and tenor of economic policy issues. Part of the chaos is a result of deep-rooted ideological differences among the disparate constituents of the NDA and some of it is a direct consequence of the compulsions of coalition politics.

There is considerable evidence of the pulls and pressures of coalition politics on economic decision-making. One instance was the indecision on increasing the then officially administered prices of petroleum products in 1998-99. Whereas the United Front government had dilly-dallied and agonised for months over such a decision in 1997, the second Vajpayee government too succumbed to pressure from NDA partners not to hike the prices of petroleum products between March 1998 and April 1999. Eventually, just before the BJP-led NDA coalition was sworn in to power again in October 1999—exactly a day after the last round of polling—the then caretaker government of Vajpayee hiked the politically-sensitive price of diesel by a whopping 40 per cent in the face of a sharp rise in world oil prices.

There has been a gradual convergence of political opinion on many economic issues cutting across party lines—with the exception of the left—notwithstanding the fact that this consensus among opposing parties and formations has periodically broken down and keeps breaking down on particular issues. Within the largest political parties in the country, the Congress and the BJP, there has been internal divergence of opinion on economic policy issues.

The two major political formations that are opposed to the broad direction of the economic reforms and not just the details are the left, consisting mainly of the two communist parties, and the Swadeshi Jagaran Manch (SJM), an offshoot of the RSS. Both have had to compromise on economic policy issues because of over-riding political compulsions. While the left may not have liked the direction of economic policy formulated by the United Front government, it could not threaten to withdraw from the UF coalition since that would have meant helping either the BJP or the Congress. A similar TINA (There Is No Alternative) factor has constrained the SJM in its opposition to the policies followed by the BJP-led NDA government. Thus, the ideological pulls and pressures on economic policy issues have often taken place—and continue to take place—within political parties and their ideological fraternities rather than merely among them.

It can, therefore, be argued that instead of a genuine consensus on economic policy issues what is often witnessed is an illusion of consensus. This is on account of the fact that there are a number of similarities between the economic policy prescriptions espoused by the BJP and the Congress. Both parties now apparently reject the 'socialist' policies that were put in place in the 1950s by Jawaharlal Nehru (although, of late, there are signs that the economic programme of the Congress, or more precisely its rhetoric, is veering leftwards). Both parties today argue in favour of a more 'market friendly' policy package. It is a separate matter altogether that Nehru himself had advocated a 'mixed' economy for India, one that he saw as incorporating the best elements of both capitalism and socialism.

In practice, what happened was arguably a mix of the worst of both systems. Successive Congress governments (before the Narasimha Rao regime) set up an excessively bureaucratic economic system that stifled entrepreneurship and private initiative on the one hand and failed to provide primary education and basic health-care to the majority of Indians, on the other. While the rest of the world generally perceived Nehru to have tilted in favour of the Soviet Union and his economic policies to be socialist in character, his critics at home argued that he pandered to the interests of big business and thus encouraged capitalist practices.

What muddied the waters further was the spurious differentiation that was drawn between the public and the private sectors in the country. Virtually throughout the first half century after India became politically independent, public sector corporations served as the personal fiefdoms of politicians and bureaucrats in power—the state thus became the private property of the privileged few. At the same time, private corporate groups prospered thanks to a generous infusion of funds from government-controlled banks and financial institutions. Thus, the losses of the public sector got translated into the profits of the private sector and, more often than not, the gap between the 'right' and the 'left' became obliterated insofar as economic policies were concerned.

While the BJP and the Congress today both loudly proclaim the virtues of economic liberalisation in public, there are in fact deep differences of opinion within both political parties on the direction and pace of economic reforms. What has compounded the confusion is that while the BJP is the single-largest constituent of the ruling NDA coalition, as the largest Opposition party the Congress is invariably obliged to criticise the NDA government's economic policies even if these are not substantially different from the policies that were pursued by the earlier Congress government headed by Narasimha Rao.

The fact of a political party opposing another's policies for 'the sake of opposition' is also illustrated by the turnaround in the BJP's *swadeshi* rhetoric. Before the party came to power in March 1998, it had asserted that the economic reforms process had till then not been sufficiently pro-Indian. The BJP's slogan used to be, 're-forming the reforms', and the party argued that reforms had been overly sensitive to the needs of foreign investors and had not provided a level playing field for Indian industry. The BJP, the party's pre-election manifesto had proclaimed, would aim at an India 'built by Indians, for Indians'. Six years later, most economic analysts would agree that the NDA government's economic policy thrust has not been substantially different from what a Congress government would have followed.

While the manifestation of the 'India for Indians' view of the reforms was evident in the first budget presented by Finance Minister Yashwant Sinha in June 1998 (Sinha imposed an across-the-board hike of 8 per cent on all customs duty, subsequently reduced to 4 per cent), the same budget also reflected the compelling need for the government to assuage foreign investors to counter the impact of the economic sanctions imposed on India as a result of the nuclear tests conducted in May.

Within a year, the situation had changed radically. *Swadeshi* was no longer the flavour of the month in the BJP. After the return of the BJP-led NDA to power in October 1999, the government pushed through the bill to allow entry of the private sector—Indian and foreign—into the insurance business. It may be recalled that the BJP had resisted a similar bill in 1997, proposed by Chidambaram, on the grounds that the insurance business should be opened up initially only to private Indian firms. In 1999, it was not as if there were no sections within the Sangh Parivar which were opposed to the insurance bill. The SJM and the Bharatiya Mazdoor Sangh, the trade union affiliate of the RSS, continued to have reservations. Yet, since 1997, the balance of power within the Sangh Parivar had clearly shifted in favour of the pro-reforms section.

Just as Sinha's first budget was derided by the reformists, his second budget (of February 1999) was hailed as one of the most pro-reform budgets. For the first time, a Finance Minister had openly announced the government's intention to privatise public sector undertakings, not just disinvest shares in them. Sinha's budget speech also spoke of a 'second wave of reforms'. After he had to rollback many of the proposals contained in his first budget, Sinha had been severely criticised for bowing to populist pressures.

But this was not the only time Sinha bowed to pressure. He had to once again rollback his budget proposals in 2002 following strident criticism from his own colleagues in the BJP. Even the fact that his party lost the municipal elections in Delhi in March 2002 was attributed to the Finance Minister's anti-middle-class budget. Vice President of the BJP, Sahib Singh Verma, put in his papers.

Budget proposals, as Sinha often stated, are not meant to be static. He claimed he had merely responded to public opinion. But there were a few questions that remained unanswered. What prevented the Finance Minister from eliciting the opinion of the people at large during the series of pre-budget consultations he had with, among others, representatives of industry, the small-scale sector, trade unions, farmers and economists? What stopped Sinha from seeking the views of his own party stalwarts, not to mention the BJP's allies in the NDA? Did he think he would be able to get away with a 'tough' budget without the support of his compatriots in the Union Cabinet and the Council of Ministers? What happened during meetings of the Cabinet Committee on Economic Affairs when budget proposals are supposed to be discussed threadbare and then approved?

In a coalition government, decision-makers from the largest party should seek and find an area of consensus among the ideologically disparate constituents of the coalition. The rollback drama showed that the NDA clearly had a long way to go before it learnt the *dharma* of coalition politics.

The RSS and the SJM had been critical of some of the government's economic advisers who had held important positions in earlier Congress governments: individuals like N.K. Singh and Montek Singh Ahluwalia. During a public function organised by the SJM, George Fernandes (who was yet to be reinducted as Defence Minister at that juncture) flayed a report on employment that had been prepared by an official panel headed by Ahluwalia. Fernandes said the report should have been prepared in six months; instead it took two-and-a-half years. Saying there was little in the recommendations of the report that would help create 10 million new jobs each year, Fernandes went on to derogatorily describe Ahluwalia as an 'acolyte of the World Bank'.

Though certain leaders of the RSS and the SJM were privately unhappy about the actions taken by the then Finance Minister Sinha to check a fall in the value of the Unit Scheme of 1964 (US–64) run by the country's oldest and largest mutual funds organisation, the government-controlled Unit Trust of India, they did not openly express their disagreement. However, other individuals known to be close to the RSS were far less restrained in their attacks on the Finance Minister. Consider, for instance, an article written by management expert Bharat Jhunjhunwala that was published by the *Indian Express* (August 1, 2001). RSS chief Sudarshan had earlier extolled the virtues of Jhunjhunwala and suggested that it should be individuals like him who should be advising the government on economic policy issues rather than unnamed 'rootless wonders'. (Despite his influence, Sudarshan's advice was not heeded, at least not in this instance.)

In the article, Jhunjhunwala lamented that the BJP in power had not behaved very differently from the Congress. He wrote:

> Any bureaucrat or minister can subvert governance to favour his near and dear ones and yet claim that he is clean. The BJP has continued with this ignoble tradition... the income tax department had issued notices to Mauritius-based FIIs [foreign institutional investors] seeking to deny them benefits of the Double Taxation Avoidance Treaty with that country because their head offices were located in USA or other countries. The Finance Minister intervened and instructed that a certificate of registration issued by the government of Mauritius was adequate and final proof of the FII's domicile and asked the income tax department to withdraw their notices. The Finance Minister's *bahu* [daughter-in-law] was one beneficiary of the minister's intervention. Yet, this was considered clean because the Finance Minister had disclosed his interest to the Prime Minister. Whether the decision was taken in the interests of the country or the *bahu* can never be answered....

Jhunjhunwala was hardly the only RSS sympathiser who attacked a top functionary of the Vajpayee government. Into this category fell former Chief Minister of Delhi Madan Lal Khurana and former BJP General Secretary K.N. Govindacharya. Both were very critical of what they alleged were the Vajpayee government's moves to bend over backwards to accommodate the interests of the WTO.

Even as the BMS, the SJM and, to a lesser extent, the RSS continue to fret and crib about the Vajpayee government's economic policies, these organisations would certainly stop short of doing anything drastic that could have the potential of destabilising the government. Simultaneously, the BMS would join hands with trade unions close to the Congress and the communist parties on specific issues—for instance, on the question of opposing the government's move to allow foreign firms to hold 26 per cent equity in companies manufacturing goods for the defence services.

During the 1980s, under the influence of individuals like Nanaji Deshmukh, the BJP used to claim that the party believed in what it called 'Gandhian socialism'. In 1991, after Manmohan Singh initiated his policies of economic liberalisation, there were quite a few BJP leaders who argued that the Congress had 'hijacked' its economic agenda. Even as the confusion on economic policy issues continues in the BJP, the situation is not very different in the largest Opposition party, the Congress. The same party that had earlier championed the cause of privatisation and had begun the sale of shares of public sector undertakings found itself in a curious position in which it opposed the manner in which Bharat Aluminium Company (BALCO) was privatised.

That the Congress too is far from united on the composition of economic reforms was evident during meetings to review the party's poor performance in the 1999 elections. The divide between the pro- and anti-reform groups became all too evident with several senior leaders including Rajesh Pilot and Arjun Singh targeting Manmohan Singh for allegedly giving the party an anti-poor image. The reforms ushered in during Singh's tenure from 1991 to 1996, they argued, had given the party the image of being concerned only with promoting the economic interests of the elite, while ignoring the concerns of the poor. Singh predictably offered to resign from his position as Leader of the Opposition in the Rajya Sabha and counter-attacked by asking why these leaders had chosen to remain silent for so many years. However, Sonia Gandhi persuaded Manmohan Singh, who has a squeaky clean image, to desist from any such drastic step.

Within the Congress, a debate continues about whether India's grand old party has of late lost much of its political support base because its policies of economic liberalisation were perceived by the electorate to be pro-rich. In a country where one out of four individuals still lives on less than one US dollar a day, policies that are not seen to be helping the poor can never ensure support for a political party, whatever be its true ideological complexion. An opposition party like the Congress can afford to speak in different voices when it is out of power. The BJP was not dissimilar when it was opposing the Congress.

Apart from these differences within these political parties, another reason why the economic policies followed by coalition governments have not been significantly different from those followed during single-party rule is simply because such governments—with the exception of the current one—have not been around long enough to radically alter the broad direction and content of economic policy. Even when attempts have been made to change this direction, these have not been followed through sufficiently as, till 1999, no coalition government had been able to present more than two successive Union budgets leave alone see through their implementation. The budget in India is used as an annual event that is not a mere presentation of the country's accounts, but an occasion for governments to propagate, shape and highlight their economic policies.

There are a variety of reasons which explain why the economic policies followed by coalition governments are not very different from those followed by single-party governments. Sociologist M.N. Panini has argued that the emergence of backward-caste politics could have a direct bearing on economic policy. The crux of Panini's argument is that since parties that project themselves as champions of the backward castes have focused on job reservations in government as a key element of their strategy, they must have a vested interest in the perpetuation of an economy in which the state continues to play a dominant role. To the extent that economic liberalisation seeks to do exactly the opposite—namely, to reduce the role of the state and enhance the role of markets—the OBCs would tend to be opposed to it. Conversely, the upper castes, who see reservations as eroding their strength in the government, will tend to support liberalisation. This is because liberalisation encourages free competition and free competition in turn benefits those who are already endowed with skills and resources, in this case the upper castes.

While the argument is difficult to refute in theory, the actual politics of the OBC-dominated parties has not quite matched this theory. H.D. Deve Gowda and Chandrababu Naidu are obvious examples of leaders espousing the cause of OBCs who are also liberalisers. One reason for this rift between precept and practice could be that these parties are dominated by the most privileged among the OBCs. Hence, the sections that are in the leadership of these parties are not as underprivileged in terms of existing resources and skills as might be presumed. Another factor could be that while liberalisation may in the long run reduce discretionary controls and hence the ability of those in power to milk the system, in the short run this may not be the case. Some left economists, for instance, have argued that the economic reforms, far from reducing the scope for corruption, have only increased it while centralising discretionary powers (the proverbial single-window clearance for projects). Also, since the reforms entail the entry of the private sector into areas hitherto monopolised by the government, these areas can now yield kickbacks that they would not have earlier.

A third important reason for the OBC-dominated parties not being as virulently anti-reforms as might be expected could be that most of these are as yet young parties. During their short lives, they have concentrated on building a political programme and have had little time to formulate a coherent long-term economic strategy. Their positions on economic policy, therefore, have varied from issue to issue and have been dictated largely by short-term political expediency.

While coalition governments have sought to change economic policy priorities, these attempts have met with mixed success. Moreover, the proposition that coalitions have not been able to significantly change the course of economic policies in India does not run contrary to whatever one perceives to be the relationship between political uncertainty and economic development. It might seem logical that uncertainty of any kind, including political uncertainty, is not good for economic development. There are others who would, on the contrary, argue that a period of economic adversity spurs the political leadership to take tough decisions that it may not otherwise take. True, the period of coalition governments in India has witnessed considerable political uncertainty. But it is far from clear that political instability has been bad for the economy. But more on that later.

The first non-Congress government in New Delhi in 1977 was headed by Morarji Desai, who had earlier broken away from the Congress headed by Indira Gandhi on account of a large number of differences, not the least among them being differences on economic policy issues. Morarji Desai was never enamoured of

Indira Gandhi's socialist rhetoric and the ushering in of ostensibly radical land reform programmes, among other things. But the
Janata Party government headed by Desai was not substantially
different from its Congress predecessors insofar as economic policies were concerned, with a few notable exceptions of course.

While Desai was considered to be conservative and pro-capitalist in
his economic ideology and outlook, the government he headed
became better known for its 'leftist' stance. As Union Industry Minister, the 'socialist' George Fernandes, created a sensation when
he told two of the world's biggest multinational corporations,
Coca-Cola and IBM (once International Business Machines), that
they should wind up their operations in the country unless they
reduced their equity holdings in their Indian affiliates to less than
40 per cent under the provisions of the Foreign Exchange Regulation Act. Fernandes also actively advocated a 'small is beautiful'
industrial policy and the Union government enlarged the list of
items whose production was reserved for small-scale industrial
units. The same Fernandes who had compared sections of businessmen to vermin, however, also pushed through a controversial technical collaboration agreement between German multinational Siemens and India's government-owned Bharat Heavy
Electricals Limited (BHEL), which is one of Asia's largest manu-
facturers of power equipment. This agreement was considered by
some to be against the interests of BHEL.

Despite Fernandes' positions on various economic issues, the
Janata Party government headed by Morarji Desai is not remem-
bered for having radically changed India's economic policies. If
anything, there was considerable continuity in the policies followed despite the personal predilections of Morarji Desai and his
Industry Minister. The Charan Singh government that followed
Desai's government was avowedly pro-farmer. Charan Singh considered himself a leader of the country's farmers, although his
support base was largely confined to the agriculturally prosperous districts of northern India, especially western Uttar Pradesh
and Haryana. His shortlived government could do little or nothing to influence the Union government's economic policies, including its policies for the agricultural sector.

The second phase of non-Congress governments at the Union
level started in December 1989 after the National Front government
led by V.P. Singh came to power. Earlier, as Finance Minister in

Rajiv Gandhi's government, V.P. Singh had pursued what many saw as a carrot-and-stick economic policy of sorts. On the one hand, he slashed direct tax rates, including personal income tax rates, arguing that the high income tax rates were effectively dissuading compliance among tax-payers and, in fact, encouraging more and more people to evade taxes. This apparently had the 'Laffer curve' effect of increasing revenue collections while bringing down the propensity of tax-payers to evade paying personal income tax. (Briefly, the Laffer curve effect is economic jargon that means a reduction in direct tax rates encourages more people to pay taxes, which, in turn, results in the tax net widening and revenue collections going up.)

This reduction in income tax rates would not have worked in isolation. Singh probably would not have been half as successful in raising revenues had it not been for his unstated policy of conducting raids against rich and powerful individuals accused of tax evasion. For a while, it seemed that lowly and often ill-paid tax officials had suddenly discovered a new-found confidence to book affluent and influential industrialists and sometimes even send them to jail for brief periods. The problem was that India's cumbersome and time-consuming legal system would ensure that many of those accused would be released on bail while litigation would continue and the process of prosecution would drag on for years. The other problem was that over-zealous officials sometimes took vicarious pleasure in humiliating and harassing well-to-do entrepreneurs and traders on the ostensible plea that the law was above no individual.

During Singh's brief tenure as Prime Minister, veteran socialist from Maharashtra, Madhu Dandavate, served as Union Finance Minister. In the February 1990 budget, Dandavate sought to impart a leftward shift to the government's economic policies—taxes on affluent sections were upped and public sector enterprises were sought to be strengthened.

But well before the financial year was over, in November 1990, the V.P. Singh government was toppled and a Congress-supported minority government headed by Chandra Shekhar was installed in its place. A then little-known former bureaucrat from Bihar, Yashwant Sinha, became the new Finance Minister, a post he was to hold again more than seven years later in March 1998. The Chandra Shekhar government was very keen on presenting the

Union budget, but the Congress under Rajiv Gandhi was adamant that the government should only present a vote-on-account and not a full-fledged budget. Since the Chandra Shekhar government was totally dependent on Congress support for its survival, it reluctantly agreed and in February 1991, Sinha presented a bland statement of accounts without any policy pronouncements.

The reason for the Congress not agreeing to the government presenting a full budget became evident less than a week after the vote-on-account was placed in Parliament. On March 4, 1991, the Congress suddenly decided to withdraw support to the Chandra Shekhar government apparently because a couple of policemen from Haryana were conducting a surveillance operation outside the residence of Rajiv Gandhi. This was also the time when international confidence in the Indian economy was on the verge of a collapse. Non-resident Indians panicked and began withdrawing their hard currency deposits from Indian banks. As the foreign exchange reserves dipped and the country's balance of payments started deteriorating, the caretaker government with Sinha as Finance Minister realised, much to its dismay, that there was a real danger of the country defaulting on its external financial obligations. For the first time in independent India's history, the Union government pawned a part of the official gold reserves held by the Reserve Bank of India (RBI).

This decision predictably raised a huge hue and cry. Indians, more than citizens of almost any other country, are crazy about the yellow metal and the government's action sent out alarm signals to the public at large. Here was a caretaker minority government mortgaging the country's most precious wealth to keep its head above water. Congress leaders like former Finance Minister Pranab Mukherjee roundly criticised the government (which the party had been supporting just a few weeks earlier) for mismanaging the economy. Even Manmohan Singh, who had by then become Economic Adviser to the Prime Minister in Chandra Shekhar's government after the completion of his tenure as Secretary General of the Geneva-based South Commission, realised there were few options before the government to stave off a balance of payments crisis.

Even as the country was on the verge of defaulting on its external financial obligations, India went in for the 10th general elections in May 1991. By the time the P.V. Narasimha Rao government came to power the following month, the country's hard currency reserves had plunged to an unprecedented low and, at one stage, were equivalent to barely two weeks' import requirements. Inflation was also running at a high level by Indian standards of around 12 per cent (it reached a peak of 17 per cent later that year in September). This was, of course, the annual rate of inflation as measured by the official wholesale price index; the actual increase in retail prices to the consumer as measured by various consumer price indices was much higher.

Finance Minister Manmohan Singh, holding a political position for the first time after a long and illustrious career as an academic and a bureaucrat—he had headed the Planning Commission and the RBI—knew from the outset that he would have to act and act fast to avert an impending economic disaster. He first drastically devalued the Indian currency in two stages in early July—this was the first time since 1966 that the rupee was officially devalued by the government. With an eye towards obtaining a hefty 'structural adjustment loan' from the International Monetary Fund (IMF), Manmohan Singh's first Union budget presented in July, dramatically altered the direction of India's economic policy regime. He slashed customs duties thereby reducing the protection given to domestic industry, while at the same time he sought to do away with the industrial licensing system and other controls on industry and trade. Over the next five years, the pace of economic reforms decelerated considerably.

The 13-day government of Atal Bihari Vajpayee in May 1996 took one major economic decision during its all-too-brief tenure: the decision to offer a counter-guarantee to Enron Power Corporation of the US, which was the first foreign company to set up a power project in the country at Dabhol near the west coast in Maharashtra.

Even as it became clear that the first Vajpayee government would not last for any length of time, the United Front had come together to arrive at a Common Minimum Programme which formed the basis of the formation of the country's first coalition government of its kind headed by H.D. Deve Gowda. The UF government received 'outside' support from the second and third largest political parties after the BJP, namely, the Congress and the CPI(M). While the Congress did not exert much influence in shaping the UF government's economic polices, the CPI(M) did manage to do so to some extent because of its presence in various commit-tees set up to coordinate the activities of the 13 constituents of the government.

The Finance Minister in the UF government was the savvy lawyer–politician Palaniappan Chidambaram from the Tamil Maanila Congress. Chidambaram had served in two Congress governments under Rajiv Gandhi and P.V. Narasimha Rao. In the Rao government, Chidambaram had served as Union Commerce Minister. He was considered to be an enthusiastic liberaliser, an admirer of Manmohan Singh's economic policies (though on occasions he is said to have crossed swords with Singh at Cabinet meetings). As the man responsible to a considerable degree for drafting the UF's CMP, it was not surprising that Chidambaram imbued it with a pro-reform stance.

It was inevitable that Chidambaram's economic ideology (and the policies that stemmed from it) would be opposed by the CPI in the UF government and by the CPI(M) in the coordination and steering committees. This was precisely what happened, although the differences of opinion never reached a head or caused a ma-jor crisis of governance. As pointed out earlier, one major reason for this was the dearth of options open to the left. However much the left may have disagreed with the economic policy framework of the UF government, it could not do very much more than ex-press its reservations. Having reached the conclusion that keep-ing the BJP and the Congress out of power was top priority, the left could not have actually withdrawn from the UF.

The most apparent evidence of the differences within the UF government on economic policy issues was the inordinate delay in arriving at a decision to hike the prices of petroleum products. For weeks on end, the committees attached to the UF government debated and deliberated on the issue and repeatedly failed to arrive at any decision. It had become obvious that the government's finances would become difficult to manage if the losses on the 'oil pool account' of the Union Ministry of Petroleum and Natural Gas continued to mount. The UF government realised it had been saddled with an unpopular decision that had become inevitable since the previous Congress government had failed to increase the administered prices of different petroleum products (because it believed that such a move would alienate the party from large sections of voters). The UF government did eventually bite the bullet, but only after considerable heartburn.

To those opposed to the UF, the government's procrastination was evidence of the inefficient manner in which a coalition government worked. As far as the UF government's supporters were concerned, the government had responded to popular sentiments and had extensively debated the pros and cons of the decision before it was taken. Another occasion on which Chidambaram's differences with the left led to a standoff was when he tried to push through legislation allowing private Indian and foreign firms to enter the insurance business (but more on that later).

Chidambaram's first budget presented on July 26, 1996 appeared to many to continue along the path laid out by Manmohan Singh. The process of reduction of import duties and de-bureaucratisation was sought to be continued. The government set up the Disinvestment Commission headed by senior bureaucrat G.V. Ramakrishna, who had earlier headed the official watchdog body for the country's capital markets, the Securities and Exchange Board of India (SEBI). At one stage, Chidambaram stated that the government would 'invariably' accept the Disinvestment Commission's recommendations. Later, however, the Commission found that it had been reduced to a body that would only recommend the modalities of disinvesting the equity shares of specific public sector enterprises and not one which would be responsible for implementing and monitoring the entire process of divesting the government's stake in these corporations. Chidambaram's second budget, presented at the end of February 1997, was hailed by sections of the media as a 'dream budget' for it sought to reduce the incidence of income tax on individuals and companies while at the same time projecting an increase in revenue collections.

A month later, political upheavals ensured that the dream budget would soon turn into a nightmare. Congress President Sitaram Kesri pulled the rug from under Prime Minister H.D. Deve Gowda and had him replaced by Inder Kumar Gujral. At one stage, in April 1997, it appeared that the budget would not be approved by Parliament but the crisis was averted. More than a year later, Chidambaram was to state that political uncertainty—and the toppling of two UF governments by the Congress—was responsible for destroying the confidence of investors as well as consumers, resulting in the projections contained in his budget going completely awry. He had assumed that the fiscal deficit as a proportion of the country's gross domestic product (GDP) would be contained at 4.5 per cent, but the actual figure by the end of the year worked out to more than 6 per cent. To be fair to Chidambaram, however, his predecessors and successors had also not been particularly successful in containing the fiscal deficit to the levels projected at the time when the budget proposals were announced. Another important reason why the UF government's budget calculations went haywire was the decision to accept many of the recommendations of the 5th Central Pay Commission, which recommended increases in the salaries and remuneration paid to government employees.

After Vajpayee became Prime Minister for the second time in March 1998, it was widely reported that he wanted Jaswant Singh to be the Finance Minister in his Cabinet. (Singh, who had served as Finance Minister during the first 13-day Vajpayee government in 1996, had lost the elections from Chittorgarh in Rajasthan.) However, leaders of the RSS were not particularly happy with Vajpayee's choice and 'persuaded' him to select Sinha for the position. Sinha had the unenviable task before him of preventing the growth rate of the country's economy, segments of which were slipping into recession, from slowing down further. Sinha sought to define his plans to kick-start the Indian economy through a series of rather vague statements-of-intent that payed ritual obeisance to the Vajpayee government's National Agenda for Governance. The agenda, like the President's address to Parliament spelling out the government's priorities, was full of pious pronouncements that were not just unexceptional and non-controversial, but predictably couched in the rhetoric of 'consensus' politics. The Finance Minister said the regular budget to be presented later would 'seek to impart the necessary stimulus to agriculture and industry, restore dynamism to exports, encourage larger flows of foreign investment...take decisive initiatives to improve the state of the infrastructure, strengthen the financial system...'. He said the 'inherent strength of our economy...has enabled us to hold our heads high and not succumb to the economic gales that have been sweeping through the Asian region.'

Meanwhile, within the BJP and the larger Sangh Parivar, a tussle was underway about what should be the government's economic policy thrust, with the *swadeshi* group on one side and the 'liberal' group on the other. The BJP, which had earlier sworn by Gandhian socialism, became critical of the Rao regime's economic policies on the ground that the economy had been exposed to international competition too quickly. Before the May 1996 general elections, the BJP would often say what India needed was technology for computer chips and not potato chips. In this regard, the BJP and some of its allies like the Samata Party (headed by George Fernandes who insists that he continues to vociferously espouse the cause of socialism) appeared to be speaking the same language as the two main communist parties. A large section of opinion within all these otherwise diverse political parties argued in favour of a slow, selective and cautious opening up of the Indian economy to international competition.

The pro-*swadeshi* argument that emerged in the mid-1990s could be summarised thus: The Congress government headed by P.V. Narasimha Rao with Manmohan Singh as Finance Minister had, since the middle of 1991, rolled out the red carpet for foreign firms and lowered import duties under pressure from multilateral funding agencies like the IMF. Since the bulk of the biggest Indian corporations, whether privately owned or controlled by the state, were midgets by world standards and needed government support (if not protection) to survive, leave alone prosper, domestic companies were severely handicapped. The argument further ran that governments the world over offer more than a modicum of support to local entrepreneurs, that the same developed countries which shout the loudest about free trade in global fora are the very nations which protect inefficient industries at home on account of the political influence wielded by home-grown industrialists and workers' unions.

There is a slightly more sophisticated variant of the pro-*swadeshi* argument, which draws on the analogy of the need for the *mai-baap sarkar* (literally, the mother-father government) to protect 'infant' industries from foreign competition. But what happens when the infant fails to grow up, to mature and then go into the big, bad world outside to make his or her living? What do parents do with their pampered, overgrown brats? Do they throw them to the wolves and hope for the best? Or should they adopt a more humane approach towards their spoilt offspring?

Those in favour of expediting the pace of external liberalisation of the economy contend that Indian industry has been protected too much and for too long. The fact that domestic capitalists were shielded from competition by the government's policies of encouraging import substitution at any cost, including building high tariff walls, resulted in consumers getting a raw deal. Thus, while corporate profits soared and official revenues remained buoyant, the least-organised segment of the economy, the consumers, had no choice but to make do with over-priced, shoddy products and sub-standard services.

Proponents of both points of view marshal reams of facts and figures to bolster their contentions. And, there is more than an element of truth in the arguments put forward both by the supporters as well as the critics of *swadeshi*.

Nobody would dissuade international capital from flowing into infrastructure projects, be these roads, bridges, ports or airports, particularly if such inflows also involve access to technology not available within the country. Yet it is also true that these are the very projects that are not inherently profitable, that is, unless the risks are heavily underwritten by the government. At the same time, no Indian politician worth his salt can oppose foreign or multinational investors in today's situation, so long as new jobs are created. (For example, the longest-serving Chief Minister Jyoti Basu, a communist, had repeatedly urged multinationals to invest in his state of West Bengal, a practice that his successor has continued.) Yet, the debate on whether India can afford to adopt a selective approach towards foreign investments and keep such inflows out of particular areas, notably, consumer goods, is far from over. The chances are that whichever government is in power would hum and haw, move back and forth, while not excessively antagonising either local corporate bigwigs or representatives of multinational concerns.

Addressing his first formal meeting with corporate captains at the Federation of Indian Chambers of Commerce and Industry (FICCI) in March 1998, Finance Minister Sinha said low public investments in infrastructure had contributed to the economic slowdown even as he warned of 'hard decisions' to arrest the downturn in his forthcoming budget. At the meeting, Sinha recalled how his decision to mortgage the country's gold stocks in 1991 had saved the government from defaulting on its external financial obligations, even though it made him personally unpopular. Before his parleys with domestic industrialists, Sinha had spoken in Washington and London, where he sought to assuage apprehensions that his government's policy of *swadeshi* was protectionist and would dissuade foreign investors from coming to the country. Addressing representatives of the World Bank and the IMF, Sinha again attempted to allay fears that populist spending by his government would increase budgetary deficits.

Vajpayee too went on record stating that *swadeshi* did not mean 'we don't value direct foreign investment'. Speaking for the first time to industrialists in his capacity as Prime Minister in April 1998, Vajpayee told the annual session of the CII that he had 'inherited a weak, deficit-ridden economy, but I'm not complaining'. While stating that 'we cannot afford to play politics with the nation's economy any more,' the Prime Minister argued that the steps taken to free the economy since 1991 had not been backed by checks and balances. The social sectors of the economy as well as the infrastructure had not improved. While outlining a 90-day agenda for action (which, as subsequent events showed, was not implemented), Vajpayee sought to explain what he meant when he claimed that there was an urgent need to 'reform the reforms process'.

He said industry had three main complaints against the government—it felt the government was responsible for avoidable delays in setting up projects, that the government took too much and provided too little, and that the government was in areas of business 'it had no business' to be in. The Prime Minister went on to enumerate the three main complaints the government had about industry. He said industry did not share the government's social responsibilities and that it preached the virtues of transparency to the government but did not itself operate in a transparent manner, nor did it fulfil its obligations to workers and consumers. Finally, industrialists wanted competition but not in the industries they were in. Vajpayee then identified the three complaints ordinary citizens of the country had against both industry and government. First, most people believed that government and business were hand-in-glove helping each other, the rest be damned. Secondly, it was perceived that both industry and government did not care about the real needs of the people. Finally, it was felt that there were two sets of laws in the country, one for ordinary people and the other for politicians and industrialists.

Perceptive as these observations were, the track record of the Vajpayee government as far as economic policy went was quite different. A little over two weeks after the government conducted nuclear tests at Pokhran, on the first day of June 1998, Sinha presented the budget for 1998-99 that came to be derogatorily known as the 'rollback' budget. Never in the last half-century of independent India had any Union Finance Minister changed his own budget proposals as quickly and as drastically as Yashwant Sinha did in the first fortnight of the month. It seemed the maiden budget of the new government was jinxed. Sinha announced two major changes in his budget proposals in less than 24 hours. The first was the reduction in the prices of petrol from what had been stated by the Ministry of Petroleum. The second was the decision to halve the increase in the administered price of urea fertiliser. Then, 10 days later, the Finance Minister completely rolled back urea prices and at the same time, halved the proposed increase in customs tariffs covering roughly one-third of the country's total imports. He also withdrew the witholding tax on foreign borrowings by Indian corporates.

The lobbying to make the changes in the budget came from various quarters, including industry associations, but the greatest pressure to rollback urea prices came from the BJP's own allies, notably the Shiromani Akali Dal of Punjab (the state which accounts for the lion's share of the country's total consumption of urea). Jayalalithaa was equally adamant about opposing any hike in urea prices. Thus, Sinha's hopes of redressing the growing imbalance in the pattern of usage of fertiliser (among the three principal groups of nutrients) in India, which had worsened on account of imperfect methods of pricing and distribution of subsidies, remained a pipedream.

By September 1998, the dissensions within the BJP and the Sangh Parivar over the government's economic policies appeared to be coming to a head. The criticism of the Vajpayee government's economic policies by the SJM became extremely strident, thereby embarrassing the BJP and its supporters no end. BJP spokespersons sought to distance the party from the SJM's position and argued that even in the past some of the views expressed by the SJM were different from those of the BJP. At the same time, late BJP spokesperson K.L. Sharma told journalists that the BJP-led government would seriously consider the opinions of the SJM.

The SJM was also peeved at Industry Minister Sikandar Bakht's 'sudden' proposal that 100 per cent foreign-owned companies be allowed to manufacture cigarettes and tobacco products. The SJM argued that instead of encouraging such companies, the government should be discouraging smoking. On this issue, the SJM received support from former Mizoram Governor, Rajya Sabha MP Swaraj Kaushal, who also happens to be the husband of Sushma Swaraj, a Minister in Vajpayee's cabinet. Kaushal had stated that the decision to allow foreign firms to produce cigarettes 'defies the logic of *swadeshi* and was contrary to the BJP's stated policy of encouraging foreign investment only in 'core' areas like infrastructure. The SJM also pointed out that while the government was encouraging the manufacture of 'sinful' products, it had 'succumbed' to business lobbies by 'banning' the production of common non-iodised salt. Manch spokesperson P. Muralidhar Rao said iodised salt was required only in areas where goitre is endemic and that common salt produced from seawater had certain properties that iodised salt did not possess. The SJM even claimed that it would launch a new 'salt *satyagraha*' on this issue.

The SJM also opposed the BJP-led government on other issues like the move to allow foreign equity in private companies wanting to enter the insurance business, 'needless' counter-guarantees given by the Union government to foreign-funded power projects and the Bakht-brokered deal to resolve a dispute between the government and Japan's Suzuki Motor Company on appointing the chief executive of Maruti Udyog Limited. The two, the Union government and Suzuki, were equal partners in the car manufacturing joint venture. Then, the SJM attacked the then Commerce Minister Ramakrishna Hegde's foreign trade policies, specifically the shifting of 380 items to the open general licence (OGL) list of imports and 140 items to the special import licence (SIL) list. These decisions were described as a sell-out to the World Trade Organisation (WTO). Much of the SJM's strategy is credited to Gurumurthy, a diminutive Chennai-based accountant and journalist turned economic ideologue. He is publicly very critical of the consequences of economic globalisation and opposed to the unfettered entry of multinational corporations. Gurumurthy was quoted by *Outlook* magazine as saying he would even start a campaign against western-style toilets.

As part of the Sangh Parivar, the SJM was clearly in a predicament because the BJP-led government had not really gone back on the economic reforms policies followed by previous governments. The BJP argued that it would not implement its own economic agenda since it was part of a coalition and had to go strictly by the National Agenda for Governance.

Towards the end of 1998, the BJP and the Sangh Parivar were racked with internal dissension on the issue of allowing foreign companies to enter the insurance business in the country. Insurance was the last segment of India's financial sector that remained barred to foreigners. On October 22, 1998, a high-powered group of ministers led by Vajpayee confidante, Jaswant Singh (who was then Deputy Chairman of the Planning Commission) arrived at a 'unanimous' decision that foreign companies (including foreign institutional investors, non-resident Indians and overseas corporate bodies controlled by them) would be allowed to hold up to 26 per cent of the equity capital of privately-controlled insurance companies in the country. This was an important recommendation of a committee of Parliamentarians headed by Congress MP Murli Deora. A day before the group of ministers met, Finance Minister Yashwant Sinha said at a seminar on infrastructure that new legislation would be introduced in the coming (winter) session of Parliament in late November 1998 to set up and empower a statutory insurance regulatory authority (IRA) to oversee the removal of the government's monopoly on the insurance business.

A section within the government was clearly of the view that in the situation which prevailed after the nuclear tests, a 'positive signal' should be sent to foreign investors by allowing them to enter the insurance business. Besides, it was argued that India needed to mobilise long-term funds for infrastructure projects. The Indian government, first under Jawaharlal Nehru and then under Indira Gandhi, had nationalised the life insurance business in 1956 and the general insurance business in 1972. Foreign firms were allowed to operate in very restricted areas like shipping re-insurance. The proposed IRA bill was aimed at not merely allowing the regulatory authority to issue licences to new players from the private corporate sector but also to lay down stringent guidelines for them. The government had also intended simultaneously to introduce bills to amend the Acts of Parliament that govern the working of two giant, monolithic, state-owned organisations, namely, the Life Insurance Corporation (LIC) and the General Insurance Corporation (GIC) which has four subsidiaries: Oriental Insurance, National Insurance, New India Assurance and United India Insurance.

In 1994, an official committee (set up during the Narasimha Rao government and headed by the former Governor of the Reserve Bank of India R.N. Malhotra) had recommended that the government allow private firms to compete with these state-owned monopolies after the establishment of a suitably empowered regulatory authority. Thereafter, all successive governments dilly-dallied on the question of opening up the country's insurance business to competition from private firms. In February 1997, P. Chidambaram, as Finance Minister in the centre-left United Front government, had allowed private companies to offer health insurance policies for the first time. In August 1997, the government headed by I.K. Gujral had moved the IRA bill in Parliament but it was withdrawn after strident opposition, not only from the left parties (which were supporting the UF government then) but also from the BJP which made it clear that it would not be adopted. At that time, the BJP said that it was not averse to Indian companies entering the insurance business but was not favourably inclined towards foreign companies getting into this industry. On June 1, 1998, Finance Minister Sinha proposed in his budget speech that private domestic insurance concerns be allowed to enter this hitherto exclusive preserve of the government, leaving open the question of whether (and to what extent) international insurance companies could enter the fray.

By November 1998, differences in the Sangh Parivar over the issue of allowing foreign investment in insurance had reached a climax. RSS and SJM leader Dattopant Thengadi castigated Finance Minister Sinha at a public meeting and derogatorily dubbed him 'incompetent' and 'useless'. (There was more than a touch of irony in what Thengadi said. because it was the RSS leader K.S. Sudarshan who had reportedly persuaded Vajpayee to make Sinha the Finance Minister instead of Jaswant Singh who was Vajpayee's first choice for the post.) In early December, during a heated session of Parliament, arch political opponents from the left and the right came together to oppose the Insurance Bill causing considerable embarrassment to the government since, by then, the Union Cabinet had resolved to allow foreign companies to hold up to 26 per cent shares in Indian insurance companies.

At one stage it even appeared that the then BJP president Kushabhau Thakre might oppose the government's decision. He and other party functionaries had pointed out that when the UF government sought to introduce a similar bill in Parliament in August 1997, the BJP had staunchly opposed it. During a party meeting, Vajpayee had to publicly tell the then Youth and Sports Affairs Minister Uma Bharati (who had opposed the government decision on insurance) to shut up and not interrupt him. Following hectic parleys, the BJP finally presented a united face; Vajpayee's view had apparently prevailed and the hardliners marginalised. But, by then, the damage had already been done. Though the Insurance Regulatory Authority Bill was moved by the government, it could not be passed by both houses of Parliament and had to be shelved. The government had hoped to get the Bill adopted during the 1999 budget session, but it fell before this could happen. The bill was finally adopted by both houses of Parliament in the winter session of 1999. It was the first major economic decision taken by the third Vajpayee government.

Even as the government's decision to privatise the insurance industry and open it to foreign investors was facing resistance in 1998, the BJP-led coalition moved more cautiously to amend the country's patent laws to bring these in line with the norms laid down by the WTO. As in the case of the IRA Bill, the government referred a bill to amend the Indian Patents Act of 1970 to a Parliamentary committee. In December, the Vajpayee government decided that it would try and convert the bill into law after the main Opposition party, the Congress, stated that it would support the amendment to the patent laws, subject to certain minor changes being incorporated. It was, after all, the Congress government under P.V. Narasimha Rao that had initiated policies in mid-1991 to open up India's economy and on the last day of 1992, the country had formally become a member of the WTO and had signed the agreement on TRIPS (trade related intellectual property rights).

India's laws on patents had allowed the patenting of manufacturing processes, not products, especially products like food, pharmaceuticals and agro-chemicals. As per WTO rules, India has to introduce product patents by 2005. Those in favour of the amended patent laws argue that these would attract new investments in companies producing pharmaceuticals and pesticides. The opposition to changing the country's patent laws came from farmers and social activists who argued that the new laws would not only lead to a sharp rise in the prices of medicines, but also cripple thousands of indigenously-owned small pharmaceutical concerns.

With the Congress and the BJP united on the issue, the amendments went through in the Rajya Sabha in the December 1998 winter session. The government was, however, not able to present the bill in the Lok Sabha. At one stage, the then Minister for Parliamentary Affairs Madan Lal Khurana had claimed that the presentation of the bill was delayed because the requisite approval of President K.R. Narayanan was late in coming, but a sharp rejoinder from the President resulted in the Minister hastily eating his words. The Patents Bill was eventually passed in the next session of Parliament, which was the budget session of 1999.

As has been already stated, there were contradictions galore as far as the thrust of economic policies were concerned not only in the ruling party but within the principal opposition party as well. Not everybody in the Congress was equally enthusiastic about the Bill to amend the laws on patents. While one section comprising individuals like former Finance Minister Manmohan Singh (who is often described as the chief architect of the economic liberalisation programme) was in favour of the bill, other Congress leaders argued that the party should not create an impression that it was supporting the fragile coalition government led by Prime Minister Vajpayee. The pro-change group in the Congress won the internal tussle. By this time, the Congress under Sonia Gandhi was trying to project itself as a rejuvenated political party and had become increasingly strident in its criticism of the economic policies of the Vajpayee government. 'Prices are rising, unemployment is rising...all this leads to an ominous situation,' the President of the Congress told party faithfuls at a meeting held in New Delhi. Boosting the morale of the Congress was an opinion poll predicting a clear win for the Congress if general elections were to take place.

In the aftermath of the February 1998 Lahore Declaration signed between Vajpayee and Pakistan Prime Minister Mian Nawaz Sharif, it was the turn of the Finance Minister to show that he too could deliver. Sinha's second budget, presented in February 1999, earned quite a few compliments even from his political opponents for simplifying the excise duty regime. He was able to walk a tightrope by keeping at bay both the hardliners within the Sangh Parivar (namely, the SJM) as well as the gang of liberalisers. More importantly, Sinha also paid lip service to the cause of a 'second wave' of reforms and promised that he intended to downsize the bureaucracy. One major component of the second wave of reforms was the government's decision not merely to disinvest its equity in public sector firms, but to privatise some of them.

Privatisation of this sort, however, ultimately took place only in 2000, when Hindustan Lever, the Indian arm of the MNC Unilever, bought a majority stake in Modern Food Industries, a public sector unit making bread and other food products. Subsequently, there have been a few other 'strategic sales' of PSUs to private firms, including the sale of BALCO, Indian Petrochemicals Corporation Ltd (IPCL) and Videsh Sanchar Nigam Ltd (VSNL). However, each of these sales has been surrounded by controversy and the government's privatisation programme has not really taken off, with the privatisation of oil sector PSUs in particular coming to a grinding halt. To begin with, two major oil sector PSUs—Hindustan Petroleum Corporation Ltd (HPCL) and Bharat Petroleum Corporation Ltd (BPCL)—could not be privatised because of dissensions within the government. By the time the government did reach a compromise on the issue among its feuding ministers, it was overtaken by developments. Ruling on a public interest petition, the Supreme Court ruled that HPCL and BPCL could not be privatised without obtaining the prior approval of Parliament, since these companies had been created under Acts of Parliament by nationalising the assets of foreign-owned oil companies in the 1970s.

The fact is that privatisation is a dirty word in the lexicon of many of India's politicians, union leaders and opinion makers. These sections were brought up to believe not only in the virtues of a socialist economy in which the public sector would attain the 'commanding heights' of the economy, but also in the merits of the government acting as the model employer. Many people in India are unsure about the benefits that would accrue from Margaret Thatcher-style privatisation. At one level, a large section of the intelligentsia is clear that the country's political leadership and its bureaucracy must not continue to run a host of loss-making ventures which own hotels and manufacture products ranging from bread and bicycles to automotive tyres and watches. Put differently, it is widely perceived (at least within the middle class) that the government has no business to be in such businesses, especially since the Indian state is doing a pretty bad job of providing what it should be providing—primary education and basic health care.

Having said this, the next question which arises is what needs to be done to close down, sell (transfer managerial control) or rehabilitate chronically ill PSUs humanely while keeping in mind the interests of workers and the overall economic environment of a country in which large numbers are unemployed or under-employed. This is indeed the crux of the problem. As stated earlier, in 1996, the UF government had set up a Disinvestment Commission which, over a two-and-a-half-year period, recommended a slew of measures to tone up the functioning of over 40 PSUs. However, the UF government as well as the BJP-led government were rather sluggish in acting on the Commission's recommendations.

The government has a long way to go before it is able to convince most people in India about the efficacy of privatisation as a means of reviving the country's bloated and inefficient public sector enterprises. The fact that the disinvestment strategy pursued so far has concentrated largely on profitable PSUs has certainly not helped. These companies are in monopoly positions, have a high profile and thus, their shares are quoted at reasonably attractive rates. There are a number of problems with this strategy. While it is easy to sell the shares of profit-making PSUs, such sales can only be one-time events and do not address the problems of chronic loss-making PSUs. Besides, the government has used the proceeds of privatisation/divestment to bridge the budget deficit. Such a policy would be, to use a phrase coined by British Labour leader Jim Callaghan while referring to Margaret Thatcher's policies of privatisation, akin to selling the family silver to pay the butler.

There has been a gap between rhetoric and practice on other aspects of reforms as well. For instance, after the government ostensibly dismantled the administered pricing mechanism (APM) for petroleum products on April 1, 2002, Petroleum Minister Ram Naik 'persuaded' the public sector oil companies led by the Indian Oil Corporation (IOC) to not increase petrol prices for three months despite a sharp and sudden increase in international prices of crude oil from around $20 a barrel to over $27 a barrel. As a result, the oil PSUs incurred a huge loss of around Rs. 200 crore per month, while privately-owned oil refining companies (including Reliance Petroleum) continued to receive prices for their products that were benchmarked to international rates.

The Vajpayee government's privatisation programme has been particularly controversial after Arun Shourie took over as Union Minister for Disinvestment in August 2000. Shourie is a Minister with a difference. For one, he has a reputation of being absolutely clean. He also works with amazing zeal. But in the process, Shourie also painted himself into a corner. He became the favourite whipping boy of many of his Cabinet colleagues and his ideological compatriots in the BJP, not to mention his allies in the NDA coalition. A former economist with the World Bank, erstwhile editor of the *Indian Express* chain of newspapers, and the winner of the 1982 Ramon Magsaysay Award for Journalism, Literature and Creative Communication Arts, Shourie was declared 'Business Leader of the Year' by the *Economic Times*, India's largest circulated financial daily. Business magazines have regularly published his photograph on their covers.

Despite such impressive credentials, why did Shourie fail to forge a consensus about the need for big-ticket privatisation? Why did he find himself so isolated and why was he unable to convince his own government's ministers and supporters of the need to hand over managerial control of PSUs to private entrepreneurs? Shourie's privatisation programme was placed in cold storage not on account of his political opponents in the Congress or among the communist parties. His own colleagues in the Vajpayee government and his friends in the RSS proved to be the biggest enemies of his grandiose plans of privatisation. Other sections of the Sangh Parivar like the SJM and the trade union Bharatiya Mazdoor Sangh also expressed their staunch opposition to Shourie's privatisation policies.

It appeared as if Minister for Petroleum and Natural Gas Ram Naik did not want his Ministry to lose control over HPCL and BPCL, the second and third largest oil refining and distribution companies in the country. Both companies are also profitable. Nor did the then Coal and Mines Minister Uma Bharati seem happy with the manner in which the Ministry of Disinvestment sought to privatise the Orissa-based National Aluminium Company (NALCO). The entire political class in this eastern state—including the ruling Biju Janata Dal and its rival, the Congress—came together to oppose the privatisation of NALCO. The privatisation of NALCO, the world's lowest-cost aluminium manufacturer, was also opposed on the ground that the timing would be inopportune since international aluminium prices were at their lowest in the last five years.

It should be noted that both Ram Naik and Uma Bharati belong to the BJP. The same story was repeated in the case of Fertilisers and Chemicals Minister Sukhdev Singh Dhindsa (belonging to the Shiromani Akali Dal) and National Fertilisers Limited. After Videsh Sanchar Nigam Limited (VNSL)—once India's monopoly international telecommunications service provider—was privatised and management control handed over to the Tata group, the then high-profile BJP Minister for Communications and Information Technology Pramod Mahajan opposed the decision of VSNL's new private owners to transfer a large chunk of money to a Tata group company. Yet, curiously, none of these ministers has ever publicly said they are opposed to privatisation. They merely contend they are opposed to the methodology of privatisation adopted by Shourie's ministry.

Besides Petroleum Minister Naik, the move to privatise HPCL and BPCL was staunchly opposed by Defence Minister George Fernandes. He had earlier written a letter to Prime Minister Vajpayee calling for a mid-course correction in the government's privatisation policy. Besides concurring with Naik that the petroleum sector was strategically important—India currently imports more than 70 per cent of its requirement of crude oil—Fernandes also said privatisation should not result in public monopolies being replaced by private monopolies.

All monopolies are bad but a private monopoly is certainly worse than a public one. After all, bureaucrats can be transferred and politicians have to get re-elected. However, a private promoter and his children's children can stay put for years on end and be accountable to no one. An example was the way in which the Reliance group took over the management of Indian Petrochemicals Corporation Limited (IPCL) in May 2002. After privatisation, the combined Reliance–IPCL conglomerate currently controls between 80 and 90 per cent of the Indian market for a wide range of petrochemical products. (It seems strange to recall that in the mid-1980s, as editor of the *Indian Express*, Shourie had written a series of articles that were scathing in their criticism of Reliance and the Ambani family that controls India's largest private corporate group.)

In early January 2003, the DMK, then a part of the NDA, issued a strongly-worded resolution against the Vajpayee government's policy of privatisation and its alleged attempts to subvert the socialistic character of the country's Constitution. Political observers felt that the DMK's statement had been prompted by the attempts made by its arch political rival in the state, the AIADMK, to come close to the BJP and the NDA.

After its fifth national conference held in Hyderabad in the first week of January 2003, the SJM issued a resolution criticising virtually every aspect of the Vajpayee government's privatisation programme although the RSS-affiliated outfit maintained that it was not against disinvestment in principle. Stating that it had serious reservations over the procedures being adopted by the government towards the PSUs being sought to be disinvested, the SJM said it 'is convinced that disinvestment should not be the first option, but the last one, after all other alternatives have been exhausted'. It suggested that the government deal with PSUs on a case-by-case basis by following a sequence of logical steps that included de-bureaucratisation and corporatisation, diagnosis of problems and their solutions, strategic sale, valuation and share disposal.

Meanwhile, in January, the BJP's cell dealing with scheduled castes urged the party leadership to protect the interests of dalits who would be denied 'reserved' jobs after the management of particular PSUs passed into the hands of private promoters. At the meeting of the national executive of the BJP Scheduled Castes' Morcha, it was pointed out that the new owners of privatised PSUs would no longer feel obliged to fill up posts reserved for SCs as well as STs. A number of the dalit leaders of the BJP said during the meeting that the underprivileged sections of Indian society were the worst affected by the changes brought about by the so-called economic reforms policies of the government.

All over the world, privatisation has proved to be controversial. In India, it has become one of the most contentious and divisive issues confronting the NDA government led by Vajpayee.

Changing labour laws is another area in which there are conflicting viewpoints in the Vajpayee government. The BMS is a leading trade union organisation and its representatives contend that it is 'independent' of the BJP. In the same breath, BMS leaders concede that they have close ideological affinity with the RSS. In February 1999, less than a year after Vajpayee had been sworn in as Prime Minister for the second time, speaking at a national convention of the trade union, BMS founder and veteran RSS leader

Dattopant Thengadi had used unusually harsh language when he described Finance Minister Sinha as an *anarth mantri* (literally, a minister who causes chaos) instead of *arth mantri* (or a minister who handles the economy). The octogenarian Thengadi did not stop there. In April 2001, the BMS founder again attacked Sinha in public, this time during a rally held at New Delhi's Ram Lila grounds. On this occasion, the Finance Minister was accused of being a 'criminal' for encroaching on the territorial preserve of the then Labour Minister, Satyanarain Jatiya, who also happens to be a BMS leader.

The provocation for the uncharitable remark was a reference in Sinha's speech on the last day of February announcing the proposals for the Union budget for 2001-2002. The Finance Minister had stated that the government wanted to remove certain 'rigidities' in the country's labour laws by amending the Industrial Disputes Act to enable industrial establishments employing up to 1,000 employees to retrench workers without obtaining the prior permission of the appropriate government authority. The law as it stands grants such a facility only to industrial organisations employing up to 100 workers. Sinha also mentioned the need to change the laws pertaining to contract labourers.

Thengadi's outburst reportedly upset Sinha so much that he threatened to resign. The Finance Minister was, however, persuaded not to put in his papers after various leaders of the RSS and the BJP (including the then Party President K. Jana Krishnamurthy) distanced themselves from Thengadi's views and told him not to take the BMS leader's remarks seriously. Though the BMS leader's views were described as 'his own', the trade union body never formally disowned Thengadi's remarks. What happened instead was that Labour Minister Jatiya was removed from his post. This decision was widely interpreted by the media as having been taken because Jatiya was perceived to be opposing the 'reform' of the country's labour laws.

The Cabinet sought to approve a bill to amend the Industrial Disputes Act on the eve of the presentation of the Union budget for 2002-2003 on the last day of February 2002, presumably to enable the Finance Minister to state that he had been able to fulfil the promise contained in his budget speech made a year earlier. That was, however, not to take place. Strong opposition to the move from many of Sinha's colleagues in the Cabinet has ensured that the Industrial Disputes Act is yet to be amended.

The pulls and pressures within the NDA were evident again after Sinha's fifth budget was presented on February 28, 2002. History was repeated a fortnight later when Sinha had to again roll-back his budget proposals. While he had announced a Rs. 40 hike in the price of a cylinder of cooking gas, he had to halve the increase following intense pressure from the BJP's allies in the NDA coalition. Some of Sinha's colleagues in the BJP were openly unhappy with his proposals to increase the incidence of income tax on the middle-class and his decision to pare the interest rates on small savings schemes run by the government. Former Delhi Chief Minister and former BJP Vice President Sahib Singh Verma resigned his post as BJP Vice President after his party received a drubbing in the capital's municipal corporation elections. Verma publicly blamed Sinha for having antagonised middle-class tax-payers by his budget, as already stated.

Subsequently, there was tremendous pressure on Sinha from his party compatriots at the BJP's Goa conclave. Newspapers reported that there were vicious attacks on Sinha at the party's national executive meeting. It was claimed that the Finance Minister and his officials tried very hard to preserve the 'integrity' of his budget, However, he was reportedly overruled by the Prime Minister himself. On April 26, 2002, Sinha removed the service tax on life insurance. He relaxed the provisions of Section 88 of the Income Tax Act to provide relief to tax-payers with annual assessable incomes varying between Rs. 1.5 lakh and Rs. 5 lakh. He has also helped the middle-class by partially restoring the manner in which income from dividends and mutual funds were taxed. These moves would benefit around one-seventh of the 28 million income tax assessees in the country. The Finance Minister also reduced the excise duty rates on certain textile processes as well as products used by the middle-class, notably, umbrellas and bicycles.

Sinha claimed that the changes in the budget proposals would result in the national exchequer losing an amount in the region of Rs. 2,850 crore. He was able to 'save face' because the reduction of the administered interest rates on small savings schemes was not reversed, nor was the new 'security' surcharge on income tax. The face-savers, however, could not help Sinha keep his job. Later that year, Vajpayee reshuffled his Cabinet and Sinha was shunted out to the External Affairs Ministry, while Jaswant Singh, Vajpayee's first choice for the job, finally became Finance Minister once again.

One of the first decisions taken by Jaswant Singh was to switch the portfolios of the two junior ministers (Ministers of State) in his ministry. This decision had to be reversed following a complaint by Shiv Sena supremo Bal Thackeray. The 'rollback' phenomenon had also afflicted Singh. Also, like Sinha, Singh unsuccessfully tried to persuade Labour Minister Sahib Singh Verma to bring down the interest rate on employees' provident fund deposits.

Jaswant Singh was an officer in the army before joining the BJP. He had served as Deputy Chairman, Planning Commission and Foreign Minister. In his second stint as Finance Minister—the first was in the short Vajpayee government in May 1996—his first Union budget was described as a populist one. One of his first public statements as Finance Minister was that he would try and place grain in the stomach of the indigent and money in the purse of the housewife (*garib ke pet me dana, grihani ke tukia me anna*). Since then, Singh has adopted a distinctly more populist stance than Sinha had. In particular, the middle-class has clearly been targeted as a section that needs to be wooed back to the BJP's fold. How much of this is because of differences between Singh's and Sinha's economic strategy is a moot question, given the fact that Singh's sops to the electorate have all come at times when important elections have been round the corner.

The 2003-2004 budget—like all budgets before it—was certainly political. Nevertheless, it did contain some unpopular decisions. Though he repeatedly assured everybody that there would be no rolling back of his unpopular decisions, the new Finance Minister's arm was twisted by his own colleagues in government. In his budget speech, Jaswant Singh had said that in view of the likely increase in the prices of naphtha and gas—in view of the hike in the prices of all petroleum products in the run-up to the Iraq war—he wished to 'at least' contain the fertiliser subsidy bill. He, therefore, proposed that the issue price of urea be raised by a 'modest' amount of Rs. 12 per 50 kg bag. The proposed increase in the administered prices of di-ammonium phosphate and muriate of potash was Rs. 10 per 50 kg bag. This move was widely opposed by influential members of Singh's own government. Barely a fortnight after the presentation of the budget, on March 11, the Finance Minister announced in Parliament that he was withdrawing his proposal to increase fertiliser prices. The rollback virus had struck again.

Finance Minister Singh was eager to implement a new value added tax (VAT) regime that is considered to be far superior to the existing sales tax system in the country. In his February 28, 2003, budget speech, he said the 'coming year would be historic' with states switching over to a VAT system. 'The central government has been a partner with the states, in the highest tradition of cooperative federalism, in this path-breaking reform,' he stated. Less than two months later, Jaswant Singh was singing a different tune. On April 24, he told the Lok Sabha: 'A poorly implemented VAT won't work. Therefore, VAT cannot be implemented unless all states adopt it together.'

What happened was that the Finance Minister could not go ahead with these tax reforms not so much on account of opposition from representatives of rival political parties, but because of staunch resistance from some of his own colleagues in the BJP (like Madan Lal Khurana). These BJP politicians took up cudgels on behalf of sections of traders who are against the implementation of VAT, an important reason being that the new system would check widespread tax evasion. Sections within the BJP also apprehended that VAT may result in an inflationary spurt in the short run that could spoil the party's electoral aspirations later in the year in states like Rajasthan, Madhya Pradesh, Delhi and Chhattisgarh. The BJP's political opponents have in the past derogatorily described it as a 'party of traders'.

The Finance Minister's intentions have also been opposed by another of his Cabinet colleagues, Labour Minister Sahib Singh Verma. At a time when almost all interest rates in the country were ruling at their lowest levels in nominal terms in three decades, the board of trustees of the Employees' Provident Fund Organisation (EPFO) staunchly resisted a lowering of the interest rate on deposits from a level of 9.5 per cent per annum to 8 per cent. The EPFO has over 30 million industrial workers as its members. Now it may have made good economic sense to pare the interest rate on such deposits, but such a move would certainly not have pleased the workers and their leaders in the trade unions—particularly not at a time when job opportunities in the organised sector are growing at barely 1 per cent per annum and the ranks of the unemployed are swelling.

On May 31, after a considerable amount of haggling, the government lowered the EPF interest rate by 0.5 per cent to 9 per cent for the current financial year. In order to sugar-coat the bitter pill and not convey an impression that the government was against the interests of the working class, the central board of trustees of the EPFO agreed to pay a bonus of 0.5 per cent. This bonus, ostensibly paid to celebrate the golden jubilee of the EPFO, meant that the effective rate of interest on deposits remained at 9.5 per cent. Among the biggest opponents to the move to cut the interest rate of EPF deposits have been representatives of the BMS.

What was not officially admitted by government spokespersons during the first half of 2003 was that populism had become the order of the day and that no decision would be taken that could offend any interest group or lobby in view of the state assembly elections scheduled to take place later in the year, as also the forthcoming general elections. Deputy Prime Minister Advani acknowledged in a newspaper interview that 'the pace of reforms has been affected' and that this is 'an experience other democracies have gone through'. 'Everything that is economically correct may not be electorally popular,' Advani observed, adding that changes in labour laws 'will be slow' (*Business Standard*, June 2, 2003).

There are problems galore as far as the economy is concerned. Job opportunities are not expanding fast enough, the inflation rate has picked up and regional imbalances have widened. These issues are all politically sensitive and are being used by the Opposition to beat the government with. In such a scenario, the powers-that-be would prefer inaction rather than risk acting decisively and offending one section of the population or the other.

It is often argued that on account of a growing political consensus on many economic policy issues, the overall direction of economic reforms would not change even if there be political uncertainty or upheavals. Even if this is the case, what is apparent is that the momentum of economic reforms can never be sustained without political consensus. Thus, in the absence of such a consensus, the government will find it extremely tough to open the country's doors wider to foreign investment, significantly lower interest rates on deposits in the employees' provident fund, implement a new value added tax regime or expeditiously privatise profit-making PSUs.

The point worth emphasising is that while it is well to talk about the need for sustaining the pace of economic reforms, this laudable objective cannot be realised until and unless there is a broad-based political consensus within and outside the government to achieve such a goal. That consensus still eludes India.

One of the most obvious manifestations of the failure of the NDA government's economic policies was the growth of a 'food mountain' at a time when several states faced drought and even starvation deaths. The Food Corporation of India had around 60 million tonnes of foodgrain in its godowns in the middle of 2002. This was three-and-a-half times the 'minimum buffer norm' of 17 million tonnes. The explanation for this problem of plenty lay in the fact that the Union government had been procuring increasingly higher quantities of wheat and rice—especially from—Punjab, Haryana, Uttar Pradesh, and Andhra Pradesh—by regularly increasing the minimum support prices paid to farmers. It was no coincidence that three of the BJP's crucial allies in the NDA were major political parties in these regions—the Akali Dal, the INLD, the RLD and the TDP. More importantly, the support base of the SAD, the INLD and the RLD is predominantly among farmers.

The food economy is only one example of the kinds of compromises that a coalition government has to make merely to ensure its survival. But these compromises extract a heavy toll on the exchequer. Economic commentators like Prem Shankar Jha contend that with coalition governments becoming a 'permanent feature' of governance in India, the capacity of the government to impose short-term sacrifices on the people for long-term benefits has disappeared. In his book, *A Jobless Future: Political Causes of Economic Crisis* (Rupa, 2002), Jha has remarked:

> The starting point for reviving the economy, making future growth sustainable, reversing the decline of employment in the organised sector and averting the threat of de-industrialisation is to admit that the 1991 [economic] reforms [initiated by Manmohan Singh, the then Finance Minister in the P. V. Narasimha Rao government] have failed. They have failed because they were left incomplete. This incompleteness is preventing India from becoming a beneficiary of globalisation and turning it into one of its victims.

To return to the question raised in the early part of this chapter, has the period of political instability that followed the May 1996 elections, and which also coincided with the phase of coalition governments in New Delhi, been good or bad for the Indian economy? In a paper entitled 'Electoral Cycles and Economic Policies of Governments of India' by Kausik Chaudhuri and Sugato Dasgupta

(*India Development Report 2002*, Indira Gandhi Institute of Development Research, Oxford University Press), it has been indicated that more investments take place when coalition governments are in power. One reason why this happens is because various regional interests are held together by 'generous distribution of infrastructure projects'.

Economist Surjit S. Bhalla wrote in the week before Yashwant Sinha presented his second budget on February 27, 1999:

> Political instability does not matter. The conventional wisdom is that political wisdom is bad for the economy. In its survey of investment houses in mid-July [1998], 'Asia Pacific Consensus Forecasts' reported that the most unfavourable factor affecting the economic prospects of India was 'political uncertainty' followed by international sanctions [after the nuclear tests of May 1998] and the Asian crisis. There is a different, more compelling view. Political instability is actually good for economic reform. The contention is that lack of political dominance means that politicians in power will make the extra reform in order to fight for marginal votes in a future election. And if political stability is present, the politicians are unlikely to make an effort because of their inherent 'short-sightedness', or complacency.

Bhalla cites what he calls six 'pieces of evidence' to support his claim that economic reforms occur when there is political instability and do not occur when there is stability.

> The first example is from late 1984 when Rajiv Gandhi assumed his dynastic post with 415 seats or more than three-fourths majority.... Mr. Gandhi had talked of reforms and expectations were high. The rapidity with which the prospect of reforms disappeared can only be compared with the speed with which a BMW zooms towards 60 mph—or the speed with which Mr Gandhi reduced his party's seats to less than half in late 1989 (197 seats in a 543 seat parliament). Second, the Narasimha Rao–Manmohan Singh reforms were undertaken by a minority government and amidst considerable political and economic uncertainty in 1991. Third, once Narasimha Rao got comfortable with a majority in Parliament (political stability) the reforms stopped. Fourth, the United Front government undertook significant reforms with the political disadvantages of two Prime Ministers in eighteen months....

Bhalla goes on to list the reforms made by the UF government: reduction in the maximum rate of personal taxes to only 30 per

cent, rationalising of petroleum products pricing, movement towards privatisation (albeit painfully slow), beginning of deregu-
lation of interest rates and movement towards capital account
convertibility by easing gold imports. The fifth example is the
change in the BJP's position on spiralling onion prices before and
after the November 1998 assembly elections. Before the elections,
the party was complacent but not after it was roundly defeated in
Delhi, Rajasthan and Madhya Pradesh. Bhalla, who runs his own
consulting unit, went on to extol the virtues of the Vajpayee government in his sixth and final example.

> After the defeat [in the assembly elections], the BJP has been a
> changed economic and political animal, The Jekyll–Hyde reality
> of the BJP is now exposed, and exposed by reform [Jekyll] ele-
> ments within the BJP. There is a liberal outlook on both political
> and economic matters. The Hyde wing of the BJP is still there, is
> still vocal, but it is being relegated to the sidelines. It is contended
> that this radical change for the better was precipitated by the im-
> pending ouster of the BJP—i.e. increased instability makes for
> good political and economic policy. Since December 1 [1998], the
> BJP has moved considerably forward on economic reforms—the
> beginnings of a cut in interest rates, the heightened concern with
> government borrowings and the fiscal deficit, introduction of re-
> forms on insurance and the conviction that large-scale
> privatisation is needed are all hallmarks of a 'new' BJP.... When
> the history of BJP rule is written, it is likely that 1998 will be
> remembered as the year of the great BJP divide—and as the begin-
> ning of its avatar as a liberal reform party. The fringe elements of
> the BJP (lumpen elements who would like to take India back to
> the authoritarian, inquisition, sixteenth century political era and
> to leftist, protectionist, *swadeshi* economic policies) are being
> sidelined—they have nowhere to go. Why this was not realised
> earlier by the BJP is a mystery—though it must be said that the
> party caught on to the reality in less than a year.

These views can be countered, since at the heart of the issue is
what constitutes 'real' economic reforms. Bhalla's praise for the
BJP's heightened concern for high government borrowings or high
deficits may be premature. No politician would agree entirely with
the thesis that governments act only when pushed to the corner,
that political instability would invariably lead to economic
reforms. Some amount of instability may be good for keeping

those in power on their toes and preventing them from becoming complacent.

How much political instability—or how little—is desirable is a far more difficult question to answer. As is evident, mere talk of reform is not enough. If these reforms are not perceived to be improving the lot of the majority of Indians, the electorate would throw out those who initiated them. Witness the humiliating defeat that was suffered by the Congress party in the May 1996 elections. Even if one-third of India's population remains functionally illiterate and even if at least one out of four Indians lives below the poverty line (whichever way one may choose to define it), the electorate of the country has shown time and again that it is capable of taking mature, considered decisions regarding those who claim to represent it.

Economist Deepak Nayyar and political scientist Pranab Bardhan (*Democracy in India,* edited by Nirja Gopal Jayal, Oxford University Press) have argued that the current political climate is not favourable for the kind of reforms being ushered in. Their arguments are not of the usual 'instability is bad for reforms' or 'populism versus reforms' variety. They make a rather more substantive point. Nayyar points out that the economics of markets excludes those without the requisite entitlements, whereas democracy seeks to include. This, he says, is the 'essence of the tension between the economics of markets and the politics of democracy'. He goes on to say that the economic reforms programme introduced in 1991 'was simply not related to the institutional framework of political democracy'. 'It was, therefore, neither shaped by political processes nor rooted in social formations, which could have provided constituencies in polity and society.' As a result, he goes on to add: 'In the sphere of economics, the old consensus has broken down while a new consensus has not emerged.'

Bardhan points out that the shift of political power from the centre to the states in recent years has been accompanied by a shift of power towards the intermediate and lower castes. This, he argues, means that the earlier practice by which economic decision-making was institutionally insulated, is getting eroded. The concern for group equity and group rights—as against individual rights—runs counter to the market philosophy and hence creates a context which is not favourable for reforms aimed at making the economy market-friendly.

In conclusion, the three broad propositions on the relationship between coalition governments and economic policies mentioned at the beginning of this chapter, bear reiteration.

First, there has been no obvious or clear-cut pattern in the relationship in India thus far. The performance of the country's economy has not been noticeably different under different coalition governments from what it has been when single-party governments have ruled India. Nor has the economic policy framework been significantly different.

Second, coalition governments have not been able to change certain structural imbalances in the economy: for instance, regional imbalances in economic development between the west and the east, the north and the south. Western India has done better than eastern India, the south has moved ahead much faster than the north in many respects. Has the presence of coalition governments made much of a difference in redressing these regional disparities in development? Not really. Certainly not as yet. While political parties have apparently come closer together on issues of economic ideology, the so-called 'consensus' on economic reforms has periodically broken down on crucial questions. Such questions relate to privatisation or revival of ailing PSUs as well as the speed at which the economy should be 'globalised' or exposed to international competition. Thus, even as parties have appeared to come closer to one another on economic policy issues, there is considerable internal dissension on economic policy issues within the the BJP and the Congress.

Finally, unlike Japan or Italy where the nitty-gritty of economic decision-making may not change that much with each new coalition government, in a developing country like India, politics has dominated—and will continue to exert influence over—every minor economic decision, from the price at which the Food Corporation of India should procure grain to the question of whether export of onions should be allowed at any given point in time.

Chapter 9

Gazing at a Crystal Ball

How long will the era of coalition politics continue in India? Is it never going to be possible for a single party, be it the BJP or the Congress, to dominate the country's polity? The answer to the latter question is relatively easy: it seems unlikely in the foreseeable future. The answer to the first question is a more difficult one. Is India then heading towards a two-party system? Certainly not in a hurry, if it is at all doing so. The country may remain multipolar for quite a while. If anything, the polity could get even further fragmented in the immediate future.

So what is 'new' about the era of coalition politics in India? The Congress ruled the country for more than four-and-a-half decades because it had the character of a coalition. Under Mohandas Karamchand Gandhi, the party was a unique non-violent force against colonial rule and it represented almost all sections of society when India became politically independent in 1947. For the next 20 years, the coalitional character of the Congress remained more or less intact. The umbrella nature of the Congress was first seriously challenged in 1967, but the manifestation of the symptom was largely restricted to state assemblies. A decade later, the Congress lost Parliamentary elections for the first time in independent India. With the benefit of hindsight we can now see that the process of a single-party coalition giving way to more explicit coalitional arrangements had already begun.

It could be argued that but for two dramatic assassinations—Indira Gandhi's in 1984 and Rajiv Gandhi in 1991—the decline of the Congress' electoral fortunes would already have reached an advanced stage as early as the second half of the 1980s. Perhaps the 'new' era of coalition politics in India would have started well before it ultimately did. Since there can be no counter-factual to this hypothesis, it might seem that it really does not matter whether we accept it or not. That is not quite true. If the elections of 1984 and 1991 are recognised as ones in which the Congress performed much better than it would have if no dramatic events had influenced them, the picture one gets is of a party that has been on a more or less steady decline since as far back as 1967 (remember the 1972 general elections were soon after an Indo–Pak war in which Indira Gandhi could bask in the glory of having contributed to the break-up of Pakistan, pushing domestic issues into the background). The elections of 1980–1981 then become the only general elections since 1967 in which the Congress has come to power without the assistance of issues either extraneous to domestic politics (though one can quarrel with the description of an Indo–Pak war as being extraneous to Indian politics) or with cathartic events like the assassination of a Prime Minister.

Such a perspective must also mean that the decline in the fortunes of the Congress is not the result of mismanagement by one leader or the other, but has a more lasting structural basis. The foibles of individual leaders may have contributed to the process, perhaps even hastened it, but they cannot be held solely responsible for the decay. A question that arises from such an understanding would be whether the process is peculiar to the Congress or is more generic in nature. Could it be the case that the very model of a coalition within a single party has become unviable? The evidence certainly seems to suggest that this is the case.

Whether one sees the Mandal–Kamandal standoff as a cause of the fragmentation of the polity or as its consequence, what is undisputable today is that many parts of the country—in particular the Hindi heartland—are experiencing a sharpening of divisions within society, whether on the basis of caste, religion or ethnicity. It is difficult to see any party being able to hold together groups with such hostility towards each other for very long. A case in point was the BJP's attempt at forging a coalition between the upper-castes represented by leaders like Rajnath Singh and Kalraj Mishra and the intermediate castes represented by Kalyan Singh.

There are empirical reasons as well for foreseeing a reasonably long period of coalitional politics in India. Historically, Parliamentary

elections in India have by an large delivered fairly decisive mandates in each state. It is another matter that since each state may
have voted decisively for one or the other of two contending fronts
or parties, the aggregate result may have thrown up an uncertain
verdict. In 1996, for instance, the Janata Dal and its allies swept
states like Bihar, Karnataka and Tamil Nadu. The BJP and its allies
had unquestioned dominance in Uttar Pradesh, Madhya Pradesh,
Gujarat and Maharashtra. The Congress and its allies secured
equally decisive verdicts in Andhra Pradesh, Orissa and the north-
eastern states. The net result was a hung Parliament with the
single-largest party, the BJP, getting less than one-fourth of the
total number of Lok Sabha seats. This pattern of decisive state-
level verdicts has begun to change. Uttar Pradesh no longer yields
any one victor, nor do states like Maharashtra, Karnataka, Tamil
Nadu or Andhra Pradesh always give clear mandates.

As for the much talked about bipolarity of the Indian polity, as
we have already shown in such great detail, it is more wishful thinking than actual fact. Here's a thought that might have seemed
shocking till not very long ago, but can by no means be ruled out
any longer. We could in the near future, perhaps as early as the
14th general elections in 2004, have a Lok Sabha in which the BJP
and the Congress put together cannot muster a majority. This may
or may not happen, but it does not seem impossible as it once
would have.

There's a more difficult question to answer in the context of
coalition politics: Will coalition governments necessarily remain
unstable? That's a more difficult prediction to make. As the old
saying goes, a week is a long time in politics. The proposition may
be particularly true for the new, highly fluid and unpredictable
phase that politics in the world's largest democracy is currently
going through. What can be said though is that the sooner parties
recognise that ideological affinity is the best guarantor of the
longevity of alliances, the shorter will be the period of unstable
governments.

Why are we not gripped by despondency at the thought of coalitions continuing to rule India in the foreseeable future? Given
the conventional wisdom that coalitions tend to slow down
decision-making and make official policy a prisoner of conflicting
claims, it might seem that a future dominated by coalitions is quite
a depressing scenario. But then, are these not the same 'problems'

that are mentioned when democracies are compared with dictatorial regimes? That is no coincidence. Indeed, the reason why we are not alarmed by the thought that coalitions could be here to stay is precisely because they could make a major contribution to deepening and strengthening Indian democracy. If they have arisen because large sections of the people of India felt excluded from the process of development, they will survive only if they are able to reverse that exclusion. It is possible, of course, that the era of coalitions will make electoral politics more cyncical, sectarian and opportunistic, but we are optimistic that the same groundswell that rejected earlier regimes for not being responsive enough will prevent such a denouement, at least in the medium- to long-term.

The burden of expectations that coalition governments will have to bear is by no means small. At least one out of four Indians is steeped in poverty. That's one-fourth of one billion people, more than the population of the United States. Almost half the population of India is denied basic education and health care. Nearly two-thirds of the country's girl children do not receive any education worth the name. Yet, India's institutions of higher learning, like the Indian Institutes of Technology and the Indian Institutes of Management, produce students who have made their mark the world over. One estimate was that at the turn of the century, some 15 per cent of all computer software professionals in the world were persons of Indian origin. Academic Shiv Visvanathan comments that the problem with many of India's institutions of higher learning are that these have become transformed into intellectual assembly lines of the world, clearing houses for ideas, both good and bad, which the world gratefully accepts or summarily rejects.

There is a similar stark contrast in the area of health care. Nobody seriously disputes that the country's health care system needs drastic overhauling. The government used to spend more per head during the 1950s and 1960s than it does at present. The governments of India's less developed and smaller neighbouring countries have better health care facilities than large parts of the country (especially the north). Only Kerala has a health care system that is comparable to that in the US. On the other hand, there is no dearth of Indian doctors who have made it big in the US, while the British National Health Service is dominated by Indian doctors. Surely there is nothing basically wrong with the quality of education provided in the country's medical colleges. India's pharmaceuticals manufacturing industry is one of the few industries which is bigger than its counterpart in China. Yet the fact is that the Indian pharma industry produces and sells huge quantities of the kinds of drugs we don't really need: cough and cold mixtures and digestive aids are two examples. Many drugs banned in most countries of the world are freely sold in India—there is even a plethora of what doctors call 'irrational' formulations. While Indian companies export bulk drugs all over the world and some have expanded the frontiers of medical science with their research, the average Indian has no access to health care worth the name.

There is no dearth of such examples of the gulf between the achievements and possessions of India's elite and the poverty of resources among the rest. It is not without reason that India is seen as a land of amazing contrasts and contradictions. More often than not, this fact is stated with a sense of pride. It is time we recognised that those on the wrong side of these contrasts see the situation rather differently. Unlike in the past, they are no longer willing to lament their fate. They have chosen to express themselves and in the process the Indian polity has got fragmented like never before. But the beneficiaries of this process—the small regional or caste-based parties—would take their support base for granted at their own peril.

The programme of economic reforms has used the disillusionment with the Nehruvian model of development as its moral justification. Ironically, however, whatever little consensus exists on the contours of the reform package is restricted to those who were not the worst sufferers of the controlled economy—the middle-class and those at the highest rungs of the economic ladder. As one descends that ladder, the consensus is replaced by scepticism if not suspicion, which explains why anti-reform measures are still labelled 'populist'. The scepticism is not without basis. The have-nots have seen this same elite sell them the Nehruvian dream. They are understandably not too keen to trust the elite today when it tells them that the reforms will usher in a better tomorrow.

The exclusion, of course, is not only in the economic sphere. Almost one-third of the country's citizens still suffer social discrimination on account of the caste system more than 55 years after Independence. The peoples of this country are divided along every conceivable line: class, religion, language, region, race, and overlapping all of these, the caste system. Unless India's inequalities in terms of social and economic classes narrow considerably, the country will not be able to 'develop' or move ahead in the international arena, certainly not fast enough. It might seem difficult to sustain the people's faith in a democracy that repeatedly fails to deliver even basic human needs to them. Conversely, many of the non-economic divisions in Indian society would conceivably become less oppressive and perhaps gradually disappear if the economic divide is reduced.

That then is the challenge facing coalition governments of the future. It is certainly a huge challenge. Coalitions, however, are arguably better equipped to face up to the challenge than any single party in India at the moment.

Index

About The Authors

PARANJOY GUHA THAKURTA started his career in journalism in 1977 and is currently Director of the School of Convergence, an educational institution. He has worked with *Business India, Business World, The Telegraph, India Today,* and *The Pioneer;* been associated with Television Eighteen India Limited (CNBC); is a freelance contributor to various publications, websites, radio and television channels; has anchored for six years a daily interview and discussion programme on CNBC; and, has directed a documentary on India's experience with television. Paranjoy lectures on topics close to his heart—like the working of India's polity, the economy, and media—and teaches and trains aspiring media professionals.

SHANKAR RAGHURAMAN has been a journalist since 1986. Now Senior Editor with *The Economic Times,* Shankar has previously worked with the Press Trust of India, *The Pioneer,* and TVI. His main areas of interest are Indian politics, macroeconomics and sports. He is a regular panelist/commentator on television programmes on current affairs.